D1132380

Emil W. Haury's
Prehistory of the
American Southwest

Emil W. Haury's Prehistory of the American Southwest

EDITED BY

J. Jefferson Reid

and

David E. Doyel

The University of Arizona Press

Tucson & London

About the Author

EMIL W. HAURY, past president of the Society for American Archaeology and of the American Anthropological Association, received the Viking Fund Medal in 1950 and the A. V. Kidder Medal in 1977. From the late 1930s until 1964 he served as director of the Arizona State Museum and as head of the department of anthropology at the University of Arizona, where he was also the Fred A. Riecker distinguished professor in anthropology from 1970 to 1980. During his career he was elected to the National Academy of Sciences, the American Academy of Arts and Sciences, and the American Philosophical Society.

About the Editors

J. JEFFERSON REID, professor of anthropology at the University of Arizona, became director of the Archaeological Field School at Grasshopper in 1979. His research has emphasized the Mogollon culture and the history of the development of southwestern archaeology. He received his doctoral degree in 1973 from the University of Arizona, where he studied with Emil Haury.

DAVID E. DOYEL is an anthropologist who specializes in the cultures of the American Southwest. He is the former chief archaeologist for the Navajo Nation, director of the Navajo Nation Museum, and city archaeologist and director of the Pueblo Grande Museum for the city of Phoenix, Arizona. He has conducted extensive archaeological research in Arizona and New Mexico. He received his Ph.D. in 1977 from the University of Arizona, where he studied southwestern prehistory with Emil Haury.

Second printing, 1992, with an updated bibliography of the author's works.

THE UNIVERSITY OF ARIZONA PRESS

Copyright © 1986
The Arizona Board of Regents
All Rights Reserved

This book was set in 10/12 Linotron Baskerville.
Manufactured in the U.S.A.
⊗ This book is printed on acid-free, archival-quality paper.

Library of Congress Cataloging-in-Publication Data

Haury, Emil W. (Emil Walter), 1904–
    Emil W. Haury's Prehistory of the American Southwest.

    Bibliography: p.
    Includes index.
    1. Indians of North America—Southwest, New—
Antiquities—Addresses, essays, lectures.   2. Southwest,
New—Antiquities—Addresses, essays, lectures.
3. Haury, Emil W. (Emil Walter), 1904–   —Addresses,
essays, lectures.   I. Reid, J. Jefferson.   II. Doyel,
David.   III. Title.   IV. Title: Prehistory of the
American Southwest.
E78.S7H37   1986   979'.01   85-20900
ISBN 0-8165-0896-8
Paper ISBN 0-8165-1313-9

Publication of this book is made possible in part by financial support from The Arizona Archaeological and Historical Society.

To
HULDA PENNER HAURY

Contents

PART FOUR

HOHOKAM
People of the Desert

All photographs in this book were provided through courtesy of the
Arizona State Museum, University of Arizona, Tucson, Arizona.
Photographers include: B. Cummings (Fig. 1.1), O. C. Havens (Figs. 1.2
and specimens in Chapters 11 and 13), L. F. H. Lowe (Figs. 9.14, 9.16,
9.20), E. B. Sayles (Figs. 1.4, 7.8, 8.12), H. Teiwes (Fig. 1.6), C. Turner
(Figs. 9.2, 9.4, 9.6, 9.7, 9.8, 9.12, 9.13), J. B. Wheat (Fig. 1.3), and the
Gila Pueblo Staff (Fig. 1.5). All other photographs, and all line
drawings, are by Emil W. Haury.

Prehistoric sites in the Southwest

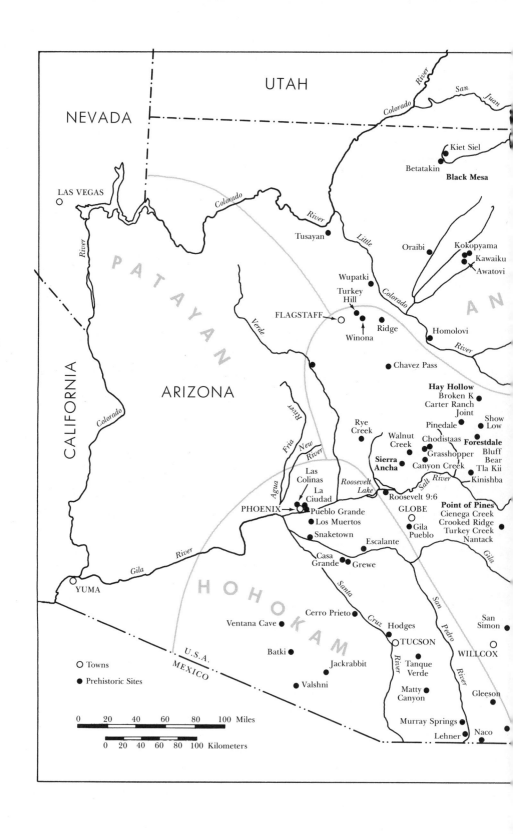

PART ONE
Overview

Emil Walter Haury

The Archaeologist as Humanist and Scientist

J. Jefferson Reid

Archaeologists are renowned as explorers of remote places, as discoverers, as puzzlers patiently fitting together the pieces of the past. These popular portrayals find substance in the archaeological career of Emil Haury, whose uniquely southwestern adventure story is amply highlighted by successful solutions to puzzles of prehistory. The conspicuous absence from the American Southwest of gold-laden tombs does not diminish the explorations, the discoveries, or the story of the archaeologist whose travels and personal encounters spanned sixty years of active research.

Famous men and their careers are often more complicated than they seem, and Emil Haury is no exception. His life, as he recounts it, embodies a simplicity that obscures deeper, more complicated themes and circumstances. A probing of this veneer provides an understanding of his times and a sense of the man as humanist, as scientist, and as the most prominent southwestern archaeologist of this century.

FORMATIVE YEARS

Professor Gustav A. Haury taught Latin at Bethel College in Newton, Kansas. His wife, Clara K. Ruth Haury, was the mother of four sons. Emil, the youngest, was born on May 2, 1904, and reared in a

3

small Mennonite academic community of the American Midwest. Familial warmth and example encouraged development of the intellectual, artistic, and manual skills that would serve him throughout his archaeological career.

One envisions the thoughtful young Emil, daydreaming about American Indians from the pages of *American Boy Magazine*. Youthful thoughtfulness grew into scientific thoroughness and a sincere, gentlemanly regard for other people. It became entwined with sensitivity—perhaps even a touch of shyness, with personal loyalty, with dedication, responsibility, deliberation, and close attention to detail.

Reserve was balanced by an exuberant sense of humor often expressed in practical jokes, as when he and John McGregor, while students working with Cummings on the San Carlos Apache Reservation, created the illusion of an Apache raid for a naive peer recently arrived from the East. His archaeological "hoaxes" served both as pranks on his fellow students and as tests of their visual acuity, a sense with which Haury was unusually gifted. Good humor was a valuable companion throughout his life.

Most impressive was Emil's ability to perceive in bits of archaeological information patterns that eluded others. His discoveries and insights into southwestern prehistory stemmed initially from his keen perception, a special mind-eye coordination that allowed him to shape facts into novel configurations; where others described finds in isolation, he selected the meaningful pieces and arranged them into interpretable patterns. His analytic insights were substantiated by amassing additional information and made understandable through documentation and concise exposition, qualities that characterize the mature scientific intellect.

In profiling Emil Haury's career one must not overlook the advantages that imposing stature, strength, and health conferred on an archaeologist traversing the backwoods and deserts of Arizona in the 1920s, 1930s, and 1940s. The stamina and leverage of his six-foot-three-inch frame contributed directly to his archaeological research by making it easier to endure the hardships of fieldwork. Only by traveling widely, often on horseback, subsisting on a basic diet of his own design, and living in the open could he observe the archaeological remains of Arizona. These observations, securely filed in his mind, formed the essential substance from which his insights were made. Physical characteristics played a valuable role in permitting Emil to gain a broad exposure to variability in the archaeological record and in directing him to focus research on data collection in the field.

Slim Ellison, an Arizona cowboy who served as Haury's guide on several field trips under the Mogollon Rim, provided an accurate summation:

> Haury was edjicated and smart. It had took on him, and I'd tell a hand Haury wasn't no softie, he was plumb full of vim and vigor, knew what he wanted to do, and was organized to do it, down to a gnat's eye. . . . I'll tell a man, Haury was a ramblin, scramblin, driftin, climbin, edjicated son-of-a-gun. You know, if our gover'ment could organize and work like Haury did that job [Canyon Creek Ruin in 1932], we'd have a sound, 100-cent dollar! (Ellison 1968:266–268).

CUMMINGS, DOUGLASS, AND GLADWIN YEARS (1925–1937)

Emil Haury's archaeological skills were shaped during twelve years of apprenticeship under Byron Cummings, A. E. Douglass, and Harold Gladwin. During this time he progressed from inexperienced student to seasoned professional archaeologist. That this passage was made so rapidly is largely due to the unusual circumstance of working under three remarkably different, intellectually energetic men whose sequence of association with Emil was as momentous to his professional development as was the particular character of each man's contribution.

Emil was twenty-one in 1925 when he joined Cummings's excavation at Cuicuilco on the outskirts of Mexico City (Fig. 1.1). Afterwards he transferred to the Department of Archaeology at the University of Arizona, where he completed his junior and senior years, his M.A. degree, and where, during the 1928–1929 academic year, he held his first teaching position. Emil was far more than a student; he was Cummings' right-hand man, research assistant, and chauffeur. It was as chauffeur for Cummings, Acting University President in 1927, that Emil was introduced to prominent people throughout Arizona. This job also took him to the first Pecos Conference, where he and Clara Lee Fraps (Tanner) were among the handful of students in attendance. Also in their party was Hulda Penner, daughter of Reverend and Mrs. H. D. Penner of Newton, Kansas; she and Emil were wed in June of the following year. (See Woodbury [1983] for a short history of the Pecos Conference.)

Figure 1.1. Emil Haury at the site of Cuicuilco outside Mexico City, 1925.

Cummings, the indefatigable explorer, frequently took students to the field on weekends and holidays. It was on one of these trips, in response to a call from a teacher at the Double Adobe School, that Emil first encountered evidence for the association of artifacts with remains of extinct animals. The 1926 Double Adobe finds were not promoted by Cummings and were soon overshadowed by the discoveries that same year at Folsom, New Mexico. Twenty-five years later Emil would respond to the call of ranchers in the upper San Pedro River area to uncover the important mammoth kills at Naco and Lehner.

As a classics scholar and Victorian moralist, Cummings employed an antiquarian approach to archaeological record keeping and inference, one with which Emil became increasingly uncomfortable. This uneasiness and the awkwardness of his first year of teaching prompted him to look elsewhere for additional archaeological training and experience. Even so, his archaeological perspective was given its initial shape through the humanistic approach and humanitarian concern of the dynamic Byron Cummings.

In 1929 Emil accepted a job with A. E. Douglass, the astronomer and father of dendrochronology, as Douglass was organizing the Third Beam Expedition. It was as members of the expedition team in June of that year that Haury and Lyndon Hargrave unearthed a tree-ring sample in Show Low, Arizona, that bridged the apparent gap between Douglass's prehistoric and historic tree-ring chronologies. Bridging this gap permitted the first accurate dating of the Southwest's major pueblos. Although in Emil's own words this was the most dramatic event of his archaeological career, his subsequent year with Douglass had a deeper, more pervasive impact upon his later archaeological research. (See Webb [1983] for a biography of Douglass.)

Of immediate significance were the contrasting approaches of Cummings and Douglass; while Cummings observed broadly with an eye toward general humanistic implications, Douglass attended to minute detail in a precise, scientific fashion. Douglass's example was not lost on young Emil, who quickly absorbed the scientific method, but decided that the microscopic investigation of tree-rings was not to be the major subject of his research career. He did, however, continue to play a prominent role in the development of tree-ring research.

Working with Douglass on the nascent science of dendrochronology gave Emil a thorough appreciation for the value of its archaeological applications as well as for the importance of chronological concerns to all of prehistory. Very early in his own career, and before these new techniques were widely available or understood, he had demonstrated a sophisticated grasp of chronometric method and the inestimable value of pieces of burned wood for resolving questions of chronology and past behavior. The importance of dating prehistoric events, especially of establishing archaeological chronologies, pervades all of his research and imbues his reconstructions of prehistory with lasting scientific usefulness as well as controversy. A large measure of this concern for archaeological chronometry must be attributed to the experiences gained under Douglass.

Harold Sterling Gladwin was a financier who fell in love with the Southwest and its prehistory. In 1928, with Winifred MacCurdy, he founded the Gila Pueblo Archaeological Foundation in Globe, Arizona. Under his direction the Foundation's archaeological research became the most innovative and productive of the Depression Era. From a number of job opportunities available to him in 1930, Emil elected

Figure 1.2. Members of the Gila Pueblo Archaeological Foundation at Grand Canyon in 1930: (*seated, left to right*) Harold S. Gladwin holding Paddy, Winifred Jones MacCurdy (Gladwin), Nora MacCurdy, Hulda Haury, Emil Haury, Russell Hastings; (*standing, left to right*) Edith Sangster, Evelyn Dennis, George Dennis. (Photograph courtesy of Mrs. Priscilla Gladwin.)

to become assistant director of Gila Pueblo (Fig. 1.2) because Gladwin promised fieldwork and publication opportunities and support for doctoral studies.

The fieldwork proved to be ample and varied. It was during his Gila Pueblo years that Emil broadened his exposure to archaeological remains throughout Arizona and adjacent New Mexico. At this time he also participated in the definition of Hohokam culture and was provided the research opportunities that led him to define the Mogollon culture. A frenetic schedule of fieldwork and publication, guided and supported by Gladwin's intellect, iconoclasm, and personal fortune, was translated into significant archaeological results by the resilient young Emil Haury. Under Gila Pueblo's aegis Emil excavated at Tusayan Ruin (Haury 1931), Rye Creek Ruin, Roosevelt 9:6 (Haury 1932; see Chapter 11), Canyon Creek Ruin (Haury 1934b), Mogollon Village and Harris Village (Haury 1936a; see Chapter 13), Snake-town (Gladwin and others 1937), and White Mound Village (Gladwin 1945). He surveyed in the Grand Canyon and throughout the mountains of Central Arizona and New Mexico, and in the Gladwins' field vehicle, remodeled from a Pierce Arrow town car, he traveled farther afield into Utah, Nevada, and California.

In the midst of this activity Emil devoted two academic years to a doctoral degree, which was completed at Harvard in 1934. Although the specific influences of one's professors and fellow graduate students is difficult to gauge, the Harvard intellectual environment left significant marks upon the content and direction of Emil's career. This influence was clearly the case in the later development of his dissertation research, directed by Roland B. Dixon, which compiled and analyzed information from Frank Hamilton Cushing's 1887–1888 excavations at Los Muertos, a Classic period Hohokam settlement south of Phoenix.

In 1937 Haury returned to the University of Arizona to become head of the Department of Archaeology. His first task was to broaden the scope of the Department by renaming it one of Anthropology. The following year he assumed the directorship of the Arizona State Museum, a position which, along with the headship, he held until 1964.

By the age of thirty-three he had worked under the most prominent figures in Arizona archaeology; he had surveyed, excavated, and published widely. His own special character, the requirements of the times, and unique circumstances placed him in a position to direct the course of Arizona archaeology for the next forty years. His accomplishments form the foundation of Arizona prehistory.

LEADERSHIP AND STYLE IN SOUTHWESTERN ARCHAEOLOGY

Although much of Haury's time was taken up with teaching, administration, and public service, he continued field research at the pace to which he had become accustomed; from the onset he incorporated student training. His tradition of archaeological field schools began in 1939 in the Forestdale Valley and continued there through the summer of 1941. After the war he moved the Field School to Point of

Figure 1.3. Staff of the University of Arizona Archaeological Field School at Point of Pines, 1948: (*left to right*) Emil Haury, Pat Wheat, Dick Wenker, Charles Chidsie, Molly Kendall, Ray Thompson, John Ellis, Donald Lehmer, E. B. Sayles, Hulda Haury, Barbara Chidsie, Don Swartz.

Pines where, from 1946 until its closing in 1960, he directed a broad research program characterized by the productivity of the students. While the field schools at Forestdale and Point of Pines represented an extension of Haury's personal research interest in Mogollon prehistory, the Point of Pines work signaled a dramatic shift in its fulfillment. Under Haury's supervision advanced students took major responsibilities for fieldwork, analysis, and exposition—the approach to archaeological field training that has come to distinguish the University of Arizona Archaeological Field Schools (Fig. 1.3).

The Field School occupied his summers; other field studies consumed available time during the academic year. A program of research on the Papago Indian Reservation began in 1938 and ended in 1942 with the completion of excavations at Ventana Cave (Haury 1950a). Over the years other duties provided increasingly less time for fieldwork during the academic year. Even so, Haury's sense of the importance of archaeological discoveries compelled him to adjust his schedule to include field research. As a result, he uncovered the mammoth kill sites at Naco in 1952 and at Lehner in 1955 and 1956.

After the excavation at Ventana Cave, he did little work on the Hohokam, but one suspects it was never far from his mind, especially given that critiques of his original Snaketown chronology had gone unanswered for two decades. By 1964 he felt it was time to mount a major Hohokam field project. At this time Doc Haury stepped down from his positions as head of the Department of Anthropology and director of the Arizona State Museum to devote himself to the Hohokam and to emerging issues affecting American archaeology.

Throughout his leadership years Doc Haury shaped generations of archaeological research. He did so through a particular style—one that was expressed in the face of decades of debate and controversy. The Haury style is a composite of characteristics that owe much to elements of personality, professional and academic associations, and the state of knowledge of southwestern prehistory. The elegance, economy, and enthusiasm of an archaeological Edison characterize his style and his work, and within this frame it is most readily comprehended. He focused on the basic questions of prehistory—who, when, what, why, and how—and designed field research, eloquent in its simplicity, to resolve these questions.

How is Archaeology Done?

How an archaeologist goes about answering the basic questions of prehistory is illustrated in all of Haury's research. Two fundamental methodological principles are exemplified: one is the selection of analytically appropriate archaeological sites for investigation and the second is making interpretations of prehistory that are consistent with the quality and character of the data.

How did Haury identify analytically appropriate sites? He was always intellectually clever and on occasion he was just lucky, but luck explains little and provides no direction for others. Principally, he surveyed widely and, with a definite problem in mind, selected the site best suited to the research problem.

Let's look at the Mogollon. Haury spent the summer of 1931 surveying ruins throughout the central mountains of Arizona and New Mexico. He returned in 1933 and 1934 to excavate the two sites in New Mexico—Mogollon Village and Harris—on which he defined the concept of Mogollon. Haury's achievement of a new synthesis is

remarkable when one considers that his fieldwork was not the first
done in west-central New Mexico; in fact, by the mid-1930s that region was among the most thoroughly explored areas outside of the
San Juan Basin. What Haury did was to select sites very carefully for
their potential to yield high-quality information, with which he was
able to make interpretations not perceived by others regarding the reconstruction of past behavior.

Who Were the People?

In addressing the question of who was there, Haury has provided
more answers than any other southwestern archaeologist, and probably more than any other American archaeologist. Although he has
charted cultural variability during the Paleoindian and Archaic periods, he is best known for defining the Mogollon and for being a
coauthor with Harold Gladwin of the Hohokam concept. These are
two of the four generic cultural groups of the American Southwest;
the other two are Anasazi and Patayan.

When he and Gladwin defined the Hohokam, there was general
acceptance of the concept; Mogollon was a different matter altogether. First proposed in 1936, the concept existed for at least the
next two decades under a shroud of skepticism and accusations of ille-
gitimacy. During this time Haury concentrated his Field School program in the Forestdale Valley and at Point of Pines to support through
field research his original proposition of Mogollon authenticity and
antiquity.

Haury's Mogollon work also presents an interesting historical twist.
In defining the Mogollon, Haury broke with the established view of
southwestern prehistory to initiate a dramatic conceptual shift. In the
1930s there was reluctance to modify the hypothesis of Basketmaker-
Pueblo (Anasazi) as culture-bearer to the Southwest; the personality
and authority of the remarkable A. V. Kidder (Fig. 1.4) were linked to
this conservative stance. (See Woodbury [1973] for a biography of
Kidder.) Earl Morris (1939:248) outlined the situation well:

> Most of us under the grip of the northern bias were content to
> accept the Basket Maker–Pueblo cycle as basic, presumably
> representative of neighboring districts which had not yet been
> measured by its standards, and probably parental to the rela-
> tively late culture variants known to have existed in regions to
> the southeast, south and southwest of the San Juan center.

Figure 1.4. A. V. Kidder (*left*) and Emil
Haury at Point of Pines, 1948.

It remained for the Gladwins and their coworkers of Gila
Pueblo to jar the kaleidoscope. Disturb the picture they certainly have . . . by showing that there are major provinces in
the Southwest to which it is not applicable. Due to their efforts
the Hohokam of the Gila are as firmly established as are the
Basket Maker–Pueblo of the north. . . .

Gila Pueblo advocates a third parent stem in the Southwestern complex—the Mogollon culture of southwestern New
Mexico. . . . The claims of the Mogollon culture to fundamental individuality and antiquity so far are not as well confirmed
as those of the Hohokam. It is, however, the opinion of Gladwin and Haury that additional excavation would carry it back to
parallel the earliest Hohokam phase now known. No clearer
minds than theirs have grappled with Southwestern problems,
and in regard to this point, I would expect time to prove them
right.

Several years later Erik Reed (1942:31) described Haury's Mogollon proposition as a concept that "completes the breakup of traditionalist thought."

When Did it Happen?

Chronometric concerns were always paramount in Haury's research. What young archaeologist would not have been marked by the dramatic moment in 1929 when A. E. Douglass first dated the major ruins of the Southwest? Haury's experiences with tree-ring dating under the direction of Douglass instilled in him the knowledge that questions of rate, change, direction, sequence, and movement depend for a reliable answer on the ability to estimate time at an appropriate level of resolution.

Haury's attention to chronology was a blessing with burdens, and his handling of the burdensome aspects gives added insight into his style. Being attuned to the value of tree-ring dating, he secured data to document when sites were occupied, and his Mogollon work was strengthened through this documentation. The Hohokam, on the other hand, were not blessed with a habitat that included abundant, easily datable trees, nor, it seems, were they inclined to use the datable pines available in the surrounding mountains. Dendrochronology was of no direct use to Haury's formulation of the original Hohokam chronology.

Research carried out at Snaketown in 1934–1935 by Gila Pueblo (Fig. 1.5) led to Haury's formulation of the Hohokam phase sequence and chronology based on his analysis of ceramics in Mound 29 at Snaketown. Reevaluation of this analysis—leading to reinterpretation of the chronology—has occupied an increasing number of archaeologists over the years. For the first thirty years of alternative chronological arguments, some of which were couched in personal attacks, Haury remained quiet in print, principally because he possessed no new data with which to confirm or reject his original scheme. In 1964 he returned to Snaketown to collect new chronometric data, which, though they support the phase sequence, do not resolve all chronological problems. In accord with Haury's approach, the resolution of the remaining chronological problems will be found in new evidence.

What Did People Do?

Answers to questions of what prehistoric peoples were doing are embodied in Haury's site reports; they are clearly expressed, for example, in his depiction of the Hohokam as desert farmers and crafts-

Figure 1.5. The Gila Pueblo staff at Snaketown in 1935: (*left to right*) Emil Haury, Julian Hayden, Evelyn Dennis, Irwin Hayden, E. B. Sayles, Nancy Pinkley, Erik Reed, Fisher Motz.

men (Haury 1976). His restraint in behavioral reconstruction is a result of his commitment to the character of the data and the nature of the research problems that directed him to select a site for investigation. For example, he returned to Snaketown explicitly to resolve problems of Hohokam chronology. In pursuing this question in the field, he came across remains that permitted him to expand his portrayal of the adjustment of Hohokam people to the Sonoran Desert. New data also caused him to revise his notion of their ancestral tree.

Haury's work in the early 1940s at Ventana Cave (Haury 1950a) led him to a hypothesis of cultural continuity between the Late Archaic peoples of the Sonoran Desert and the Hohokam; his interpretation of the remains at the Cienega Creek Site supported this continuity hypothesis. Analysis of materials from the 1964–1965 Snaketown excavations, however, required that he abandon the original hypothesis

Figure 1.6. Emil Haury with a group of students on a field trip to Snaketown in 1974.

in favor of one proposing a movement of people into Arizona from
somewhere in present-day Mexico. This question of origin, like so
many in Hohokam prehistory, was still unresolved in 1985. In Haury's
hands the search for a solution to it was open minded and faithful to
the available evidence: new evidence demanded another hypothesis,
which was clearly announced in the literature (Haury 1976: 351–353).

Why Did It Happen?

In considering the question why, Haury grappled with problems
of explanation that have become a focus of contemporary theory in
archaeology. He, however, never felt comfortable with what we, today,

call theory, though he was sensitive to the reasons behind the behavior of prehistoric peoples. Two conditions have influenced perceptions of Haury's stance regarding theory and the explanation of past behavior. The first condition reflects the essence of his style: reliable reconstructions of behavior must be well grounded in the archaeological evidence. Without a secure knowledge of who, when, and what, the why explanations of prehistory would remain nebulous hypotheses; Haury called it speculation. He devoted his intellect and energy to the solution of fundamental issues, and thereby provided substance for the synthetic, explanatory research of future archaeologists.

The second condition is that Haury is perceived to have avoided explanatory statements more than he actually did because he did not employ the terminology associated with contemporary explanation. His style and experience prompted him to express himself in refreshingly clear language, both in his written reports and in his discussions with students (Fig. 1.6). Through close observation of the Arizona landscape and the prehistoric evidence upon it, Haury developed firm hypotheses for why people behaved as they did. These thoughts have been expressed in concise language throughout his career and in the concluding chapter of this book.

POSTSCRIPT AS PROLOGUE

This anthology of Emil Haury's thoughts presents the essence of his contribution to southwestern archaeology and prehistory. By bringing together his writings with introductions by his colleagues, it also codifies Haury's position on major issues and celebrates his accomplishments by facilitating future research into southwestern prehistory. Emil Haury surveyed more territory and excavated more sites than would be possible for an archaeologist of today. His thoughts, informed by unparalleled personal experience with the archaeological record, form a basis for future knowledge of the past.

2

The Greater American Southwest

Emil W. Haury

By long-standing usage among archaeologists, the Southwest of the United States is defined as encompassing all the state of Arizona, all but the eastern third of New Mexico, the southwestern and far-western margin of Colorado, the southern two-thirds of Utah, eastern and southern Nevada, and the states of Sonora and Chihuahua in northern Mexico. As Kroeber has aptly pointed out, the geographical delineation of culture wholes is beset with numerous problems, one of which is that sharply drawn boundaries convey the impression of a cleavage that actually does not exist. Within the structure of the culture-area concept, boundaries are intended to indicate only some notion of the lateral spread of elements and through them our understanding of a way of life reaching out from centers of cultural florescence. If we recognize this limitation, the Southwest as noted above has some utility.

Reprinted by permission from "Courses Toward Urban Life: Archaeological Considerations of Some Cultural Alternates," edited by Robert J. Braidwood and Gordon R. Willey. *Viking Fund Publications in Anthropology* 32. Copyright 1962 by the Wenner-Gren Foundation for Anthropological Research, Incorporated, New York.

For our purposes, it is pointless to consider at length the history of the development of the culture-area concept per se and how it has been applied to the Southwest. Suffice it to say that the efforts of Mason (1896) focused on ethnic environments and that Wissler's (1922) work depended upon natural-cultural area relationships. Beals's studies (1932) represent essentially the analytical trait approach for a small part of continental America, and Kroeber's important contribution (1939) looks—as does Wissler's, but far more perceptively—at the natural-cultural area correspondences. Kidder's (1924) analysis and, more recently, the Seminars in Archaeology: 1955 (Wauchope 1956) have been motivated by archaeological considerations, the latter having concerned itself with areal and focal shifts on a multichronological basis.

The foregoing delineations present us with an area too restricted for delving into the problem that confronts this symposium. A larger unit of study will provide us first with wider environmental and cultural ranges that, through comparison, will yield more rewarding results than if the area were kept smaller. For this reason I wish to use as the basis for my remarks that portion of the western United States and northern Mexico characterized by Kirchhoff (1954) as the greater Southwest (Figure 2.1). Areally, this includes "Central, Southern, and Baja California, the great Basin, Arizona, New Mexico, Southern Coastal Texas, and Northern Mexico to the Sinaloa and Panuco River" (Kirchhoff 1954:533). This constitutes a region from one-half to one-third the size of the Near East as outlined by Braidwood (1958:1419).

Whether this geographical subdivision of North America is a true cultural entity or not rests on one's taxonomic precepts, a problem that does not concern us here. It is important, however, to note that, in a broad sense, the greater Southwest is a natural area that locally harbors limited habitats. These differ sharply from the main pattern of aridity and maximum sunshine that characterizes the region as a whole.

This large area supported varied culture types historically, and for some of these a long evolutionary record is demonstrable.

It is also evident that different groups of peoples, living in similar environments, followed divergent paths and at variable speeds in the progression of their ways of life from the simple to the more complex. It is these facts that make the region an especially attractive one for reviewing the core problem of this symposium.

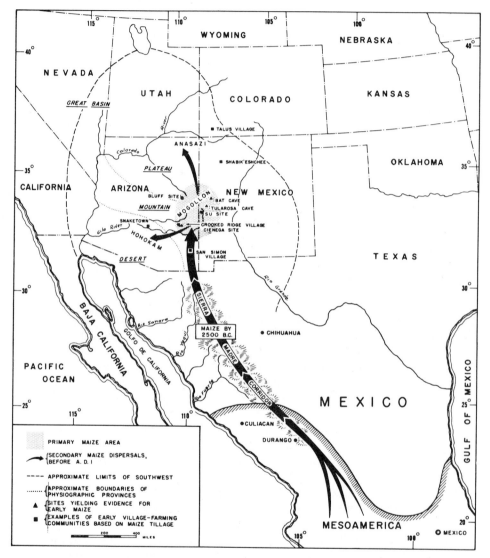

Figure 2.1. Map of the greater Southwest, illustrating the probable route over which maize was diffused from Mesoamerica to the southwestern archaeological zone and its subsequent dispersal to other cultural areas.

ENVIRONMENTAL CONSIDERATIONS

Kroeber (1939) has done us a notable service in synthesizing the work of numerous botanists who have looked at the problem of vegetation areas. It is apparent immediately that the greater Southwest constitutes one of the most complex natural regions in all the New World, characterized by environmental ranges from extreme desert to high mountain forest.

For our purposes it will be sufficient to point out some of the broad distinctions by vegetation type (after Shelford 1926) and to identify the areas:

1. *Broad-leafed Evergreen Semidesert:* south coast of California and north Pacific coast of Baja California.
2. *Extreme Desert:* south interior California, southern Nevada, western Arizona, Coahuila.
3. *Desert:* Great Basin, much of the Arizona plateau, most of Baja California, western Sonora, and Sinaloa.
4. *Succulent Desert:* central and southern Arizona stretching south into Sonora, Rio Grande Valley from central New Mexico to the Pecos confluence with the Rio Grande, eastern Chihuahua, and Durango.
5. *Dry Grassland:* parts of western New Mexico, southeastern Arizona, northern Chihuahua, eastern New Mexico, isolates in eastern Durango, including a portion of western Coahuila and Zacatecas.
6. *Desert Coniferous Forest:* eastern Utah, much of north- and east-central Arizona, west and east flanks of Sierra Madre Occidental.
7. *Moist and High Mountain Coniferous Forest:* the backbone of the Sierra Madre Occidental.

It becomes apparent from the foregoing that no smooth transition from one environmental extreme to the other exists. On the contrary, the distribution of vegetation areas is spotty and dramatically changing. At the same time it is worth noting, as a possible favorable condition for south-to-north diffusion of cultural factors, that transits could have been made over long distances through either desertic or mountainous environments without radically departing from either of them.

More important, however, is the fact that these vegetation areas provide the range of climate, terrain, and plant resources on which man could work out a variety of subsistence activities. The adaptive process in a nearly universally harsh environment was eased because of the varied resources. And somewhere within the area agricultural stimuli, as a prelude to the development of a higher societal order, should have found fertile ground. One of our problems is to determine where and when this took place.

Except for coastal regions, diurnal temperature extremes are typical, and it is obvious that, as a function of the altitudinal extremes, mean temperatures also manifest a wide range. For most of the greater Southwest, rainfall comes in two seasons: the general storms of winter, bringing snow to the higher elevations and rain elsewhere, and the local intense thunderstorms of the summer. These are often separated by many months of intense heat and drought. In short, sharp variation in climate as between the dry and the wet season are the norm.

ETHNOGRAPHIC SYNOPSIS

We need to view the native peoples of historic times only in the most meager detail to give us some feeling for the spectrum of culture types. The range is as dramatic as was the ecological, from Seri fishermen to Zuñi farmer. Some of these differences are attributable to the responses of people to habitat, and the present may be taken to mirror the past.

For south coastal California, Baja California, and the coast of western Mexico, semimaritime cultures existed, drawing both upon the sea and the land for subsistence. They were non-agricultural, as were also some of the interior tribes. To exist under harsh living conditions and seasonal food sources, scattering and mobility were required. The nearest approach to sizable populations and permanent residences is met among the coastal groups, where the Gabrielino and Chumash reached a cultural climax (Kroeber 1939:44). Neither historically nor archaeologically was food production a significant factor. These areas, thus, play no part in our problem except in helping to establish a primitive economic base over a wide geographical range.

Moving eastward from California, we encounter immediately the Colorado River, which, like the Nile, is flanked in its lower reaches by desert and mountains. It was a slender lifeline for the Yuman tribes who farmed the bottom lands without benefit of rain or irrigation, depending on the ever present ground moisture arising from a high water table.

East of the Yumans, the upper Pimas and Papagos, while living in villages, depended about evenly on natural resources and on farming. This is the giant cactus belt upon the fruits of which heavy reliance was placed.

In northwestern Arizona, other Yuman tribes—the Yavapai, Walapai, and Havasupai—had farming of sorts, but for at least half the year they were collectors, following the economy of other desert neighbors.

To the north, the Great Basin, the southern part of which concerns us, by climate and vegetation belongs to the Southwest (Kroeber 1939:50). Historically, its people, like the Paiutes, are characterized by a meagerness of culture and collecting subsistence habits.

Following the circuit clockwise, we next have the sedentary Pueblo farmers, whose towns contrast sharply with the mobile and scattered life of the adjacent Navajo and Apache. Here in the same environment we see two subsistence patterns that are poles apart.

Finally, in the northern Sierra Madre are the mountain-dwelling Tarahumara. By geography, they should have benefited by and perhaps retained the higher cultural attributes from Mesoamerica. But this seems not to have been the case as far as food dependence is concerned, for their economy is little above the level of subsistence farming. To the west of them the Cahitans and Pimans farmed the rich bottom lands of a series of rivers that rise in the Sierra Madre and empty into the Gulf of California.

The population density for the Southwest is given by Kroeber (1939:143) as 10.7 per 100 square kilometers, exceeded only by the Northwest Coast and California in all North America north of Mexico. Yet, looking at the greater Southwest, the density range is from 2 to 5 in the Great Basin to more than 75 per 100 square kilometers in the Pueblo area, which, except for a small part of California, is the highest value for native populations north of Mexico. Kroeber also rates high the culture intensity of the Pueblos as a concomitant, in this case, of population density (1939:Map 28), and comparably low intensities where the population was thin. Human resources in historic times thus match the extremes already noted for the natural setting of the greater Southwest.

LATE QUATERNARY HISTORY

Geological studies in the greater Southwest bearing on terminal Pleistocene and Recent history have been late in getting started. It was the archaeologists' interest in early human history and the perpetual need to develop water resources in an arid environment that stimulated much of the work that has been done. On the basis of this we conclude that within the last 15,000 years, in fact since mid-Pleistocene times, there have been no large-scale changes in surface relief. Although the region surely felt the fringe effects of the large ice masses far to the north, glaciation as such played no part in shaping the landscape save for a few isolated instances, such as the San Francisco Peaks. Stream terraces are discernible in many places, but these have not yet been convincingly correlated directly with the glacial and interglacial episodes. Climatic shifts from cool to warm and moist to dry, phenomena that do leave an imprint upon the land, have been attributed to the wide-ranging northern hemispheric climatic patterns. For our purposes it will be enough to note that within the time of the archaeological record, conservatively 15,000 years, there has been progressive desiccation, intensified during the altithermal drought of about 4,500–7,000 years ago (Antevs 1955). Since 5,000 years ago essentially modern conditions have prevailed.

The effects of vulcanism upon man were minimal because only localized activity is known. Sunset Crater, near Flagstaff, which erupted in the eleventh century A.D. is one, and its effects upon the region's residents have been studied (Colton 1932). The Pinacate volcanic field in northwestern Sonora may have been active within the last 15,000 years, and some suspect that Capulin Mountain's eruptions were witnessed by Folsom man. I do not see vulcanism as a factor of any consequence.

The principal forces at work were the epicycles of erosion and sedimentation, evidences of which are best preserved in the inner valleys of the major drainage systems. This was fortunate, for it was along the main drainages that man congregated by reason of richer natural resources, upon which he was dependent. The locally changing landscape, by alternate scouring and filling, provided the opportunity for the preservation of human traces, fires, camps, and remains of animals killed, often in a decipherable geological context. The recent erosion cycle, starting in the 1880s, is now providentially exposing these often deeply buried evidences, the location of which could never be predicted. It is obvious, too, that unless knowing eyes are present at the moment of exposure the traces may forever be lost by the destructive force of the next flood.

Detailed geochronological studies are only now well under way, and until these begin to produce meaningful results we must rest upon generalities in our efforts to relate man to nature on the incipient exploitative level.

PROGRESSION OF CULTURE PATTERNS

A hypothetical and simple approach to the problem of culture history is one in which a single pattern is recognized at the time of origin, or first appearance, out of which there emerged a complex of patterns, the product of diverse responses to various forces. The evidence for the New World begins to hint that no such simplified scheme is supportable. Taking the chronological short view of 10,000–12,000 years as the base line, at least two culture types are already in evidence. These show up in the greater Southwest, which invites our attention to them.

The readily identifiable elements of these two patterns are the stemmed and the lanceolate projectile point traditions. The former represents the Desert culture as seen in Danger Cave occurring as early as 9,000 years ago (Jennings 1957:265) and was associated with tools designed for seed-grinding and preparation of plant foods. This was a clear indication of an adaptation to wring the most out of an essentially arid environment. In all probability this pattern has a substantially greater antiquity than the dates presently indicate. It is predictable, on the basis of the Great Basin and western distribution of the Desert culture, that the oldest manifestations will be found in the West. Old World ties are not establishable on the data now available, but one may speculate that the complex was related somehow to the chopping-tool tradition of eastern Asia. Gidding's recent Alaskan studies of beach ridges and associated cultural remains may provide a much needed connection, for his oldest complexes consist of chopping tools and stemmed points.

The second pattern, that of the lanceolate blade, was used by the big-game hunter and was associated predominantly with meat and hide-dressing tools, as judged by the slim data now available. The distribution of this complex is wide, but chiefly east of the Rockies, with a southwesterly extension into the Southwest. At best, the age for lanceolate blades does not appear to extend much beyond 12,000 years ago, but, as with the Desert culture, a greater age would ease some of the problems related to the distribution of the type. And when older occurrences are found, they should be east of the Rockies. Old World connections for the lanceolate blade are not easily demonstrable, but, if there was a link, it doubtless arose from a quite different tradition than did the stemmed point of the Desert culture. The fluting technique, as has already been noted by others, was undoubtedly a New World invention.

The points relevant to our discussions are:

1. Within the last 15,000 years, two culture types seem to have entered the New World deriving from different Old World patterns, and distributionally they converged in the greater Southwest.
2. We see plant-food exploitation, on the one hand, and animal-food dependence, on the other, though obviously not to the complete exclusion of the opposite in either case.
3. Irrespective of the precise temporal relationship of these two patterns, they must have impinged on each other. The question here arises as to what the consequences were.
4. Central to our problem is an assessment of the survival potential of the two systems under conditions of increasing aridity.

Retracing our steps somewhat now, we find that Desert-culture remains are infrequently found in association with extinct fauna, the Sulphur Spring stage of the Cochise culture being an exception. Taking the Desert culture of Danger Cave in the Great Basin as the expression best suiting our needs, the Pleistocene fauna of 10,000 years ago was already gone, whereas it was still extant to the east. Thus, if the Desert culture ever depended on big game, it was forced early to rely heavily on plant resources and to develop the appropriate technologies. The long and intimate experience of a wide range of plant life undoubtedly saved them during adverse climatic shifts, for changing the dependency from desirable to less-desirable, and perhaps hardier, plants was made relatively easy. Under the conditions of marginal subsistence, with some fluctuations in the degree of impoverishment, florescence was unlikely, if not impossible. As a consequence, we see a truly phenomenal situation of a near-static way of life from a remote 10,000 years ago to the ethnological present, a classic example of man's tenacity in a little-changing and harsh environment. This is in specific reference to the Great Basin.

The big-game hunters on the fringes of the greater Southwest were faced with a distinct hazard. Extinction of the game, brought on by increasing aridity, loss of forage, and by man's own cutting-down of the herds, demanded a shift in economic dependence if life and residence were to be maintained. The temporal relationship of the collector and the hunter now becomes important in our speculative reconstruction, for if the collector was first, as has been held (Jennings 1956:72), then the hunter had a ready model to follow when he was forced to change his ways. The full transition from butchering to seed-grinding, as symbols of essential dependence, took time, and it is doubtful that the wrench was as severe as we would like to think. Hunters also collect, just as plant-collectors hunt, and the shift was therefore one of emphasis.

The urge to exploit vegetal resources possibly meant infiltration into previously unsettled or lightly populated areas, the higher altitudes, which may have been less desirable as haunts of big game and therefore had been bypassed by man. Extensions of habitat brought new challenges and gave societies experience in subsisting in environments ranging from desert to forest. This now established the broad base from which we must operate in assessing subsequent developments. The time is roughly 7000 B.C. and later.

Speaking of the Southwest proper, several points need to be noted: (1) On the local scene, the level of cultural achievement, a subsistence economy that required maximum energy from a maximum number of people, must have been receptive to the addition of any resource to the cultural inventory that would ease the quest for food. (2) The invention or acquisition of tools, the milling stones, and the mastery of their use in grinding native foods, certainly by 8000 B.C. (Jennings 1957:285), demanded no major overhauling of food-preparation practices when a new plant became available. (3) On the foreign scene Mesoamerican societies were flourishing and were already in possession of maize, whose durable influence was soon to be felt in the frontiers to the north.

The earliest appearance of maize in the greater Southwest, and here I assume—without detailing supporting arguments—that it came out of the south, has been determined in the order of 3000 B.C. by radiocarbon means (this date is revised in Chapter 17). The places are Bat Cave (Mangelsdorf and Smith 1949), Tularosa and Cordova caves (Martin and others 1952) in New Mexico, all in altitudes over 6,000 feet; and at Point of Pines, Arizona (Ariz. W:10:112), in a valley floor geological context of first, possibly second, millennium B.C. age (Martin and Schoenwetter 1960). The latter identification is based on pollen extracted from silts in a mountain valley at 6,000 feet above sea level. These stations are within a little more than a hundred miles of each other, a geographical clustering of the evidence that I believe to have significance.

Maize—whether cob, plant, or pollen—of comparable age has not yet been found in the subarid desert, though it was a staple by the beginning of the Christian Era. For most of the Great Basin, Southern California, and presumably Baja California, maize was not accepted. We are left, then, with the inference that the earliest maize, probably a variety adjusted for higher altitudes, spread along the cordilleran spine of the greater Southwest and found lodging in east-central Arizona and west-central New Mexico. Mangelsdorf and Lister (1956) conclude this to have been the case after a detailed review of the botanical evidence.

As an early cultigen companion to maize we must also add squash and, by 1000 B.C., the bean, thereby completing the conventional trinity of food plants that characterized so much of North America. We may think of this mountain region as nuclear in the sense that it represents the earliest seed-planting—involving a grass in process of domestication—anywhere in the northern part of the greater Southwest. We assume that equally early and even earlier stations may be found stretching southward into Mesoamerica. Maize without pottery, possibly as early as that from the Arizona–New Mexico frontier, has been reported from caves in the Sierra Madre of Chihuahua (Mangelsdorf and Lister 1956), but it has not been radiocarbon determined. For this area, then, incipient cultivation may be set at a time from 2500 to 3000 B.C. (see Chapter 17).

The recipient people, the Cochise culture, a regional manifestation of the wider-spread Desert culture, are still imperfectly known. Their residence pattern and architectural forms, if any, have not been established, except that we know that caves were used for shelter where available and that, more commonly, settlements or camps in the open are deduced from implement and hearth concentrations in geological contexts exposed by recent erosion. The deep blanket of soil under which most of these remains occur has slowed the research on fuller definition of the culture. We know it chiefly through the stone implements that were geared to the collection and preparation of plant food, such as grinding stones and percussion-flaked choppers.

These reflect typological stability over a long period of time.

For at least 2,000 years the advent of the new cereal grain that ultimately was to shape societies left no measurable effect upon the recipients, either in the complexity of the culture or upon the speed with which it progressed. It is evident that effective food production was long in coming, a subject to which we will return later.

Continuing now with our survey, some 2,000 years after the arrival of maize, a new craft reached the core of the greater Southwest, again a gift from nuclear Mesoamerica. This was the knowledge of pottery-making. The earliest dated pottery comes from within the area of oldest maize, from Tularosa Cave in west-central New Mexico (Martin and others 1952:483) with a radiocarbon determination of about 150 B.C. Clearly here, as well as elsewhere in the world, pottery was not a direct concomitant of agriculture, but after A.D. 1 both flourished as correlates.

With this new trait, responsive in reflecting regional clay and mineral resources, susceptible to change through time, and a hallmark of cultural or tribal differences, the opportunity was enormously increased for eventual archaeological analysis and identification. Before pottery, the relatively undifferentiated lithic typology of the far-flung Desert culture (Cochise) does not permit recognition of sharp or specific regional differences except over large areas and long stretches of time. After pottery, regional manifestations become evident not only in the pottery itself but in related attributes. As a consequence of this fact, the archaeologist has recognized three main cultural streams: the Anasazi, centering in the plateau of the Four Corners area; the Hohokam of the Arizona desert; and the Mogollon of the mountain zone extending southward along the corridor far into Mexico. These are the so-called higher cultures of the Southwest. This is not the place to argue the ethnic separateness of these groups. We are interested, however, in cultural responses to the settling-down process in three strikingly different environments. These may be taken up as a series of problems.

Settling Down

As background for the cultural build-ups beginning roughly with the Christian Era, we need to dip deeply again into the time of food-collectors. It is axiomatic that in the New World, except for some maritime groups, the settling-down process was a correlate of maize tillage. This concept, I believe, needs some modification, at least for the

Southwest. Because of their special attraction, caves cannot be used as a test of stationary living. The evidence must be found in open sites. The vast accumulations of grinding stones in stations of the Cochise culture, as exemplified in the Cave Creek Site (Sayles and Antevs 1941:17), and the considerable accumulation of refuse strongly hint at localized and perhaps near-continuous residence. The extensive attrition of milling stones and the subsurface storage pits occasionally seen favor this idea. Some of these sites are datable to pre-maize times; others are within the first and second millennia B.C. after the advent of corn, but we have no knowledge that maize was grown in these sites.

It is not beyond probability that as early as 4000 B.C. the Cochise culture was engaged in deliberate plant cultivation of native species, as, for example, *chenopods* and *amaranths*. This experience with plants plus the possession of implements for processing plant foods, as noted earlier, predisposed the people to accept maize culture easily. For a long time maize did nothing to alter the mode of living beyond what was already known, though it must have supplied a greater measure of security achieved by the storage of surpluses.

We are still in the dark regarding the detailed nature of houses, their arrangement, or their number in a community during this period of incipient maize cultivation. Pit houses, with shallowly sunken floors, with dirt-covered beam and brush superstructures, and with entrance through the sides were probably the norm. This is predicated on architectural evidence of the first millennium B.C. (Sayles and Antevs 1941:27) and on the established architectural pattern observable in such villages as at Pine Lawn, the Vahki phase at Snaketown, and at Forestdale, dating near the time of Christ. All these are surely well up the ladder of architectural history.

The important point to reiterate, however, is that over much of the greater Southwest some experience had already been gained in settled living before the arrival of maize and other seed crops. At least two thousand years were to pass before formalized communities arose.

Which Subenvironment the Best for the Transformation?

The greater Southwest, as already indicated, provided a wide variety of ecological systems in which food-getting advances could have been made. It is also evident that the achievements were not uniform over the area but, instead, were spotty. Polar differences, as between the Great Basin collectors and the Plateau planters, are found within the space of a few hundred miles. Is there anything to be learned by a closer inspection of this problem?

Jennings states (1957:286) that "the Basin provides the semi-arid climate regarded by many as prerequisite to the beginnings of plant domestication." Prerequisites and antecedents, however, did not appear to be enough because the record does not support plant domestication as a Basin achievement or yet even tillage to any extent. This holds true also for the Succulent Desert, where, in modern times, tribes like the Papago depended upon native plants for 50–60 per cent of their food and agriculture at best was desultory (Castetter and Bell 1942:56). Sauer (1952: Plate 2) shows the Southwest as a recipient rather than a donor area.

Being on the receiving end of a diffusion pattern, three initial conditions were, I believe, primarily responsible in making the transition from collector to producer a reality. First was propinquity, the geographical closeness to the avenue through which elements were passing from nuclear Mesoamerica northward. The opportunity to acquire these had to be present. Second, the biogeographical setting needed to be similar in kind to that of the donor area, and, third, an optimum cultural environment was needed, a willingness to accept, to modify, and to build. These three requisites were met in the Sierra Madre corridor and, for our purposes, in the northern extension thereof—the higher regions and mountains of the Arizona–New Mexico border country.

For the most part, this was an open forested setting endowed with some natural clearings, with sufficient precipitation at the right times of the year for farming on a simple level without water-control devices. Both European and American scholars are holding the view that agriculture arose in wooded lands (Clark 1946:57–71; Braidwood 1948; Sauer 1952:21–22), and it would seem logical that, during the initial dispersal of plant and technique, it would stick to this environment. At least the southwestern data support this view.

Not until agriculture was well established here did it flow out into the less favorable environments as a secondary expansion to the arid plateau and the desert (see Figure 2.1). The harshest part of the Southwest in terms of water scarcity was the desert. Farming, except in river bottoms, was impossible without water control, and measures to control water took some time in developing. But, once gained, the desert was ripe for full exploitation. Perhaps not until the beginning of the Christian Era did maize cultivation become significant among the Hohokam of the desert, as a result of simple canal development. It appears to have been no earlier on the Plateau among the Anasazi, whose planting was limited to small plots situated where ground moisture was concentrated and held after floods.

Kirchhoff's "Oasis America" (1954) centers in the "Great Sonoran Desert," a construct based on ethnology. But in a historical sense the desert appears to have been conquered late.

I conclude that the initial transformation took place in the uplands, that the truly great advances in agriculture came in some of the more arid regions but not until the techniques of canal irrigation were learned. Other arid sections, as the Great Basin, did not experience the same course. The road to stability was not obligatory.

Delayed Effects of Agriculture

The earlier observation with respect to the retarded effects of agriculture bears further discussion because it stands in sharp contrast to the usually accepted opinion that rapid cultural evolution followed as a consequence of food production. Childe's use of "revolution" (1952) has perhaps influenced our thinking, although he is careful to point out (1950:3) that "revolution" denotes the "culmination of a progressive change." Redfield's "transformation" (1953:5) is better suited, it seems to me, to describe what actually happened.

In any event, as previously noted, some two thousand years elapsed between the earliest record of maize in the Southwest and the appearance of village life and other concomitants signaling full sedentary living (Jennings 1956:76). A possible explanation for this may reside in the early knowledge and practice of seed-planting of non-domesticated forms. The addition of maize to the list of existing seed crops was valued as only one more. Early maize was also a primitive form— pod corn—and the yield was relatively small. Its introduction required no new tools for processing, thereby allowing the introduction to pass as a commonplace.

Another factor, perhaps even more important than the foregoing, was the later evolutionary change of maize. Left alone, changes in a single race were gradual, but the introduction of new races of maize produced striking evolutionary spurts. Mangelsdorf and Lister (1956: 172–173) have demonstrated a rapid change in maize in northwestern Mexico at about A.D. 750 ± 250, when, in a few centuries at the most, a primitive race was almost completely transformed by the introduction of two new entities. The date above is too recent for our situation, but, given a similar circumstance in the core area of the Southwest shortly before the time of Christ, one begins to sense the possibility of explosive changes. Improved strains meant increased yields. Larger harvests spelled surpluses. The principle of storage, in underground pits or even in baskets, was already known, so now the economy was shifting from mere subsistence to one of relative abundance. When this happened, there was undoubtedly a real premium attached to the acceptance of maize as something new and prized. As a postulate, I would say that, with this event, new diffusion took place. The northern reaches of the greater Southwest and the Sonoran Desert now came under its influence. Basketmaker (Anasazi) and Hohokam farming was becoming a reality. It is significant that the oldest villages yet recognized, Falls Creek in southwestern Colorado (Morris and Burgh 1954), the Pine Lawn villages (Martin 1940, 1943; Martin and Rinaldo 1947; Martin and others 1949), the Bluff Site (Haury and Sayles 1947), and Snaketown (Gladwin and others 1937), all date near the beginning of the Christian Era, following the postulated improvement in the races of maize. Furthermore, these villages represent the three main culture types—Anasazi, Mogollon, and Hohokam—a strong indication that the factor operating to stimulate the formation of village life cut freely across cultural boundaries. Maize and its related domesticates stand as the logical candidates for bringing this about. I know of nothing in the climatic history of the region, another force operating without respect to culture, that might be called upon to help explain the rise of villages.

The full transformation, then, from collector to producer, was long in coming, attributable primarily to the primitive nature of maize. Its improvement, by introduction of new races, did produce the kind of revolutionary changes within a few centuries usually thought of as following the first farming.

Animal Domesticates

Unlike the Near East and other parts of the Old World, where domestication means both plant and animal, the North American problem is simple. Herd animals were never domesticated, and the only animal that clearly falls within this domesticated category was the dog. Archaeological evidence indicates (Haury 1950a:158) that the dog was already present several thousand years before Christ. The inference is indicated that the dog was not even domesticated here but was brought to the New World from the Old by its human masters.

Of uncertain status in the greater Southwest was the turkey. Some argue that it was domesticated, while others hold to the idea that it was kept. Whatever the outcome, it will have little bearing on our problem, for we must conclude that the people of the Southwest were seed-planters and that they could not count domesticated animals as having any real economic importance among their resources.

The Village: Pattern, Size, and Longevity

According to the previously stated postulate, the improvement in the race or races of maize, shortly before the time of Christ, greatly stimulated its planting in the core area and was responsible for its quick spread to all the greater Southwest except the Far West. Close upon the heels of this advance we see for the first time what Braidwood has aptly called (1958:1428) "village-farming communities." I see these as distinct from the earlier long-occupied camps of the Cochise culture, whether in caves or in the open, because of formalized architecture, perhaps a closer clustering of the houses, usually the presence of a larger, apparently non-domestic structure, and a greater complexity of the material possessions. Of whatever cultural identity, that is, Hohokam, Mogollon, or Anasazi, the house pits remaining reflect a solidity of construction and an investment of labor that would arise only from a need for prolonged residence. These were not temporary camps, evidenced particularly by the Bluff Site (Haury and Sayles 1947), where house pits were scooped out of solid sandstone. Although direct evidence of maize is not available for all, it does exist for some, and for the others the inference that maize was the dependent crop may be drawn from the types of metate or milling tools present.

In evaluating such factors as house distribution and size of community, we are seriously handicapped (in the early 1960s) by the nature of the archaeological digging. Few total villages have been cleared. Hence estimates must be based on what was dug and by extrapolation. A tacit assumption must also be made that, except where demonstrably different ages of houses can be established, all structures were simultaneously inhabited. Against these uncertainties let us examine a few test cases.

MOGOLLON CULTURE
Bluff Site (Haury and Sayles 1947). Occupies the sloping top of a bluff; about 6,600 feet above sea level; 22 of a probable 30 domestic houses excavated; one large communal or (?) cere-

monial structure, near village's center; house distribution random, separated from each other 5–25 meters; several structures date later than main occupation. Assuming 20 houses to have been simultaneously inhabited, and an average family-size factor of 4–5, the village population was 80–100 persons. Age of village: Mogollon I, *ca.* A.D. 300, by tree-ring dating. No direct evidence of domesticated plants, but maize cultivation is inferred.

Crooked Ridge Village (Wheat 1954). Situated on a long, well-drained ridge, 6,200 feet above sea level; 24 of a probable 100 rooms excavated; two large ceremonial structures are near apparent center of village; house distribution random, nearest about 5 meters apart. Some difference in age of houses is indicated, so, assuming that 50 houses were simultaneously occupied and applying the family-size factor of 4–5, the population was 200–250. Age of village, oldest horizon: Mogollon I, Circle Prairie phase, estimated pre-A.D. 400 (Wheat 1955:213). Charred maize present (Wheat 1954:164).

SU Site (Martin 1940, 1943; Martin and Rinaldo 1947). Located on low flat-topped ridge at 6,440 feet above sea level; 28 of a probable 34 houses were dug, randomly scattered in two groups each with nearly central ceremonial house. If 20 houses were occupied at once, probable population was 80–100. Age: Mogollon I, Pine Lawn phase, estimated pre-A.D. 500 (Martin and others 1949:222). Maize inferred from presence in same time period at Tularosa Cave.

San Simon Village (Sayles 1945). On low terrace at 3,600 feet above sea level; 66 structures located, undetermined number remaining undug; no ceremonial structure. Architectural sequence greatly complicated by overbuilding during 6 phases. Oldest houses number about 12, yielding population of 48–60. Age: Mogollon I, Peñasco phase, estimated to be early centuries of Christian Era. No direct evidence of maize, but presence inferred.

ANASAZI

Talus Village (Morris and Burgh 1954). Houses terraced on 25° slope, Animas Valley, Colorado, at approximately 6,800 feet above sea level. A probable 9 houses, floors cleared, closely spaced; indeterminate number not excavated. No ceremonial structure recognized. Population estimate not valid, but at best community was probably small, 75–100. Age: Basketmaker II, pre-A.D. 400, by tree rings. Maize and pumpkin or squash inferred from presence of same in nearby shelter of same age.

Shabik'eshchee Village (Roberts 1929). On mesa top, about 6,600 feet above sea level; village completely dug, 18 houses and one ceremonial room; random distribution, 2–8 meters apart. Presumed population 75–90. Age: Basketmaker III, A.D. 400–700, dating by association. Maize culture inferred.

HOHOKAM

Snaketown (Gladwin and others 1937). Desert environment on terrace above Gila River at about 1,200 feet above sea level. A site of long occupation and only 2 houses recognized representing oldest horizon; initial village probably small, no population estimate possible; house size suggests extended family use. Age: near A.D. 1, dating by stratigraphy and association. Maize agriculture inferred.

In selecting the foregoing villages, I have concentrated on the earliest ones of which we have a record. It is evident that the data are woefully lacking and hardly comparable, especially for the Anasazi and Hohokam. Regardless, they may certainly be recognized as the Southwest's incipient villages, arising from the oldest architectural tradition for the whole of the area in the late Cochise times (Sayles 1945:1–3).

While these villages cut across cultural and environmental boundaries, they were all roughly of the same age. This synchronous build-up supports the idea that the time of village-founding under differing circumstances was the true threshold of settled living. Similarity in village plan is evident, a random scattering of units, with a centrally located ceremonial structure (temple?), especially early in Mogollon villages and somewhat later in those of the Anasazi. This feature remains to be identified among the Hohokam. Village population, by our gross estimates, seems to have been a hundred souls or fewer on the average, though Crooked Ridge Village appears to be an exception. The evidence for maize culture in all is good, and we can accept it as the key factor in accounting for the new phenomenon in settlement history.

The volume of refuse and the lateral extent of it in late Cochise culture sites suggests a community size roughly comparable to that of the village-farming communities. One must agree, on our meager data, with Redfield (1953:6) that the transition from food-collecting to food-producing was not accompanied by an immediate increase in community size.

It may be an accident of more intensive excavation that the Mogo-llon villages appear somewhat more solidly established than do those of the other groups, but these also coincide in distribution with the area from which the earliest maize data and the earliest pottery have come and which was ecologically similar to the donor area of maize. No sites comparable to these villages are known elsewhere in the greater Southwest, though they may well exist to the south in the Cordilleras. The advance from camp to farming village here lagged behind the Near East by at least 4,000 years.

The question of village longevity bids brief reference. Most of the aforementioned villages enjoyed a comparatively short life, at most through several developmental phases of the archaeologist's time scale. The San Simon Village, and especially Snaketown, had a demonstrably long life, 1,200 to 1,400 years for the latter, or 2,000 years if the historic Pima are admitted as the descendants of the Hohokam. Snaketown's is the outstanding stratigraphic record for a southwestern open site. I view village life span as the probable consequence of a particular advance in farming technology. This was water control by ditches. While our oldest readily supportable date for canalization at Snaketown is A.D. 700 (Haury 1936c), the sophistication of the canal of that date and the length of the ditch, more than 3 miles, presupposes a developmental period of considerable time. In view of the survival problem facing even a small community in the desert without some form of water control, I do not find it difficult to believe that ditch irrigation in simple form was already known by A.D. 1. The enormous labor investment in canal construction rooted people to the spot. As the canals grew in length and complexity, bringing ever more acreage under cultivation, new villages would, as a matter of course, be established; but there would have been little reason to abandon the original settlement. So it grew, experiencing local shift in house sites, piling up ever deeper-layered deposits of refuse, and in the end giving the impression of maturity that only long occupancy supplies.

As for the San Simon Village, initially of Mogollon identity and later carrying a Hohokam veneer, the reason for longevity is less readily explained. Neither terrain nor water resources were such as to permit canal irrigation, so the reason must rest on presently unrecognized advantages of the site. While other villages of the Mogollon and Anasazi were frequently overbuilt by later peoples, there were hiatuses in the occupational sequence. Canal irrigation was not employed by them, although simple forms of water control were known. In short, from the slim data we have for the Southwest, village longevity appears to be directly related to the level of hydraulic advances.

Subsequent histories of village and town development in the three areas took different paths. The Mogollon passed the scattered pit-house-living stage largely as the result of having come heavily under the Anasazi sphere of influence. Among the latter a new architectural form was emerging, rooms were joined to rooms, making a cellular structure, and rooms were built on top of one another, the ceiling of one becoming the floor of the next. The plaza or courtyard also puts in an appearance. Thus, Mogollon and Anasazi settlements of later times, certainly classifiable as towns, were essentially the same in composition.

The Hohokam, however, except for a short-lived intrusion of puebloid architecture into their domain in the fourteenth century, abided by the old tradition and lived in sprawling villages of shallow pit dwellings. This is all the more surprising because they had achieved a farming status not matched by the other societies. The reason obviously lies in cultural factors. One may guess that the security given by canal irrigation, a source of water for thirsty fields less capricious than rain, somehow must be taken into account. This dependability required fewer group efforts in formalized rain-making ceremonies and on religious structures per se. Also descent—patrilineal, if we may judge by the modern Pima analogy—and lack of emphasis on the extended family and clan may have been factors. Expertness in husbandry did not automatically determine the compactness or form of community development.

Land Use and Irrigation

The variety of environments in the greater Southwest into which agriculture eventually spread called for the adoption of various methods before effective farming could be established. These would have come only after long familiarity with the habitat. For the core area, the Mogollon, I would reason that there was ample time for this, in the order of 2,000 years. For the rest of the area it may be argued that some knowledge of method spread with material, so that adaptations dictated by the diverse environments were more quickly achieved. The flood-water farming described by Bryan (1929) undoubtedly mirrors the system employed literally from the beginning of planting in the plateau. For the mountains, where land was at a premium, some form of water run-off controls, such as low terraces and check dams, worked effectively to hold and spread the natural water that came as rain or snow (Woodbury 1961). This system, too, must be old. Dating the tangible remains is notoriously difficult because the plots were in use into late prehistoric times. But, without these conjectures, I do not see how the oldest villages described could have reached the permanency indicated.

Irrigation by canal, however, is another matter. Here we must deal with a trait that, in developed form, required engineering skills and labor recruitment not demanded by the simpler systems. Since agriculture came out of the south, it is also tempting to attribute canal irrigation to the same source. I have been willing to accept this as probable, but recently serious doubts have arisen in my mind. Irrigation was only nominally practiced in Mesoamerica, with which most southwestern interconnections seem to have been established, and the antiquity has not yet been certainly determined beyond the Toltec era (Palerm 1955:35–36). Only in the Rio Balsas does one find systems comparable to Hohokam and, beyond that, northern Peru. If the germinal idea did come with maize, it would appear that the Hohokam, by the early centuries of the Christian era, had seized it and, spurred by their favorable topographical environment, achieved full mastery in quick order. The alternative is to entertain the thought that canals were spontaneous, inspired by the fingering-out of waters during flood stage in the Gila and Salt rivers into numerous shallow channels on the flood plain. Nature's example would not have gone unnoticed, for before irrigation farming could have been only on flood plains.

A unique outcome of canal irrigation was the removal of restrictions that dictated village location (Haury 1956:9; Chapter 16). For farming communities in the Southwest two requirements ruled the place of residence: available water and land. Now with water control via ditch, naturally occurring water was no longer requisite, and, so long as the topography permitted it, canals could be made to reach out to farmlands far from rivers, with villages built adjacent. Actually, this emancipation of residence came late, not until the thirteenth or fourteenth century.

The chief significance for us in the foregoing discussion is that different systems of land utilization arose among the three subcultures, required by varied habitats, and that these systems were sufficient to engender subsequent florescences.

Elsewhere in the greater Southwest, especially in the northern and eastern perimeter, farming was little more than a subsistence activity. To the south, as one approaches Mesoamerica one infers intensification of planting where permitted by the environment. The irrigators of the lower Yaqui River in Sonora—because of the shallowness of archaeological time and of what little is known of their historic relationships—may be presumed to have learned the art from the north.

Other Consequences of Village Life

The assessment of the kind and extent of cultural reorientation that followed full dependence on agriculture, beyond the more easily observed phenomena of architectural form and tool complexes, has not been undertaken. It is a difficult subject but one that begs attention, even though most of what can be said is still speculation.

Systematic efforts to note the influence of sedentary living on trade have not been made. It may be observed, however, that trade during most of prehistory in the Southwest was seldom more than a nominal exchange of goods, far below the level of commerce, as evident in the early settlements of the Old World. The liveliest exchange for the longest time of which we have any record appears to have been in marine shell from the west. This began even in the early-man horizon (Sayles and Antevs 1941:67; Haury 1950a:189–190), but it did not reach its peak until after A.D. 1000.

Exchange of pottery is the most readily identifiable evidence of trade, and this we know took place on the village-farming community level between neighboring tribes. Again, not until late in prehistory, however—in the fourteenth century—do we see this reaching significant proportions, that is, when the volume became large enough to make commerce in pottery appear as an institutionalized activity.

The initial appearance of maize, pottery, and the figurine complex from the south I regard as the product of diffusion. This continued through time, ultimately heavily affecting the Hohokam in particular. Direct importations of metal objects, notably copper bells, probably from Michoacan; the mosaic pyrites-encrusted plaques from still farther south; and the military macaw represent trade over the greatest distances. This long-range trade came, not as an antecedent to village and town development, but as a consequence of it. As far as the Southwest is concerned, it is my opinion that diffusion, principally of the stimulus category, was always more important in shaping the native societies than was direct commerce, the imposition of culture elements or patterns by minority immigrant groups or by large immigrant groups who initiated a life way *de novo*. (See Chapter 17 for a revision of this view.)

Coming now to a brief consideration of religion, our ideas clearly must be based on a few tangible remains, and they may be wide of the mark. Mural pictography, usually associated on the early level with the sacred rather than the secular, does not help us. No art of this kind has been surely identified to be as old as the incipient village level. The oldest mural paintings in the Southwest are probably those of Basketmaker II (Anasazi), and the subjects do not reveal to us any clear religious motivation.

Buildings are a somewhat surer base for making judgments. These are the "great houses" or "great kivas." They are major features in all Mogollon villages of pre-A.D. 400 age so far dug except the San Simon Village (Wheat 1955:213), and they usually occupy a central spot in the village. The consistency of their appearance at this early time, the greater engineering skill required to build them over that required to build domestic structures, and the community of effort their construction demanded certainly means that the trait was not new even at this time level. While the origin of the kiva in space and time remains obscure, one may look to the south for its source, where religious systems were already crystallized. From Mogollon, the great kiva went to the Anasazi, where by A.D. 600 it was firmly established.

Curiously, the Hohokam, who were drawing on Mexico for cultural inspiration, especially by the end of the first millennium A.D., and who we know had also merged with the Mogollon in the overlapping frontier of the two groups, never seem to have acquired the great kiva. It is tempting at this point to reevaluate the data from Snaketown (Gladwin and others 1937:74–77), referring to two large Vahki-phase houses by identifying them as great kivas. Typologically, this is supportable, but it would leave the Vahki phase without any domestic structures. If structures 1:7H and 8 were houses in fact, then the place of the great kiva may have been taken by the ballcourt, the idea having come out of the south perhaps as early as A.D. 500–700.

Reading backward in time from the modern pueblo analogy of the priesthood-kiva linkage, one may guess that a priesthood in its formative stages, or some kind of institutionalized religious leadership, was an associate of the oldest Mogollon kivas. Beyond this any assertions lose touch with reality.

The idea of a "kingship" appears to have been foreign in all the greater Southwest. At least there are no modern survivals among native peoples, and there is nothing in the archaeological record to support it. Sociopolitical or socioreligious leadership, however, may be inferred. For Mogollon and Anasazi, the dispersal of houses around the great kiva hints the latter. For the Hohokam, no such distribution is observable. Here I would hold that the emphasis was on civil leadership, for this was more important in canal-building and maintenance than in organized ceremonialism oriented to producing rain.

A still further suggestion of effective political leadership is seen in the multi-village service given by one canal. The welfare of a number of villages depended upon cooperative efforts, and some form of centralized authority must have existed (Haury 1956:8; Chapter 16). But these achievements, along with concepts of water and land rights, are already far beyond the beginnings of village-farming settlements in time. They are to be reckoned among the consequences of the technological advances of a hydraulic society.

FINAL CONSIDERATIONS

We have now passed in quick review some of the major aspects of the culture build-ups in the American Southwest (Figure 2.2). On the collector level, from about 5000 B.C. to 3000 B.C., cultural uniformity characterized the region as a whole; but the subsequent routes were far from uniform. Progress was impressively unequal. Some tribes, as those in parts of Southern California, Baja California, and the Great Basin were essentially static, maintaining the old collector patterns for a probable 10,000 years. Others, starting from the same base, particularly the Hohokam, Mogollon, and Anasazi, reached the highest cultural evolution seen in the area. At any one time after A.D. 1 a cross section of economic patterns would have revealed a spectrum of all the variants ever present except the big-game hunter. In short, in only a part of the greater Southwest did the transition from food-collector to efficient food-producer become a reality (see Figure 2.1).

The dictates of environment were partly responsible. The shortage of rain, the high evaporation rate, and the absence of live streams in most of the varieties of desert previously listed kept large parts of it uncultivable. Land tenure was possible only under a simple subsistence economy except in the Succulent Desert, where natural conditions favored a higher development. It is observable that a correlation existed between the better-endowed areas and the higher cultural achievements, but under these circumstances the environment was permissive and not compulsive. Cultural initiative and determination

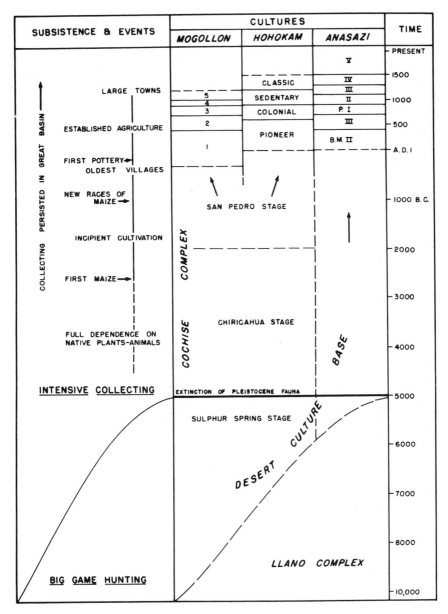

Figure 2.2. Synoptic chart of southwestern culture horizons and approximate timetable of advances leading to urbanism.

must also be reckoned with as dominant factors. Intensification of food-producing came as a happy combination of ecology, cultural outlook, and availability of outside stimuli.

In order of time, agricultural exploitation of the greater Southwest's subenvironments appears to have been oldest in the Desert Coniferous Forest, then spreading into the Dry Grassland, and the more favored parts of the Desert and the Succulent Desert as a nearly simultaneous expansion.

Viewed as a cultural process, the achievement of food production on a high level was far from explosive and not entirely indigenous in nature. Rather, it resulted from a combination of, first, several millennia of experience with and dependence upon native plants and, second, the introduction from the outside of new plants with nutritional and yield potentials higher than any of those in the local flora. Principal among these was maize from Mexico. Initially it was a primitive form, grown for perhaps 2,000 years by simple and desultory cultivation before its full capabilities were realized. In the Southwest, at least, the transition from incipient to advanced cultivation was a slow process.

The reconstruction that I have proposed, briefly summarized, holds that the northern Sierra Madre and the mountain country of Arizona and New Mexico were the core area of the Southwest so far as the transition from food collection to food production was concerned. This is predicated on the presence of the oldest maize, the oldest villages with "temple" structures, the oldest pottery, and a geographical setting favorable for simple agriculture at the end of the corridor along which elements of higher culture traveled from Mesoamerica. Improvement of the primitive maize in the first millennium B.C. by the arrival of new races, or perhaps by teosinte introgression, accounted for a second dispersal of the cereal to its ultimate limits in the greater Southwest. Then followed the development of agricultural techniques suited to differing ecosystems and the ultimate rise of the higher, more complex societies. It was not until these events occurred, at a time coinciding roughly with the beginning of the Christian Era, that we have reasons to consider effective food production a reality. Oddly, the climax areas, the riverine Hohokam of southern Arizona, and the plateau Anasazi of the Four Corners did not coincide with the original core area, where the mountain environment or cultural inertia seems to have had a suppressive effect in spite of having been congenial at the start. The Mogollon, although the initiators of what may be regarded as a good start toward the better life, lost their momentum and were eventually surpassed by their neighbors.

In late prehistory after A.D. 1000, we recognize the existence of large Hohokam villages—for example Snaketown, with perhaps a thousand inhabitants (14 houses excavated, an estimated 5 per cent of those present)—and the towns of the Anasazi, like Pueblo Bonito, with an estimated population of 1,000 (Judd 1954:1). Settlement expansion from the hundred or so inhabitants of the village-farming community to the large village or town of a thousand or more souls was ten centuries in coming. With this increase we see also, especially among the Anasazi, formalized architecture, religious concepts made real to us by kiva architecture, expanding arts and crafts, with perhaps some specialists, some increase in trade, and public works in the Hohokam canals. At the root of these advances were, first, the food surplus, which permitted concentrated populations, and, second, what Childe (1950) refers to as the "social surplus," members of the society who were not needed for food production. This level of attainment was maintained for 300–400 years, whence began a substantial reorientation of the societies, which took the form of shrinking boundaries accompanied by an increase in town populations. The Point of Pines Ruin had a probable population of between 2,000 and 3,000 in the fourteenth century. This trend continued until the advent of the Spanish in the sixteenth century. Actually, the pueblos (Anasazi) of historic times added little to the pattern that was not already established long before. The Hohokam seem to have suffered almost complete eclipse after A.D. 1400, and the glory of their culture is but faintly echoed by the modern Pima Indians. The reasons for the decline are not readily apparent and do not concern us at present except in one aspect. Because the decline was already under way before the Spanish conquest, we can say that both Anasazi and Hohokam had reached their cultural climax before this disrupting influence arrived. It is thus pointless to speculate whether greater heights would have been reached by the native peoples if the Europeans had not come.

Turning to the final problem now, the evaluation of southwestern native cultural evolution against Childe's criteria for cities and civilized life (1950), the following brief observations may be made. The settlements of southwestern societies did not reach the status of cities, and their way of life fell short of civilization as defined, in spite of impressive accomplishments. Advances toward this state are seen in large aggregations of people, an increase by a factor of 10 or more over the early village-farming communities and a beginning of the development of public works, the canals of the Hohokam, to a limited extent canals among the Anasazi, and possibly the great kiva. But this is about all that can be said on the positive side. On the negative side, we have no data that would hint at centralized wealth arising from taxation, no writing, no developed foreign trade for raw materials controlled by segments of the population, no truly developed mercantile centers, no organized warfare, and no ruling class per se. Among the predictive sciences, only astronomy appears to lay claim to any recognition. The movements of the heavenly bodies and the equinoxes, important in modern Pueblo ceremonialism, undoubtedly stem from an old and deep-seated knowledge. But it was rudimentary at best and known principally by priests, who were the combined religious and political leaders. Archaeology does not clearly tell us whether or not full-time specialists existed or what the rules of residence were.

The most we can say for the greater Southwest is that in a part of it, roughly the geographical core area, the necessary foundation for achieving urbanization was laid in the first millennium B.C. and that the ensuing centuries witnessed substantial advances. But innate cultural factors more than environmental restrictions set the boundaries of high accomplishments. Civilization as such, with its related cities and other attributes, was not to be. For the rest of the area the native people never rose above the level of a subsistence economy.

A significant sidelight on the greater Southwest is the fact that its archaeological record of human progress is exceptionally complete up to the point of city achievement. We cannot yet say with certainty that all the historical processes of cultural evolution manifested in the region were experienced by one and the same people; but, at least until late prehistory, this appears to be a likely possibility.

PART TWO

Trees of Time

◄3►

Archaeology and Dendrochronology

Bryant Bannister and William J. Robinson

When Emil W. Haury first became associated with tree-ring research in the late spring of 1929, archaeology and dendrochronology had been bedfellows for over a decade. Ever since A. E. Douglass, the father of dendrochronology, had succeeded in crossdating a small group of prehistoric wooden beams from Aztec Ruin in 1919, it had been clear that the newly formulated tree-ring dating method offered the most promising approach to achieving the long-sought goal of establishing calendrical dates for southwestern ruins. But success came neither easily nor quickly.

Douglass defined his research strategy in a 1919 letter to Clark Wissler of the American Museum of Natural History: "[It] consists in obtaining groups of timbers of different ages so that one group will overlap another, and after combining them (by crossdating) we may bridge over a great many hundred years in the past." If all went well, the resulting prehistoric tree-ring chronologies would eventually be linked to a firmly dated chronology derived from living trees. The first real test of this idea was based on a collection of Pueblo Bonito beam sections sent to Douglass by Wissler. Douglass succeeded in crossdating the Bonito samples with the previously examined Aztec

timbers, and in 1921 he announced that Aztec Ruin had been constructed some forty to forty-five years later than Pueblo Bonito. Stimulated by this exciting revelation, Neil M. Judd, who was just beginning his many years of research at Pueblo Bonito, arranged for the
National Geographic Society to support Douglass's novel approach to
the absolute dating of southwestern ruins. Thus was born the First
Beam Expedition which took to the field in the summer of 1923 to
procure the tree-ring samples required to establish a dated chronology
at least back to the time of Pueblo Bonito. By 1928 two important results had been obtained. First, a continuous tree-ring sequence, firmly
anchored to living trees and including materials from mission churches
and occupied pueblos, had been extended back with confidence to
about A.D. 1400. Second, an internally crossdated floating tree-ring
chronology of 585 years had been constructed from several hundred
samples from about thirty prehistoric ruins that today would be classified as Pueblo III (A.D. 1150 to A.D. 1300). The time had come to plan
a second expedition to locate those elusive timbers that would bridge
the gap between the absolute and floating series and provide the archaeologists, for the first time, with a true chronological perspective
on southwestern prehistory.

The Second Beam Expedition was launched in the spring of 1928
when Lyndon L. Hargrave, then an advanced student at the University of Arizona, was sent to collect beam samples from the old
and abandoned sections of the Hopi villages, particularly Oraibi.
Nearly three hundred new samples were obtained, and the dated tree-
ring chronology was extended back with certainty to A.D. 1300. One
Douglas-fir beam from Oraibi even seemed to carry the record a bit
farther back, to A.D. 1260. Nevertheless, the results were disappoint-
ing because the dated chronology still had not been linked to the prehistoric sequence.

The stage was now set for the Third Beam Expedition of 1929.
Douglass, Judd, Harold S. Colton of the Museum of Northern Arizona, and others had become convinced that a successful solution
would entail excavation of charcoal-bearing ruins carefully selected
on the basis of their temporal placement within the known pottery sequence of northern Arizona. One such site was the Whipple Ruin at
Show Low, Arizona, and Hargrave, by then employed by Colton, was
assigned to work there. But another assistant was needed and, on the
recommendation of Byron Cummings of the University of Arizona,

a "promising young instructor" from the university was sent to join Hargrave. That young man of promise was Emil Haury, and he could not possibly have entered the field of dendrochronology at a more propitious moment, for it was Hargrave and Haury who soon discovered (and gave their initials to) HH-39, the charred specimen that allowed Douglass to bridge the gap and assign construction dates to scores of the most important ruins in the Southwest. Haury's reminiscences of this event in "HH-39: Recollections of a Dramatic Moment in Southwestern Archaeology" (Chapter 4) tell the story as only a participant can. Douglass's ten-year quest had been successfully concluded, and Haury had been a major figure in its most rewarding moment. The disciplines of archaeology and dendrochronology were inextricably joined, and Emil Haury became a leading practitioner of both.

Perhaps it is difficult for a younger generation of archaeologists, a generation constantly exposed to the radiocarbon method and a host of other dating techniques, to fully appreciate the impact of dendrochronology on southwestern studies in the 1930s. Prior to that fateful evening of June 22, 1929, in Show Low, when Douglass spontaneously presented a short course in the temporal placement of southwestern ruins to his fascinated audience of Judd, Hargrave, and Haury, archaeologists literally had no idea how old these great pre-Spanish ruins actually were. The existence of a reliable chronological framework on which to chart the development of prehistoric cultures not only profoundly changed the structure of southwestern investigations, but also altered the thinking of all New World archaeologists. Firm time controls, in the absolute sense, had for the first time been introduced into the study of a pre-literate society. Haury, a man not given to overindulgence in hyperbole, summarized it best in his 1935 report "Tree Rings—The Archaeologist's Time-Piece" (Chapter 5): "In fact, it may be stated without equivocation that the tree-ring approach has been the greatest single contribution ever made to American archaeology," and ". . . dendrochronology has brought about perhaps the most revolutionary single element in archaeological thought."

It is no wonder, then, that Haury chose to continue his association with tree-ring research. Immediately following the exhilaration of the "bridging of the gap" episode, he became Douglass's laboratory assistant, working first in Flagstaff and later in Tucson. In his National Geographic Society monograph of 1935, *Dating Pueblo Bonito and*

Other Ruins of the Southwest, Douglass explained how he "tricked" his young assistant into independently reconfirming the tree-ring chronology across the "gap" by training him on unidentified specimens which Douglass had previously used in his own chronology construction work. It was because of this period of training, which obviously provided Haury's exposure to the mechanics of tree-ring dating, that his final notes on the project showed many of the characteristics that permeated his later works: organization, accuracy and attention to detail, and strict adherence to logic. It seems clear that the time spent with Douglass was formative in Haury's appreciation of rigorous methodology in science.

In the spring of the 1929–1930 academic year, Haury assisted Douglass in teaching a course in dendrochronology. One member of that class was Harold Gladwin, founder of the newly created Gila Pueblo Archaeological Foundation, and in 1930 Haury left the University of Arizona to accept employment at Gila Pueblo, where he was able to blend his skills and interests in archaeology and dendrochronology. At Mogollon Village and Harris Village, at White Mound Village, and at Canyon Creek Ruin and the Sierra Ancha cliff dwellings these interests were pervasive. Indeed, in his landmark volume of 1934, *The Canyon Creek Ruin and the Cliff Dwellings of the Sierra Ancha*, Haury was the first to make significant use of tree-ring dates beyond their bare numeric value. His discussion of the dating of the Canyon Creek Ruin introduced the vitally important concepts of date clustering along with the clustering of cultural traits, seasonality of cutting, and reuse of timbers, and in the mid-1980s it still stood as one of the best models for the integration of tree-ring dates with associated archaeology. Certainly one of Haury's major contributions to dendrochronology was the initial formulation of a body of theory bearing on the use of tree-ring dates in a variety of archaeological contexts. His 1935 "Time Piece" article, in particular, defined the fundamental concepts of archaeological tree-ring interpretation that all later dendrochronologists employed (Robinson 1967; Bannister 1969, 1977; Dean 1978, 1981).

The 1930s were the halcyon days of the relationship between archaeology and dendrochronology. Douglass was actively engaged in archaeological dating, and archaeologists trained by him were active at numerous sites and institutions in the Southwest: Haury at Gila

Pueblo, Florence Hawley at Chaco Canyon, W. S. Stallings at the Laboratory of Anthropology, and John McGregor at the Museum of Northern Arizona. In 1934 the Tree-Ring Society was founded and the *Tree-Ring Bulletin* became its official journal. Haury was an initial member of the Society and was also listed as one of the first editors and publishers of the *Bulletin*. He was elected a fellow of the Society at the annual meeting of 1936 in Flagstaff and served as managing editor of the *Bulletin* from 1937 to 1939. During this period, he also served as treasurer of the Society.

It is not surprising that Haury's impact on the creation of a firm chronological foundation for southwestern archaeology was considerable: through his fieldwork and laboratory dating and through his involvement with the organizational aspects of dendrochronology, he contributed as much as any individual, particularly in terms of balance between the two disciplines. It could be argued, in fact, that Haury's perceptions which led him to define the Mogollon culture—a definition of lasting impact in southwestern archaeology—were substantially aided by his knowledge and use of dendrochronology. If the Mogollon had not been firmly anchored in time, with a long period of preceding development, the culture might well have remained just a branch of the Anasazi, but with a development proven as old or even older than Basketmaker, Haury's arguments of distinct cultural development of the Mogollon came to be accepted.

After his departure from Gila Pueblo and return to the University of Arizona in 1937, Haury continued his deep interest in dendrochronology, as evidenced by his work in the Forestdale Valley, but he left the technical processing in Douglass's hands. His last official participation in the organizational part of dendrochronology came when he, Douglass, and Edmund Carpenter, of the Steward Observatory, were named as founding personnel for the formal creation of the Laboratory of Tree-Ring Research at the University of Arizona on December 5, 1937.

The years after World War II brought a new era in the relationship between archaeology and dendrochronology. The first flush of excitement resulting from absolute dating of prehistoric remains was gone. Tree-ring dating became a routine practice, and more and more effort among dendrochronologists was directed to new applications of tree-ring data in nonarchaeological fields. Haury's personal role in dendrochronology was restricted by increasing departmental and field-school responsibilities; yet, in a specific way, he continued to contribute to the field by including dendrochronology in student training. Tree-ring dating was emphasized at the Point of Pines field school with lectures, demonstrations, and deep commitment to its value as the essential time control required by a sophisticated archaeological science. Students were encouraged to take more formal classroom training in dendrochronology whether they intended to apply this training directly or not. It is hardly surprising, then, that many who "deserted" archaeology as a home department to practice dendrochronology were Haury students.

One cannot close without reporting a little-known fact that must be considered the one Haury contribution to the field of dendrochronology that transcends all others. There came a time when A. E. Douglass, at the age of ninety, relinquished his founding directorship of the Laboratory of Tree-Ring Research and the question was raised by many as to whether the pioneering program in dendrochronology at the University of Arizona should be continued at its then current level of activity. The details are not important; it is sufficient simply to state that it was Haury who stepped forward and persuasively argued that the work of the Laboratory should be maintained and vigorously supported. The Laboratory was preserved, and by the mid-1980s tree-ring research had expanded to all parts of the globe.

⊰ 4 ⊱

HH-39

Recollections of a Dramatic Moment in Southwestern Archaeology

Emil W. Haury

The chronicle of A. E. Douglass's experiences in developing his world-renowned studies into the growth behavior of trees is laden with the insight of a scientist, hard work, frustrations, heartwarming episodes and high drama. Although the complete story of his experiences has not been written and the full impact of his contributions to archaeology has not yet been assessed, one event, which stands out above all the rest, bears recounting on this occasion.

Let us turn time back, as Douglass so successfully did on a grand scale, to the late 1920s. Judd was putting the finishing touches on Pueblo Bonito; Morris was making his uniquely effective contributions to our knowledge of the Basketmakers by urging his battered little truck into the canyons of the Red Rock country; Colton and Gladwin were launching the Museum of Northern Arizona and Gila Pueblo respectively. And there were others, too numerous to mention. It was a time of great activity, spurred in part by the first codification

Reprinted by permission from *Tree-Ring Bulletin* 24(3–4):11–14. Tucson: The Tree-Ring Society, 1962. Presented in a symposium, Tree-Ring Dating, at the 27th Annual Meeting of the Society for American Archaeology, May 5, 1962, Tucson, Arizona.

of the knowledge of the Southwest by the Pecos Conference in 1927. Lacking at that time was any acceptable basis for pinning age labels on the periods of culture development, Basketmaker I to III and Pueblo I to IV, which grew out of the Pecos Conference discussions. Only Pueblo V was securely anchored in the historical present. But, for earlier periods, even the best-informed estimates varied widely. One heard reference to the Basketmakers at 2000 B.C. without provoking an argumentative ripple. Where did the great population centers of Chaco Canyon, Mesa Verde, of the Tsegi, and countless other well-known ruins fit into the Christian calendar? The uncertainty bore down on everyone's thinking, for descriptions of ruins, studies of pots and pans, and efforts to recreate ancient history were sterile without a valid sense of time. All eyes, some skeptical, were turned on the astronomer Douglass; his mind and hands were developing a method that might yield the key to unlock this chronological impasse.

By 1929 Douglass reached the break-through point in his studies. Had this been achieved a decade or two earlier, he would certainly have experienced agonizing delays for the necessary advances in archaeological knowledge had not been made and the mood of the archaeologists was not then ready for him. But, by happy coincidence in the accident of history, the man's idea and the technique were introduced to the discipline about to be vastly enriched at the right moment in its progress.

The Third National Geographic Society Beam Expedition was set into operation in 1929. Its program, arising out of the experiences of the First and Second Beam Expeditions, was to make an all-out attack on the problem of uniting two separate chronologies resulting from Douglass's work up to that moment. The first segment was the chronology beginning with the records in the then-growing trees and extending back in time to about A.D. 1260. To achieve this, Douglass had made use of the timbers from Old Oraibi and even charcoal dug from the ruins of Kawaiku. The second segment of the chronology he called the Relative Dating Series. It was developed from the ring records of wood provided him by the archaeologists, beams from Aztec, Pueblo Bonito, Cliff Palace, Betatakin and others. This series was 585 years in length. It was clear that if this sequence of rings could be joined to the ring record of known age, the time of occupancy of these ruins would immediately become known. Bridging the gap, therefore, became the prime preoccupation, and it was this task to which the Third Beam Expedition was directed.

At this point, knowledge of regional archaeology became important, and the predictive aspect of science had to be called upon. It was known that in northern Arizona, color gradations in the evolution of pottery ranged from red, then orange to yellow. The wood providing the ring record in the oldest part of the historic sequence came from a time when yellow pottery was produced. The youngest logs of the Relative Dating sequence came from ruins that produced red pottery. The answer seemed clear: locate ruins with a predominance of orange pottery, for in them there might be found the architectural wood whose rings would bind the two sequences together.

There was also the factor of geographical location, for the right kinds of trees had to be available to the ancient builders. This presented something of a dilemma. Ruins with the strongest accent of orange-hued pottery were farthest from presumed timber sources, and ruins in the most favorable environments produced a predominance of red pottery, albeit of a different kind than the red pottery of earlier times.

Colton, Judd, and Hargrave worked closely with Douglass in selecting the most promising sites. Four were eventually decided upon: the Whipple Ruin at Showlow, the Pinedale Ruin 15 miles to the west, Kintiel and Kokopnyama more than 100 miles to the north. Hargrave and Haury were signed on to guide the field operations. The party first moved to Show Low in mid-June, 1929, and took up residence in the local hostelry, a converted two-story red brick home. Telephone service was uncertain at best and electric lights were not yet contributing to the luxury of local living. The advantage was that the hotel was just across the street from the ruin.

I cannot say that our first glimpse of the ruin filled us with a sense of destiny. The location of the site on the highest ground adjacent to the flat Showlow valley had made it attractive for homesites for the people who settled there just before the turn of the century. Three houses and sundry barns, sheds, and outhouses occupied flattened parts of the site and many of the original building stones had been put to modern use. Furthermore, much of the ruin had been turned over by one of the owners in search of pottery. It seemed a dismal prospect to do worthwhile archaeology here.

By Tuesday, June 18, a small crew of laborers had been enlisted and the first ground was broken. We had to remember that this was a charcoal-hunting junket and no matter how interesting the test, if no "black gold" appeared, it had to be abandoned in favor of another.

For several days diary entries reveal a tone of discouragement by such notations as "nothing out of the ordinary today." To spur the laborers to maximum effort a bonus of $5 was offered to the man finding a specimen with a hundred rings or more.

Hargrave and I had devised a code system for numbering the specimens found, employing the beginning letter of our surnames, followed by a serial number, which recorded the order of discovery. The register shows HH-1 as a miscellaneous collection of 13 charcoal scraps recovered in a clean-up operation of previous testing. Most of these were no larger than a walnut, and the cataloguing of them was a sign of sheer desperation, although we would not view the keeping of small pieces in such a way today.

A stone-wall property line cut off the major part of the ruin from a small appendage at the far north end. Just what prompted digging in this inconspicuous part of the village beyond the wall I do not recall, but let's attribute it to the desire to sample broadly. Close to the surface a laborer's shovel brought up black, the color to which our eyes were now geared. But how could anything so shallowly buried serve our ends? Could it be a piece of recent wood, the residue of modern occupation? Further digging soon showed it to be the surface-charred end of an ancient roof timber, the heart wood unaffected by the heat long since turned to dust. But, happily, the preserving effects of the charring extended from near the center of the log to near its outer surface. It was by all odds the largest piece of charcoal yet found. This was Saturday morning, June 22. My notes of the discovery are a model of brevity and incompleteness—"Reed Whipple opened up Test 11, Room 4 this morning and shortly exposed a good-sized timber near the surface. Douglass and Judd arrived from Flagstaff just in time to take pictures of it in situ and to help take it out." Then follows the understatement of the decade: "This piece proved to be very valuable; the center ring dated 1237." The latter was obviously an afterthought but written before the full significance of the log was realized.

Douglass and Judd could not have arrived at a more opportune moment. The specimen was exceptionally fragile and its removal would require the combined skills of all hands present. Finally, carefully wrapped and treated, the log was tagged. The number was HH-39.

Douglass immediately retired to a nearby shed, commandeered as a laboratory, and proceeded to do a quick field analysis. Characteristic ring patterns of the thirteenth and fourteenth centuries in the historically anchored sequence were quickly identified, and by counting back in time the innermost ring proved to be the year 1237. The range of the historic chronology was thus extended by more than two decades. This, at least, was in the direction of the gap and Douglass made no effort to conceal his enthusiasm. He continued the examination throughout the afternoon, completely engrossed in his work, intent upon extracting the last bit of information from the carbonized fragments of the beam.

At the dinner table that evening, the conversation suffered long lapses of silence, Douglass turning over in his mind the findings of the day, the rest of us waiting for any pronouncement he might be ready to make.

We moved into the living room for a further review of the problem. Douglass seated himself near the center of the room at a small square table which provided barely sufficient space for a few charcoal fragments, his skeleton plots, and hand lens. Judd, Hargrave, and I arranged ourselves around the room, expectant, but choosing not to talk. Yet one question was uppermost in everyone's mind. Could the extension of the historic chronology by 23 years possibly close the gap? Judd finally broke the silence by the observation: "Maybe the gap is not very big." We felt certain that this thought had been in Douglass' mind most of the day, for he had with him the plots of the prehistoric sequence and was, in fact, already testing a possible overlap. We waited, listened to the uncertain hissing of the gasoline lamp that supplied the only light, watched his every move, and noted with concealed amusement the ever-enlarging smudge of charcoal on his nose as he repeatedly cross-checked the specimen against his paper records.

Finally, the answer came; and here I must quote from memory. If the words are not exact, the meaning is: "I think we have it. Ring patterns between 1240 and 1300 of the historic sequence correspond in all important respects to the patterns in the youngest part of the prehistoric sequence. This means that there was no gap at all. The overlap of the two chronologies was only 26 years and there was no possible way to join the two on the evidence we had. Beam HH-39 has established the bridge." This was a moment of great truth, and at a time like this, the truth sinks in slowly. No one spoke. Douglass was busy making mental calculations, correcting his relative dates for ruins to the years of the Christian calendar. He broke the silence in his gentle way and told the spellbound archaeologists: "This means that

Pueblo Bonito was occupied in the eleventh and early twelfth centuries and the other large ruins of Chaco Canyon were of the same age. The ruins of Mesa Verde, Betatakin and Keet Seel are a little younger, mid-thirteenth century." He continued his recitation, revealing his phenomenal memory, by listing all the major sites from which he obtained wood for developing the prehistoric sequence, and delivering at the same time, a totally new and vital short course in southwestern prehistory.

For the three of us, the experience was unforgettable. To be present at the instant of the celebrated break-through in science that set the chronological house in order for the southwestern United States was reward enough. But beyond that, was the privilege to work for a time at the side of Douglass, the scholar, the astronomer turned archaeologist.

5

Tree Rings
The Archaeologist's Time-Piece

Emil W. Haury

Since 1929 southwestern archaeology has stood on a much surer footing than at any other time in the history of its development. This stabilization is due to the research of Dr. A. E. Douglass of Tucson, Arizona, whose inquiries into the reaction of trees to weather, from an astronomic standpoint, led, as a ramification, to the use of the annual growth rings in trees in dating the pre-Spanish remains of man in the Southwest. From the standpoint of the archaeologist, the most significant progress date in Dr. Douglass's study was June 22, 1929. On that day ended a long search for a particular sequence of rings needed to complete the ring record. This sequence was found in a log in the Show Low Ruin, and united two chronologies then extant, the one a floating series of five hundred and eighty years, the other an historic series extending from 1929 to about A.D. 1280. The great value of the joining of these two series lay in the fact that it became possible, for

Reprinted by permission from *American Antiquity*, 1935, 1(2):98–108. This chapter began as a paper presented at a symposium on "Trees: Recorders of History and Climate," held at Santa Fe, New Mexico, on May 1, 1935, in connection with the Southwestern Division Meeting of the American Association for the Advancement of Science.

the first time, to speak of the age of the Southwest's foremost ruins in terms of the Christian calendar. By this one step, forty old villages, occupied by the Pueblo Indians before the arrival of Europeans, were placed historically. That this achievement was possible where written records were not kept seemed unbelievable; that the discovery was made by an astronomer who utilized material thought worthless by the archaeologist seemed still more incredible. But, in the brief six years which have elapsed since the Show Low log was found, the southwestern student has come to take dendrochronology, or "tree time," as a matter of course, giving data gained through this medium precedence over knowledge gleaned in any other way. In fact, it may be stated without equivocation that the tree-ring approach has been the greatest single contribution ever made to American archaeology. In the regimentation of facts it has taken priority over typological and associational studies, even over stratigraphy which heretofore had proven itself the most valuable control. Tree rings and stratigraphy have shown themselves to be complementary and have combined to build a chronology which shall endure. The whole-hearted acceptance and the continued use of the tree-ring approach by the southwesternist will be an undying tribute to Dr. A. E. Douglass, the inventor of the system.

Since the finding of the first date ever to be derived from a pre-Spanish ruin, Kawiakuh in the Jeddito Valley, in 1928, many ruins, large and small, aggregating well over two hundred, have been dated by Dr. Douglass and his students. Impressive as this figure is, it is nevertheless admittedly small and forms but a very meager percentage of the ruins for which a potential date is possible.

The locality now affected by tree-ring dating in the Southwest may be limited by Mesa Verde on the north, Prescott on the west, Globe on the south, and Pecos on the east; thus including practically all of the plateau and mountain area. In the main, this area includes the sections where Basketmaker and Pueblo remains are the most dense. It is not too much to hope that extensions will be made from this region to include other cultures whose position in time can now be determined only by less satisfactory means. Especially bright are the prospects of carrying the system to other archaeological areas, as, for example, the Mississippi Valley.

Through painstaking research and the application of a rigorous procedure in the study of tree rings, Dr. Douglass has been able to establish a chronology for the Southwest extending in an unbroken line from the present almost to the time of Christ. Quoting from the Annual Report of the Chairman of the Division of Plant Biology of the Carnegie Institution, (Year Book No. 33, for the year 1933–1934), Dr. Douglass writes:

> The long southwestern tree-ring records . . . have given a rainfall history, back to about 650 A.D. Two earlier sequences of "Basket Maker" age, secured by Earl H. Morris, were joined together in March 1933, making a total length of about 800 years. Since January 1932, a definite relationship of the more recent of these to modern chronology has been under consideration. This connection was found in a superb specimen from Chetro Ketl collected and dated by Miss Florence M. Hawley in December 1931. This has been supported by many others, and has enabled us to carry a well-established chronology back to about 200 A.D. and a somewhat complacent record to 11 A.D. A few excellent charcoal sections of prehistoric beams collected in 1927 by Mr. Morris have been identified as dating near 350 A.D.

This chronology has a two-fold value for the archaeologist. First, it holds the key for dating countless other ruins that fall within its span, for wood which has not yet been excavated may be compared with this ring record at any time in the future; second, it offers a weather record, a story of years of drought and of plenty, which opens a large field for study along ecological lines. Owing to local variations in the ring patterns, the master plot or chart of the rings which we now possess does not operate over the entire Southwest. Rapid strides are being made annually to remedy this by the construction of new chronologies. The net result of these studies will bring an even wider area into the picture where dates may be obtained from ruins. In that section where the chronology has functioned with the most success, we find that ruins have yielded dates which fall into a span of more than thirteen centuries, beginning with about the year A.D. 1700 for the latest, and extending to about A.D. 350 for the earliest. It may be fairly stated that the lower limit has not yet been reached. The significance of this naturally is that, where so great a span of time is involved, a new means is supplied for arranging antiquities into stages without the need of cumbersome and often inexact nomenclatures. But more than this, the span of years into which we now know that Basketmaker III and Pueblo IV ruins fall has been an eye-opener as to the rate of culture growth. The ages estimated for some of the major and late ruins on purely empirical grounds were shown to be somewhat too high by the actual dates, but the discrepancy was not inordinately large. Further, the order of periods was unchanged, which in itself is an excellent commentary on the reliability of the methods developed in local research prior to the addition of dendrochronology. For the earlier stages in Basketmaker-Pueblo growth, however, the estimates were considerably in excess of the actual dates. To be specific, dates for those Basketmakers who possessed pottery, which were generally placed before Christ, can now be carried forward to at least A.D. 700. As a consequence, the periods following Basketmaker III are later than heretofore supposed, Pueblo I, for example, dating from the late 700s to approximately A.D. 900, and Pueblo III at its zenith dates about A.D. 1100. The evident fact is that the development from primitive beginnings to the peak of achievement was a swift one, and did not require the centuries of laborious evolution generally imagined. In this point, then, dendrochronology has brought about perhaps the most revolutionary single element in archaeological thought. We have also learned that the development did not progress equally over a wide area; in marginal areas a Pueblo II stage had been reached when at other points Pueblo III was already in full flower.

Reviewing the distribution of dated ruins within the present time scale, we find that sites placed culturally in Pueblo III and IV, dating from A.D. 1000 to A.D. 1350, are most numerous, thus giving us the fullest data on those stages. With the exception of the Flagstaff area, Pueblo II is practically undated and, for Pueblo I, dates are available for both the eastern and western variants. From this point back, the information is very sketchy.

As I see it, there are three angles in the tree-ring-archaeological relationship which must be considered. These are: the field angle, covering the collecting of the beam material; the laboratory angle, embracing the dating of the wood or charcoal samples; and the interpretative angle, in which the facts discovered in the preceding step are integrated and fitted into the background.

For the first of these, it is unnecessary to go into detail, as the field man is already acquainted with the general methods and requirements (McGregor 1930). Sampling in standing ruins requires specialized equipment, and should be done with due regard for the antiquities involved. The recovery of charcoal and decayed wood from open sites is also beset with special problems which must be met as they arise. Success or failure in getting a satisfactory date for the final growth layer of the tree may depend upon the method of handling the beam material in the field by the field technician, for neglect or improper treatment may cause a partial loss of outer rings on fragile specimens.

Looking at the problem from the angle of one who dates the wood, I believe it cannot be too strongly urged that the excavator himself should have a fundamental knowledge of woods, and the utility of ring types. With such knowledge, laboratory work could be reduced to a minimum. However, a wise policy to pursue at all times, whether conversant with the subject or not, is to save all material about which there may be any doubt. The excavator's task does not stop with the selection and care of the material, for, if improperly recorded, certain desired information will assuredly be lost. Wood should receive the same careful attention that is accorded to all other types of specimens. The fullness of the results will depend to a degree upon the thoroughness and wideness of the sampling. The more rooms giving beam material, the better the growth changes of the structure and the history of the culture will be understood.

The second phase, the dating of the wood, is beyond a doubt the most important and crucial step of the three, for inaccuracies will inevitably lead to chaos in the third step, the interpretation. This is to say that to express the cutting date of a log as A.D. 1100 definitely places it; the quantity is unchanging; it is either right or wrong. The weight of the decision naturally rests upon the individual who undertakes the dating, and his responsibility is therefore very great. This dictates that he should proceed with sound and discerning judgment based upon substantial facts. By common consent, it was decided at the tree-ring conference at Flagstaff in 1934 that at least two competent individuals should agree on any date before such a date is published, thus verifying its accuracy.

Some misunderstanding has been created in the past by the failure to specify whether a published date was the bark date—the final layer of woody tissue grown by the tree, occurring beneath the bark—or that of the innermost ring of the log. For the archaeologist, the bark date only has real or primary value. On the other hand, the innermost ring and those intervening are of interest to the student concerned with chronology-building and cycle studies. It is therefore the further duty of the examiner of the wood to state the true condition of the date, whether derived from the final ring or from the last ring on a specimen with an indeterminate number missing. All these points must be seriously considered in the interpretive angle.

A few words may be said at this point in connection with the release of tree-ring data. It is naturally desirable that dates be released
as soon as possible after they have been determined. It is realized,
however, that the reports in which they should properly be published
may be years in preparation, and that their immediate publication
through normal channels may not be feasible. To meet this contin-
gency and others, the idea of issuing a tree-ring bulletin was con-
ceived less than a year ago by those vitally interested in dendrochronology. It was felt that the long delay in the issuance of dates might
retard the advancement of the study, especially in chronology building, and at the same time withhold vital information from the archaeologist. The publication of the dates in a small quarterly in no way de-
tracts from their value in the final published form. To endow such
information with maximum value, it is desirable that together with
data as to the origin of the wood, the sap-heart date, bark date, etc.,
the culture affiliation should also be stated as clearly as possible. Without this the dates have little or no meaning to the archaeologist. If, in
the tabular form of presentation, the lack of space demands the use of
Pueblo I, Pueblo II, etc., the variants of these periods should be explicitly stated. For the benefit of those concerned with the dating of
wood, a combined chronology reproduced in a line cut would also be
invaluable, for, by this means, information as to local differences in
the ring records could be uniformly and inexpensively disseminated.
I should like to emphasize the fact that, since the student's reliance on
or rejection of, tree-ring data will depend largely upon its fullness and
the form of publication, this step should be carefully planned.

We now come to the third consideration, namely the interpretation
of tree-ring facts from the standpoint of archaeology. We may ask at
once, are there any standards of correlation which may be offered for
general acceptance? While to answer this question requires some discussion, it may be admitted from the start that each case in which tree-
ring dates have contributed to our knowledge of ruins, special circumstances demanded special consideration in the interpretation, and
that a formula or group of standards cannot be absolutely set down.
To restate the query put a moment ago, to what extent can we rely
upon wood from a room in order to date the masonry and the associated artifacts? An answer can be given only after a careful inspection
of the related facts, as wholly different explanations may be controlled
by these.

One of the first points to be considered is the question of cutting date, versus deadwood date. This is to say, does the bark date on a log represent the actual time of cutting by the people who built it into their dwelling, or does it represent the last year of the life of the tree which died through natural causes and stood or lay in the forest for a long period before being selected by man? It is generally believed that deadwood or wind-fallen trees were infrequently utilized, first, because this type of wood is much more resistant to the axe than green or live wood, and secondly, in the case of pine and most woods in the local forests, it soon decays and becomes unfit for use. If used, however, it must have been rarely, since the task of hunting out proper deadwood in the forest would probably exceed that of cutting fresh logs. An occasional piece thus incorporated into a structure in which the beams were dominantly live wood, would give an earlier date. It could be largely discounted since precedence, in most instances, must be given to the most recent dates. Exceptions to this would be cases of remodelling or replacements, that is, fresh logs built into an existing building. Further support for the use of live wood is obtained in cases where a series of logs from a single room terminate with the same ring, representing the same year. In one instance with which I am acquainted, twenty-four logs from a pit house gave the same terminal date. The probability of the occurrence of this condition, if deadwood has been selected for the structural beams, is extremely small. Repetitions of this case call for a generalization to the effect that live wood was generally used, and that the final ring can be accepted as representing the construction time. One condition that may introduce error is the possibility that beams once cut were not immediately used, but were allowed to season in order to avoid sagging. Although seasoning of logs is practiced by the Pueblos to some extent, it cannot be positively asserted that this procedure obtained in ancient times. A variation of a year or two in the dates of logs of a given house may suggest this. If seasoning prevailed, house-building was definitely planned a year or two in advance, a condition which was probably not general. Emergency situations must also have arisen which demanded immediate construction. Admitting that a year or two elapsed between cutting and construction time, the factor is so small as to be trivial, and the problem resolves itself into a very minor one.

While wood found within a room is most apt to be related to it structurally, several other conditions may also prevail which might prove to be disturbing factors in the interpretation. For example, charcoal from the fireplace might conceivably give far more recent dates than the roof beams. Where the structure has been burned, it may not always be possible to segregate wood from the two sources. A further confusing situation might be created by the dumping of discarded wood into an abandoned room which was being filled with rubbish; however, here the nature of the wood and its position in the fill will usually give some clue as to its origin. Logs found as an integral part of the house, i.e., built into the walls or lying on the floor in such a position as to indicate clearly that they were once in the roof, are naturally the most convincing in offering construction dates. Let us take an ideal case to see what possibilities might arise where definite structural wood is being dealt with. Say that six major logs supporting a roof give, in each case, the same bark date of A.D. 1300. Little leeway is possible here in interpretation, for the odds overwhelmingly favor that date as the time of construction, or within a year or two in case of seasoning. Should one of the logs give a date of A.D. 1150, the obvious discrepancy of 150 years can best be explained by supposing that that particular log was salvaged from an older structure. This situation is known to have occurred in the past, as witness the log taken from a house in Oraibi a few years ago which was cut in the late fourteenth century (Douglass 1929:754). Or we may find that one or more of the logs gives a reading of A.D. 1350, fifty years later than the remaining five. In this event, a repair or replacement may be indicated. It is further conceivable that each of the six logs will give different dates, probably indicating a heterogeneous collection of beams, in which event only the latest date will be of any particular value. Such a condition must be rated as highly unsatisfactory. It will be readily seen that the various situations thus outlined will, in one way or another, affect the interpretation. Each set of circumstances presents a particular problem, the solution of which cannot be reached by pre-arranged standards.

A similar set of conditions may be visualized in working out the relationship of the dates of a room to those of the artifacts contained within. To put this as a question: Are the artifacts within a house approximately the same age as the house itself? Generally speaking, they are; however, in some instances they may be more recent. This is said with full recognition of the possibility of finding old pottery and the like in recent rooms, and recent materials in rooms which have been occupied for a long time. In this case judgment must be influenced by the archaeological conditions. The best form of proof for dating artifacts in this manner lies in the consistent appearance of a trait or traits within rooms of the same general age. This is to say that group data became the decisive factor. For example, the Canyon Creek Cliff Ruin (Haury 1934b), located on the Fort Apache Indian Reservation, offered eighteen datable rooms out of a total of about sixty. These rooms are scattered throughout the length and breadth of the structure in both the first and second stories. The artifacts from all rooms were uniformly of the same generic kind, reflecting no period changes, and the range of dates from the eighteen rooms was between A.D. 1326 and A.D. 1348. From this it may be concluded that the material culture is of comparable age, or perhaps a little later. It can be unerringly dated to the fourteenth century. This angle of tree rings and archaeology is one of the most vital, and, because of its admitted importance, a correlation should not be attempted without full comprehension of all related information.

Once material culture has been satisfactorily dated in a region, objects native to that place, but alien to another, become valuable time indicators. In such cases tree rings are directly responsible for ordering the data in the primary area, and indirectly in the adjoining area. The value of this approach is particularly high in such regions where, owing to physiographic and other conditions, tree rings may never be utilized. The time status of the Hohokam of the Gila Basin has been worked out chiefly by this method. The same principle will doubtless be brought into play in the study of Mexican and Mississippian cultures.

Exact as a date may be, it is not possible to value each one equally. Distinctions arise which are governed to a certain extent by conditions already outlined, and by others which will be mentioned presently. We need to consider the value of a single date versus many dates, first, from a one-type site, that is, one in which the occupation was short and the material culture all of one phase, and second, from a site long occupied, in which growth changes are apparent. An individual date from a one-type ruin can be more rigidly interpreted than one from a large complex site, since, in the former, there was little opportunity for old beams to be re-used and for other disturbing factors to creep in. Single dates may be strengthened by dates from other sites of approximately the same age and cultural association. As an example, two dates from Gila Pueblo, a one-type ruin, are A.D. 1345 and A.D. 1385. While these are indicative of the age, there is of course room for

error. However, with dates ranging from A.D. 1326 to A.D. 1348 in the
Canyon Creek Ruin, and with a terminal date of A.D. 1383 for the
Show Low Ruin, both of which manifest cultural ties with Gila Pueblo,
the dates procured at Gila Pueblo may be admitted as valid.

In the case of a site giving several stages, group data only will give
satisfactory results, for individual dates offer too great an opportunity
for misinterpretation owing to the possibility of reused beams. One
important case of this character is now before us. The earliest date
from a ruin in the Southwest is about A.D. 350. This was obtained
from a log found by Mr. Earl H. Morris in Mummy Cave, Canyon del
Muerto. Archaeologically, it is known that this cave was occupied from
Basketmaker II times, but the conditions were so confused that the
association of the beam in question could not be positively determined. No matter how strong the temptation may be to date the culture on the strength of this log, it cannot legitimately be done until
further dates or relevant facts have been gathered.

While we have been concerned so far mainly with dates from structural wood, Dr. Florence M. Hawley has also demonstrated the utility
of charcoal fragments from rubbish heaps in the case of Chetro Ketl
(Hawley 1934). The value of pottery sequences obtained from the
study of daily sweepings of broken pottery and charcoal, as a check
against information obtained in the building itself, needs hardly to be
pointed out. This study also helps in solving the problem of the length
of time involved in the accumulating of rubbish mounds.

So far, the climatic angle of tree rings and archaeology has only
been mentioned. Yet here lies a very fertile field, for past weather and
human activity are intimately related. In the present chronology, which
just falls short of 2000 years, one extended drought and several short
ones are recorded. We suspect that the most severe of these, the
drought lasting from A.D. 1276 to A.D. 1299, profoundly affected certain of the southwestern peoples, and was responsible in the main for
shifts in the population at about that time. But so far we have done
little more than look at the raw and isolated facts. Here the archaeologist must cooperate with the climatologist whose interpretation of the
tree-ring calendar from the weather angle is needed before it is possible to carry the study forward along strictly archaeological lines.

We would do well to ask ourselves at this point whether or not the
tree-ring data we now have conflicts with the archaeological evidence.
It has already been intimated that, before the benefits of dendro-

chronology were available, the error of age estimates of culture stages increased progressively from recent to remote times. However, since this adjustment has been made in the minds of students of southwestern archaeology, it can be said that no glaring conflicts, such as radically differing dates for the same cultural stage, have occurred. Indeed, should a violent disagreement occur, it would be well to look into the possibility of irregular conditions in the archaeological evidence. Improper release of dates and too rigid an interpretation, may tend to throw the facts out of alignment. On this last point, it is well to remember that, while a date may generally place a developmental stage, it does not delimit it. A problem relating to this part of the discussion has recently been raised by Mr. John C. McGregor, who, in dating wood from pit houses excavated by the Museum of Northern Arizona, found a span of 150 years in bark dates from the wood of a single pit house. Upon first consideration, one might say that the house was occupied for this period, and that towards the end of the occupancy, log replacements were made, thus accounting for the great difference in time. The improbability of a 150-year life for an underground house, and the lack of change in the material culture associated with it, in view of the more rapid changes general over the Southwest, tend to temper this idea. But the problem is not easily solved. A likely explanation is that, in the construction of the house, the builders robbed an old dwelling for useful beams, adding to them others cut currently, and consequently of much later date.

Much, very much indeed, has been accomplished in the few years that dendrochronology and archaeology have joined hands, but the work has literally only begun. Some ramifications of the subject have been almost entirely neglected. Along lines of basic research more work is necessary. For example, master plots covering zones or more restricted areas than we now possess, would be invaluable in hastening the dating in marginal areas, as in the Mimbres, where certain fundamentals shown in the Flagstaff chronology were apparently not repeated. Fortunately Dr. Douglass and Mr. H. S. Gladwin are now at work on this problem and results may soon be expected. Research on woods other than those now used should lead to worthwhile results.

Extension of tree-ring dating to other areas is a challenge which cannot be overlooked. First steps outside of the nuclear area in the Flagstaff–Chaco Canyon sector, were made to the east in the Rio Grande where Mr. W. S. Stallings, of the Laboratory of Anthropology, has succeeded in the difficult task of building up a basic chronology extending to A.D. 1100 (Stallings 1933). In the Tennessee Valley, Dr. Hawley has obtained significant results from wood found in Mound-builder remains. Northern Mexico and possibly parts of South America may similarly prove to be rich fields. For the tropics, the outlook is not bright, although not altogether hopeless. In my opinion, illuminating work might well be done in Egypt where an abundance of useful wood of dynastic times is available. While the Egyptian chronology has been worked out with reliability on astronomic and historic ground, I believe it is not unlikely that tree-rings might well substantiate and possibly amplify this.

The degree to which success will come in the relationship of American archaeology and dendrochronology will depend largely upon the degree of cooperation among those vitally concerned in the study. Due to its involved nature, the welfare of the subject depends upon coordinated efforts. Lacking this, the most unique check yet discovered on the changing quality of human culture cannot bear its richest fruit.

PART THREE

The First Southwesterners

Paleoindian and Archaic People

◄ 6 ►

Discovering Early Man in Arizona

C. Vance Haynes

The breakthrough in conclusively demonstrating that North American Paleoindians did indeed successfully hunt Pleistocene megafauna came in 1926 near Folsom, New Mexico, where scientists found projectile points in undeniable association with bones of a Pleistocene species of bison. That same year, Emil W. Haury accompanied Byron Cummings to Whitewater Draw in southeastern Arizona, where they excavated the nearly complete skull of a mammoth from deposits overlying artifacts of the Sulphur Springs stage of the Cochise culture. From that day forward Emil Haury maintained his strong interest in early man in the New World, and that formative experience was just the beginning of a career devoted to the archaeology of the Southwest and to Paleoindian studies.

An early appreciation for the contributions that other disciplines can bring to archaeology was manifest in all of his work. His understanding of the importance of geology to interpreting archaeological stratigraphy was born out in 1941 by his enlisting the aid of Harvard geomorphologist Kirk Bryan, who prepared a chapter on the geological interpretation of the deposits of Ventana Cave, Arizona. *The Stratigraphy and Archaeology of Ventana Cave, Arizona* (Haury 1950a) is one of Haury's truly monumental contributions. Ventana Cave, the first multicomponent site in Arizona with a Paleoindian occupation, produced an assemblage of stone artifacts in association with bones of extinct game animals. One of the projectile points is clearly related to the fluting tradition, either Folsom or Clovis, but the possibility of an earlier occupation was raised by the occurrence of two problematic artifacts in the underlying conglomerate. Haury's scientific objectivity was expressed in his caution that the evidence was "of such a scanty nature in the light of more positive data . . . from the volcanic debris layer that it may be regarded as inconclusive." Less cautious investigators, promoting the more sensational aspects, might have insisted that these artifacts were the earliest evidence of man in North America. The occurrence of three Archaic occupations at Ventana Cave above the Paleoindian volcanic debris layer and below Hohokam and Papago levels established an archaeological sequence that became a major reference for which archaeologists in the mid-1980s were still developing a chronology through radiocarbon dating.

Intense rains during the summer of 1951 exposed mammoth bones in Greenbush Draw near Naco, Arizona. Soon after Fred and Marc Navarrete reported two projectile points in association with these bones, Haury arrived with geologist Ernst Antevs and paleontologist John Lance to investigate what became known as the Naco Site, the first Clovis site to be found west of the continental divide. Haury's report, a model of concise, interdisciplinary reporting, concluded that the single mammoth represented by the bones had been attacked and killed by Clovis hunters, who had dispatched no less than eight projectile points into the beast. Basing his conclusions on geologic evidence, Antevs estimated the time of this kill at 10,000 to 11,000 years ago. The fact that this estimate was later verified by radiocarbon dating attests to the remarkable accuracy of his geologic-climatic dating model for the Southwest. Lance identified the mammoth as *Mammuthus columbi*, reviewed the problem of probocidean taxonomy, and called for a systematic reexamination of the taxonomy of mammoths with Paleoindian associations.

While the Naco excavations were in progress, Edward F. Lehner came to Haury to report his discovery of mammoth bones protruding from the bank of an arroyo only ten miles northwest of the Naco Site. Three years later Haury was advised by Lehner that summer rains had exposed a bone bed of impressive extent. Subsequently, the Arizona team, joined by E. B. Sayles and William W. Wasley, excavated what became known as the Lehner Site and discovered thirteen Clovis projectile points in and among the bones of nine Columbian mammoths, a bison, a horse, and a tapir. Eight miscellaneous tools were also found in situ, as well as two fire hearths with charcoal that provided the first radiocarbon dates for the culture. The first results, which varied by 5,000 years, led Haury to remark that "no aboriginal fire was kept burning that long!" Subsequent replication of radiocarbon dates by several laboratories established a date of 11,200 B.P. for the Clovis culture in Arizona, a radiocarbon date that was later determined at several other Clovis sites.

In the Lehner Site report Haury addressed questions that were still current in the mid-1980s, such as how Clovis points might have been employed, how mammoths may have been held at bay and attacked, and the temporal position of Clovis relative to the Sulphur Springs stage. His call for observations of what happens to elephant carcasses around modern water holes anticipated the current trends toward taphonomy and experimental archaeology.

With the Lehner Site, Haury became the first archaeologist to have the good fortune of excavating two significant Clovis sites during his career. If we include the Murray Springs, Leikem, Escapule, and Navarrete sites, with which he was personally involved as either collaborator or advisor, he can claim direct personal experience with four of the known Clovis sites plus two probables, and it may be that in the future another Clovis site will appear in the San Pedro Valley to attract the attention of his special genius.

Artifacts With Mammoth Remains Naco, Arizona

Discovery of the Naco Mammoth and the Associated Projectile Points

Emil W. Haury

HISTORY

On September 22, 1951, Marc Navarrete brought word to the Arizona State Museum of the discovery of two large projectile points in association with mammoth bones exposed in an arroyo eroded by Greenbush Creek one mile northwest of Naco, Arizona (Figure 7.1). Marc Navarrete and his father, Fred, for some fifteen years have been watching the arroyo for fossils as erosion widened and deepened it.

A bone concentration, though known for some time, was freshly exposed by floods resulting from heavy summer rains in August, 1951. This encouraged Fred Navarrete to dig in an attempt to salvage what appeared to be a part of a skull with teeth and tusk of a large animal. In the course of this work he found near the skull a projectile point in what appeared to be undisturbed matrix. Additional excavations by Marc Navarrete soon revealed the left foreleg, scapula, humerus, and ulna and, near the superior margin of the scapula, again in the undisturbed clay, a second projectile point came to light.

Reprinted by permission from *American Antiquity*, 1953, 19(1):1–14.

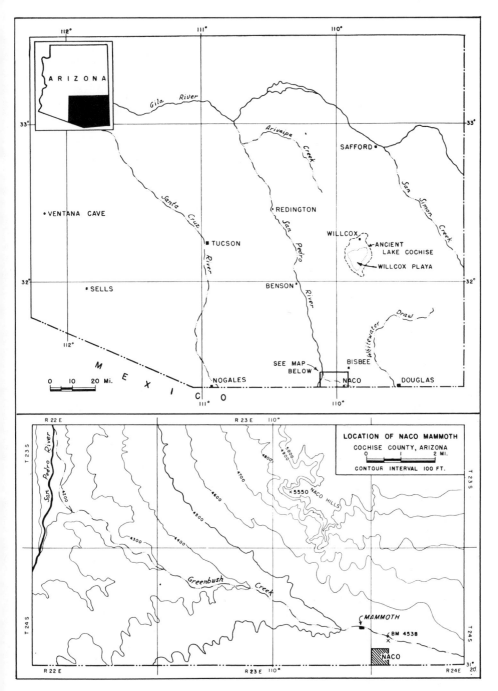

Figure 7.1. General map of southeastern Arizona (*above*) and enlargement of Naco area (*below*), giving location of mammoth station.

The excavations herein reported were made from April 14 to 18, 1952, with the following persons participating: Ernst Antevs, whose analysis of the geology accompanies this report; John Lance, paleontologist, Department of Geology, University of Arizona, whose report is also related hereto; E. B. Sayles, Curator of the Arizona State Museum; Garland Marrs, Alan Olson, George Cattanach, and Hayden Russell, students in the Department of Anthropology; and the writer.

The exemplary attitude and the alertness of the Navarretes shine as a beacon on the relationship between the interested amateur and the specialist. It is my sincere hope that the vital part these men have played in adding to a clearer understanding of early man in the Southwest will be a lasting satisfaction to them. Special acknowledgment is also made to Reid Gardner, then President of the Arizona Edison Company (now the Arizona Public Service Company) for having expedited the permit to excavate on company property.

The digging procedure was as follows: a) removal of recent surface deposits and outlining the extent of prior excavations; b) removal of overburden to bone layer and delimiting the extent of the bone deposit; c) exposure of all bones; d) preparation of elements and sections for preservation by jacketing. All steps were given adequate photographic coverage.

TOPOGRAPHY

The San Pedro River rises in northern Sonora, Mexico, flowing through southeastern Arizona in a northwesterly direction where it eventually joins the Gila River. The San Pedro Valley along its entire course is narrow, bordered on each side by mountain chains, and falls from 4275 feet above sea level at the international boundary to about 1900 feet at its juncture with the Gila. The upper basin, extending from Benson southward, contains extensive deposits of Pleistocene and Pliocene Age. Recent alluvium in the valley's axis is quite deep, quickly deposited and quickly eroded because of the steep gradient. Fossil remains are found chiefly in the older alluvial deposits along the edges of the inner valley and away from it in tributaries.

Greenbush Creek is one of these. It rises almost parallel to the Mexican border about seven miles due south of Bisbee near the southern tip of the Mule Mountains, extending west by north for twelve miles where it empties into the San Pedro River (see Figure 7.1). The elephant locality is a little over nine air miles from the river.

Figure 7.2. The mammoth locality (Arizona FF:9:1) on Greenbush Creek, one mile northwest of Naco, Arizona. Arizona Public Service Company plant in background.

This drainage has an average fall of about 30 feet per mile. The flood plain, beginning a mile east of Naco, gradually widens to one-half mile or so at the lower end. Until a few decades ago the valley floor was heavily grassed and locally quite marshy. The erosion of the San Pedro channel, which began in 1883 (Bryan 1925:342), extended into the tributary systems and by 1922, headward cutting in Green-bush Creek reached a point north of Naco. This exposed the fossil-producing beds. The mammoth locality is one mile north by west of Naco on the south bank of the draw at an elevation of 4515 feet above the sea (Cochise County, R23E, T24S, S13, NE1/4; Arizona State Museum Survey No.: Arizona FF:9:1). At this point the arroyo has a depth of 3 meters and a width of 12 to 15 meters (Figure 7.2).

OCCURRENCE OF BONES

The San Pedro Valley has long been known as a fertile source of paleontological material. In the 1920s Gidley removed an extensive fauna from upper Pliocene and Pleistocene beds near Benson (Gidley 1922, 1926; Gazin 1942); the territory north of Redington has been a productive hunting ground for camel and other remains of Pliocene age. Elephant bones, stray elements and otherwise, have frequently come to notice, especially in the middle and upper reaches of the drainage. The discovery of these has been hastened by the accelerated erosion of the beds of the main stream and its tributaries. This is mentioned only to point out the fact that the San Pedro Valley, which has already contributed information on the late stage of the Cochise culture (Sayles and Antevs 1941:21–26) may be expected to continue to yield information of early man. It would be folly to believe that the Naco elephant was the only such evidence.

At the start of the excavations, the only bones known were a few scattered elements at the edge of the arroyo lightly covered with sand and gravel and some 3 meters from the arroyo bank. The space between the gravelly arroyo floor and the bank sloped gently upwards towards the bank (Figure 7.3) and consisted of laminated silts and clays and a thin blanket of drift material (Figure 7.4, bed e and *supra*). The laminated clay-silt bed, being somewhat more resistant to erosion than the softer overlying deposits, remained as a bench.

The removal of bed e revealed the fact that the bones were encased in it but rested on, and in the case of the larger elements, somewhat pressed into, the underlying sand layer d (see Figure 7.4). Locally among the bones there were small sandy lenses, evidently the result of current action which brought coarse material into the pond from higher parts of the sand bar. Over most of the area, however, the clay-sand cleavage was sharp. The position of the bones on the sand and the nature of the matrix makes it clear that the animal fell on the sandy surface and had not become mired. Lance (1953:19) has identified the animal as a Columbian mammoth, *Mammuthus* (*Parelephas*) *columbi*.

Insofar as revealed by our excavations, the bones were scattered over an area of approximately 7 meters east-west by 4 meters north-south (see Figure 7.4). The lowering of the arroyo bed below the bone level along the northeastern margin may have removed some of the elements. The larger bones, as skull, jaw and tusk, forelimbs, scapulae, ribs and vertebrae, were fairly well concentrated though disarticulated. The smaller foot bones were scattered as shown, the most distant ones being downward on what was then the gently sloping surface of a sand bar. The hind legs, pelvic girdle and lumbar vertebrae

Figure 7.3. Laminated clay-silt bed (see also Figure 7.4e) in base of which mammoth bones occurred. Trowels mark locations of bones encountered early in excavations, and dotted line indicates extent of Navarrete excavation.

were not recovered, having either been carted away by the hunters when the animal was butchered, or washed away by the recent erosion. The latter possibility could only have taken place if these bones had become quite widely scattered from the rest, placing them in the present arroyo's path.

The bones rested on a sand deposit (bed d) which sloped uniformly over the area exposed with an east-west strike and a constant dip of 90° to the north. This slope in itself may account in part for the disarticulation of the bones, but the occurrence of the lower jaw up-slope from the skull, which may be presumed to have been near its original position when the animal fell, suggests that other agencies as predators, possibly man, also dragged some of the bones about. The ribs and cervical vertebrae, though jumbled, were well concentrated (Figure 7.5).

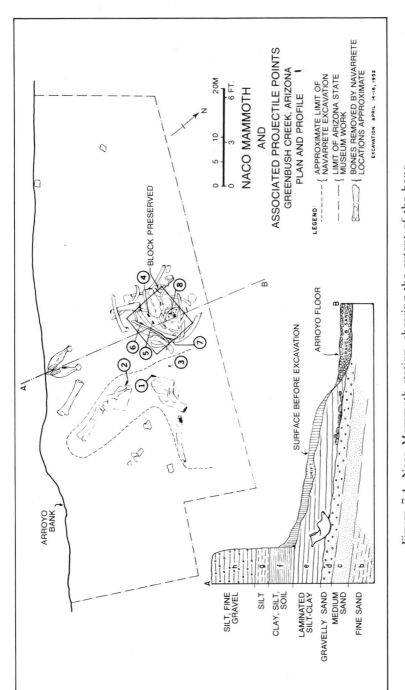

Figure 7.4. Naco Mammoth station, showing the extent of the bone bed, location of spear points, and the geology. Lettering of the deposits coincides with those assigned by Dr. Antevs (1953). Enumeration of projectile points is in order of discovery; location of points 1 and 2 approximate only.

Figure 7.5. General view of mammoth bones in early stage of uncovery. Lower jaw (*center*); ribs and vertebrae (*foreground*).

We may visualize the sequence of events leading to the preservation of these bones, somewhat as follows: killing of the animal,
slaughtering, decay of remaining tissues, scattering of bones, and
within a few years, the ponding of the adjacent stream providing the
conditions for the formation of the clays which preserved them. That
this took place within a few years of the death of the animal is indicated by the good preservation of the delicate parts of the bones. It
may also be inferred that between the time of the "kill" and nature's
burial of it, man did not revisit the spot, for it would appear likely that
the spear points would have been retrieved. Several of these most certainly must have lain in plain view.

POINTS

Table 7.1 presents the essential characteristics of the eight points
associated with the mammoth and one found in the arroyo upstream.
Excluding the latter, we have in these a remarkable sample of un-
damaged projectile points, found in situ and used in the killing of a
single large mammal. Their chief value lies in demonstrating what
variations may be expected in contemporaneous weapons. While the
Arizona State Museum actually removed but five of the eight points
from their original spots, there is no reason whatsoever to doubt that
the remaining three, two of which were taken out by the Navarretes
and one by us in disturbed ground, were hurled on spears at the same
time and by the same hunters as the others. The eight points will be
regarded as a single association. Leaving the weapons in the cadaver
seems a wasteful procedure in our eyes. But the task of searching for
them in the butchering process must have been regarded as not
worthwhile. I do not believe the wounded animal escaped the hunters
and died far from the scene of the attack.

The location of the points is given in Figure 7.4. Number 1
(A-11912) has been placed approximately but Fred Navarrete is
positive in his statements that the specimen was at the base or nuchal
area of the skull. The position of Number 2 (A-11913) in relation to
the left scapula has been established on the basis of a kodachrome
slide in possession of Marc Navarrete. The rest were plotted during
our work. Number 3 (A-10904) must have lain originally within the
area excavated by the Navarretes, but exactly where, is not known.
Numbers 4, 5, 6, 7, and 8 (A-10899, A-10902, A-10901, A-10903, and
A-10900) rested among, between, and on bones in a meter-square

Figure 7.6. Meter-square block of ribs, vertebrae, and scapula, showing locations of five spear points. This block was jacketed and removed intact to the Arizona State Museum.

area but none was imbedded in bone (Figure 7.6). Numbers 6 and 7 were lying flat and wedged between ribs and Number 8 rested squarely against one of the anterior articular facets of the atlas vertebra. This occurrence is strikingly like the spear and atlas vertebra of a mammoth reported by Sellards (1938: Plate 1) from Roberts County, Texas. Assuming that there was little or no shifting of the points since the death of the animals, the angle and place of penetration was about the same in each case, from the upper right side of the elephants and at the base of the skull, the spot in the elephant's anatomy where the spinal cord was most vulnerable. In the case of the Naco mammoth, this spear might have been the disabling one. It is worth noting that all the points recovered at Naco were between the skull base and fore part of the rib cage.

If the projectile point-bone association of itself is not convincing of contemporaneity, the concentration of the points in the vital target area of an animal should dispel any doubts. It may also be inferred

Table 7.1
Naco Projectile Points
(Measurements in millimeters; color reference to
Munsell Soil Color Charts, Hues 7.5R through 5Y)

Arizona State Museum Cat. No.	Figures 7.7 & 7.8	Location of Points Shown in Figure 7.4	Material and Color	Total Length	Maximum Width	Basal Width	Maximum Thickness	Extent of Dull Edges Above Base	Remarks
A-11912	d	Near nuchal area of skull. No. 1	Chert; dusky red, 10R, 3/2 to 10R, 2/1; reddish black near tip and base	96	25	23	9	32	Found by Fred Navarrete Aug. 1951. Pronounced median ridge both faces. Same material as No. A-10904
A-11913	f	About 10 cm. from superior margin of left scapula; point towards bone. No. 2	Chert; reddish gray, 5YR, 5/2 to dark gray, 5YR, 4/1. Some mottling	97	30	27	9.5	35	Found by Marc Navarrete Sept. 1951
A-10899	b	In rib area. No. 4	Chert; dark brown, 7.5YR, 4/2 grading to brown, 10YR, 5/3. Banded	72	26	19	8	31	Same material as No. A-10903
A-10900	h	On anterior articular facet of atlas vertebra. No. 8	Felsite; very dark gray, 2.5YR, 3/0	68	27	27	8	35	One ear broken. Same material as A-10901

Catalog No.	Fig.	Provenience	Material						Remarks
A-10901	g	Between overlapping ribs. No. 6	Felsite; very dark gray, 2.5YR, 3/0	81	30	27	8	35	Fluting by multiple flaking. About 3mm. lost at tip, not included in measurement. Same material as A-10900
A-10902	c	In rib area. No. 5	Chert; dark gray, 2.5YR, 4/0 grading to very dark gray, 2.5YR, 3/0. Banded, translucent at edges	68	31	27	8	30	Ears rounded. Poorest workmanship.
A-10903	e	Between and in contact with overlapping ribs. No. 7	Chert; gray, 10YR, 4/1 to light brownish gray, 10YR, 6/2. Mottled	116	34	27	9.5	36	One ear broken. Same material as No. A-10899
A-10904	a	In back dirt, Navarrete excavation. No. 3	Chert; dusky red, 10R, 3/2	58	23	22	7.5	28	Same material as A-11912
A-11914	Fig. 7.9	In arroyo ¼ mile upstream from elephant locality	Chert; gray, 10YR, 6/1	81.5	32	30	10	32	Large horizontal flakes. Fine edge retouching

that these were weapons and not knives used in butchering the animal. Tools used in the dismembering process were not recovered. The recent evidence from Mexico (Aveleyra and Maldonado-Koerdell 1952) suggests that small cutting tools were employed in the slaughtering of the mammoth at Iztapan.

The materials used in the manufacture of the Naco points are of two classes, chert and felsite (identification by Richard T. Moore, Assistant Mineralogist, Arizona Bureau of Mines). The chert varies in color from dusky red through browns to gray and shows some banding and mottling. The felsite, dark gray in color, is exceptionally homogeneous and well suited for pressure chipping.

The interesting observation may be made that three pairs of points were made of the same stone: 6 and 8, dark gray felsite (Figures 7.7 and 7.8, g,h); 1 and 3, dusky red chert (Figures 7.7 and 7.8, a,d); and 4 and 7, brown chert (Figures 7.7 and 7.8, b,e). This indicates that materials were obtained in good-sized chunks and that the source of supply was quite adequate. Where that source was is impossible to say now, although it should be noted that both limestone, the probable source of the chert, and volcanics, the source of the felsite, occur locally. There is no patination evident in the specimens.

Figures 7.7 and 7.8 illustrate the eight points, obverse and reverse. Even including the smallest point in the series (3, Figures 7.7 and 7.8, a) both maximum and basal widths are quite uniform. These range from 23 to 34 millimeters and 19 to 27 millimeters respectively. The lengths show a far greater range, from 58 millimeters (3, Figures 7.7 and 7.8, a) to 116 millimeters (7, Figures 7.7, e, and 7.8, e). Six of the points range between 68 and 97 millimeters which, as far as this sample is concerned, appear to best express the normal size. It is important, however, to recognize the smallest (3) and the largest (7) specimens as emphasizing the lack of standardization in length of this kind of projectile. This size range sounds a note of caution to the taxonomist who would use length as a rigid criterion. It also makes clear that the largest of animals known to ancient hunters were not always hunted with only the largest tips on their spears.

Without exception the place of maximum width is at the approximate mid-point of the blade. Edges curve gently from the point baseward except in 1, 2, and 8 (Figures 7.7 and 7.8, d, f, and h) which show slight recurving near the bases.

Bases are concave in all specimens, ranging from 2 to 5 millimeters in depth.

Figure 7.7. The eight points recovered among the bones of the Naco mammoth: a, Number 3(A-10904); b, Number 4(A-10899); c, Number 5(A-10902); d, Number 1(A-11912); e, Number 7(A-10903); f, Number 2(A-11913); g, Number 6(A-10901); h, Number 8(A-10900). Length of e, 116 millimeters.

Figure 7.8. The Naco points, reverse faces.

The flaking on all points may be classed as horizontal to irregular with high variability in flake size. One and 7 (Figures 7.7 and 7.8, d, e) best illustrate the horizontal arrangement of the flake scars. The techniques of collateral and oblique parallel flaking, commonly associated with early chipped tools, are not represented at all. Fine edge retouching generally is lacking though locally it occurs in an apparent effort to bring the edges to more perfect symmetry. The irregularity of the flaking did not lead to the formation of a median range, except in 1, and, as a consequence, its section is lozenge-shaped.

Fluting occurs on both faces of all points. This was done by removing usually one large flake from the base pointwards and occasional small flakes. A good example of multiple flakes is seen in 6 (Figures 7.7 and 7.8, g). The length of the fluting varies from one-fourth to one-half the length of the point.

Ground edges are consistently present. Evidently this was done to prevent cutting of the hafting materials by what otherwise would have been sharp edges. The dulling includes the concave base and the edges from the base upwards for about one-third to one-half the total length of the point. There is close correlation between length of fluting and extent of edge smoothing which reflects, in my opinion, the functional relationship of these two characteristics.

Reference was made above to the fact that in three instances 2 points were manufactured from the same stone. In actual workmanship, there is a striking similarity in all points, yet it is probable that those pairs of identical materials were produced by the same craftsman. If this inference is allowed, it becomes evident that one individual made points as variable in size as 1 and 3 (Figures 7.7 and 7.8, a, d) and in shape as 6 and 8 (Figures 7.7 and 7.8, g, h).

ADDITIONAL DISCOVERIES

Some years prior to the discovery of the Naco elephant, Marc Navarrete picked up a fluted point in the arroyo bed of Greenbush Creek about one-quarter mile above the elephant locality. Made of gray flint, it measures 81.5 millimeters in length, 32 millimeters in width and 10 millimeters in greatest thickness. In all characteristics, form, size, chipping, basal thinning, dulled edges at base (Figure 7.9), it agrees with the projectiles recovered among the bones of the elephant and may also be labelled as of the Clovis Fluted type. Evidently eroded from some buried resting place, this point hints at a wider distribution of the type than is indicated by the elephant locality.

About 25 miles northeast of Benson (see Figure 7.1) between the headwaters of Arivaipa Creek on the north and Whitewater Creek on the south, lies a land-locked basin where, in past times, waters collected to form a lake covering approximately 120 square miles (Meinzer and Kelton 1913:34). The Willcox Playa, a salt flat, is the modern inner remnant of the old lake floor of pluvial Lake Cochise. Well developed gravel beaches, especially on the west and south sides, testify to the former extent and permanency of the lake. Antevs regards the

Figure 7.9. Clovis Fluted point (*reverse face on right*) from Greenbush arroyo floor. Lateral lines indicate extent above base of dulled edges. Length, 81.5 millimeters. (Drawing by Barton Wright.)

most recent maximum stand of the lake to have been during the last pluvial (Sayles and Antevs 1941:33).

Sayles and Antevs during their studies of the Cochise culture and representatives of the Arizona State Museum have, on numerous occasions, found traces of human occupation on the old beaches. While much of this has been surface evidence, extensive workings of the beaches for highway ballast and a few shallow erosion channels have revealed lithic materials well within the beach gravels also. Most of the specimens have been the tools of the Cochise culture, notably those designed for grinding. The head of a human femur, heavily mineralized was recovered from a gravel pit (Ariz. CC:13:3, Arizona State Museum Survey) in the southwestern beach by the Arizona State Museum. Shore deposits are also known to contain vertebrate fossil remains (Bryan and Gidley 1926).

In November, 1952, one of the gravel pits (Ariz. CC:13:5) was revisited and in the course of examining the standing profile of the pit, a projectile point was found in situ at a depth of .9 meters in the highest part of the beach (Figure 7.10). It rested horizontally on one of its flat faces among the uncemented beach pebbles which, at this level, are in a liberal dirt matrix. The point, of opaque lusterless obsidian, is 40 millimeters in length and 24 millimeters in width. The chipping is of an inferior quality (Figure 7.11) and the edges are not ground.

Figure 7.10. Profile of gravel pit in Lake Cochise beach, showing the projectile point (*circled*) detailed in Figure 7.11 in situ at a depth of .9 meters. Object pointed at is a stone chip.

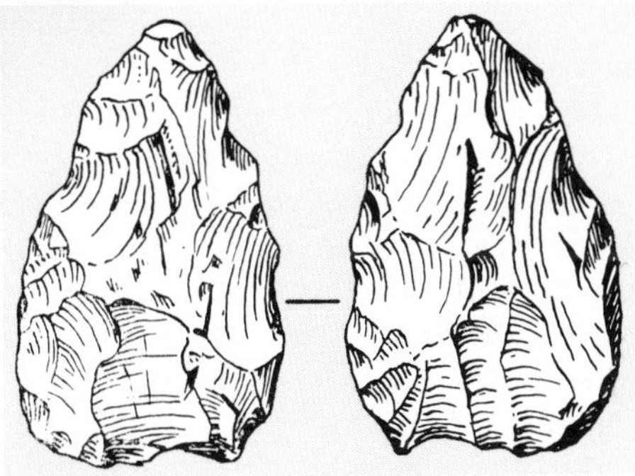

Figure 7.11. Projectile point (*reverse face on right*) from beach gravels, pluvial Lake Cochise. Actual size.

Basal thinning has been attempted. Grinding stones and several stone chips, though not formalized tools, were observed close by and at about the same depth.

Reference is made to these occurrences here for two reasons: first, that the Willcox Playa area holds promise to early man studies and has up to now been quite neglected, and second, that the point in particular may be drawn into the consideration of the Naco points. Since, in an exposure of several hundred meters in this gravel pit, there is no evidence of downward artificial penetrations into the gravels, I believe that the specimens are in a true geological context. If this is the case the cultural items would have been lost or strewn on the beach surface, *before* the climax of beach-building was reached, for nearly a meter of depth was added before the lake receded. This would place the time as within the last pluvial or in excess of 10,000 years ago, and roughly the equivalent in time of the Naco elephant.

Typologically the Lake Cochise point cannot be classified as a Clovis fluted, but we wonder if it is not within the expectable range of that type which certainly would have included some of inferior quality. Its association with grinding stones introduces the timely question of the relationship between the gathering economy of the Cochise culture and the hunting economy reflected by the Clovis fluted projectiles. More will be said about this later.

DISCUSSION

Typological placement of the Naco projectiles, including the one from the arroyo, presents no serious problem. All manifest a high degree of regularity except in length and the norms thus set closely agree with the characteristics of the type now known as the Clovis fluted. Sellards (1952:38) accepts this identification as do Roberts, Krieger, and Wormington (personal communications). Only the smallest one in the lot (3) has been questioned. *If found alone*, it probably would not have been classed as a Clovis fluted. Identification of single specimens has often been difficult, but in this case where eight occurred in one animal, its inclusion in the type is inescapable. The value of the sample lies in the size variation it reveals and we have a suggestion in it that our concept of the type may be too narrow.

In other places where Clovis fluted points have been found in association with faunal remains the animals represented are elephants. The evidence for this has been summed up in Sellards (1952:17–46). The tools of the elephant hunters, imperfectly known as to typological range, he calls the Llano complex and the makers of them Llano man. The name is derived from the Llano Estacado or Staked Plains of New Mexico and Texas, for it is in this region that the principal discoveries of elephant kills have been made. The Naco station extends the area of distribution of Clovis fluted points farther to the south and west than heretofore known and the Iztapan mammoth (Martínez del Río 1952; Aveleyra and Maldonado-Koerdell 1952) in the Valley of Mexico greatly extended the range of elephant hunters southward.

Since the Naco station has provided us with but a single type of tool, we can view the early hunters only through the narrow objective thus provided. The presence of Llano man in this part of the Southwest is attested by them but we are still in the dark about him personally or about other aspects of his culture.

Two problems, however, may be discussed briefly. The first of these concerns the age; the second, the Cochise culture–Llano man relationship.

Antevs, on geological grounds, has assigned the age of the bone deposit to a period between 10,000 and 11,000 years ago. We have, as yet, no supporting radiocarbon dates. Elsewhere, the occurrence of Clovis fluted points with mammoth, the geological contexts, and the wide dispersion of the type hint at a respectable age. For the Clovis, New Mexico, sites Antevs holds the Clovis formation "to be at most 13,000 and at least 10,000 years old" (Antevs 1949:190). Krieger, in his recent summary of New World culture history (1953:241) states that "Clovis points are somewhat older than 11,000 years, possibly as much as 15,000 to 18,000 years." Even though our dating methods today still lack explicitness, the historical position of the Naco weapons appears to be early in the predictable range. In my opinion, the Naco "kill" was older than the oldest cultural horizon in Ventana Cave with a minimum date of 10,000 (Bryan 1950:125–126), and both of these were anterior to the Sulphur Spring stage of the Cochise culture, dated by climatic history to more than 10,000 years ago (Sayles and Antevs 1941:55) and by radiocarbon means to 7756 ± 370 (Libby 1952:84). Whether this is early or late in the life of the stage is not known.

This brings us to the question of the relationship of Llano man— the hunter—and Cochise man—the collector. Our knowledge of the Cochise culture has come chiefly from buried campsites along old streams and bogs where grinding stones, used in food preparation, have been found literally by the ton. In the earliest stage, the Sulphur Spring, chipped tools and, most of all, projectile points, are rare to absent. Subsequently during the Chiricahua and San Pedro stages, and especially the latter, flaked tools appear in abundance.

Three possibilities suggest themselves: first, that from the start, the area of greatest concentration of Cochise culture sites, southeastern Arizona, was inhabited by collectors, and that the Naco points signal an intrusion into their territory by the Llano hunter. Second, that historically, the hunters were here first and that in response to changing environment which set in at the end of the last pluvial, the economic dependence of these people gradually shifted to include gathering along with hunting. Third, the Llano hunter and the Cochise collector were one and the same from the beginning and that the strikingly different tool assemblages are related to seasonally differing food sources and habits—winter hunting and summer gathering.

In terms of what little data we have for the western United States, I favor the second of these possibilities not ignoring, however, the third as part of the problem, too. In the Plains, grinding tools are not included in the Llano complex though the age is high. So far, diligent search in the Greenbush Creek has produced no grinding stones, suggesting that if any camps were nearby, they were those of hunters. In the Ventana complex (Haury 1950a:176–199) there was but one grinding tool in a sample of ninety specimens. In higher and later deposits they were present by the hundreds. Hence, the inference drawn above. If the point from the ancient Lake Cochise beach, previously noted, is as old as it appears to be, the coexistence of the two tool types is apparent, although in accordance with this reconstruction, the time would have been somewhat later than the Naco discovery.

CONCLUSIONS

From the foregoing observations, and including also those of Antevs and Lance, the following conclusions may be drawn:

1) Prior to 10,000 years ago, during the last pluvial maximum, a Columbian mammoth (*Mammuthus* [*Parelephas*] *columbi*) was killed by hunters who hurled no less than eight stone-tipped spears into it. The locality was in what we know today as the San Pedro Valley in southern Arizona.

2) The animal fell on a sand bar adjoining a stream and what remained of the carcass after the hunters had salvaged the parts they wanted was soon covered by a succession of deposits which register the subsequent climatic history of the region.

3) Though variable in size, the spear points were all of one kind, called by students of early man the Clovis fluted type. These are almost identical with others found to the east and northeast in the Plains, thereby extending the known distribution well to the west.

4) The relationship of the Llano complex of which these points are but one element and the Cochise culture remains to be determined but they undoubtedly represent a hunting antecedent of the latter.

⊰ 8 ⊱

The Lehner Mammoth Site
Southeastern Arizona

Emil W. Haury, E. B. Sayles, and William W. Wasley

In the spring of 1952, while the Arizona State Museum of the University of Arizona was engaged in the excavation of the Naco Mammoth Site, Edward F. Lehner was inspecting property he anticipated purchasing about two miles south of Hereford on the west side of the San Pedro River in Cochise County, southeastern Arizona (Figure 8.1). Lehner noted and examined the stratified deposits exposed in the vertical bank of an arroyo channel which crossed the property. At the base of this bank, about 2.5 meters below the modern surface, he noticed bones exposed by the erosion of the channel. Lehner's natural curiosity was piqued by the occurrence of bones at this depth. He probed a bit and concluded that the bones might be those of some extinct animal life and therefore ought to be of scientific interest or value. He carefully removed a few of the fragments and took them to the Arizona State Museum where some of them were identified as the tooth plates of mammoth.

Reprinted by permission from *American Antiquity*, 1959, 25(1):2–30. Contribution Number 11, Program in Geochronology, University of Arizona.

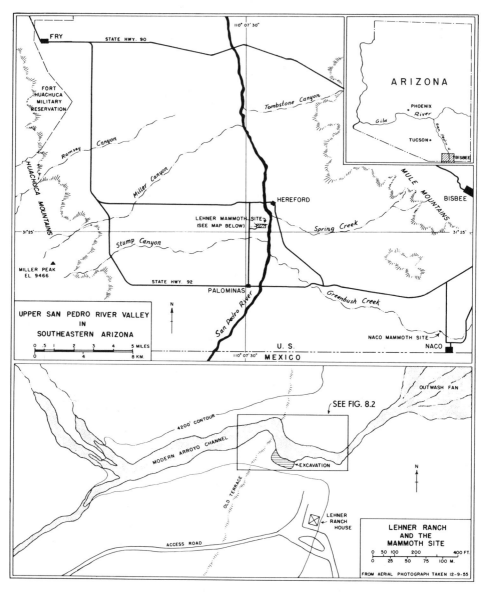

Figure 8.1. General map of the Hereford area, southeastern Arizona (*above*) and detail map of the Lehner ranch (*below*), showing location of the mammoth excavation.

A few days later Haury examined the site and observed that the geology generally duplicated the situation at Naco (Haury and others 1953:5, Figure 3) where work was then in progress. The age of the deposit appeared to be recent enough to warrant the hope that associated human artifacts might be present. However, no direct evidence of this association was observed. During the next two years the mammoth exposure was revisited several times. Ernst Antevs examined the locality and concurred in the belief that the mammoth remains could have been deposited within the time range of human habitation in the Southwest.

After the particularly heavy summer rains of 1955, Lehner, who by then had acquired the property, advised Haury on September 17 that much more bone had been exposed. The following week the site was visited by John F. Lance and Wasley. Bone was exposed laterally for about 15 meters in the same stratigraphic horizon. No articulation of bone was observed, but the relationship of skeletal elements and the general condition of the bones seemed to preclude the chance that they were redeposited, although even then, with much more bone exposed, no evidence of man was noted. Nevertheless, the decision was reached that exploratory excavation was justifiable.

CLIMATE AND ECOLOGY

The upper San Pedro Valley is a broad, relatively flat, alluvium-filled valley of the Basin and Range physiographic province. On the west it is flanked, in the general vicinity of the Lehner ranch, by the rugged Huachuca Mountains which reach an elevation of 9466 feet at Miller Peak (Figure 8.1). On the east the valley is bordered by the less imposing Escabrosa-Mule Mountains. The San Pedro River rises at an elevation of about 5000 feet in the rolling prairie country north and east of Cananea, Sonora, Mexico. The upper valley of the river extends northward across the international border to the area around Charleston, Arizona, which has an elevation of about 4000 feet. At the Lehner ranch the width of the San Pedro Valley is about ten miles. The San Pedro River has cut its valley and present channel near the eastern margin and, as a consequence, most of the tributary drainages trend eastward. Over a series of low terraces these drop about 700 feet in elevation from the base of the Huachuca Mountains to the river which, opposite the Lehner ranch, is at an altitude of about 4160 feet. At this point the flood plain of the river is about one mile wide.

The drainage of the upper San Pedro Valley has the dendritic pattern typical of Basin and Range topography. It is characterized throughout by the arroyo cutting (Antevs 1952:375) of the present erosion cycle. In the San Pedro Valley this type of erosion has exposed a number of early man sites, including the Naco station. Greenbush Creek, in the banks of which the Naco Site was discovered, is one of the major tributaries from the east joining the San Pedro River about one mile south of the site (see Figure 8.1).

The Present

In general terms the climate of the upper San Pedro Valley may be described as semi-arid and mesothermal. The precipitation of the region averages 12.75 inches a year, with almost two-thirds of this total falling during the July to September rainy period. In April and May the average is 0.2 and 0.15 inches, respectively, and 0.5 to 0.8 inches are expectable during each remaining month. Temperatures roughly match those at Douglas, Arizona, where the means are 44.5° F. for January, 79° for July, and 62° for the year. The flow of the San Pedro is perennial but in the dry season the discharge is minimal or subsurface along many stretches of the valley. In terms of Thornthwaite's (1948: Plate 1) more detailed classification, the valley is characterized as semi-arid, with a moisture deficiency surplus index of −20 to −40; third mesothermal with a thermal efficiency of 33.66 inches to 39.27 inches; no water surplus in any season; and a temperature-efficiency regime normal to fourth mesothermal, having a summer concentration of thermal efficiency from 48% to 51.9%.

On the basis of ecological classification, the upper San Pedro Valley belongs to the Apachian biotic province described by Dice (1943:56–58). Although this biotic province is characterized by four life zone belts, desert, arid grassland, encinal, and montane, only the last three are represented in the upper valley of the San Pedro River, which is at a higher altitude than that required for the desert. The arid grassland which characterizes the valley floor is composed primarily of short grasses, although taller grasses are common along the drainages. Black grama and blue grama predominate among the short grasses, but at this altitude there are also other grama species as well as grasses such as dropseed and seed muhly. The tall grasses are represented chiefly by sacaton which grows in swales in competition with tobosa (Nichol 1952:206–207). Encroaching upon the arid grassland belt are mesquite and blackbrush or tarbush, usually occurring separately in relatively pure stands, but occasionally mixed. The latter situation is sometimes accompanied by small colonies of creosote bush and cat's-claw (Nichol 1952:211). Small relict islands of cottonwood, willow, ash, and oak are mainly confined to the stream channel of the San Pedro River.

The encinal belt of the hills along the sides of the valley is characterized by various oak species of which Emory is the commoner form in this area. Ground cover is provided to some extent by the curly mesquite grass. Cat's-claw, desert hackberry, and mesquite are also common in this belt (Nichol 1952:207–208), and in the higher altitudes there are some juniper stands (Dice 1943:58). The montane belt of the Huachuca Mountains consists largely of pines, some spruce, Mexican ash, and oak.

The Recent Past

Less than a century ago the general aspect of the San Pedro Valley was different from today in a number of respects. The entrenchment of the stream began at the mouth of the San Pedro River in 1883 and proceeded headward at a rate of about 125 miles in ten years by a process of progressive arroyo cutting (Bryan 1925:342). Roe Martin and Jack Parker, longtime residents of the upper valley, recall that about 1910 to 1914 the channel of the river at Hereford was narrow and only 2 to 3 feet deep. F. B. Moson, another early rancher, remembers the Hereford area in the 1880s and 1890s before entrenchment began. He recalls when the stream was no more than a series of grassy swales and when springs and seeps occurred along the valley floor. During these years the present tributary arroyo on the Lehner ranch was itself only a swale in which there was a seep. Channel cutting began in this tributary in the 1920s.

The literature of the nineteenth century provides descriptions of conditions seen in the San Pedro Valley prior to 1860: by James Ohio Pattie in 1825 (Thwaites 1905:99–104), by Cooke in 1846 (Bieber and Bender 1938:140–147), by Parry (1854:18) in 1852, by Parke (1857:123–125), and by Hutton (1859:79–80, 87–88). These consistently describe a grass-covered valley with small stands of cottonwood, walnut, ash and some oak along the water course. The river supported beaver and some fish. Mesquite trees growing along portions of the valley were large enough to provide timbers for Spanish and early American buildings. Descriptions of the upper San Pedro Valley of Kino's time in the early eighteenth century by Velarde (Wyllys

1931:126–130) and by Mange (Karns 1954:77–83) indicate that the environment was about the same as it was in the first half of the nineteenth century.

Cattle and horses were introduced to the San Pedro Valley by Kino in 1696 when he left "a few cattle and a small drove of mares" at Quiburi, near modern Fairbank (Bolton 1948, Vol. 1:165). Throughout the Spanish period there appear to have been some cattle in the area at all times, but large herds occurred only periodically (Di Peso 1953b:34). However, during the early 1800s sizable herds of cattle were raised in southeastern Arizona, particularly at the San Bernardino ranch east of Douglas and in the upper San Pedro Valley (Cooke 1848:555). During the middle and late 1830s the Apache succeeded in driving the Mexicans from southeastern Arizona, seizing their horse herds, and leaving the cattle to revert to the wild state in which they were found by the early Anglo-American explorers and the hundreds of forty-niners who took the southern route to California (Bartlett 1854, Vol. 1:256; Bieber and Bender 1938:133). It was not until the 1870s that cattle ranching was reintroduced to the upper San Pedro Valley (Wagoner 1952:42). Since that time the cattle industry has taken on great importance in southeastern Arizona.

The preceding sketch is an attempt to present a diachronic view of the region. Several noticeable environmental changes took place in the brief span of a hundred years: (1) denudation of grassland areas by overgrazing of cattle, (2) encroachment of mesquite and black-brush upon the weakened grassland areas, (3) decided lowering of the water table and the consequent complete disappearance of beaver and fish and the near disappearance of the large deciduous tree growth along the river, and (4) extensive arroyo cutting to a mean depth of 15 to 20 feet (Humphrey 1958). While it is generally felt that these changes might have come eventually as a natural consequence of climatic change, it is also a concensus that overgrazing and other activities of man probably triggered and hastened these changes. If the present cyclonic storm pattern, which produces excessive precipitation during the summer months and virtually none at all during the remainder of the year, began in the 1880s, as has been suggested by some observers, then the coincidence of this timing may also be drawn upon to explain the rapidity of the change. Whatever the cause or causes for these recent changes the analogy is clear that past changes of similar or even greater magnitude must be envisioned to provide the physical setting for the evidence in the Lehner Site.

We can only conjecture what the upper San Pedro Valley may have looked like to the big-game hunters of 10,000 years ago. The environment may still have presented essentially a grassland, dotted with small stands of trees and shrubs, and dominated by species which thrived in a cooler climate than the present. Pollen studies now in progress should shed light on this problem. Dillon (1956:168–169) has suggested that perhaps a decrease of 10°F. in the mean annual temperature and more moisture would produce the conditions presumed to have existed in the period of maximum glaciation during the Wisconsin. Considerably less change in temperature and precipitation would have been required to duplicate the conditions believed to have been prevalent 10,000 years ago.

LOCATION OF THE SITE

The Lehner Mammoth Site (Cochise County, T23S, R22E, Sec. 21, n1/2 nw1/4 nw1/4 nw1/4) is designated as Arizona EE:12:1 in the Arizona State Museum archaeological survey (Wasley 1957). It is about 0.4 miles west of the present channel of the San Pedro River, on a small tributary entrenched by arroyo cutting for a distance of about 0.25 miles above (west of) the site and for about 0.1 miles below the bone bed. At the lower end of this arroyo the tributary fans out onto the flood plain of the San Pedro River so that it does not now actually extend to the entrenched river (see Figure 8.1). In the immediate vicinity of the site, the source of the arroyo channel has been deflected southward by a partially buried terrace remnant composed of sediments older and more resistant to erosion than the more recent deposits of the valley fill. This deflection of the channel was a happy circumstance, for a less acute change would not have brought the bones to view. At this point the modern arroyo channel is about 25 meters wide (Figure 8.2). The elevation of the site is 4190 feet.

EXCAVATION PROCEDURE

The work on the Lehner Mammoth Site was carried out in two phases: excavation of the bone bed in December, 1955 (Figures 8.3 and 8.4), and excavation of the hearth area in February, 1956. The latter extended westward from the western limit of greatest bone concentration. With the exception of minor differences in detail to be noted later, the excavation procedures followed at the bone bed and

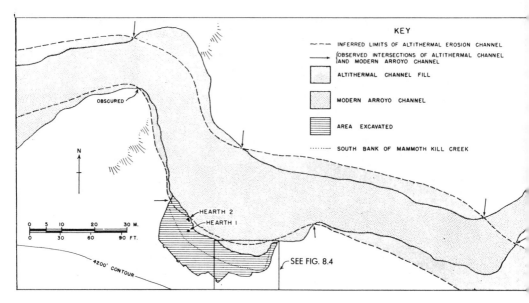

Figure 8.2. Detail map of the Lehner Mammoth Site in
relation to the modern and Altithermal arroyo channels.

at the hearth area were similar. The overburden above the areas to be
excavated was removed by means of a power shovel. A "cushion" of
soil about 50 centimeters thick was left over the bone bed to prevent
crushing and disturbance of the bones. This was stripped by hand labor as the second step. When the complexity and extent of the bone
bed became known, a 1-meter grid system was superimposed over it
to facilitate mapping and recording of pertinent data. The grid was
extended westward to encompass the area containing the hearths exposed during the second phase of excavation. The rapid deterioration
of the bone after exposure to the drying air, the complicated arrangement of the bones, and their vertical distribution precluded complete
excavation and mapping of the site as a unit. Expediency dictated that
as one segment or level was exposed, mapped, and recorded, the
bones should be removed before proceeding to the next segment or
level of the excavation. Photographic procedures, necessarily, had to
conform to this scheme. For this reason it was not possible to include
in a single photograph the completely excavated bone bed showing its
relationship to the relevant geological features.

Figure 8.3. Area of bone and artifact concentration uncovered by first phase of the excavation. Looking west. Scaling stick in background is 3 meters long.

THE BONE BED

The top 2 meters of silty deposits over the bone bed were progressively less sandy and more clayey from top to bottom. Underlying this was a distinctive dark band, almost black in color, representing a silty clay soil with some humic content. The thickness of this deposit varied from 5 to 25 centimeters with an average of 15 centimeters. The exposed bones in the arroyo bank prior to excavation appeared to lie directly below this black layer, a fact substantiated later by digging. The extent of the area from which the overburden was removed by power shovel was about 11 meters back into the bank and 17 meters along the face of the arroyo bank—where the bones seemed to be most heavily concentrated.

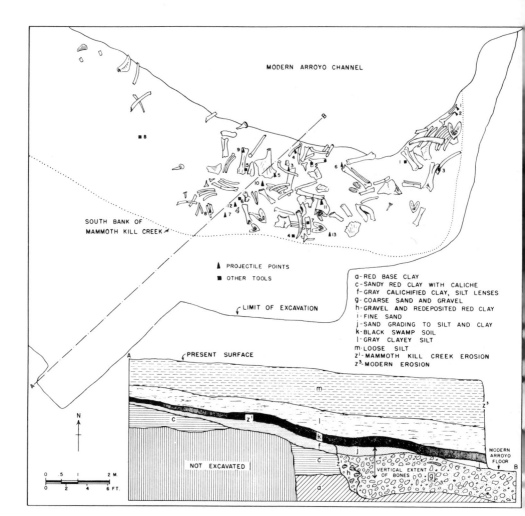

Figure 8.4. Geological profile of area of bone and artifact concentration. Main bone elements only are shown. Deposits b, d, e, n, o and erosion Z^2 do not appear in this profile but are shown in Figure 8.9. Bones occurred in deposits g–j.

The uncovering of the bones began at the eastern edge of the excavation and the first artifacts were found shortly afterwards within 20 centimeters of the arroyo face. These consisted of two Clovis fluted projectile points, one touching and the other near rib fragments (Numbers 1 and 2, Figure 8.4). About this same time a few flecks of charcoal were observed in the sandy matrix surrounding the bones. These finds amply justified continuation of the project because they demonstrated some sort of association of man and mammoth.

Figure 8.5. Clear quartz projectile point (Figure 8.12c) in situ among ribs, probably of young mammoth. Two overlying rib sections were removed to allow photography.

By the time the first phase of the excavation was completed, elements of eight mammoths, identified by lower jaws, were counted. Bones of bison, represented definitely by a jaw fragment containing three teeth and vertebral fragments, emerged near the western edge of the bone bed. Found directly with the bones, either near bone as between two ribs (Figure 8.5) or actually touching bone, were 13 projectile points, eight cutting and scraping implements, one chopper and eight miscellaneous chips and flakes. The latter probably represent refuse from tool making on or near the spot. In no instance were the projectile points observed to have penetrated bone. Small scraps of charcoal became somewhat more abundant towards the western, or upstream, end of the excavation. As much as possible of this was saved for radiocarbon dating. The source of this charcoal became apparent only after the second phase of the excavation was undertaken in February, 1956.

The condition of the bone encountered was uniformly poor. The structure was spongy upon fresh exposure and often the articular surfaces were disintegrated. For this reason, fully articulated bones could be demonstrated in only one instance. This was a fragmentary maxilla with tusk, containing a tooth in perfect occlusion with its mate in the mandible (Figure 8.6). Nevertheless, articulation was strongly suggested in other instances: a radius and ulna side by side, their proximal ends close to the distal end of a humerus, assuming a semi-

Figure 8.6. Excavation detail. At extreme left is clay bank (see Figure 8.4a) of Mammoth Kill Creek. Fill in center is mixed clay and gravel (see Figure 8.4h). At right is the coarse sand and gravel bar (see Figure 8.4g). Tusk of young mammoth extends downward under caliche block; directly above, at top of column, is basal portion of the black swamp soil (see Figure 8.4k). The tusk and supporting maxilla with tooth rests on matching tooth in lower jaw (*arrow*). Looking southwest.

flexed position with respect to the latter; a tibia in similar relationship to a femur; sets of ribs found in sequence with respect to size, the ribs of each set oriented in the same direction. These instances of presumed articulation occurred for the most part toward the eastern end of the bone bed.

The matrix surrounding the bones consisted partly of a white, uniform, fine sand (see Figure 8.4i) locally grading to silt and clay (see Figure 8.4j), partly of sand mixed with gravel (see Figure 8.4g), and partly of a redeposited reddish clay with caliche inclusions (see Figure 8.4h), which was moderately interfingered with gravel. The fine white sand occurred most continuously at the eastern end of the bone bed thinning towards the west to lenses and pockets in low spots in the uneven surface of the gravel. Where thickest at the eastern end, this sand may have helped to preserve the bone by acting as a close-fitting pad or cushion which provided better subsurface drainage, thereby resulting in the best examples of articulation.

In the face of the evidence at hand it was concluded early in the excavation of the site that the animals represented in the deposit, or at least some of them, were killed by man. Further, it seemed clear that the slaughter took place on a sand and gravel bar of an ancient perennial stream channel, hereafter referred to as Mammoth Kill Creek. In tracing the south bank of this stream, we were able to determine that Mammoth Kill Creek took a course roughly paralleled by the modern arroyo (see Figure 8.2), although the south bank, in the area of excavation, was about 4 meters south of the modern arroyo. The same buried terrace which diverted the course of the modern arroyo also diverted in a similar manner the channel of Mammoth Kill Creek, so that a sharp bend was formed. At one time the current of Mammoth Kill Creek ran along the south bank, or the outside of the bend, carving an almost vertical bank 1.8 meters high, and scouring its channel most deeply in this place. Eventually, when aggrading began, the south side of the channel filled with gravel and with tumbled portions of the red clay bank, while the main stream may have cut a shorter course somewhat farther to the north. The area along the south bank then became a relatively quiet, shallow, freshwater pool, an ideal watering place for game animals and an ideal hunting place for man. In this pool the fine white sand was deposited during the time of the mammoth hunts and perhaps for a short time afterwards.

In one or two places the depth of the bone bed between the highest projection and the lowest submergence of bone in a vertical line was a little over 1 meter. The highest bone, primarily elements of some of the lower jaws, protruded into the black soil overlying the bone bed. The lowest bone, consisting of the tip of a tusk and a pelvic section, extended downward near the bottom of the stream channel of Mammoth Kill Creek. The tusk was buried in material that had sloughed off the south bank (see Figure 8.6) while the section of pelvis was in the zone of the interfingering of the bank material and the bar gravel. This situation suggests that the first animals were killed while the gravel bar was still forming and before the deposition of the white sand, and that the last animals were killed after at least a portion of the white sand had been deposited. Thus, there is a strong indication that not all of the animals were killed at one time, but that this was the site of a series of elephant hunts extending over an indeterminate, though probably short, period of time.

The highest and lowest artifacts were separated by a vertical distance of about 70 centimeters. The highest artifact, projectile point 12 (see Figure 8.12j, Table 8.1), was found about 10 centimeters below the black soil, while the lowest, projectile point 11 (Figure 8.12m), was found near the upper portion of the pelvis fragment mentioned previously. These two projectile points are similar enough from a technological standpoint to have been made by the same craftsman. On this cultural evidence it would seem unwise to postulate any great length of time between the first kill and the last at this locality. That the lower of these two points was found essentially in situ and had not worked down through the bar deposit during the wallowing or thrashing of mammoths at the water hole is suggested by its position close to and pointing towards a wing of the pelvis mentioned previously, and by its broken tip as if it had actually struck this bone. The higher projectile point, in common with several of the others, was on top, or near the top, of the gravel bar, and certainly had not worked upward through the gravel deposit. For both bone and artifacts, the highest and lowest specimens occurred near the south bank of Mammoth Kill Creek where both bones and artifacts were most heavily concentrated.

Although the mandibles of eight mammoths were recovered from the bone bed during the first phase of the excavation, most of them in fair condition, it should be noted that not a single skull was found intact. The fragment of maxilla containing a tooth and a tusk (see Figure 8.6) was one of two instances in which only a small part of a cranium was preserved. Two or three masses of badly crushed flat bone were encountered which may have been parts of skulls, but these by no means account for all that once must have been there. While mammoth tongue and brains may well have been considered delicacies by the hunters, these parts could easily have been recovered without total destruction of the skull. Since a cranium was present at the Naco Site (Haury and others 1953:3), we must conclude that at the Lehner Site skulls simply failed to survive both time and the hunter.

THE HEARTH AREA

Upon the completion of the work in the bone bed, it was apparent that at the eastern and southern margins of the excavation the extent of the bone concentration had been approximately delimited (see Figure 8.4). However, a number of problems were still unanswered with reference to what might lie to the west, or upstream. Tool 8 (see Figure 8.4) came from the face of the west bank of the excavation (see

Figure 8.7. Second phase of excavation. Looking west.

Figure 8.3) left at the end of the first phase of the operations. Some elements of bone were also visible here. Were there still more artifacts and more animals in the area beyond? Flecks of charcoal in the upper zone of the bone bed were observed to increase in abundance towards the upstream end of the area exposed and they were still to be found in the face of the west bank of the excavation. What was the source of this charcoal? Moreover, we wanted more information about Mammoth Kill Creek and about the geological events which preceded and followed it. These were the deciding factors which inspired the second phase of the excavation. This step, undertaken in February, 1956, involved opening an area immediately to the west of the initial excavation for a distance of about 19 meters and southward into the bank about 13 meters (Figure 8.7). Overburden was removed by power shovel to the top of the black soil, so that less hand labor would be required. We now knew that the pay dirt was entirely underneath the black soil, and we risked crushing bone in order to save time and expense.

For convenience we have called this section of the excavation the hearth area to distinguish it from the bone bed. Relatively little bone

Figure 8.8. Hearth Number 1 seen in cross section.

was uncovered during this phase of the excavation. Those elements found included a portion of the lower jaw of a tapir, a horse podial, and the ninth mammoth jaw, all on the sand and gravel bar in Mammoth Kill Creek, and in the same geological context as the other bones. The south bank of this early stream was exposed in two more places. These, with the portions exposed during the first step of the digging, permitted us to plot the south bank of Mammoth Kill Creek (see Figure 8.2). Although no more artifacts were recovered in this area, further welcome evidence of man's activity was represented by two charcoal-laden hearths. These occurred on the sand and gravel bar. At its western end the bar consisted of a uniform medium sand, somewhat tan or grayish in color and at least 50 centimeters thick. In the area of the hearths no excavation was made to the bottom of the sand deposit or to the bottom of the channel of Mammoth Kill Creek.

About 10 centimeters of the tan sand deposit covered the top of Hearth 1, separating it from contact with the overlying black soil. This may be taken to indicate some flooding of the bar after the hearth was used. Hearth 1 was a pit of irregular basin shape in cross section, which measured 40 centimeters in diameter at the top and was 35 centimeters deep (Figure 8.8). Hearth 2 was merely an extensive fire area, irregular in outline and without a pit or depression. A dense concentration of charcoal, consisting of a nearly solid mat 3 centimeters or more thick, covered an area roughly 1.25 meters long and 70 centimeters wide. Hearth 2 was on top of the sand bar's surface. The charcoal was separated locally from the black soil by small patches of fine white sand about 1 centimeter thick and in a few spots it extended slightly into the overlying black soil.

The suggestion that these hearths were used for cooking meat lends credence to the idea that they were contemporaneous with the time the animals were killed. In an area where bone was rather scarce, shattered elements of unidentifiable bone lay over the south edge of Hearth 1, while the tapir jaw fragment, slightly charred, was only 20 centimeters from the northwest edge of the same pit. The difference in stratigraphic position suggests that Hearth 1 was the older of the two, but in all probability this does not represent a significant interval of time.

Charcoal from both hearths was saved for radiocarbon dating, the results of which are reported below. Pieces in excess of 1 centimeter in diameter were preserved for botanical identification. On the basis of determinations made by the Forest Products Laboratory at the University of Wisconsin and by T. L. Smiley of the University of Arizona Geochronology Laboratories, pine, ash, and oak were represented. Species of oak and ash are known to have grown along the San Pedro River in historic times, while pine is now confined to the Huachuca Mountains, some ten miles to the west. Hence, information from this source sheds little light on the problem of ecological differences that may have existed between the time of the kill and the present. The hearths underline the real motive for the chase—food—and hint that no time was lost in satisfying the hunger pangs of the hunters.

THE GEOLOGICAL EVENTS: A PREVIEW

Antevs' detailed analysis of the geology of the Lehner Site follows this report. At this point it seems appropriate to review briefly the sequence of formations and events to provide the reader with some knowledge of the physical nature of the station before discussing the artifacts and the dating and before embarking on the concluding section. We are not now concerned with the oldest deposits revealed by the excavations. Into these Mammoth Kill Creek eroded its channel

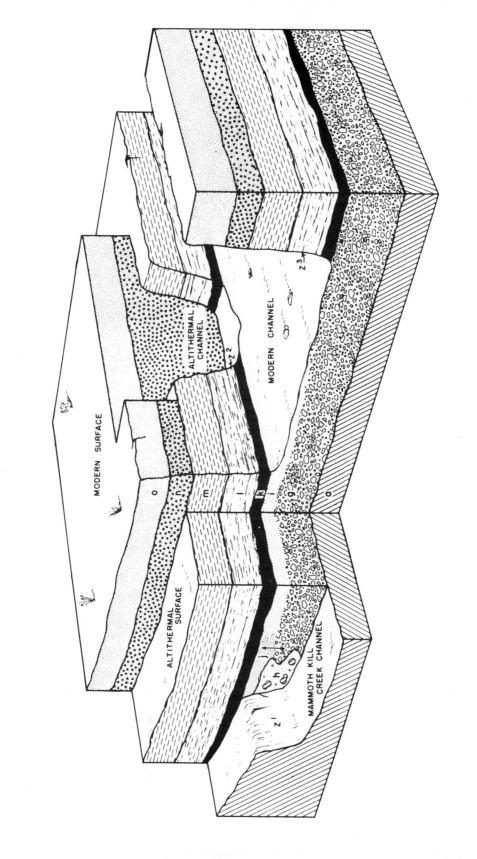

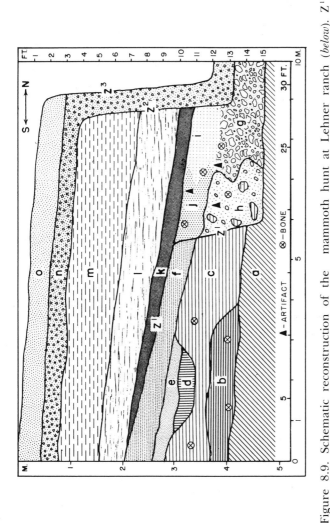

Figure 8.9. Schematic reconstruction of the geological history of the Lehner Mammoth Site. Periods of sedimentation and erosion (*above*) are shown in true chronological order and in proportional scale, but license has been taken with the axial relationship of the arroyos for clarity. Beds b–f, older than Z^1, have been omitted, but are shown in bottom drawing. Composite south-to-north profile of the site of the mammoth hunt at Lehner ranch (*below*). Z^1 marks the old stream channel in which bones and artifacts were deposited. Z^2 indicates the Altithermal, and Z^3 the modern arroyo. Arrow indicates vertical distribution of bones in deposits g–i. Erosion periods are: Z^1, south bank of Mammoth Kill Creek; Z^2, Altithermal arroyo channel (see Figure 8.11); Z^3, modern arroyo.

(Figure 8.9Z[1]). This perennial stream was in existence and started filling before the animals were killed. From the distribution of the bones in the gravels and sands (Figures 8.9g–i, 8.10g–j) it appears that much of the filling took place during the time of the hunts.

Rapid deposition was then interrupted and local conditions were favorable for the development of a swamp. The record of this event is preserved by a distinctive, carbon-laden black layer (Figures 8.9k, 8.10k). The evidence suggests that this swamp was basin-shaped in profile and semilunar in outline, curving around the base of an old hill which diverted the course of the older and younger streams. The swamp soil sloped upward more rapidly to the south than to the east and west. This reconstruction is partly conjectural because subsequent erosion removed all traces of its northern limits. The organic content of the swamp soil was sufficient to make possible radiocarbon assays.

The swamp soil was overlain by clayey silt (Figures 8.9l, 8.10l) which, in turn was blanketed by loose silt (Figures 8.9m, 8.10m). This period of deposition was followed by one of erosion of presumed Altithermal age. The resultant arroyo channel was easily observed at no less than seven places where the modern arroyo cut through it (see Figure 8.2) and was best illustrated by the exposure directly east of the bone bed (Figures 8.11, 8.9Z[2]). In several places the Altithermal arroyo removed the swamp soil and it is presumed that it also destroyed a portion of the bone bed. Subsequent events include the complete filling of the Altithermal arroyo (Figures 8.9n, 8.11n) and the accumulation of recent deposits (Figure 8.9o). The modern erosion cycle which began in the final decades of the last century has produced the present channel (Figure 8.9Z[3]).

THE ARTIFACTS

The artifacts, whether points or cutting tools, clearly occurred in direct association with the bones (see Figure 8.4). In lateral and vertical distribution the greatest densities of bones and tools coincided. From this it is inferred, even though little evidence of bone articulation was observed, that negligible displacement of either tools or bones has taken place since the time of the kill. The possibility of accidental association of tools and animal remains through secondary deposition is certainly to be ruled out. It goes beyond all logic to attribute this kind of sorting to nature. Any lingering doubts as to the

Figure 8.10. Geological profile. See Figure 8.4 for key to lettered beds. Arrow indicates jaw of young mammoth. Scaling stick is 3 meters long.

Figure 8.11. Altithermal arroyo channel, cutting into black swamp soil, as exposed in modern arroyo 13 meters downstream from east end of excavation. See Figure 8.4 for key to lettered beds.

contemporaneity of animals and man are eliminated by the two hearths adjacent to and on the same level as the bones.

There are 13 projectile points, two of which were seriously damaged. The essential data for each are given in Table 8.1. All exhibit the same basic outline, oblanceolate with concave base. Minor variations range from essentially straight sides (Figures 8.12c, 8.13c) to convex sides (Figures 8.12m, 8.13m) to slightly concave near the base (Figures 8.12i, 8.13i). The latter example approaches in form the Cumberland type of the eastern United States. This basal narrowing is barely discernable on several of the other examples in the collection. It seems to stem from the custom of dulling the edges by grinding. The maximum width on all occurs about midway between the point and the base. All intact bases are concave. The angle of inclination noted by Di Peso (1953a:85) on the Willcox Playa and Texas Canyon points is a

Figure 8.12. The projectile points from the Lehner
Site. Length of j, 97 millimeters.

measure of unequal tang length. It does not appear to be a significant
feature of the present sample.

The flaking on all points is horizontal and highly variable as to
flake size. Fine edge retouching is observed on one point (see Figures
8.12j; 8.13j). The poorest control of the pressure technique is seen in
the three small, clear quartz points (see Figures 8.12a–c, 8.13a–c)

Table 8.1
Projectile Points at the Lehner Site

Specimen Number*	Figure Number	Location	Description**	Length	Width	Basal Width	Thickness	Extent of Basal Grinding
				Measurements in Millimeters***				
1 (A-12674)	8.12l, 8.13l	Tip near mammoth rib fragment in fine sand; .15 m. below swamp soil.	15–20 mm. missing. Chalcedony; translucent, very dark gray, 10YR, 3/1, clouded with black, 10YR, 2/1.	(87)	31	(27)	8	(22)
2 (A-12675)	8.12f, 8.13f	Tip against mammoth vertebral spine in fine sand; .10 m. below swamp soil.	Long splinter broken from side; slightly re-shaped and corners of thick edge ground. Chert; opaque, dark gray-brown, 2.5Y, 4/2.	79	(22)	(19)	7	32
3 (A-12676)	8.12i, 8.13i	In gravel bar; .12 m. from bison jaw fragment and .05 m. from mam-moth rib; .25 m. below swamp soil.	Chalcedony; translucent dark gray mottled with light and dark shades of brown, 10YR, 3/2.	83	29	27	10	43
4 (A-12677)	8.12g, 8.13g	Under mammoth rib fragment near center of bone bed in gravel bar; .25 m. below swamp soil.	Chert; translucent dark gray 7.5R, 4/0 with bands of darker gray, 5YR, 4/1.	74	28	23	8	28
5 (A-12678)	8.12b, 8.13b	Under mammoth ilium .25 m. below swamp soil, in gravel bar.	Point missing. Clear quartz.	(36)	17	15	7	12
6 (A-12679)	8.12h, 8.13h	Flat against distal end of mammoth leg bone; .15 m. below swamp soil in gravel bar.	Possibly reshaped. Chert; translucent gray, 2.5Y, 6/0, mottled with lighter and darker specks of gray.	62	31	25	8	29

Cat. No.	Code	Provenience	Material					
(A-12680)	8.12x, 8.13x	In mixed clay and gravel, .05 m. below swamp soil.	About 15 mm. missing. Chert; opaque light brownish-gray, 10YR, 6/2 with a band of light gray, 10YR, 7/1.	(81)	29	(25)	7	(25)
8 (A-12681)	8.12c, 8.13c	Between ribs (? bison), .10 m. below swamp soil in mixed clay and sand near S. bank of Mammoth Kill Creek (see Figure 8.5)	Clear quartz.	47	21	21	7	13
9 (A-12682)	8.12d, 8.13d	Flat against mammoth long bone; .20 m. below swamp soil in gravel bar.	Chalcedony; translucent gray, 10YR, 5/1, mottled with specks of pale red, 7.5YR, 5/4.	56	25	23	7	22
10 (A-12683)	8.12a, 8.13a	.15 m. from mammoth ribs; .40 m. below swamp soil in the gravel bar.	Clear quartz.	31	17	16	5	12
11 (A-12684)	8.12m, 8.13m	Tip touching mammoth ilium in mixed clay and gravel; .40 m. below swamp layer in area of deepest bone concentration; .30 m. north of mammoth jaw No. 4.	Tip impact fluted. Chalcedony; translucent gray, 7.5R, 5/1 mottled with dark gray-brown spots, 10YR, 4/2.	(78)	30	22	8	32
12 (A-12685)	8.12j; 8.13j	.10 m. from a mammoth vertebral corpus in mixed clay and gravel; .15 m. below swamp soil and .75 m. west of mammoth jaw No. 7.	Chert; opaque gray-brown, 10YR, 5/2 streaked light gray and red brown, 10R, 3/6.	97	30	26	8	35
13 (A-12686)	8.12e, 8.13e	.15 m. from mammoth jaw No. 5 in sloughed clay from south bank of Mammoth Kill Creek; .25 m. below swamp soil.	Jasper; opaque, pale red, 7.5R, 4/2.	52	28	26	7	22

*Listed in order of discovery. Numbers coincide with those shown in Figure 8.4. Parenthesized numbers are Arizona State Museum catalogue designations.
**Code designations refer to Munsell Soil Color Chart.
***Parentheses indicate estimated measurement.

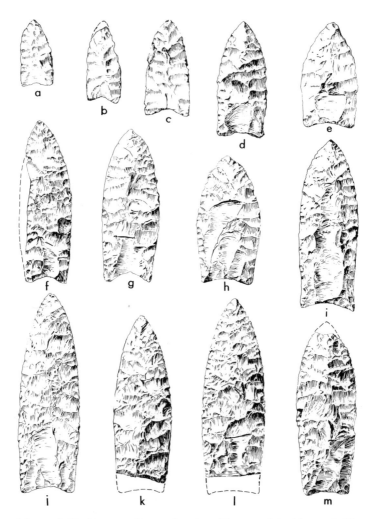

Figure 8.13. Reverse faces of points illustrated in Figure 8.12.

where it is attributable to the nature of the material. Only the three
quartz points do not show fluting, though some basal thinning is apparent. Fluting occurs on both faces of the rest of the points. On the
whole the flutes are short and sometimes flanked by short narrow
flake scars along the margins at the base. Close study of the fluting
suggests that no further edge chipping was done after making the

channel. What can happen when a stone spear tip strikes bone is indicated by the point with tip missing and impact fluting extending from the tip baseward (see Figures 8.12m, 8.13m). It was found in contact with a mammoth ilium. Bases and edges, extending about one-third the distance to the tip, were ground smooth. This treatment was also accorded the fractured edges of one point (see Figures 8.12f, 8.13f) from which a long sliver was broken. These two points suggest that retrieving of projectile points was practiced.

The size range of these points, from 31 to 97 millimeters, roughly duplicates the situation encountered in the Naco sample (Haury and others 1953:7), underscoring the fact that there probably is no significant correlation between the size of a projectile point and the size of the game hunted. We think that the material source, clear quartz crystals, was the size-limiting factor in the production of the three small points (see Figures 8.12a–c, 8.13a–c) rather than the kind of game to be hunted with them. One of these was found next to a mammoth pelvis and the largest of the three was wedged between ribs tentatively identified as those of a bison. It seems obvious that the makers of these points were strongly form conscious but not bound to any compelling size ideal. Recognition of this ought to reflect itself in our analytical treatment and categorization of projectile points.

The eight tools, other than points, may be functionally labeled as scrapers, a knife, and a chopper. Pertinent information about these is given in Table 8.2. The scraper category, accounting for five and probably six of the specimens, is the largest and best represents the tools associated with butchering. The implication here is that the larger scrapers may also have been equally useful as slashing and cutting tools. All scrapers are distinguished by unifacial edge chipping and a thick body. Form duplication suggests two types: pointed and keeled tools, steeply chipped along both edges (Figure 8.14a, b); and primary flakes with chipping principally along one edge (Figure 8.14d, f, g). The fragment shown in Figure 8.14c undoubtedly fits here also. We have identified as a knife a primary flake (Figure 8.14e) the thin, naturally sharp edge of which bears small shallow chipping scars on one face. Whether these were intentionally made or were the product of shearing cannot be determined. The final tool is a stream cobble from which a few flakes have been detached (Figure 8.14h). These flakes were driven from the naturally flat side of the stone. It resembles simple chopper forms common in early sites of the Desert culture.

A few additional comments on the scrapers are in order. The simi-

Table 8.2
Other Tools at the Lehner Site

Specimen Number*	Figure Number	Type	Location	Description**	Measurements in Millimeters***		
					Length	Width	Thickness
1 (A-12687)	8.14d	Side Scraper	Beside mammoth leg bone about .15 m. below swamp soil in mixed sand and clay.	Chalcedony; translucent grayish-brown, 2.5Y,6/2, streaked with dark brown, 10YR, 4/3.	66	46	16
2 (A-12688)	8.14h	Cobble Chopper	Under mammoth tibia in gravel bar; .15 m. below swamp soil.	Natural pebble with at least three thick flakes removed by striking the same face. Rhyolite; grayish-brown 10YR, ranging from 5/2 through 7/2.	120	110	40
3 (A-12689)	8.14f	Side Scraper	Under mammoth rib and next to proximal end of humerus of nearly articulated long bones; .30 m. below swamp soil in mixed clay and sand.	Finely retouched convex edge. Chalcedony; opaque, dark gray, 5Y,4/1, with clouds of dusky red, 10R,3/3.	112	58	18
4 (A-12690)	8.14c	Tool Fragment	Under mammoth vertebra fragment and .10 m. west of tip of tusk belonging to jaw No. 8; .25 m. below swamp soil in mixed clay and sand.	Fragments showing chipped edge. Andesite; gray patina, 5Y,6/1.	(35)	40	6

* Listed in order of discovery. Numbers coincide with those shown in Figure 8.4. Numbers in parentheses are Arizona State Museum catalogue designations.
** Code designations refer to Munsell Soil Color Chart.
*** Parentheses indicate estimated measurement.

larity in size and form of the two pointed, keeled tools suggests that these represent a formalized type in the minds of the makers, designed to perform special and possibly heavy-duty work. The points were snapped off the remainder of the tool at the same places and by a force applied from the same direction. While these have not been

Table 8.2 (*continued*)
Other Tools at the Lehner Site

Specimen Number*	Figure Number	Type	Location	Description**	Measurements in Millimeters***		
					Length	Width	Thickness
5 (A-12691)	8.14a	Keeled Scraper	Under same mammoth long bone as point A-12682 but at the opposite end and .10 m. lower; in gravel.	Fragmentary; coarse flaking with some fine retouching. Chalcedony; translucent light gray 7.5R,7/10, mottled with specks of white, 10R,9/1, and weak red, 10R, 4/4.	(65)	33	15
6 (A-12692)	8.14g	Side Scraper	Near scattered mammoth teeth .30 m. below swamp soil in gravel bar.	Flake scars shallow, some fine retouching; edge dulled. Andesite; black, 7.5R,2/0.	130	73	20
7 (A-12693)	8.14e	Knife	.40 m. below swamp soil in mixed clay and gravel.	Thin edge of flake finely retouched or sheared. Andesite; very dark gray, 7.5R, 3/0.	70	60	12
8 (A-12694)	8.14b	Keeled Scraper	West of the main area of bone concentration in base of fine sand lense on gravel bar; .15 m. below swamp soil.	Fragmentary; coarse flaking heavily retouched or sheared. Rhyolite; pale brown, 10YR,6/3, speckled with dark brown, 10YR,4/3.	(63)	28	15

reported heretofore as associates of Clovis fluted points, similar artifacts are seen in the pre-ceramic horizons of the California desert (Campbell and others 1937: Plate 33d), southern Arizona (Haury 1950a: Figure 34f), and interestingly enough in the possibly early site of El Jobo in northwestern Venezuela (Cruxent and Rouse 1956: Figure 3). Tools labeled as side scrapers, distinguished by having a well-developed point but lacking the keel, accompany the fluted points from both the Shoop Site (Witthoft 1952: Plates 2, 13, 15, 16) and the Bull Brook Site (Byers 1954: Figure 92i) in the eastern United States.

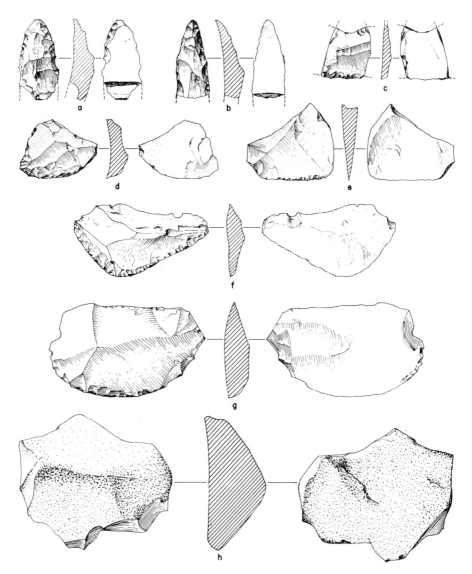

Figure 8.14. Tools other than projectile points from
the Lehner Site. Length of g, 130 millimeters.

These occurrences suggest that a pointed and keeled scraper form is not only early but may prove to be one of the diagnostics of the Llano complex. The other scrapers in the collection with side chipping are perhaps too generalized to permit comparison, since their form was largely determined by the shape of the original flake.

The real meaning of the tools other than projectile points from the Lehner Site is that they begin to fill out the Llano or Clovis complex (Figure 8.15) and provide us with some idea of the equipment used in butchering.

The identification of the rock types from which the points and other tools were made are listed in Tables 8.1 and 8.2. These determinations were made in the Arizona Bureau of Mines, University of Arizona, by microscopic study and spectrometric tests on materials believed to be identical with the rock type from which the artifacts were made. The chief interest in doing this was to determine if some of the materials could have come from distant sources. Since all materials used originated in either volcanic or sedimentary rocks and both of these are present in the area, it is probable that tool stone was local in origin. Raw material for the three crystalline quartz points probably came from the Huachuca Mountains where local deposits of sizable crystals are known.

NACO-LEHNER COMPARISON

Before leaving the discussion of the tools of the Lehner Site, a few words are in order about the similarities and differences of the Naco and Lehner stations. It should be noted that the accident of discovery has allowed us to exhume within the span of a few years and from two places only 12 miles apart evidence bearing significantly on early man's activities. The two stations differ in that Naco yielded but a single animal while the Lehner Site yielded numerous units both in animals and species. Only projectile points were recovered at Naco while Lehner, in addition, produced other tools and two hearths. The scattered, small charcoal flecks in the Naco matrix probably signal a fire in the vicinity of the kill. The projectile point similarity is impressive because the two lots could be merged into one typological assemblage. The geologic history in both localities is essentially the same, recording a similar succession of events of about the same time magnitude. The Lehner swamp soil, certainly a local phenomenon, is missing at Naco.

The date assignments are equivocal. Antevs originally placed the

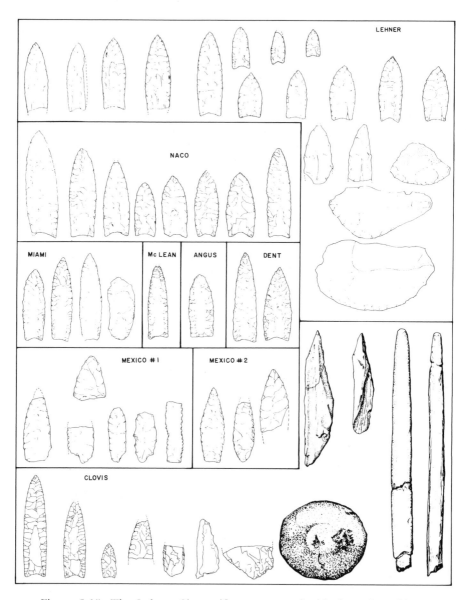

Figure 8.15. The Lehner Site artifacts compared with those from Naco and other sites which have produced tools in association with mammoth remains. Sources for artifacts other than those from Lehner Site are: Naco—Haury and others 1953: Figures 6, 7; Miami—Sellards 1952: Figures 8, 9; McLean—Sellards 1952: Figure 20b; Angus—Figgins 1931; Dent—Figgins 1933; Mexico No. 1—Martínez del Río 1952; Mexico No. 2—Aveleyra Arroyo de Anda 1955: Plates 25, 26; Clovis (Blackwater No. 1)—Sellards 1952: Figures 13–18.

Naco kill between 10,000 and 11,000 years ago (Haury and others 1953:17) but he has since revised the figure to 13,000 or more years. The radiocarbon date for Naco at 9250 ± 300 is some 2000 years younger than the probable age of the Lehner Site at more than 11,000 years ago. Notwithstanding these discrepancies, the artifactual evidence suggests that the same people, perhaps the same band, were responsible for the kills, and that the time separating the two occurrences may have been no longer than a few years. If, however, the dates noted above are correct, the time difference has an important bearing upon our concept of the elephant hunter's tenancy of this part of the Southwest and of the stability of his projectile point form. There is no way presently to settle this problem. Nonetheless, the two localities go a long way towards establishing elephant hunting as a pattern for a part of the Southwest in which such evidence has been lacking and gives strong hope that the camp sites will some day be found.

THE LLANO COMPLEX

Sellards (1952:17–46) recently consolidated the known data on certain artifacts which occurred in association with extinct animals, principally the mammoth, and called the assemblage the Llano complex. In addition to the main sites, largely limited to the southern High Plains, he also included the Naco station because it produced Clovis fluted points, the chief diagnostic element of the complex. Small, unfluted points, scrapers, hammerstones, and crude bone implements were also recognized as elements of the pattern. In all, the aggregate number of specimens is small, so small in fact that the evidence seems slim to support so basic a concept of an old elephant-hunting society. However, the age of the Llano complex, certainly older in the main than Folsom, and a wide geographic range, show there is something to the idea. Amplification of the complex by adding to the trait inventory, the discovery of camp sites in datable geological contexts, and the recovery of the bones of Llano man himself are pressing problems.

The artifacts from the Lehner Site clearly come within the pattern of the Llano complex on the basis of the fluted points and the small unfluted points, the associated fauna, and the age of the remains. The pointed scrapers and the large side scrapers have not been exactly duplicated by the materials from other Llano complex sites but they may be taken as examples of tools representative of the assemblage. Herein, perhaps, lies one of the more significant contributions of the Lehner Site to our knowledge of the period.

The consistency and the range of the Llano complex artifacts recovered up to now from mammoth-kill sites are shown in the sketches of Figure 8.15. Included for comparative purposes are the tools associated with the remains of two mammoths in the Valley of Mexico. Fluted points were not found here but the stations may be roughly contemporaneous with the kill sites in the United States. The implement yield from slaughtering grounds gives us an activity-selected sample and hence a one-sided view of the probable tool inventory. The bone tools from the Blackwater No. 1 (Clovis) locality are hints of a wider range of artifact type, as are also the hammerstones. The latter have particular interest because Sellards notes (1952:42) these "may also have served the purpose of a grinding stone." Similar handstones are a characteristic trait of the Sulphur Spring stage of the Cochise culture (Sayles and Antevs 1941: Plate 3, a, d). Further definition of this element in the Llano complex may prove to bear significantly on Llano-Cochise relationships.

On a tentative basis, it would appear possible to expand the Llano complex as to components and range by taking into account the materials recovered with Clovis points in surface sites, especially in the West, providing that no mixture of artifacts from different horizons is represented. Many of these occurrences have been summarized by Daugherty (1956), Jennings and Norbeck (1955), Wormington (1957), and others. Inspection of the large Campbell (1940) collection from near Tonapah, Nevada, would bear fruit. The wide-ranging distribution of the fluted point in the eastern United States, as at the Bull Brook (Byers 1954), the Shoop (Witthoft 1952), the Quad (Soday 1954) sites and the surveys that have been made such as the impressive array of points examined by Ritchie (1957) in New York, once brought into some meaningful relationship with the Llano complex, would have far-reaching implications in Paleoindian history. A step in this direction has already been taken by Mason (1958:44) who regards the Michigan Clovis-like points as a Great Lakes manifestation of the Llano complex. The problem that exists here, as with other eastern occurrences of fluted points and related tools, is that they have not been found as yet with the late Pleistocene faunal forms. This association has greatly aided the definition of the complex in the West. It is not our intent here to launch a study of this problem but someone should attempt it.

Until a more unified picture can be drawn, the Llano complex must stand as a western manifestation. The Lehner and Naco increments may be taken to represent the southwesternmost extent of the range. Both support the definition of the complex as a big-game hunting pattern.

DATING THE LEHNER SITE

Two methods for determining how long ago the mammoths and other animals fell prey to human hunters are presently available: estimates based on the geological history, and radiocarbon dating. Antevs's careful study of the geological record follows. It is not necessary to dwell on his report now beyond noting that he finds an age of 13,000 or more years for the event supportable.

Radiocarbon results have been obtained from three laboratories. Most of them are from the University of Arizona Carbon [14] Age Determination Laboratory (Wise and Shutler 1958), which then used the solid carbon method. Single dates each were run by the Radiocarbon Dating Laboratory, University of Copenhagen through the cooperation of Henrik Tauber, and the University of Michigan Phoenix-Memorial Project Laboratory through the assistance of James B. Griffin. Both of these laboratories employ the carbon dioxide method. The results are given in Figure 8.16. A review of the values reveals some disturbing internal inconsistencies as well as several gratifying correspondences.

Radiocarbon dates, as well as all other kinds of data, require evaluation in terms of reliability, consistency, and meaning. The present lot is no exception. Taking up the swamp soil (Figure 8.4k) results first we see altogether too large a range represented in the three dates from a thin bed to convince one that the assays were really good. The nature of the samples, carbonaceous soil, is suspect in itself for such material is probably more subject to contamination than is solid charcoal. Furthermore, these dates were obtained early in the history of the University of Arizona Laboratory and later refinements in the techniques are believed to have given better results. Antevs rejects the swamp soil dates on the grounds that these place the swamp in the onset of the Altithermal Drought, an improbability, and favors a late pluvial date. An argument in favor of this position is the stratigraphic relationship between the swamp soil and the bone and culture bearing layers directly below. In some instances the black layer was in direct contact with

LEHNER SITE PROFILE	RADIOCARBON DATES			ANTEVS' GEOLOGICAL ESTIMATES
	U. ARIZONA	U. COPENHAGEN	U. MICHIGAN	
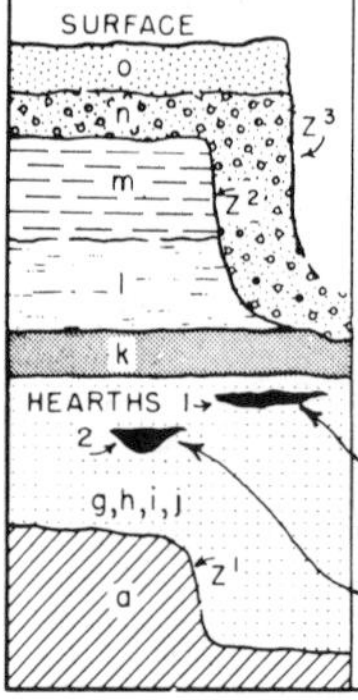	6356 ±450 } 6877 ±450 } (A-31) 7133 ± 350 (A-33) AV. 6789 ± 450 7205± 450 (A-34) 7022 ± 450 (A-32) 8330 ± 450 (A-30) 10,900 ± 450 (A-40a) 12,000± 450 (A·40b)	11,180 ± 140 (K-554)	11,290 ±500 (M-811)	Z^3 = MODERN ARROYO STARTS CUTTING 1880'S Z^2 = ALTITHERMAL ARROYO 7000−5000 B. P. k = PLUVIAL Z^1 = MAMMOTH KILL CREEK HUNTS 13,000 B. P. OR OLDER

Figure 8.16. Comparative results of radiocarbon measurements and Antevs's geological estimates. All radiocarbon dates are B.P. Beds not shown to scale; b–f omitted; g–j, the bone- and artifact-producing layers, not differentiated in drawing.

bones and everywhere it appeared to rest comfortably upon the beds beneath. If the age of the swamp soil is correct at about 6700 years and the bone bed is dated some 5000 years earlier, than we must postulate either a long period of static conditions insofar as alluviation and erosion are concerned, or that an overburden of silt was washed off, exposing some of the bones just before the swamp developed. This is unlikely for some of the charcoal of Hearth 2 was imbedded in the swamp soil and locally the two were separated by a 1-centimeter-thick layer of fine sand. We are strongly inclined to be believe that the swamp soil dates are much too young and should not be given credence.

The charcoal from Hearths 1 and 2 provided the laboratories with a nearly ideal kind of material. Nevertheless, at least three of the Arizona laboratory dates, 7205 ±450 for Hearth 1 and 7022 ± 450 and 8330 ± 450 for Hearth 2 are not acceptable. A span of some 5000 years in the assays of Hearth 2 charcoal alone goes far beyond the stretching ability of one's beliefs. No aboriginal fire was kept burning that long! Obviously something is wrong. The error in the above values can almost certainly be attributed to contamination of the charcoal. Realization of this led the laboratory technician to employ special methods to remove contaminants. The ensuing tests produced the higher figures of 10,900 ± 450 and 12,000 ± 450 with an average of 11,850 ± 50. The independent measurements in the Copenhagen and Michigan laboratories, 11,180 ± 140 and 11,290 ± 500 respectively, are in convincing agreement between themselves and they lend plausibility to the two older Arizona laboratory dates. It seems to us that a date of from 11,000 to 12,000 years ago for the time of the kills, is probably not far from the truth although this time range is short of Antevs's estimate.

The important question, of course, is how does an 11,000-to-12,000 year age correspond with such other evidence that exists for the dating of Llano man or the Clovis complex. The truth of the matter is that we haven't much evidence to draw upon and such as is available is contradictory. For example, Burnet Cave (Howard 1935) in New Mexico has yielded a radiocarbon date of 7432 ± 300 (Libby 1955:116) for charcoal from a level about 1 meter below a fluted point of Clovis type while the Lewisville Site in Denton County, Texas (Crook and Harris 1958) which also produced a Clovis point has been dated in excess of 37,000 years ago by several radiocarbon assays. The Naco mammoth (Haury and others 1953) has now been dated by the radiocarbon method at 9250 ± 300 (Wise and Shutler 1958:72) and the four oldest Lehner assays from the three laboratories give an average age of 11,340 years ago. Three reliable measurements for the Bull Brook Site on the eastern seaboard average about 9000 years ago (Byers 1959), a date which agrees well with the Naco date. However, the Burnet Cave, Naco, and the Bull Brook dates seem too young and the Lewisville date much too old for the Llano complex. In consideration of the generally accepted age of the Folsom complex at from 9000 to 10,000 years ago (Wormington 1957:39) and the geological estimates we have, a date of 11,000 to 12,000 for Clovis points as seen at Lehner is reasonable. Antevs holds that both the Naco and Lehner sites predate the relatively warm and dry Datil Interval (12,500 to 10,800 B.P.) because the geology of both stations suggests a relatively moist, subarid climate, and therefore ought to be earlier than the Datil Drought. For many students of early man such an adjustment downward in time would be palatable. If the idea is accepted that the southeastern Arizona occurrences of the Llano complex are geographically marginal in its total distribution, then it may well be that the Lehner age assignment of nearly 12 millennia ago is a minimal date for a surviving manifestation of the complex.

Closely linked with dating studies nowadays is the information to be derived from fossil pollen. A spectrum of pollen taken from the sedimentary deposits of the Lehner Site would undoubtedly yield significant information of paleoclimatic changes and provide added support for the age inferred from geology and more directly derived from radiocarbon. Although a liberal number of pollen samples were taken, the results of the analyses are not yet available. The principle work to date has been done by Lindsay (1958) centering upon the relative merits of three pollen recovery methods. Pollen was extracted from all geological horizons tested, including the artifact and bone-producing layers (see Figure 8.4g, h, i, j). Systematic identificaton of the pollen grains has not been attempted, but Lindsay (1958:61) notes that Sample 11-1, taken from between the rami of mammoth jaw Number 7 and probably best representing the pollen rain conditions of the time, showed the following pollen distribution: pine, 39%; composites, 28%; grass, 4%; spores, 5%; unknown, 23%. These results, of course, are so slender that little weight may be given them. However, taking the geology and the faunal assemblage into account, the evidence suggests somewhat less aridity, an abundance of forage, and perhaps a lower forest border than now prevails.

BIG-GAME HUNTERS AND PLANT GATHERERS

The relationship between the Llano big-game hunter and the Desert-culture plant collector stands as one of the major problems of Paleoindian history. The Lehner Site contributes little towards its solution directly. But indirectly, because it is the second kill site in the San Pedro drainage, the original Naco discovery is lifted, at least part way, from its apparent out-of-context situation and the two together may be taken as a reflection of a well-established hunting tradition where it was unknown previously. Southeastern Arizona ought to be joined to the larger big-game hunting territory that stretches far to the east and north. In the whole of this area, only the southwestern fringe, specifically southeastern Arizona, yields the abundant traces of the Cochise complex as well as those of the Llano complex. It is the presence of these two divergent tool patterns that confronts us with a provocative situation. Does this mean there was an orderly historical development from hunting to gathering? Or was it the penetration of hunter into gatherer territory; the submergence of the hunter by newly arrived collectors; or merely the shift in emphasis, perhaps seasonal or over longer time, from hunting-gathering to gathering-hunting by the same people? Or is the contrast between the two tool assemblages from which we infer different ways of life over-emphasized (Willey and Phillips 1955:733)?

The meaning of this transition is only slightly less significant for the New World than was the advance from food collecting to food producing in the Old World, for it was the dependence on plants, the knowledge about them, and the development of related grinding tools, that ultimately made the acceptance of agriculture and the settling down to village life easy. Several explanations have been suggested.

Willey and Phillips (1955:732) have minimized the typological difference, classing both in their Early Lithic stage and leaving open the question as to which complex is the older. In a later study they hold that the dates for both the Sulphur Spring and the Chiricahua stages "are no longer too early for Archaic" (Willey and Phillips 1958:91) and by implication view the early Cochise manifestations as later than their Early Lithic. As an aside, their reasoning is based on the allegedly questionable association of extinct fauna with the Sulphur Spring horizon and the occurrence of Pinto-like points (Willey and Phillips 1958:91). Lest these ideas should gain currency, we would like to set the record straight. Part of a skull and other elements of a mammoth were imbedded *in* pond beds *overlying* the culture-bearing Sulphur Spring layer at Double Adobe (Sayles and Antevs 1941:47). Furthermore in the latter deposit, amongst the Sulphur Spring artifacts and hearth stones were the bones of horse, bison, pronghorn antelope, dire wolf, coyote, and mammoth (Sayles and Antevs 1941:12). This determination is not based on a single occurrence in one site of this period but upon repetitive evidence in several sites. As for the Pinto-like points, a detailed geological study of their provenience makes it clear that they must be attributed to a somewhat later period than the Sulphur Spring stage. In short we believe that the Sulphur Spring horizon does occupy a relatively early time position, before the extinction of the late Pleistocene fauna, and that the basic question put earlier with respect to Llano-Clovis relationship cannot be settled on the premise of presumed lateness for the latter. However, it is possible to arrive at essentially the same conclusions as those reached by Willey and Phillips, but by a somewhat different route.

A point of view directly opposite to that held by Willey and Phillips was taken by the 1955 archaeological seminar group which stated

". . . that the technology of the Desert culture (of which the Cochise complex is a regional manifestation) is sufficiently distinct from that of the Paleoindian big-game hunter to testify not only to a quite different environmental adaptation but to a different cultural outlook as well" (Jennings 1956:71). Moreover, because the indicated age of the Desert culture in the Great Basin is of about the same magnitude as that for the Llano complex, the seminar concluded: "The older view, that the seed-using cultures similar to Cochise, were late developments out of a big-game hunting base, no longer seems tenable" (Jennings 1956:71; 1957:282). It was further held by the seminar group that if such a developmental sequence were the true state of affairs, the divergence took place far back in time, possibly even before man's entry into the New World.

Krieger (1953:243) and Haury (Haury and others 1953:13–14) have suggested that the transition was a logical succession following the disappearance of the game during the Anathermal warming. The change was ecologically bound and it was an enforced adaptation, if the society was to survive. This does not agree with Antevs's assessment of the geology but the idea, we feel, cannot be ignored.

Insofar as our immediately local problem is concerned, there are some arguments in support of big-game hunting as a cultural stage antecedent to the collecting stage. Briefly these are:

1. The oldest radiocarbon dates for the Sulphur Spring stage are in the order of 7000 to 8000 years (Libby 1955:112; Wise and Shutler 1958:74) as against the substantially higher age of 11,000 or more years for the Clovis assemblage at the Lehner Site.

2. The tool types of the Lehner Site, especially the fluted points and the keeled pointed scrapers, have no equivalents in the inventory of Sulphur Spring stage tools. The base of a point resembling the Clovis type from a Chiricahua stage *context* (Sayles and Antevs 1941: Plate 11a) is an exception but it may be presumed to be so much later that it would appear to have no significant bearing on this argument. The failure thus far to find diagnostic tools of the two traditions mixed in the same site strongly hints at a temporal difference.

3. Once grinding utensils and the other tools needed to collect plant foods were developed or acquired, the stage was set for the long survival of the tradition. Undoubtedly hunting

was still important in the economy, but such hunting as was practiced was not done with weapons carrying tips of the fluted lanceolate blades of the big-game hunter.

Perhaps this is drawing the obvious conclusion. In so doing no claim is made that the transition was initially centered in southeast Arizona and that it reflects, blanket-fashion, what happened broadly in western America. Our concern now is only with a local phenomenon. We estimate that the change in emphasis from hunting to collecting began before the complete extinction of the big game, witness the mammoth overlying the Sulphur Spring stage horizon in the Double Adobe station. In the post-glacial time table this was probably during the Anathermal, between 7000 and 5000 B.C. In fairness to another point of view, it must be noted that Antevs prefers the interpretation that the relatively warm and dry Datil Interval (12,000–10,800 B.P.) eliminated the mammoth (see Haury 1958a and Martin 1958 for different views on extinction). In this event the transition in economic dependence from meat to plant had to be made much earlier than has been postulated.

DISCUSSION

Two erosion periods, resulting in the Altithermal arroyo channel and the modern one, have combined to destroy a part of the bone bed. How much was washed away cannot be estimated accurately, but perhaps as much as 50%. Even so, enough has survived to make it clear that the bones of four species of animals, mammoth, horse, bison, and tapir, and at least nine individual mammoths, were present. This situation evokes a number of questions: Were all of the animals in the deposit killed by man? Were they all killed at once? If not, over what period of time were the bones accumulating? Why were the bones of so many animals restricted to such a small area?

Artifacts associated with skeletons of more than one animal are reported from the Miami locality, Texas, and Blackwater No. 1 locality in New Mexico (Sellards 1952:18–31). Hence the Lehner ranch occurrence is not unique. In all of these instances the mammoth was the predominant animal, and only at Lehner and Blackwater No. 1 were horse and bison also present. There is at present no way of settling the question as to whether or not man was responsible for the demise of all the animals in these stations. It is well known from paleontology

and by observing watering places for cattle today, that animal carcasses accumulate in limited areas without man's intervention. As for
the Lehner Site, judging from the artifact distribution, the presence
of butchering tools, and the evidence of fires, it may be inferred that
the majority, if not all, of the animals were slaughtered. Another strong
argument for this is Lance's identification of all mammoths as either
calves or young adults. This age selectivity surely was no accident. It is
explainable on the basis that the younger animals would be easier to
isolate from the herd, easier to kill, and tastier. The older animals,
those more apt to die of natural causes, are lacking.

We incline toward the idea of killing at intervals for the following
reasons:

1. It is doubtful that so many animal units, including four species, would have been watering or congregating in the same
   spot at the same time and that hunters could have dispatched
   so many at once. Large mammals, except when herds are
   driven over cliffs, are usually taken singly.
2. Wide bone dispersal for some animals and less for others,
   with some articulation present, argues for spaced kills.
3. Unequal preservation of the bones due, possibly, to differential exposure.
4. Perhaps the most significant evidence in support of this view
   is the vertical distribution of the bones, as well as some artifacts, in the gravels of Mammoth Kill Creek. This depth
   range was approximately 1 meter. While gravel and sand
   deposits may accumulate rapidly in strong current conditions, it did not appear probable, as the bones were removed
   from the matrix, that this was the case. The impact-blunted
   point (Figures 8.12m, 8.13m) was found well down in the
   gravels next to the pelvic bone which it may have struck.
   Other flat-lying bones with closely related weapons were in
   higher levels. Upon completing the excavations we were left
   with the impression that here was a favored hunting spot
   where animals, attracted by water, were periodically am-
   bushed and killed by the same band of people, but perhaps
   within a year's time.

When it became evident that more than one animal was represented in the bone bed, the question arose as to how and why this massing of bones came about. How were the animals contained? Was
there a natural trap into which they could have wandered only to be

slaughtered? The geomorphology of the station makes it clear that there was a sand and gravel floored stream bed bordered on the south by a nearly vertical bank of red clay about 1.8 meters high. The nature of the north bank is not known since it was destroyed by the Altithermal erosion. One must imagine that the animals, attracted by the water, drifted to the deepest part of the stream. This was along the outside curve of a meander bow against the clay bank. The walls of the channel, and the slopes away from them may have been too high and too slippery to be negotiated by mammoths, and access to the favored watering spot was either up or down the stream bed where trails led into it. Escape routes would have followed paths of access. At this point man probably entered the picture, for, having seen animals at the water hole, he was able with the aid of firebrands or noise, or by virtue of numbers, to contain the beasts in the channel long enough for hunters to select their prey, a young animal, and move in for the kill.

The feasibility of holding elephants at bay is demonstrated by the Nama Hottentots who, by hunting in large parties, surround the animal and repeatedly attack it from the rear as it turns against each new assailant until it falls, wounded and exhausted (Murdock 1934:481). The use of pitfalls and spearing from trees appear the less likely techniques in the present situation.

After an animal had been felled in the stream or at its edge, butchering proceeded on the spot. In time, following repeated hunts, a considerable number of bones accumulated. The work of scavengers and the trampling of bones by animals tended to scatter and break them. Left as evidence of man's part in the drama were such projectile points as he did not retrieve, the broken ones and some others that escaped him, butchering tools perhaps regarded as expendable, and the remains of fires where choice morsels were roasted on the spot. It should be noted that the tapir jaw was within a hand-span of one of these hearths and slightly charred. This, of course, is sheer speculation, but it is one way of explaining the massing of the bones. We are sorely in need of long range observations around water holes, as in Africa, to see what happens to carcasses after complete abandonment by man and scavengers. Such data might help to explain the situations encountered in the kill sites of early America.

In the preceding reconstruction, containment of the animals within the geographic area of their wounding around a water hole is implied. This seems also to have been the case at Naco, Miami, and Blackwater

No. 1 localities. These places evidently did not have the physiographic advantages offered by the Lehner Site, which leads to the suspicion that the primitive hunting techniques are a long way from being understood. African elephant hunting provides contrasts to this containment method. The African pigmy smears himself with mud from the water hole frequented by elephants and with skill and courage, creeps underneath the beast to thrust his spear deep into its belly. Then follows the arduous trailing of the animal until it perishes from its wounds (Janmart 1952:146–147). In "The Hunter," John Marshall's film of a Bushman giraffe hunt in the Kalahari Desert, the animal first received an arrow treated with slow-working poison. Trailing extended over a six-day period and many miles before the animal, in its stupefied condition, could be brought down. There is no evidence that poison was used by the early American hunter, but he seems to have had considerable success in the difficult task of holding a wounded animal close to the spot where it was first encountered.

As noted earlier, the range in projectile point length is large, from 31 to 97 millimeters. That the smallest points, all of quartz (Figures 8.12a–c, 8.13a–c), should have been used to fell mammoths seems improbable. But, since many of the mammoths were calves, the contrast between weapon and animal size is no greater than it was later when the Folsom point was used against the bison. Figure 8.5, showing a small quartz point lodged between ribs of a young mammoth (?) seems fairly conclusive. Nevertheless, the size range of the Naco points, found with a single mature animal (Haury and others 1953:7), argues for the fact that the primitive hunters did not restrict spears with small tips to small game.

Our knowledge of butchering methods is as vague as is our understanding of hunting techniques. Fortunately, the Lehner Site, more than any other to date, has given us tools whose function must have been that of cutting up the animal. The large scrapers or knives (see Figure 8.14f, g) would have served well for this, as would also a fluted point itself. The fragments of two keeled, pointed scrapers (see Figure 8.14a, b), snapped off at the same distance from the point and by a force coming from the same direction, evidently were special purpose tools designed for heavy work of unknown character. Beyond the recovery of flesh and hide, there is a hint that skulls were crushed for brains. Masses of smashed brain case bones were found, but no whole skull survived. This practice has previously been noted at the Iztapan mammoth finds (Aveleyra 1955:17–18).

Speculating once again as to how the meat was handled, it would appear that dismembering a large animal was a task of major proportions, both because of the difficulty of severing limbs and the weight of the units. In the young animals this might not have applied. The meat was most likely removed from the animal by chunk, strip, or roll, the method used by the historic bison-hunters in the Plains. This type of removal facilitated transportation of the meat to camp and doubtless was necessary anyway to preserve it by drying, a technique which must surely have been known long ago. This method of butchering would leave the skeletons intact.

In another place (Haury 1958b) attention has been called to the possible importance of the difference in the butchering techniques employed by the Old and New World big-game hunters to account for an anomolous situation of preservation in these two regions. In America a large percentage of the evidence of early man has come from kill sites (Wormington 1957). The Lehner Site must be added to the ever-growing list. For Europe, however, with its infinitely longer record of the Paleolithic and probably greater population density during all stages, references to kill situations are almost non-existent. Only two documented instances have been found, the first a Third Interglacial mastodon skeleton with an associated wooden spear shaft in Germany (Movius 1950), and the second, the bones of a young mammoth with related hearth stones and worked stones found in western Siberia outside the city of Tomsk (Movius 1950:141, footnote). In Paleolithic camp sites, however, bones of extinct animals are of common occurrence. Paleoindian camps in America also produce bones of extinct animals but thus far representing principally bison. To explain the contrast in the frequency of kill stations one must believe that in Europe they have not been found or not reported, or that glacial activity has reduced the chances of discovery if kill stations were present, or else one must believe that the difference is a significant one. If the latter situation is correct, and at the moment it seems the most plausible, then a reasonable interpretation is that the American hunter removed the meat from the carcass for transport to camp, whereas the European hunter may have dismembered the carcass, carrying the segments, including bone, away. Few traces of the kill would survive if this were the case.

CONCLUSIONS

1. The remains of nine Columbian mammoths and at least one animal each of horse, bison, and tapir, occur in a single bone bed on the Lehner ranch in southeastern Arizona, in and on the gravels of a fossil perennial stream bed.
2. Directly associated with the bones of these animals was evidence of man's pursuit and destruction of at least some of them: 13 spear points of the Clovis fluted type, eight cutting and scraping tools, and the remains of two fires.
3. Subsequent to the killing of the animals, the formation of swamp soil and then heavy alluviation concealed the bone bed, followed by the cutting of an arroyo (Altithermal) which destroyed an indeterminate part of it. Further alluviation filled this channel and elevated the local ground surface to its present position. The modern arroyo has exposed the preceding events in its banks.
4. The episodes enumerated constitute the basis for the geologic dating of the site to a time of 13,000 or more years ago. Radiocarbon measurements place the time of the kills between 11,000 and 12,000 years ago.
5. The implement typology identifies the hunters as related to the big-game hunting Llano complex best known from the High Plains.

Acknowledgments

Excavations were conducted under the over-all direction of Haury between November 28 and December 19, 1955, and between February 5 and March 4, 1956. Antevs, Lance, and Sayles participated directly in the project. The reports by Antevs and Lance, on the geological and paleontological aspects of the discovery, accompany this paper. Wasley acted as field supervisor throughout the excavations. Graduate students in the Department of Anthropology of the University of Arizona who contributed freely of their time and labor included: William J. Beeson, Rex E. Gerald, James S. Griffith, Elizabeth Ann Morris, and Arthur H. Rohn. Special acknowledgement is due Austin Jay, Cochise County Supervisor for the Bisbee District, who rendered the fullest cooperation during both phases of the excavation in providing a power shovel and crew for the removal of overburden amounting to over a thousand tons; Jack Riggs, foreman of the district highway crew; Mrs. Donna Gentry, Martin Gentry, and James MacNulty of Bisbee, and Lt. George Megginson of Fort Huachuca for services and courtesies rendered throughout the excavations. No finer example of the cooperation between the interested amateur and the professional is to be found than that provided by Mr. and Mrs. Lehner from start to finish during the protracted period of investigation. They were perfect hosts to the miscellaneous "-ologists" and to the hundreds of visitors who descended upon them during the course of the proceedings, and yet they found time to assist with the digging, to provide refreshments for the excavation crew, and to perform a variety of other services and courtesies. From the beginning Lehner manifested a deep and abiding interest in and an acute comprehension of the more involved problems of excavation, analysis, and interpretation. To the Lehners go our sincere thanks and respect for the role they have played in contributing so materially to the knowledge of early hunters in the Southwest.

An Alluvial Site on the San Carlos Indian Reservation Arizona

Emil W. Haury

The mountainous belt of east-central Arizona has produced little evidence bearing on the problem of human history prior to the introduction of pottery and agriculture and the development of village life. In terms of the Christian calendar the events since about A.D. 1 are understood with varying degrees of clarity and reliability, but before the beginning of the Christian era the record for this region is still largely a void. The nature of the terrain, composed mainly of mountains with narrow, steeply pitching, and deeply entrenched valleys, has been unfavorable for the formation of the kind of alluvial deposits in which early human remains are often found. But there is no reason to suppose that the ecology of a mountainous region was less attractive to people of a primitive subsistence economy than were the plains or the broad low-lying intermountain valleys. The work in west-central New Mexico by Martin and others (1949) and in Bat Cave by Dick (1952, 1954) has pointed up the fact that the higher altitudes

Reprinted by permission from *American Antiquity*, 1957, 23(1):2–27. Contribution Number 5, Program in Geochronology, University of Arizona, Tucson. Contribution to Point of Pines Archaeology, Number 10.

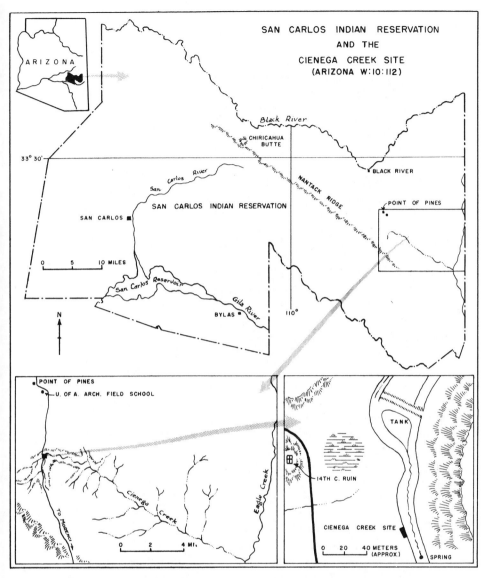

Figure 9.1. Location of the Cienega Creek Site, San Carlos Indian Reservation, Arizona.

and rough terrain were not deterrents to occupation. The discovery, therefore, of an alluvial site (Arizona W:10:112, Arizona State Museum Survey) in the Cienega Creek Valley near Point of Pines (Figure 9.1) in the summer of 1955 merely emphasizes what may be expected

Figure 9.2. Grinding stone, inverted over handstone (not visible) in Bed C-3. Trowel rests on hearthstone in Bed D-1. Profile face slopes away from camera, giving distorted impression of depth.

in the occasional valley or geologic situation in mountain country where all the conditions of man's presence, of his leaving his "tracks," and of nature's blanketing them with earth, later to uncover them again, are brought together in a way which permits decipherment.

The location of such favored spots will require a more systematic and persistent search and a closer scrutiny of the ground than is generally necessary elsewhere. The site in question abundantly illustrates this point. As early as 1941, the potential of Cienega Creek as a source of early human remains was recognized by E. B. Sayles. Here, a narrow valley, partly filled with flat-lying alluvial beds and now being exposed by arroyo trenching, provided the physical requisites for "gully archaeology." Frequent observations of the arroyo after 1946 netted occasional fragments of chipped stone in the talus but never anything in place in the arroyo walls. Finally, on July 4, 1955, Sayles and I, in company with several others, came upon a large stone imbedded in a fine-textured laminated silt deposit, which proved to be a grinding stone inverted over the companion hand stone (Figure 9.2). With this clue, indisputable evidence that man had left a functionally related combination of his tools on the spot during a period of alluviation, investigations were begun on July 6 and continued through August 3, 1955, and resumed from June 18 to June 28 in 1956.

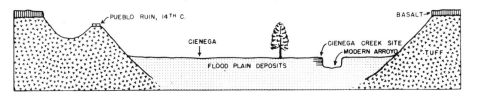

Figure 9.3. Diagrammatic section of the Cienega Creek Valley (roughly east to west), showing the relationship of the site to the local physiography.

THE CIENEGA VALLEY

Cienega Creek rises under the north rim of the Nantack Ridge at an elevation of about 7000 feet and flows in an easterly to southeasterly direction, emptying eventually into Eagle Creek 15 miles away at an elevation of 4500 feet (Figure 9.1). The several small intermittent streams which make up the head of the drainage system drop precipitously within canyons cut in tuff beds. They join at the base of the ridge to form the main valley. With the lessening of the gradient the valley broadens to 100 meters or so and is framed by steep valley sides composed of a heavy tuff bed capped by lava. Originally that part of the valley which concerns us here was deep, but aggradation has reduced this depth to approximately 45 meters and formed a flat valley floor with no appreciable altitudinal changes laterally. Mature pine trees grow sparsely on the valley floor, suggesting that stable conditions in the aggradation process were reached at least 100 years ago. Locally the valley floor becomes boggy in wet weather and, in one area of several acres, water stands for a time during the winter and summer rainy periods, producing an ephemeral marsh, or cienega, from which the creek takes its name (Figure 9.3).

The present arroyo ranges in width from 10 to 20 meters and has a depth of 4 meters or less. There are no records or observations available as to the date when arroyo cutting began. Inferentially, this was not earlier than 1885 and probably was somewhat later, judged by the "young" appearance of the arroyo itself. Youthful pines, perhaps no more than 10 to 15 years of age, have sprouted in the channel bays.

As a place to live, the valley and the adjacent mesas provided a few specific attractions. In spite of the arroyo cutting adjacent to the site here discussed, water emerges in the channel floor and trickles downstream for several hundred meters. Even during the driest parts of the year this water source is unfailing. Judged on the basis of the

Figure 9.4. Panoramic view of Cienega Creek Site (*center*) looking west. Arrow indicates fourteenth-century pueblo ruin (AZ W:10:4).

"water holes" exposed during our excavations, put down at a time when the valley floor was much lower than today, the availability of water must have been a characteristic of the spot for a long time, and therefore a feature which would have attracted people.

The mesa tops flanking the valley, though rocky, provide patches of fertile basalt-derived soil. Man-built barriers, in the form of low stone terraces designed to impede quick surface runoff, are a common sight. These are attributable to the agricultural practices of the people who have occupied the area within the last thousand years. Their village sites, too, are easily found on the benches and the mesa top. A small stone pueblo (Arizona W:10:4) occupies the top of a tuff outcrop directly west of the alluvial site (Figure 9.4). Thus, although the area was a favored spot in late prehistory, the kinds of artifacts found in these pueblo villages were not unearthed in the geological context of the valley deposits, except for a limited amount of pottery in a stratigraphically late bed. So by comparison and exclusion a long period of use of the valley may be assumed.

THE SITE

The principle human evidence in the valley deposits was limited to the area excavated, measuring 5 by 13 meters. A black carbonaceous layer (D-1), the oldest culture deposit, was traced for some 25 meters north and 75 meters south of the site and it is probable that human vestiges occur at least over this lateral spread. Some chert chips and hearthstones have been picked up on the eroded slopes of the arroyo even beyond these limits. The excavations recorded here appear to be in the heart of the area where human activity was most intense. It should be emphasized that the evidence of this was preserved within the clay, silt, sand, and gravel that make up the flood plain deposit of the valley. Human disturbances of the deposit remove all possibility of mere accidental or secondary inclusions in the alluvium. Excavations for fires, for water, and for the disposal of the dead stand in a relative temporal relationship to each other because as time passed, the rising valley floor was providing man with an ever-changing surface.

Our digging procedure was first to remove the talus material from the sloping arroyo face over a lateral width of 4 meters centering around the imbedded grinding stone which first led us to this spot. Next, the cutting of a vertical face made it clear that the deposits could be separated by character and that there was a series of them. As new cultural manifestations appeared, lateral digging of the area was eventually extended to 14 meters. Penetration into the arroyo bank varied from 3 meters at the south end to 7 meters at the north end (Figure 9.5). The maximum depth of the testing below the existing surface was 4.75 meters and the base level of the excavation below the deepest culture-bearing stratum (D-1), except for a limited test, was approximately 1.5 meters above the present arroyo floor. The face of the digging was kept vertical and the cuts into the bank varied from 0.25- to 0.50-meter slices, depending on the character of the features being dissected at the time. Approximately 200 cubic meters of dirt were removed in the operation.

Geology

The exposures of the valley deposits, visible in the present arroyo for nearly a half mile below the Cienega Creek Site, and those freshly opened by our digging reveal a succession of sediments with remarkable lateral uniformity. The maximum observed depth of the formations was about 5 meters and it is probable that they go much deeper.

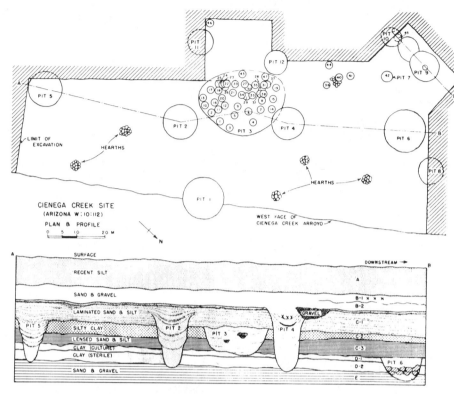

Figure 9.5. Plan and profile of the Cienega Creek Site, drawing attention to the vertical relationships of some of the cultural features. All
hearths were on the D-1 surface and Pit 1 was dug from this surface.
Circled numbers in Pit 3 and elsewhere represent cremations. Hachured
units in Pit 6 are large rocks. Pottery sources are designated by X. The
downstream dip of the beds is about 0.5 in 50.0 meters. For profile C-D
see Figure 9.9.

Vertical differentiation of the sediments into beds was based on such
physical characteristics as texture, composition, and color. No litho-
logical study was made. Marked erosional unconformities, important
in the separation of beds due to climatic fluctuations, were not seen.
Evidence for a minor erosion noted on the contact between the B-2
and C-1 beds is discussed later. The absence of such erosional features suggests a nearly continuous depositional process interrupted
by occasional pauses of variable duration when some surface stability
appears to have existed. This in itself is a hint that the recorded span
of time need not have been great.

Unfortunately the geology of the site is of little help in reading either the chronological record or in providing much useful information of past climate. No comparable sequence has been seen anywhere

Figure 9.6. The geological column of the Cienega
Creek Site. Scaling stick is 2.2 meters long.

in the area and no reference points exist which allow correlation with
other geochronologies. The absence of both vertebrate and inverte-
brate fossils handicaps stratigraphic classification. Furthermore, the
uniqueness of the archaeological complex prevents ready equation
with known cultural materials of an established sequence.

The following description of the beds proceeds from the surface
downward. It is recognized that the designation of formations in this
fashion is contrary to usual geological practice but the archaeologist
who excavates in these has need from the start to establish labels before the full profile is known. This is best done by beginning at the
surface (Figures 9.5, 9.6).

Bed A: Dark brown silt, some rounded pebbles; unconsolidated and structureless (0–1.0 meters thick).

Conformity

Bed B-1: Light brown silt, sand; soft (0.35–0.50 meters thick);
grades imperceptibly or locally changes abruptly to

Bed B-2: Light brown sand and gravel; gravel rounded tuff;
unconsolidated.

153

Conformity

Bed C-1: Light brown sand and silt, some gravel lenses; horizontal laminations of variable thickness prominent; soft. Near the top is a continuous thin (2 to 5 centimeters) organically stained clayey layer, capped by 5 to 10 centimeters of soft silt presenting a somewhat undulating and locally eroded surface (0.60–0.75 meters thick).

Conformity

Bed C-2: Light brownish gray silty clay, tuff pebbles; hard; pinches out and reappears in area of Pits 9 and 10 (0.20–0.35 meters thick).

Bed C-3: Light brown silt, sand, thin gravel lenses; prominent lenses of light tan sand and some horizontal laminations as in C-1. Bed thickens abruptly in northwest part of area excavated; wet and malodorous from organic content; plant remains identified (by C. T. Mason, Jr., Assistant Taxonomist, Department of Botany, University of Arizona) as probably Sedge (*Scirpus validus* or *S. acutus*), a marsh plant present in the area today; a seed of *Pinus*, probably *P. ponderosa*; a seed of *Chenopodium sp.*; and an unidentified seed (0.30–1.5 meters thick).

Conformity

Bed D-1: Dark gray clay, mixed with charcoal, hearthstones to depth of disturbance by man (0.15–0.25 meters thick).

Bed D-2: Dark gray clay, sterile, compact (0–0.25 meters thick).

Conformity

Bed E: Light brown sand and gravel; unconsolidated; base not exposed (1.5+ meters thick).

Fauna

Except for the cremated human bones and 2 unburned animal bone fragments associated with a cremation, no faunal remains were encountered in the excavations. Considering the food-preparing activity suggested by hearths and the few grinding tools, the absence of bone offers an interesting anomaly. This is especially true for the D bed which had all of the earmarks of a camping situation, but less so for the C bed and its components which represent a period of relatively rapid aggradation during which time people made specialized use of the spot. Since 2 unburned bone artifacts did survive in the soil

Figure 9.7. Pit 1 (*foreground*), Pit 2 (*right of scale*), and Pit 3 (*far right*). The last, containing the cremations, often with cover stones, is only partially exposed here.

one may infer that soil conditions were not such as to completely destroy bone if it was ever present. More probable is the inference that food preparation was limited to vegetal materials or that some other selective factor, not now apparent, was working.

Hearths

Shallow, circular, basin-like depressions filled with fire-stained and sometimes cracked basalt rocks and charcoal have been identified as hearths. Six main hearthstone concentrations appeared, all on the surface of layer D-1 (Figure 9.5). The amount of stones removed in the larger ones amounted to about a half bushel in volume. In addition, hearthstones were widely distributed through this bed, suggesting considerable cooking activity. The rocks themselves varied in size but seldom exceeded 20 centimeters in diameter. The heat-resisting properties of basalt influenced the choice of basalt over tuff for use in the cooking process.

In the 3 units of bed C no hearths were noted and hearthstones were rare. Their presence has no apparent connection with the cremations and must be related to food preparation practices. In passing it should be noted that the rocks associated with cremations, often as cap stones, were of unburned tuff.

Figure 9.8. Profile of Pit 3 (*center*), with cremations, and Pit 4 (*right*). Upper right margin of Pit 4 partly destroyed by erosion on C-1 surface.

It has been generally observed that the alluvial sites of the Cochise culture yield hearthstones in abundance and that they are less common in the later villages of pottery-making times. This is true of Point of Pines also where in pit-house village or pueblo they are an infrequent attribute of the site. Bed B-1, with pottery, produced none. Insofar as the local culture history is concerned the incidence of hearthstones in itself hints at some age for this site as compared with the numerous nearby ruins of pottery times.

Pits

The first feature, encountered early in the excavation, which removed all doubt about human presence on the spot and established with absolute certainty that the cultural remains were not redeposited, was a circular pit 1.5 meters in diameter and nearly as deep. Subsequent digging exposed 11 additional pits varying to some extent in size, shape, and the levels from which they were dug (Figure 9.5). The sectioning method of excavation employed made for easy differentiation of the sedimentary deposits in the pits from those of the beds into which they were dug, as it clearly brought out in Figures 9.7 and 9.8. Details of the pits are as follows:

Pit 1.   Dimensions: mouth diameter 1.5 meters, reducing to about 1 meter at bottom; bottom flat; depth 1.4 meters.

Fill: fine laminated curved silt layers with occasional hearthstones and lumps of charcoal and black clay probably derived from Bed D-1.

Level: dug from top of D-1 through this deposit and deeply into E (see Figure 9.7).

Pit 2.   Dimensions: mouth diameter 1.3 meters, with gently sloping sides converging sharply at 1 meter to make shoulder, continuing downward to form rounded bottom; depth 1.5 meters.

Fill: curved, finely laminated silt and clay layers.

Level: dug from near top of C-1, through D and into sands and gravels of E (see Figure 9.7).

Pit 3.   Dimensions: maximum diameter 3 meters; minimum diameter slightly over 2 meters; depth 1.3 meters; pit not clearly definable along western margin.

Pit 4.   Dimensions: mouth diameter 1.5 meters, sides converging to bottom diameter of 0.5 meters; depth 1.8 meters.

Fill: curved layers of laminated silts; lenticular pocket of carbon-impregnated silt near top; potsherds in upper part.

Level: excavated after C-1 was formed and from surface separating it from B-2; penetrated D and shallowly into E (see Figure 9.8).

Pit 5.   Dimensions: mouth diameter 1 meter; sides taper sharply to small rounded bottom; depth 1 meter.

Fill: curved laminated silts in upper part, grading to clay in bottom.

Level: dug at same time as Pit 3, from top of C-2 formation; penetrated D and barely into sands of E.

Pit 6.   Dimensions: diameter 1.35 meters; depth 1.75; basin-like.

Fill: silt and closely packed large rocks near bottom. Rocks suggest use of this pit as earth oven, but no direct evidence of fire seen.

Level: dug from top of D-1; penetrated E.

Pit 7.   This pit proved to be a cremation; in bed C-3; overlying bed C-2 absent in profile due to natural pinching out or to extensive human disturbance; radiocarbon age of 2150±200 suggests pit was dug at terminal C-2 time. (See also discussion under "Cremations" and Figure 9.11.)

Pit 8.   Dimensions: mouth diameter 0.9 meters; depth 1.2 meters.

Fill: sediments, numerous large and small fire-cracked rocks, and large (to 0.4 meters) sections of charred oak and pine logs.

Level: dug from C-3 surface; penetration into E not clearly defined due to excessive water.

Pit 9.   Dimensions: average diameter 1 meter; depth 3.7 meters; (Figures 9.5, 9.9, 9.10); bottom rounded, sides nearly perpendicular.

Fill: mostly clean sand, with numerous large rocks near bottom, some piled up suggesting a platform for standing; some pottery throughout fill. A late disturbance in fill was a bore of 0.25 meters in diameter and about 2 meters deep. This penetration postdates the formation of B-1 which itself formed after the digging and filling of Pit 9; it may represent one of several well-drilling efforts in the valley in recent years. Pit 9 seeped water so abundantly that excavation became extremely difficult.

Level: dug from B-2 surface and penetrated sands of E.

Pit 10.   Dimensions: mouth diameter about 0.8 meters; tapering towards bottom; depth 2.8 meters (Figures 9.5, 9.9).

Fill: clean sand and silt, no rocks, some pottery.

Level: excavated from B-2 surface.

Pit 11.   Dimensions: diameter 0.9 meters; depth 2 meters.

Fill: silts showing concave laminar structure; pottery absent.

Level: excavated from just below final surface of C-1; black clayey layer just below C-1 surface unbroken over pit; barely reached sands of E.

Pit 12. Dimensions: mouth diameter about 1 meter; depth 2.8 meters.

Fill: bottom filled with gravel derived from B-2, overlain by black silty-clay and finally sand; no pottery found but pit was dug within pottery times.

Level: excavation from surface of B-1, penetrated to E.

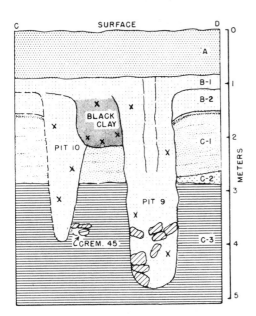

Figure 9.9. Profile C-D (see also Figure 9.5) through wells dug within a short period of time from B-2 surface about 1000 years ago. Pottery denoted by X. Bed C at this point thick and waterlogged. Note Cremation 45 in basket.

It is clear from the foregoing that functionally 4 types of pits are represented: (1) Numbers 1, 2, 4, 5, 6, 9, 10, 11, and 12, which were comparatively small but deep, each reaching the sandy E bed and filled ultimately by natural processes of sedimentation; (2) Number 3, a large shallow pit, filled with numerous pockets of cremated bone and rocks, the contents due largely to human activity and only to a minor extent to natural filling; (3) Number 7, a small pit expressly designed to receive a single cremation; and (4) Pit 8, which, judging from its contents was a large cooking pit or earth oven.

A reasonable conclusion as to the significance of the first group of pits is that they were efforts to reach water. We know that a permanent water supply exists adjacent to the site, occurring now as a spring in

Figure 9.10. Pit 9, a well nearly 4 meters deep dug from surface of B-2 layer during pottery times. Scaling stick is 2.2 meters long.

the arroyo floor. Flowage is sufficient to maintain a fairly constant water level in the modern cattle tank below the site (see Figure 9.1). Our tests, made during the dry part of the summer, showed that the water table is only 2 meters below Bed D, an inconsiderable drop in view of the drainage effects of recent arroyo cutting. All the pits in this category went through the quite impervious clay Bed D-2 into the sand and gravel below. In earlier days the water table may well have stood at the base of the D-2 bed where the supply was tapped by the pits.

As alluviation proceeded it became necessary to dig pits of increasing depth. The inference follows that no arroyo or water channel existed during deposition, otherwise surface water might have been used, making the digging of holes unnecessary. We must further infer that local inhabitants knew of this spot as a potential water source over a considerable period of time even though the periodically flooded valley floor gave no direct evidence of it. In recent years the Double Circle Cattle Company and the Indian Service built tanks and drilled

Figure 9.11. Cremation 42, Pit 7, at two stages of excavation: a, silt; b, pocket of burnt bones; c, cap stone; d, carbonaceous material with some cremated bone; e, surface from which cremation pit was dug; f, cover rocks.

wells near the site. Except during the driest part of the year, surface water is not difficult to find in the Point of Pines area and it is likely that probing for water here was a dry season activity.

The partial excavation in the Point of Pines region of large depressions 15 to 20 meters across, usually located near ruined villages dating from about A.D. 1100 or later, has shown them to be aboriginal wells (Wheat 1952). In form these resembled inverted cones, the points having been dug deeply enough (3 to 4 meters) to tap the underground water reservoir. Water was obtained by walking into the wells. Except for this feature and the size, there was little difference between the late prehistoric wells and the pits of the Cienega Creek Site. Both depended on reaching the comparatively shallow subsurface reservoir. The principle, of course, is an old one. For the Point of Pines area, this system was apparently present and used for at least 4000 years and Pit 9 (see Figure 9.10) may be regarded as a classic example of well-digging a thousand years ago.

The second and third categories of pits are related in that the excavations were for the disposal of the cremated dead. Pit 3, with its numerous individually buried lots of bones introduces the idea of the burial plot, while Pit 7 reflects the custom of the individual burial of ashes. Pit 8, of the fourth type, while perhaps originally made in search of water, was later used for pit-oven cooking. There was no evidence that it was for cremating.

THE CREMATIONS
Occurrence

Most of the cremations (40 out of 47) occurred in the restricted area of a large aboriginal excavation at least 1.3 meters deep and 3 meters in diameter. This excavation was designated Pit 3 (see Figures 9.5, 9.7, 9.8). It was made from the surface of Bed C-2 and gradually filled with clay-silt sediments. The structure of these sediments was observed in a few places which were not disturbed by subsequent use of the pit for burying cremated remains. Evidently as the pit was filling, shallow pockets ranging in size from 0.2 to 0.4 meters in diameter and 0.15 meters or less in depth, were scooped out of the matrix. The individual lots of bones were then put into these depressions and covered either with earth or with large flat unburned tuff slabs. These 2 methods of closure were about equally represented. In one case the bones were placed in a shallow stone tray (Cremation 8, see Figure 9.16a). That some time elapsed between interments is indicated by vertical super-position of cremations, four in one series. How much time is represented cannot be determined, but the absence of a well-defined surface on the C-2 bed may be taken to mean that the interval was short.

The 7 cremations not in Pit 3 were scattered at random near it (see Figure 9.5). Most of these were no more than pockets of bone deposited from the C-2 surface and therefore of about the same age as those in Pit 3. Three deserve special attention. The first, Cremation 42, in Pit 7 (see Figure 9.11a, b), was perhaps the most formal and instructive in the details preserved. This pit was 0.4 meters in diameter and 0.5 meters in depth. Some unstructured silt remained in the bottom, suggesting that either the pit was not immediately used or that it was not thoroughly cleaned out. The cremated bones were placed on the silt, capped by an unburned tuff rock. Then followed a mass of black carbonaceous material including some bone, which is presumably the ash residue from the cremating fire. Finally several covering rocks were placed over the pit which must have been visible on the surface after the interment. Eventually these were covered by water-borne silt.

Cremation 45, in the waterlogged environment of the thickened and deep-lying C-3 bed in the northwest part of the site, produced 2 coiled baskets, one of which certainly contained cremated bone. The miraculous preservation of so fragile a material as basketry (see Figure 9.20) is attributable directly to the perpetually wet condition of its resting place, a circumstance which also preserved plant parts, as discussed elsewhere. This fortunate recovery of a single basket cremation, I believe, explains the preciseness of many of the depressions in which the bones were found. It is reasonable to suppose that burying the ashes in basket containers was a common practice but that, except in this one instance, direct evidence of the custom has been destroyed. In passing it should be noted that cremations with baskets and other perishable goods dating from preceramic times and attributable to eastern variants of the Basketmaker culture have been reported from the Guadalupe Mountains (Howard 1935:67–69) in New Mexico and the mouth of the Pecos River (Cosgrove 1947:162–163) in Texas.

A third cremation (Number 36) worth special notice was the lowest in terms of its stratigraphic position (Figure 9.12; also see Figure 9.23). The bones were placed in a pit dug during the early formational stages of Bed C-3 and therefore some time before the digging of Pit 3, which became the main bone disposal area. The time interval need not have been long, yet the sequence is clear.

Cremations 36, 42, and 45 are significant in demonstrating that separate pit depositories for individual bone lots were as much a part of the burial pattern as was the concentration of ashes of many persons within a large pit. This calls to mind the oldest type of cremation known for the Hohokam (Gladwin and others 1937:93–100).

That the actual incineration process was not done in the large pit (Number 3), is indicated by the absence of fire stains and deposits of wood ashes. Furthermore the bone masses clearly rest in small artificially made pockets, which means that the ashes were transported from the crematory to their final resting place. The dirt matrix containing the bones was ashen gray in color, contrasting sharply with the brownish sediment in the large pit. Small charcoal lumps had been gathered up with the bones as had water-worn tuff pebbles. Highly carbonaceous material was observed in 4 instances. In several cases the bones formed a clinker-like mass bound together by a yellow material. Whether this was the product of firing or of long burial is not known.

Figure 9.12. Cremation 36, deposited in a pit dug during formation of Bed C-3. More than 2 meters of alluvial material was deposited over it. Scaling stick is 2.2 meters long.

Since the cremating was apparently not done in the pits where the bones were found, it is possible to speculate whether it took place in the valley or on the mesa top. If the crematories were on top of the lava-capped mesas, the soil matrix would expectably be red basalt-derived clay, and basalt pebbles might occur as inclusions rather than those of tuff because geologically the tuff beds are below the basalt flows. Cremation on the floor of the valley, however, would produce the gray clay-silt matrix noted. This matrix was probably derived from Bed D if the crematory pits were scraped out deeply enough to penetrate it. The material from this bed may have been gathered up with the bones when they were collected; or the matrix may also have been derived from the fine silt of Bed C, discolored by wood ash. Rounded tuff pebbles are present in both of these beds. These pebbles were noted with all but three of the bone lots, and in at least 4 cases the pebbles appeared to have been scorched by fire. This situation hints at the possibility that the campsite of these people was on the valley floor and may now lie deeply buried. But whether this was far or near from the place of our excavations is unknown.

Amount and Condition of Bones

The bone residue in any one cremation varies in amount from a few scraps to a double handful. In all cases this is far less than the normal amount of cremated bone coming from the funerary jars of the fourteenth century from Arizona W:10:50, the largest pueblo site of the area, where extensive studies have been conducted during the past 10 years. In the condition of the bones a similar contrast exists. The Cienega Creek Site bone is finely broken, much of it literally reduced to bone meal, and seldom are individual pieces as much as 3 centimeters long, while in later cremations pieces up to 10 centimeters are not uncommon and many fragments are identifiable as to the specific element in the skeleton. The Cienega Creek material is extremely friable in its present state, possibly a result of its long burial, and is white to gray in color. The larger pieces show thermal cracks.

In part, the difference may be due to greater destruction of the bone by fire in the earlier cremations, hinting at higher temperatures. Other factors, however, may be involved. Experimental incineration of human bone in connection with medico-legal studies (Krogman 1949:89) has indicated that, given favorable circumstances, complete destruction of the human body by fire is possible with a heat of 2500°F($+$). But to achieve this the bones must be brought from the edges to the core or maximum heat center of the fire, and when calcined the bones must be agitated or struck for fragmentation and eventual complete disintegration.

There is little likelihood that we can reconstruct accurately the degree of heat reached in the Cienega cremations, the nature of combustible materials used, or to what extent draft conditions were employed. An obsidian point (see Figure 9.14w) which passed through the fire was heated sufficiently to cause the obsidian to bubble and lose its form. George H. Roseveare, metallurgist of the Arizona Bureau of Mines, tested an obsidian chip from Pit 3 by using a thermocouple in an assay furnace muffle. He determined that incipient fusion was started in the obsidian at about 800°C (1472°F). It may be inferred therefore that temperatures of at least this magnitude were achieved. But the high fragmentation and nearly complete calcination of the bones suggests that 1472°F may have been below the actual heat developed. It is doubtful if long exposure to a low-temperature fire could produce this effect. Agitation of the brittle bones during firing may account for the extreme fragmentation. Further fracturing would result from sifting the bones from the organic fuel ashes, and from their transportation from the crematorium to the final resting place. It could also be that intentional pulverizing was practiced. One may rule out postburial conditions such as the weight of the overlying stone and soil, frost action, chemical decomposition, and the removal of the bones from the ground by the archaeologist as the primary cause for break-up. The significance of these characteristics of the Cienega Creek cremations may now seem trivial, but contrasted with the late cremations, they suggest some difference in cremation practice beyond the normal fracturing effects of heat.

One further question seems answerable: Were the dead incinerated in the flesh or were the bones defleshed and dried before burning? Raymond S. Baby, of the Ohio State Museum, studied samples of the cremations and concluded that the former alternative was the preferred one. We do not know, however, whether dismemberment of the bodies, as practiced among the Hopewell people (Baby 1954), was the custom here.

Curiously, each of 2 cremation lots yielded a single unburned chip of a tooth crown and in one instance a single bone fragment also not burned. These are attributed to accident rather than to some regular custom related to the crematory process.

Identification of Bone Fragments

The separation of the bones from the matrix in the laboratory was not a simple task. When moist and still in the ground the bones had a putty-like consistency; when dry they were extremely brittle. After some experimentation, tedious manual cleaning was found best suited for removal of the larger pieces. At best, the larger pieces, seldom more than 3 centimeters long, constituted relatively poor samples for critical identification.

To overrule any possibility that the bones may have been of animals other than man, a careful analysis was made of each lot to identify human elements. In 44 of the 47 samples specific human identification was possible. Recognizable units included skull and jaw fragments, parts of long bones, phalanges, tooth roots, and bits of tooth crowns. It may be inferred that the 3 cremations which produced too small a quantity of bone residue for the observation of recognizable parts were also human. In no case was duplication of diagnostic bones seen and it may be further assumed that the cremations were of single individuals and not multiple.

The extensive fragmentation of the bones reduced the opportunity to determine the age of the individuals at the time of death to little more than guesses. No infant remains were observed and the chances of survival of these would be limited; 8 ash lots appeared to be youths, and the rest were listed as adults, presumably ranging from young to old. Evidently the practice of cremation among the people responsible for these finds was not age limited and there is no way of telling whether or not the custom was restricted by sex.

Small calcined fragments of distinctly nonhuman bones were seen among the ashes of 6 cremations: a fragment of deer antler, a piece of leg bone probably of deer, 2 artificially tapered bits of solid bone resembling awl points, and several minute sections of leg bones of small animals. Since we know that some of the stone tools and pipes were subjected to the firing, one may suppose that other artifacts, represented by these fragments, were included too.

Artifacts Associated With the Cremations

Material goods of several kinds accompanied about half of the cremations. All of these objects, except the basketry with Cremation 45, were resistant to both time and fire. Perishable cultural items undoubtedly also accompanied the dead but these were consumed by the flames or destroyed by time.

Table 9.1 gives both the range of objects recovered and the particular associations of types of specimens with any one cremation. Most frequent were projectile points, 35 in all and ranging from one to five in individual cremation associations. Generally these were in the bone mass but near the upper part, as though they were added after most of the bones had been deposited in the earth. This is well illustrated in Cremation 39, where in addition to points, several blades were tucked in edgewise along the fringe of the bones as were also a lump of paint and 2 unburned bones, probably artifacts (Figure 9.13). Chips of chert and obsidian appear to have been fragments of artifacts, thermally fractured. No shell fragments or jewelry were observed.

There is no discernible correlation between the kind of object included with the dead and the age of the individual. Projectile points appear with all ages, though the difficulty of aging except broadly has already been pointed out.

Some of the artifacts passed through the crematory fire, whereas others did not. Projectile point w in Figure 9.14 was heated sufficiently to develop bubbles; a few chert points reveal thermal fractur-

Table 9.1
Artifacts Associated with Cremations at Cienega Creek Site

Cremation Number	Youth	Adult	Proj. Points	Blades	Obsidian Disc	Side Scraper	Obsidian and Chert Chips	Pipes	Pestle	Tray	Worked Schist	Concretions	Chalcedony Concretions	Basket	Red Paint	Burned	Not Burned
1	x																
2		x															
3		x	1														
4		x															
5		x	1	2													
6		x	2	2									x			x	
7		x					x										
8		x	1							x							
9		x	4														
10		x	4												x		
11		x					x										
12		x					x										
13		x															
14		x	3					x									
15		x			x											x	
16	x																
17		x															
18		x															
19		x					x										
20	x																
21		x															
22		x															
23		x															
24	x																
25		x	1						x								
26		x	1														
27		x															
28		?															
29		x				x											
30		x															
31		x	2				x										
32		x															
33		x															
34		x	1														
35	x															x	
36		x					x										
37	x		1	1			x					x				x	
38		x									x						
39		x	5	2											x		2
40		x															
41		x															
42		x						x									
43	x		2														
44	x																
45		x	3											x			
46		x	1	1													
47		x															
Pit 3 Misc.			2	2	x		x	x							x		

Figure 9.13. Cremation 39 (in Pit 3) and associated artifacts: unburned bone circlet and (?) deer legbone fragment (near ends of pencil), projectile points, blades, and lump of red paint (above tip of large point).

ing and two of the three complete pipes also evidence exposure to heat. Most of the material, however, appears to have escaped the ruinous effects of the fire. Why these two methods prevailed is, of course, not known. It should be observed that the same situation holds true for Hohokam cremations of later times, although in them most of the accompanying material was subjected to the fire.

It seems clear enough that, for the cultural stage represented and for the people known only by this limited material, cremation of the dead, the deposition of the bones in a limited area, and the accompaniment of earthly goods ranging from projectile points to "charm stones" (concretions), were well-established customs of the day.

CULTURAL MATERIALS

Before continuing with the examination of the artifacts, it should be emphasized that at least that part of the Cienega Creek Site exposed by the excavation is not regarded as a habitation area. Even

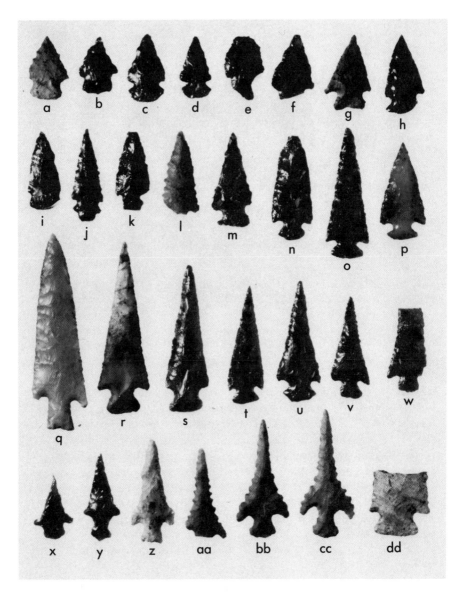

Figure 9.14. Projectile points associated with cremations, Pit 3, Bed C-2 (except a, from surface). Length of q, 8.4 centimeters.

though there was evidence of some food preparation in the form of grinding tools, hearths, and hearthstones (principally Bed D-1) there was little wastage from stone chipping and no bone refuse whatever. It seems rather to have been a watering place where some foods requiring the use of water were prepared and where, due to a special attraction not understood, the incinerated bones of the deceased were placed. The materials discussed below, therefore, while no doubt typical enough of the culture of the people who produced them, have been functionally selected. Search for the village or habitation site has proved fruitless and in all probability it lies deeply buried under a mantle of earth. If the camp is ever found, a comparison of the objects from the day-to-day trash deposit with these from the cremations should manifest few direct relationships.

Surface

As previously noted some stone chips occurred on the surface of the arroyo slopes and provided one of the clues of the presence of cultural material. During the course of the work, one whole and one fragmentary point were also found. The former (Figure 9.14a) was at a level below the D bed and had probably eroded from it. It is interesting chiefly because it closely resembles the projectile point (see Figure 9.22a) recovered from this bed in the excavation.

Bed A

Sterile within the area explored; probably contains some pottery of late prehistoric times, from the nearby site (Ariz. W:10:4) which was occupied about A.D. 1300, or from older horizons.

Beds B-1, B-2

Potsherds only, occurring chiefly towards the north end of the excavation and in the upper part of the sediments of Pit 4, throughout the silt fills of Pits 9 and 10, and in an old excavation younger than Pit 10 but older than Pit 9 (see Figure 9.9, deposit shown as black clay).

Of the 59 pieces recovered directly in B-1, 48 are from red ware vessels (14 bowls, 34 jars), 6 are plain brown ware, and one is from a mica schist tempered vessel originating among the Hohokam. The red ware, made during more than a thousand years in the Point of Pines region, exhibits only subtle differences and for that reason is not readily placeable as to time. However, by paste, color, finish, and

Figure 9.15. Pine Flat Neck Corrugated pottery from Pit 9. Width, 9 centimeters.

vessel forms, these fragments match the Reserve Red (Gifford 1957) of about A.D. 1000. Four fragments of a distinctive neck-corrugated vessel, as exemplified in Figure 9.15, (Pine Flat Neck Corrugated, Breternitz 1956: 36–39) also aid in this time identification. The eroded condition of the Hohokam fragment prevents placement as to phase but the above age is not out of reason. Six sherds from the upper fill of Pit 4 are also red ware and all are jar fragments. Pits 9, 10, and the intermediate area produced a further sample of 55 sherds, predominantly red ware but including also good examples of Pine Flat Neck Corrugated. The pottery sample from all sources represents a typological as well as a stratigraphical unit assignable to the Reserve phase.

The B-1, B-2 distinction was only locally discernible and both beds actually represent a single alluvial stage. The significance, of course, is that Bed B was formed and Pits 4, 9, and 10 became filled at about the time this pottery was produced. Pit 4 was dug by pottery-using people from the C-1 surface, and Pits 9 and 10 were penetrations from the B-2 surface. The pottery fragments we have are evidently of vessels used in gathering and transporting water. The study of walk-in wells near Point of Pines (Wheat 1952:194) has brought out the fact that red ware was preferred for this activity and that sherds of it predominate about the water holes. The evident reason is that the slipping and polishing of surfaces rendered the vessels less pervious and hence better suited for water transport and storage than the more porous brown and corrugated wares.

Figure 9.16. Stone tray of basalt (a), and pestle of quartzite (b) from Pit 3, Bed C-2. Length of a, 29.5 centimeters.

Bed C-1

Sterile; however, Pit 2 shows human activity during its formation.

Bed C-2

Within the formation itself there were a few scattered chert and obsidian flakes, useful only in revealing that some tool dressing was done nearby. Also noted were a few fragments of unshaped lava blocks which had served as grinding stones. At the termination of C-2, Pits 3 and 5 were made. Of these the former holds special interest because of the artifacts which were recovered as cremation accompaniments. This was, in fact, the chief source of specimens from the site. The inventory follows (identification of material by Arizona Bureau of Mines):

Tray (Figure 9.16a): Vesicular basalt; petal-shaped, depressed basin 1 centimeter deep, edged with a low rim; central part worn smooth from grinding; length 24 centimeters, thickness 2.5 centimeters.
Pestle (Figure 9.16b): Quartzite; dressed to form by pecking; both ends well rounded from use; length 29.5 centimeters.

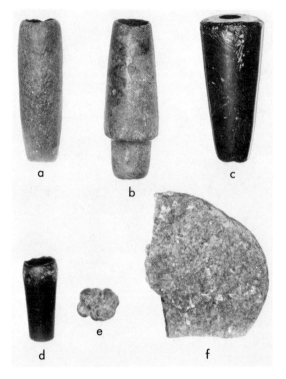

Figure 9.17. Stone pipes (a–d) and miscellaneous stones associated with cremations (e, f) from Pit 3, Bed C-2. Length of b, 5.9 centimeters.

Pipes (Figure 9.17 a–d): a, basic dike rock, altered; tubular, with slight taper; bore expands from 0.9 to 1.1 centimeters from bit to bowl end; burned; length 5.5 centimeters. b, materials as in a, above; tapered and shouldered to produce small bit; bore diameter at bit end 1.1 centimeters, at bowl end 1.3 centimeters; burned; length 5.9 centimeters. c, serpentine; reworked part of larger pipe; broad and roughly finished; pronounced taper towards bit; bore diameter 0.8 centimeters; not burned; length 5.3 centimeters. d, serpentine; bit element of composite pipe; original bowl probably stone or wood; tapered, expanded end roughened for cementing to bowl; bore expands from 0.7 centimeter to 1.1 centimeters; not burned; length 3 centimeters. Pipes, either ceramic or stone, have not been recognized as one of the hallmarks of Hohokam; but they do appear in early villages of the Mogollon culture. The 3 forms in stone represented by the specimens from the Cienega Creek Site have equivalents in pottery times (see Figure 9.25).

Spherulite (Figure 9.17e): Burned.

Stone Flake (Figure 9.17f): Mica schist; thickness 0.3 centimeter; edges trimmed; material foreign to area.

Projectile Points (see Figure 9.14, all except a): Frequency of materials, in order named: obsidian, chert, chalcedony, and jasper; form patterns represented: (1) short broad type (b–i) grading to (2) long tapered form (j–w), some with serrations; (3) slim tapered point with flared tangs (x–cc), some with pronounced serrations. Typologically Group 1 appears to derive from the Chiricahua style point (Sayles and Antevs 1941: Plate 11; Martin and others 1949: Figure 17b) and to persist into the early Mogollon Circle Prairie phase of Point of Pines (Wheat 1954: Figure 54). Group 2 establishes the pattern of the long tapered Hohokam points but is not specifically analogous (Gladwin and others 1937: Plates 75–91). Regionally Group 3 is represented by early points in Hohokam (Gladwin and others 1937: Plate 94g) and from Cordova Cave (Martin and others 1952: Figure 49l). Specimen dd (Figure 17), in size and blade pattern, suggests derivation from the San Pedro Stage type of Cochise (Haury 1950a: Plate 22) and may have been the inspiration for the long tapered points of Group 2.

Blades (Figure 9.18 a–c, g–h, j): Mostly chert, some obsidian; workmanship rough; length from 3.1 to 8.4 centimeters.

Knife-saw (Figure 9.18i): Chert; stem broken, one edge sharply serrated; length 9.1 centimeters.

Worked Flake (Figure 9.18d): Paper-thin flake of fine-grained stone; edges chipped, possibly to simulate projectile point; burned; length 2.3 centimeters.

Bilobate Object (Figure 9.18e): Obsidian; chipped to form; length 1.2 centimeters.

Disc (Figure 9.18f): Obsidian; originally chipped; faces and edge ground; diameter 1 centimeter.

Bed C-3

Stone: Only a few random flakes, hearthstones (one whole), and several grinding stone fragments. The metate and handstone which first marked the site (see Figure 9.2) were in this bed. The netherstone of the pair was a wedge-shaped lava block, not intentionally shaped, but 35 centimeters square in plan. The surface bore evidence of light use only. The handstone, likewise unshaped, was also of lava about 12 centimeters in diameter with a single worn face.

Basketry: Cremation 45 (see Figure 9.9) was deposited some time during the formation of the C-3 bed. Remnants of 2 coiled baskets were associated with it and one of these, although resting on its side, contained some of the human ashes. Preserva-

Figure 9.18. Blades and miscellaneous stone objects from Pit 3, Bed C-2. Length of i, 9.1 centimeters.

tion of the fragments was accomplished by direct transfer from the wet ground to water in which they were carefully cleaned with a soft brush; then they were given successive baths of acetone and finally extended immersion (several days) in a gasoline-paraffin mixture. Upon drying the fragments were solid enough for handling. Some shrinkage took place.

The largest fragment, half of the original specimen, represents a bowl-shaped basket about 20 to 25 centimeters in diameter. The other pieces are small. Both baskets exhibited close coiling, simple uninterlocked stitching, and a self rim, but they differed in the foundation structure (see Morris and Burgh 1941 for basketry terminology).

The first type is 1-rod foundation (Figure 9.19a) with fine texture of about 3 coils and 6 stitches per centimeter. Morris and Burgh (1941:11) list this type as infrequent in the Anasazi territory, dated to Pueblo III when it occurs, although interlocked stitching on the same foundation is common. The technique appears to have been one of the more prevalent forms of basketry among the Desert Hohokam (Haury 1950a:405).

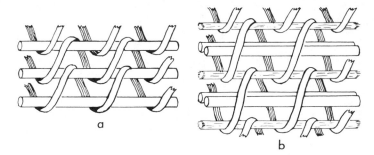

Figure 9.19. Coiling techniques in basketry with Cremation 45: a, 1-rod foundation; b, 2-rod-and-bundle foundation.

Figure 9.20. Basketry fragment from Cremation 45. Actual size.

The second type (Figures 9.19b and 9.20) is 2-rod-and-bundle foundation; bunched; texture is fine, 2.5 coils and 4 stitches per centimeter. Perhaps no basketry technique was ever so widely used and for so long a time as this one in the Southwest. In Basketmaker times it predominated (Morris and Burgh 1941:13).

Bed D-1

Although most productive of hearths and hearthstones, and most heavily impregnated with charcoal, Bed D-1 yielded few formalized artifacts. Wastage from tool fashioning in the form of chert and obsidian flakes was present but infrequent (about 30 flakes in all).

a   b

Figure 9.21. Hand-stones from Bed D-1. Maximum diameter of a, 11 centimeters.

Grinding Stones: The 2 complete and 2 fragmentary nether-stones share the characteristics of similar stones noted from the higher beds, that is, irregular unshaped blocks of lava, selected for one flat surface on which work could be done. Maximum dimensions range up to 40 centimeters. These specimens show a complete lack of attention to form and only one shows use extensive enough to produce a basin of any depth.

Two handstones (Figure 9.21) of diabase and dacite are bifacial and show edge dressing by pecking to give them symmetry. Maximum diameters are 11 centimeters. They come within the range of handstone types usually associated with the Chiricahua stage of the Cochise culture.

Figure 9.22. Projectile point (a) and scrapers (b and c) from Bed D-1. Maximum diameter of c, 6 centimeters.

Projectile Point (Figure 9.22a): Obsidian: length 2.2 centimeters. This type is a trait of the Chiricahua stage.

Scrapers (Figure 9.22b,c): Chert and quartzite; too few scrapers were recovered to establish types. Specimen b is plano-convex in section and the lower edge is steeply chipped to produce a gougelike edge. The other specimen is a roughly dressed primary flake.

Bed D-2

Bed D-2 was found to be sterile.

Bed E

Bed E was found to be sterile.

RECAPITULATION, DATING, AND RELATIONSHIPS

Figure 9.23 is presented as a means of recapitulating the evidence and as an attempt to reconstruct the geological and cultural history of the Cienega Creek Site. The features have been rearranged geographically to emphasize the continuity; the vertical scale has been exaggerated for convenience in drawing. Areas marked "Old Surfaces" represent pauses in the alluvial process of sufficient duration to produce a definable surface, either by slight erosion or by exposure and trampling.

The Age of the Deposits

We have already seen that geology alone does not yield the answer to the age of the cultural materials in terms of elapsed time. It does, however, vividly establish the stratigraphic order, and therefore the relative age, of the various features of the Cienega Creek Site. The archaeological specimens, other than pottery, are of only nominal help because some are of such generalized form that they are not critical horizon markers, and others, as some of the projectile point types, are known only from rather late deposits, too late, it would seem, to correlate satisfactorily the situation at hand. The botanical approach, as a clue to different ecological conditions, also has failed, in that the specific identification of charcoal (by T. L. Smiley, Laboratory of Tree-Ring Research, University of Arizona) shows only existing species. As of this writing the results of pollen studies have not become available. The main recourse, then, is pottery as a medium for setting certain limits, and radiocarbon dating for which, fortunately, there was sufficient material from several of the beds to permit a series of assays.

Pottery

As previously noted, the pottery, chiefly Reserve Red and the more diagnostic Pine Flat Neck Corrugated, in Bed B-1 and in the fills of Pits 4, 9, and 10 is believed to be approximately 1000 years old. The inference may be drawn from this that the surface of C-1 is that old

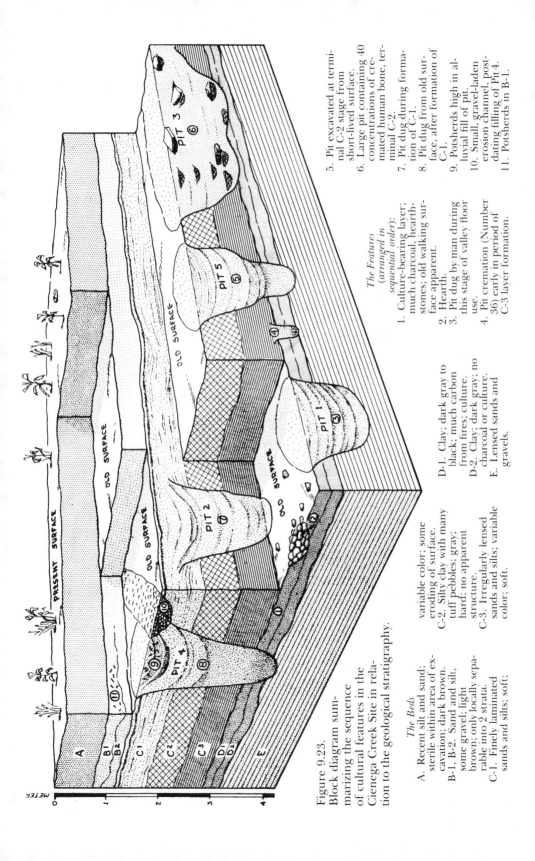

Figure 9.23.
Block diagram summarizing the sequence of cultural features in the Cienega Creek Site in relation to the geological stratigraphy.

The Beds

A. Recent silt and sand; sterile within area of excavation; dark brown.

B-1. B-2. Sand and silt, some gravel; light brown; only locally separable into 2 strata.

C-1. Finely laminated sands and silts; soft;

variable color; some eroding of surface.

C-2. Silty clay with many tuff pebbles; gray; hard; no apparent structure.

C-3. Irregularly lensed sands and silts; variable color; soft.

D-1. Clay; dark gray to black; much carbon from fires; culture.

D-2. Clay; dark gray; no charcoal or culture.

E. Lensed sands and gravels.

The Features
(arranged in sequential order):

1. Culture-bearing layer; much charcoal, hearth-stones; old walking surface apparent.
2. Hearth.
3. Pit dug by man during this stage of valley floor use.
4. Pit cremation (Number 36) early in period of C-3 layer formation.
5. Pit excavated at terminal C-2 stage from short-lived surface.
6. Large pit containing 40 concentrations of cremated human bone, terminal C-2.
7. Pit dug during formation of C-1.
8. Pit dug from old surface, after formation of C-1.
9. Potsherds high in alluvial fill of pit.
10. Small, gravel-laden erosion channel, postdating filling of Pit 4.
11. Potsherds in B-1.

or somewhat older but probably not much younger. From Bed C-1 downward through the succession of beds, pottery was absent and the deposits may be judged to be of prepottery age. Martin (Martin and others 1952:483) has listed a radiocarbon date of "150 ± 160 B.C." (Sample C-585) for the beginning of the Pine Lawn phase (Tularosa Cave) in New Mexico, some 75 air miles northeast of the Cienega Creek Site. This is the earliest date thus far obtained for a pottery-producing horizon. If we accept this as the time of appearance of pottery in the region, an age in excess of 2000 years is assignable to C-1 and the formations below. This assessment is consistent with the data provided by radiocarbon analyses made in the laboratory at the University of Arizona.

Radiocarbon

Radiocarbon determinations were obtained from 2 sources, the University of Arizona Carbon-14 Age Determination Laboratory and the University of Michigan Memorial Phoenix Project Radiocarbon Laboratory. The former employs the carbon-black method, the latter the gas-sample technique. The year of assay is 1956. All samples have been subjected to varying amounts of ground moisture.

To aid the discussion of the results obtained (see Table 9.2) from the 2 laboratories, a visual summary is given in Figure 9.24. It is immediately evident that while the dates from each laboratory are consistent on the whole with the stratigraphy of the site, there is a marked discrepancy in the values. Obviously, both sets of dates cannot be correct and it is even possible that neither set of dates is an accurate reflection of the true age. This statement may impress some as a rebel attitude but it is a way of indicating my own distrust and suspicion of the validity of many of the radiocarbon dates that have been released in recent years. The perplexing situation here underscores the fact that blind acceptance of radiocarbon analyses has led to irresolvable complications in our attempts to construct cultural chronologies. While there is no intent to belittle the technique itself, or the work of either laboratory concerned here, attention must be called to our still elementary understanding of such problems as contamination, the relative merits of solid-carbon versus the gas-sample methods, possible differences in results from various laboratories arising from conditions peculiar to a laboratory, the question of association of sample and cultural horizon, and more broadly still, the strictures and cautions that ought to be applied in the area of interpretation.

Table 9.2
Radiocarbon Determinations for Cienega Creek Site

Description	U.A. Sample No.	Age (yrs.)	U.M. Sample No.	Age (yrs.)
Fragmented charcoal of pine and oak from hearth in Bed D-1	19	4310±160	M-541	2530±300
Charcoal, highly fragmented; distributed through matrix of Bed D-1 about 2 m. east of Pit 3; 2 field samples from a 3 m. area combined	21 & 22	3980±160	M-540	2400±200
Fragmented solid charcoal from fill of Pit 6, dug from surface of Bed D-1	27	3070±150		
Finely divided carbonaceous material associated with cremations in Pit 3, Bed C-2	28	2515±300		
Charcoal, scattered fragments, 2 m. north of Pit 3 and near a hearth in Bed D-1	29	4400±150		
Scattered fragments of charcoal from Bed D-1 adjacent to U.A. Samples 21 and 22 (M-540) above			M-461	2600±250
Fragmented solid charcoal from matrix of Pit 3, Bed C-2; distributed between cremations; may be from crematory fires, brought to this location with the ashes			M-462*	1140±300
Finely pulverized charcoal, mixed with some burned bones and soil; from Pit 7, Cremation 42. Although in Bed C-3, Pit 7 was made from C-2 surface	48	2150±200‡		
Wood, partly rotted, water saturated; from Bed C-3 near Pit 8 (2 runs)	49 53	2610±200 2080±200‡ Average 2345±175		
Same sample as above, new burn	51	3380±200		
Six-pound chunk of wood slightly charred, saturated with pitch, very wet; from fill of Pit 8 (2 runs)	50 52	3250±200‡ 3025±200 Average 3135±175		

*This was a small sample and the results are not regarded as having the same validity as the other dates.
‡Samples adequate but assay regarded as grade B.

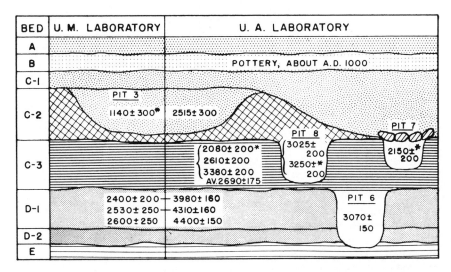

Figure 9.24. Comparative radiocarbon results from the University of Michigan and University of Arizona laboratories. Years are B.P. Asterisks denote assays of grade B quality; brackets indicate different assays of same sample in the University of Arizona laboratory; dashes between dates represent assays of the same sample by both laboratories.

Turning to the present problem: by averaging the results of samples from Bed D which were measured by both laboratories (19 and M-541; 21, 22, and M-540), we have values of 4145 versus 2465 (sigma ignored). This is so large a discrepancy, considering the small number of years involved, that markedly different interpretive results would follow if one or the other date were used. The question of differences in laboratory techniques and their effects on the results must be left to the chemist and the physicist to solve. The only means the archaeologist has to evaluate the 2 sets of dates is to introduce supporting information in search of reinforcement for his inclination to pick one set of dates over the other.

On the strength of the following information, the older values for the features of the site are favored:

1. The implement complex in the oldest culture-bearing bed (D-1) is that of the Chiricahua stage, though admittedly the identification had to be made on only a few traits. This complex in southeastern Arizona has been dated at 4006 ± 270 B.P. (Libby 1955: 113) and in

west-central New Mexico as 4508 ± 680 B.P. (Libby 1955: 113; Martin and others 1952:483). The 3-assay average for the Cienega Creek Site from the University of Arizona Laboratory is 4230 ± 105 B.P. The consistency of these dates tends to develop confidence in their validity.

2. The C layer, with three component parts, on the physical evidence of the stratigraphic column and the local archaeological pattern, has been judged to be of prepottery age, before A.D. 1 or 150 B.C. if Martin's (Martin and others 1952:483) introductory date for pottery in nearby New Mexico is accepted. The dates therefore of 2515 ± 300 B.P. for Pit 3 with its cremations and the slightly earlier values for Pit 8, Bed C-3, and Pit 6 are consistent with this reasoning. On the other hand the Michigan laboratory date of 1140 ± 300 years ago, or about ninth century A.D., for Pit 3 cannot be reconciled with the local archaeology. This substantiates Professor Crane's opinion that the date procured is not satisfactory. By that time pottery was well established, earth burial rather than cremation was the rule, and the projectile point and pipe types were not those of the artifacts associated with the cremations (Breternitz 1956). The pottery of Bed B, well above Bed C-2, represents the classes of ceramics expectable as the normal accompaniment for a ninth- to tenth-century artifact complex.

Ages of approximately 4000 years for Bed D-1, the Chiricahua stage, and 2500 years for Bed C, the time of the cremations, are supportable by collateral evidence.

It will be seen that a minor inconsistency in the values of the dates in relation to the stratigraphy occurs between Pit 8 and Bed C-3. Pit 8 is obviously more recent than the bed into which it was cut. The dates, however, indicate an inversion of a minor order. The 3 runs (49, 51, and 53) of the same sample from Bed C-3 gave a disturbing range from 2080 ± 200 to 3380 ± 200, a spread which hints at contamination or instrumentation problems. The sample from Pit 8, a chunk of pitch pine, had ideal survival properties and it is not impossible that it lay on the forest floor for many decades before being gathered for fuel. No satisfactory explanation is apparent to account for the discrepancy. It is evident, however, that radiocarbon will not always produce consistent results where narrow time limits are involved and where the organic material itself has been so excessively exposed to ground moisture.

The prehistoric wells reported in the Clovis-Portales area, New Mexico, (Evans 1951) are strikingly similar to those on Cienega Creek in their general configuration. Evans estimates the age of these wells to be later than the Folsom complex and ". . . considerably earlier than the late prehistoric Indian horizons of the region" (1951:8). In the Arizona occurrence well-digging was practiced over a long period of time, even by Indians of late prehistory; but the older wells, and those of New Mexico, would appear to be of roughly comparable age.

Correlation of Artifact Complex

A few suggestions as to possible linkages for the most definitive elements have already been made. Viewing the complex as a whole, it appears that typological connections with two later cultural forms, Hohokam and Mogollon, may be established. These connections are represented visually in Figure 9.25. Temporally, the Cienega Creek complex associated with the cremations is late in terms of the entire Cochise culture development and it may properly be recognized as a part of it, that is, late San Pedro stage. It thus stands in the right time relationship to both Hohokam and Mogollon to have contributed to these later complexes.

Two projectile point traditions, based on form, are evident and these perhaps had separate origins. The first is a long, tapered style, traceable to the kind of point that characterized the San Pedro stage and which appears to have given rise to the more elaborate forms associated with the Hohokam. The second is a short stubby point which is seen first in the Chiricahua stage and which survived into pottery times among the Mogollon people. These two traditions coexisted in the time horizon of Pit 3, or about 500 B.C. and subsequently developed along different cultural paths. Neither tradition, however, survived locally as a dominant one after about A.D. 800. This divergence is supported by a few other elements too. The pit cremation practice with offerings is clearly ancestral to the early Hohokam mortuary custom. The stone tray is the probable forerunner of the Hohokam slab palette of the Pioneer period and also of the Mogollon stone disc. Stone pipes, both the unit and composite types, are not associated with early Gila Basin Hohokam, but they do occur with some frequency in Mogollon sites.

This interpretation is possibly best considered as an accommodation of the elements known from the Cienega Creek Site at the present time. It is compatible, however, with the idea held by some (Haury 1943; Martin and others 1949:221; Martin and others 1952:500–501) that the San Pedro stage complex was parental to both Hohokam and Mogollon. The present material adds somewhat greater speci-

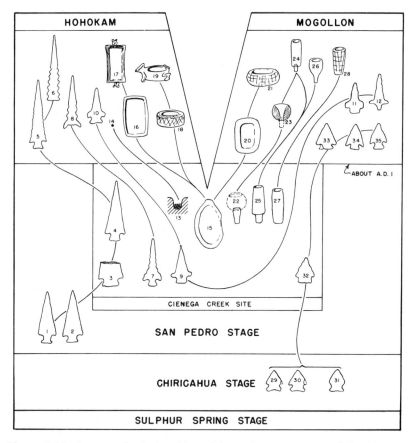

Figure 9.25. Suggested relationships of the main components of the Cienega Creek Site with comparable elements of later Hohokam and Mogollon complexes. Derivations of projectile-point traditions in stages of the Cochise culture are also indicated. Objects not drawn to scale.

1. Sayles and Antevs 1941: Plate 16d.
2. Haury 1950a: Figure 64d.
3. Cremation 37, Cienega Creek Site (A-16,047).
4. Cremation 26, Cienega Creek Site (A-16,006).
5. Gladwin and others 1937: Plate 87b.
6. Gladwin and others 1937: Plate 89a (right).
7. Cremation 39, Cienega Creek Site (A-16,045).
8. Gladwin and others 1937: Plate 89c.
9. Cremation 10, Cienega Creek Site (A-15,851).
10. Gladwin and others 1937: Plate 94g.
11. Martin and others 1952: Figure 491.

12. Haury 1936a: Plate 18f.
13. Pit Cremations 36 and 42, Cienega Creek Site.
14. Gladwin and others 1937: Figure 39, 2.
15. Stone tray, Cremation 8, Cienega Creek Site (A-15,905).
16. Gladwin and others 1937: Plate 97c.
17. Gladwin and others 1937: Plate 97e.
18. Gladwin and others 1937: Plate 58c.
19. Gladwin and others 1937: Plate 71b.
20. Wheat 1954: Figure 44b.
21. Haury 1936a: Plate 15f.
22. Pit 3, exact cremation association uncertain, Cienega Creek Site (A-15,904).
23. Haury 1936a: Plate 15c.

24. Martin and others 1952: Figure 44, lower right.
25. Cremation 14, Cienega Creek Site (A-15,872).
26. Wheat 1954: Figure 37.
27. Cremation 25, Cienega Creek Site (A-16,008).
28. Wheat 1954: Figure 52g.
29. Sayles and Antevs 1941: Plate 11c.
30. Martin and others 1949: Figure 17b.
31. Bed D-1, Cienega Creek Site (A-15,866).
32. Cremation 31, Cienega Creek Site (A-16,010).
33. Wheat 1954: Figure 54h.
34. Martin and others 1952: Figure 451.
35. Haury 1936a: Plate 17e.

ficity to tool types because those cited heretofore in favor of this continuity were of a generalized order. Furthermore, this constellation of elements, existing just before the appearance of pottery, eases to some extent the transition from no pottery to pottery. It indicates that some of the traits we have associated only with the oldest pottery horizons of the Hohokam and Mogollon actually had earlier beginnings.

One must express awareness that some analogies exist between the traits of Cienega Creek Site and elements of the Archaic horizon of the eastern United States, for example, cremations, stone pipes, and projectile point similarities. But the body of data now available seems inadequate to explore further the meaning of these parallels (see also Jennings 1956:98–99).

Summary and Conclusions

1. Traces of human activity, consisting of hearths, pits dug for water, cremations, and artifacts occur at varying depths in a flood plain deposit.
2. Aggradation, which caused a raising of the absolute level of the valley floor, was interrupted by several brief pauses.
3. The ready identification of the formational units and the direct association of some of these with the human evidences permit the relative ordering of human activity by applying the stratigraphic principle.
4. Since the succession of beds is not referable to any known sequence, geology in itself does not provide primary data as to the magnitude of the time required for the formation of the deposits. Although dating clues must therefore be sought through other approaches, the absence of marked erosional unconformities suggests a post-Altithermal period of valley filling and a depositional history of comparatively short duration.
5. Radiocarbon dates from two laboratories have been obtained. These series of dates, while not consistent with respect to each other, for the most part are compatible in relation to the provenience of the samples in the stratigraphic column. For reasons previously outlined, the older dates are regarded as most closely reflecting the true ages of the respective deposits.

6. From this evidence it may be concluded that: (1) at about 2000 B.C., Cochise people first made use of the spot, digging for water and preparing food acquired by hunting and gathering. Beyond the few stone tools they left behind nothing is known about them from this site. (2) By about 500 B.C. people were still seeking water here by digging holes and in addition they were depositing the remains of their cremated dead on the site. Although the associated material items such as basketry, projectile points, pipes, paint, and "charms" indicate a higher level of cultural complexity than the tools in the older bed, pottery was absent from the complex. (3) By about A.D. 1000 pottery was left by later Mogollon-Pueblo occupants of the region who also sought water.

7. The typology of the artifacts in Bed D-1 equates with the Chiricahua stage of the Cochise culture.

8. The inventory of traits from Pit 3 (Bed C-2) has no direct temporal or typological equivalent elsewhere and the cremations are among the earliest occurrences of this custom in the Southwest.

9. The traits are divisible, however, into 2 clusters, namely: (1) cremations with offerings; long, tapered, often serrated, obliquely notched projectile points; paint; a stone tray, which is more closely allied to the Pioneer period of the Hohokam than to any other known complex, and (2) short, stubby points and stone pipes which are known in later Mogollon horizons. Furthermore, a few of the elements, such as the large side notched point, grinding stone, and pestle, may be taken as survivals of the earlier San Pedro tradition.

10. The cultural material derived from the cremations may be viewed as ancestral Hohokam on the one hand, and Mogollon on the other hand, but not greatly antedating the oldest ceramic horizons of either. The origins of specific elements such as cremations and pipes are not known.

11. The radiocarbon date of about 500 B.C. for the potteryless assemblage of artifacts from Pit 3 and a date of 150 ± 160 B.C. for the earliest pottery horizon, the Pine Lawn phase of western New Mexico (Martin and others 1952: 483), narrow the time of appearance of this trait, in that part of the Southwest with which we are concerned, to perhaps the second or third century before Christ.

Acknowledgments

The University of Arizona Archaeological Field School was established at Point of Pines on the San Carlos Indian Reservation in 1946. Acknowledgment is made of the support given this venture during the early years by the Wenner-Gren Foundation for Anthropological Research. Credit is also due those students who worked diligently, both in the field and in the laboratory, to provide many of the data for this report. Special thanks are extended to H. R. Crane and James B. Griffin, of the University of Michigan, who responded wholeheartedly to our request for assistance in the area of radiocarbon analysis, and to the Research Corporation for its encouragement and support in the development of the Carbon-14 Age Determination Laboratory of the University of Arizona.

PART FOUR

Hohokam

People of the Desert

◄ 10 ►

A Short History of
Hohokam Research

David E. Doyel

The Hohokam differed markedly from their northern neighbors, the Mogollon and Anasazi, by adapting to the special environmental conditions of the Lower Sonoran Desert and by maintaining stronger contacts with Mesoamerican societies to the south. Archaeological investigations in the Hohokam area also proceeded along paths and at a pace distinct from research in other areas of the American Southwest. Emil Haury's pivotal role in chronicling Hohokam prehistory can only be comprehended fully within the context of the history of this research and the scientific controversy surrounding it.

Archaeological research on the Hohokam began later and developed more slowly than research in the northern areas of the American Southwest; this situation was well illustrated by the publication of Kidder's (1924, reprinted 1962) major synthesis of Anasazi prehistory prior to the beginning of systematic study of the Hohokam. The earliest work in the desert was by Cushing in the Salt River area and Fewkes in the Gila River Basin, although the results of Cushing's investigations were not to be published for sixty years (Haury 1945c). Fewkes' (1912) work at Casa Grande National Monument was significant for several reasons, one of which being that it represented one of the first attempts to preserve evidence of Native American culture with a monument framework. Fewkes distinguished what he called the Gila Valley culture from the northern pueblo culture, and discussed the apparent differences between the two traditions. Kroeber (1928) later reaffirmed this distinction by contrasting the Gila-Sonoran cultural tradition with that of the Colorado Plateau.

Kidder, relying upon pottery collections to infer cultural and chronological associations in his 1924 synthesis, was impressed by the great amount of variation in the decorated pottery from the lower Gila, which he divided into a polychrome and a red-on-gray series. He noted that the lower Gila polychrome (Gila and Tonto Polychrome), aberrant in some respects, was similar to pottery found to the north and east of the lower Gila area. It was the red-on-gray (red-on-buff) pottery that most intrigued Kidder (1962:312):

> The red-on-gray ware is especially interesting because it is so radically unlike the polychrome and, indeed, so unlike all other Southwestern pottery that it gives rise to the suspicion that it may be the result of an intrusion from some hitherto unlocated centre; or may represent an early or a late period of local work.

Kidder read with interest the account given by Cushing (1890) that the people of the lower Gila were characterized by sharply defined social classes, which were signaled by different methods of disposing of the dead. While he considered different social classes a possibility, observations of architecture permitted a further comment by Kidder (1962:302):

> It is perhaps even more likely that the two sorts of mortuary customs represent a change in culture, and accordingly a more or less considerable lapse of time.

He lamented the fact that neither Cushing nor Fewkes had conducted any stratigraphic studies to resolve these questions of culture and chronology.

GLADWIN AND THE HOHOKAM

Harold Gladwin's involvement with archaeology began at the Southwest Museum in Los Angeles, where he was a Research Fellow. He had already talked with Kidder about the pressing research problems in the Southwest, and it was Kidder who suggested that Gladwin focus on the poorly understood material from the Arizona desert (Gladwin and others 1937:14). In 1927 Gladwin arrived at Casa Grande National Monument to begin excavation of archaeological material that he would provisionally label the "red-on-buff culture" after their distinctive decorated pottery.

Gladwin's first work clearly reflected Kidder's concern with stratigraphy. His research priority was to "conduct stratigraphic tests in some one locality in the hope of being able to define a sequence of culture" (Gladwin 1928:6). Upon the Monument superintendent's suggestion, Gladwin chose the large trash mounds located near Compounds A and B at Casa Grande. He hoped to apply the results of these stratigraphic tests to the smaller ruins in the area and eventually to expand his analysis "in ever widening circles until adjoining cultures should be tapped" (Gladwin 1928:6).

On the basis of this work, Gladwin was able to discriminate basic divisions in the ceramic sequence that would serve as the base line for future research. He discovered that Kidder's suspicions were well founded: polychrome pottery always occurred late in the sequence. It was also apparent that red-on-buff pottery accompanied the polychrome, but in much reduced numbers than earlier in the sequence. Expanding his analysis outward from Casa Grande, Gladwin was able to duplicate the stratigraphic sequence and, subsequently, to define types of red-on-buff pottery antedating the appearance of polychrome ceramics.

From these observations, Gladwin made certain deductions about the cultural history of the area. He concluded that the big house at Casa Grande postdated the construction of Compound B and that, during the period before polychrome ceramics, the architectural pattern appeared to be one of individual pit houses. When additional evidence regarding burial patterns was obtained, Gladwin postulated an early period when red-on-buff pottery, pit houses, and cremation burial were typical, and a later period characterized by polychrome pottery, pueblo-style architecture, and inhumation burial. His conclusion that these later developments were attributable to an invasion of the area by an alien culture was reinforced by Schmidt's (1928) work near Phoenix.

Gladwin also proposed several interesting hypotheses about the Casa Grande itself. He was convinced that the big house had been constructed without the use of forms; this conclusion was later supported by the analysis of Wilcox and Shenk (1977). On the other hand, Gladwin's hypothesis that the Casa Grande was built as a specialized storage facility to protect food from flooding did not receive support.

GLADWIN AND HAURY AT GILA PUEBLO

Gladwin invested the five years following his work at Casa Grande in an extensive survey to determine the range of the red-on-buff culture. Using the Gila Basin as the center, the survey expanded in all directions, extending its investigations to northern Sonora on the south, the Colorado River on the west, Flagstaff on the north, and the Rio Grande on the east.

Emil Haury joined Gladwin's Gila Pueblo Archaeological Foundation as Assistant Director in 1930. One of his first duties was the excavation of Roosevelt 9:6, a site located in the Tonto Basin in central Arizona. This project was a part of the early research conducted by Gila Pueblo to determine the range and nature of the newly discovered Hohokam culture. Roosevelt 9:6 represented the Colonial period, the earliest recognized at that time. Research to describe the remains and to compare them with other known assemblages led Haury to conclude that the Hohokam at Roosevelt 9:6 clearly represented a line of development unrelated to, but contemporary with, the Basketmaker III and Pueblo I periods of the plateau sequence. By 1985 Roosevelt 9:6 was the only Hohokam site in the Tonto Basin to be reported on in detail, although similar sites had been recorded for the region. Like Snaketown, it will continue to be the site to which researchers return for analytic comparison (see Chapter 11).

Extensive reconnaissance, supplemented by the excavation of Roosevelt 9:6, permitted Gladwin and his wife, Winifred, to present the Hohokam as a new culture concept along with a tentative chronology, definitions of pottery types, and some comparisons with adjacent cultures (Gladwin and Gladwin 1933). Borrowing from Russell (1908:24), they renamed the red-on-buff culture the Hohokam, a Pima Indian expression meaning "those who have gone" or "all used up." Hohokam was interpreted as a cultural tradition unlike and unrelated to the puebloan culture of the plateau. Diagnostic material culture traits included paddle-and-anvil pottery, irrigation farming, single-pit-house architecture, cremation burial, an elaborate crafts industry, and many distinctive artifacts, in contrast to the coiled black-

on-white pottery, dry farming, and communal houses that characterized pueblo culture. The Gladwins introduced a chronological
scheme that recognized five periods: Colonial, Sedentary, Classic, Recent, and Modern. Although investigations in the desert area suffered
from the lack of a well-defined chronology, the presence of intrusive
pottery convinced them that their five periods roughly corresponded
to the five pueblo periods presented by Kidder.

The Colonial period, the earliest recognized in 1933, was envisioned as a time of population expansion into areas conducive to the
Hohokam lifeway, which included a large portion of southern and
central Arizona. A pattern of small, pit-house villages considered typical of this period had been documented at Roosevelt 9:6 in the Tonto
Basin and at the Grewe Site in the Gila Basin near Casa Grande (Woodward 1931). The Gladwins believed that the Hohokam of the Colonial
period had attained a fuller cultural development than had the puebloan groups who lived to the north, and that the "tide of civilization
flowed out of the Hohokam to affect peripheral areas" (Gladwin and
Gladwin 1933:4).

The Sedentary period, which followed the Colonial, was seen as a
time of retraction back into the Gila and Salt rivers area, where large
villages were established. Pit houses and surface houses, with or without enclosing walls, were regarded as typical of the Sedentary period.
The following Classic period was defined by the intrusion of the Salado people, who brought their polychrome pottery and knowledge
of pueblo architecture. It was during this period that irrigation systems were thought to have reached their maximum size. The Recent
period was marked by the Salado abandonment of the desert region,
at which time the Hohokam returned to their former way of life. The
Modern period was represented by the Pima and the Papago, who,
because of similar material culture and lifeways, were thought to be
modern descendants of the prehistoric Hohokam.

By 1934 the various research projects accomplished by Gila Pueblo
had recorded over 12,000 archaeological sites in an area extending from California to Texas and from Nevada to northern Mexico.
Through all of this work the origins of the Hohokam remained elusive. Gladwin nevertheless felt that the work had been productive to
the extent that the boundaries of the Hohokam area had been generally defined, a necessary step toward defining the "center." He concluded that the center of the Hohokam area must have been between
the Gila and Salt rivers, and there he returned.

Snaketown had been recorded by Gladwin in 1928. No less than sixty mounds were present at this large site, located along the Gila River a few miles downstream from the Pima community of Sacaton. Gladwin elected to excavate Snaketown, reasoning that the volume and depth of the site might contribute to the understanding of the origins of the Hohokam. Excavations began in 1934, under the direction of Emil Haury.

Snaketown proved to be a gold mine of information on the Hohokam cultural sequence, and became the standard to which all other Hohokam sites were compared. One of the most important aspects of the work was the identification of a Pioneer period preceding the Colonial. Through stratigraphic studies, the Pioneer period was subdivided into a series of phases characterized by a slow, progressive development of the Hohokam culture pattern. The Gila Butte phase of the Colonial period was identified as transitional between the earlier Pioneer period and the later Santa Cruz phase.

The discovery of the Pioneer period did not, however, clarify the origins of the Hohokam, since Gladwin could locate no equivalent for the earliest Vahki phase. He did observe similarities with the recently defined Mogollon culture; Vahki Red and the later Estrella Red-on-gray pottery were similar to the red ware and the red-on-brown pottery of the Georgetown phase of the Mogollon. He also went as far afield as Nebraska for comparative data on the pottery (Gladwin and others 1937:251).

The Gila Butte and Santa Cruz phases of the Colonial period at Snaketown were interpreted as diverging from Pioneer period affinities with the Mogollon. Traits such as carved stone, mosaic plaques, cremation, palettes, ridged axes, figurines, the shell industry, and the pottery, in conjunction with features like ball courts, mounds, and house forms, were without counterparts in adjacent Mogollon areas. The elaboration of this trait complex in the following Sedentary period further distinguished the Hohokam from their neighbors.

One of the major problems associated with the Snaketown project was the lack of chronological controls. The earliest intrusive decorated sherd found at Snaketown was a Basketmaker III type in association with Gila Butte–phase trash. The absence of intrusive ceramics from Pioneer period contexts (an occurrence consistent with the belief that pottery was not made in the northern districts during much of this time) left the beginnings of the Hohokam without any reliable dates. Haury, with Gladwin's concurrence, reasoned that the Santa

Cruz and Sacaton phases were securely dated by tree-ring-dated intrusive sherds. These dates indicated that the Santa Cruz and Sacaton phases had each lasted for approximately two hundred years between A.D. 700 and A.D. 1100. Haury's hypothesis that each of the earlier phases had also lasted two hundred years resulted in a date of 300 B.C. for the beginning of the Vahki phase. This method of chronology building had already been indirectly questioned by Roberts (1935), and was questioned by many investigators after that time (Di Peso 1956; Wilcox and Shenk 1977; McGuire and Schiffer 1982). Thus, although Gladwin and his associates had discovered the Pioneer period, a secure beginning date and the cultural origin of the Hohokam remained elusive. Nevertheless, with the landmark publication of *Excavations at Snaketown: Material Culture* in 1937, the Hohokam as a distinct culture gained acceptance from the archaeological community; no longer was it a bunch of "hokum" (Roberts 1935:26).

By 1937 Gladwin and his staff had made a substantial contribution to southwestern studies. Kidder remarked that prior to the studies in the Gila Basin, the San Juan drainage had been envisioned as the hearth area of all southwestern culture, and that this notion "was fostering a squirrel cage type of investigation only terminated by Gladwin's bold reinterpretations of Gila Basin archaeology" (Kidder 1937:vii). Although Gladwin's assertions of the preeminence of Hohokam culture were thought to be exaggerated or premature (Roberts 1935:31), they served to encourage southwestern archaeologists to expand beyond their own provincialism. Gladwin, characteristically dissatisfied with any spatial limitation, determined to explain the Hohokam in terms of their position in prehistory more broadly, and he pursued this effort up to his last publication (Gladwin 1979).

Gladwin was unimpressed by early attempts to suggest that the Hohokam were simply a northern offshoot of some undiscovered Mesoamerican culture (Roberts 1935). Alternatively, he envisioned the Hohokam and the Mesoamerican cultures as sharing certain similarities due to a common ancestry that lay in the remote past and was ultimately attributable to migrations from Asia. The earliest evidence of the Hohokam was to be found in the Paleoindian hunters of west Texas, who later adjusted to an Archaic period economy that led to plant cultivation. After 500 B.C. these Archaic people expanded westward from Texas and New Mexico to become the Mogollon and the Hohokam. Other groups moved to the Colorado Plateau, where they developed the Basketmaker culture (Gladwin and others 1937:113–119).

The work at Snaketown was only one of many significant projects accomplished by Gila Pueblo during the decade between 1930 and 1940. Haury (1936a) identified the Mogollon culture; Sayles and Antevs (1941) reported on the preceramic Cochise culture; and Sayles (1945) reported his findings from San Simon Village. Most of this work was either directly or indirectly related to Gladwin's interest in the Hohokam.

CONTINUITY IN HAURY'S HOHOKAM RESEARCH

Haury left Gila Pueblo in 1937 to become Head of the Department of Archaeology at the University of Arizona and Director of the Arizona State Museum in the following year. His research, even that devoted to the Mogollon, had implications for the Hohokam. His confidence in the Snaketown chronology was strengthened when he found Gila Butte Red-on-buff pottery, unaccompanied by other red-on-buff sherds, in association with Forestdale phase material in the Forestdale Valley south of Show Low (Haury 1940). Several years later additional tree-ring evidence from Forestdale further supported the original Hohokam chronology in reply to Gladwin's early revisions (Haury 1942).

In 1939, Haury began a research program in the Arizona Papagueria that soon outlined a sequence of culture dated between A.D. 800 and A.D. 1400. Still missing from the archaeological record was documentation of the time period A.D. 1400 to A.D. 1700 that would bring together the archaeological and the ethnographic cultures. Haury selected Batki, a historic period site which had been recorded by Kino in 1694, for investigation. Objections by the Papago to the excavation of Batki, however, prompted Haury to excavate Ventana Cave, a site most instrumental in shaping his view of Hohokam prehistory. The five meters of stratified cave deposits revealed a sequence of culture dating from the time of Paleoindian hunters and extinct fauna up to the modern Papago. The gradual development of culture represented in the deposits suggested to Haury an unbroken transition from the Archaic period hunting and gathering people to the prehistoric Hohokam. Haury (1943:222) stated:

> It is worth noting that the arrival of pottery, and doubtless agriculture also, was not accompanied by a general break in the continuity of the culture pattern. . . . When this took place may

be subject to debate, but a guess of from 1500 to 2000 years ago may be made.

Ventana Cave provided evidence for the origin of Hohokam culture out of the earlier Cochise culture and yielded information on another important problem. Typical Hohokam ceramics of the Pioneer and later periods were present in the cave deposits, but the burials present were inhumations rather than cremations. Many of the ornate items found with deceased Hohokam in the Gila Basin were not duplicated at Ventana. To account for this regional variability, Haury proposed that the Hohokam be divided into two branches—the river and the desert. The desert branch was interpreted as having been established by groups of river people who filtered into the desert and, because of the environmental restrictions imposed by this arid country, survived with a more limited range of material items (Haury 1950a, reprinted 1975).

In his report on the Cochise culture at Cienega Creek Site (see Chapter 9), Haury argued that the presence there of cremation burials in pits accompanied by offerings indicated an antecedent pattern to the Hohokam burial practice of the Pioneer period. This relationship between the two cultures was further strengthened by similarities in artifacts, such as projectile points. The available evidence suggested to Haury that the Cochise culture was ancestral to both the Hohokam and the Mogollon.

The case for cultural continuity was further developed in Haury's proposal that the Cochise culture achieved at least a partially sedentary lifeway and experimented with the cultivation of grain amaranths as early as 4000 B.C.; both of these characteristics predisposed the later folks to accept maize cultivation (Haury 1962a:115; see Chapter 2). Maize first came up the mountain corridor from Mexico to the Mogollon, and from there it radiated to the Hohokam. Although no canals at Snaketown were known to predate A.D. 700, Haury hypothesized that irrigation agriculture had appeared as early as A.D. 1 in response to the need for water control in the desert (1962a:121–122). After the Hohokam were settled, they began to assimilate additional elements from Mesoamerica.

Although he pushed forward the beginning of the Pioneer period from 300 B.C. to A.D. 1, Haury remained otherwise consistent in his view of Hohokam chronology. His confidence in the original Snaketown sequence remained unshaken even in the face of conflicting opinions and numerous revisions. Furthermore, he maintained the view that the Hohokam had developed locally from an indigenous Cochise culture, and that the Hohokam and the Mogollon were very similar during the early phases (Haury 1962a:126).

Haury also directed his attention to the related problem of contacts between the American Southwest and Mexico (Haury 1945b). In a comprehensive review, Haury concluded that, except for pottery and agriculture, the Mogollon and the Anasazi had been little affected by Mesoamerican contacts. The situation for the Hohokam was different, since there were many parallels in artifact forms and in such features as ball courts. A review of the known chronological placement of shared items, such as copper bells, macaws, effigy vessels, figurines, and weaving techniques, prompted several conclusions: these items did not enter the Southwest at the same time, they did not come from the same source, and they did not travel the same route. Haury (1945b: 65) summarized by stating that

> we should not look for a fixed route of entry, pointing back to a
> single culture group, or . . . endeavor to find traces of a band
> of people which emigrated wholesale from Mexico.

This position was echoed again in 1956, when he observed further that the absence of social classes and cities and the lack of emphasis on warfare and on religious and ceremonial architecture in the Hohokam argued against migration from the south (Haury 1956:23; see Chapter 16).

GLADWIN'S REVISIONS

Kidder (1937) noted that Gladwin had a particular dislike for loose ends, for facts that did not fit into a comprehensive theory. This unrest eventually led Gladwin to revise the conclusions of the original Snaketown report, and by 1942 he acknowledged what he considered to be major errors in Gila Pueblo's earlier interpretations, essentially those of Haury. In a major revision, Gladwin (1942) declared that the phase sequence for Snaketown had been grossly exaggerated. A reconsideration of the evidence convinced him that two hundred years was too long for the length of a phase. His suggestion that each of the earlier phases (through the Santa Cruz phase) be shortened to fifty years, resulted in a beginning date for the Vahki phase at A.D. 600 and eliminated the first nine hundred years of the original sequence. Since the original Snaketown chronology was based primarily on intrusive ceramics from the Flagstaff area, these changes demanded that Gladwin also revise the Flagstaff chronology. He concluded with the apology that he, like others, had "succumbed to the weakness which appears to affect all archaeologists when they strike something new . . . the tendency to overestimate the antiquity of the cultures which they investigate" (1942:6).

Gladwin's 1942 revisions affected only the length of the chronology; in 1948 he not only revised the chronology again but also drastically altered the original concept of the Hohokam. A major alteration concerned the position of the Pioneer period materials. Gladwin (1948: 198) became convinced that these materials were not Hohokam at all, but represented a unique occurrence of Mogollon culture in the Gila Basin, a conclusion based almost entirely upon the resemblance of the decorated ceramics to those of the Mogollon, which Haury had noted earlier. Gladwin (1948:50) also questioned the sequence of the Pioneer period pottery types that had been developed by Haury, and he concluded that the temporal ordering of these types had been in error. He felt that the Estrella, Sweetwater, and Snaketown red-on-gray types, and, thus, the associated phases, were actually overlapping and contemporaneous. Furthermore, his reanalysis of the stratigraphy of Mound 29 suggested that these Pioneer period ceramics were contemporary with the Santa Cruz and Sacaton phases. The Gila Butte phase was eliminated because Gladwin felt that the Gila Butte Red-on-buff pottery was not temporally distinct, but existed throughout the time that Mound 29 was in use. The implication of these revisions was that Gladwin no longer accepted seven distinct phases describing an orderly evolution of Hohokam culture. Instead, he postulated a parallel development of Mogollon and Hohokam at Snaketown, which was envisioned to have begun with the Vahki (Mogollon) and the Santa Cruz (Hohokam) horizons dating to between A.D. 700 and A.D. 750 (Gladwin 1948:227).

The elimination of an antecedent Pioneer period left Gladwin in a quandary to explain the appearance of the Hohokam. He also had to explain why only locally made Mogollon decorated pottery was present and why other diagnostic items of the Mogollon, such as inhumation burials, plain ware pottery, storage pits, and circular-shaped structures, were absent. To do this Gladwin (1948:231) abandoned all of his earlier ideas about Hohokam origins and suggested that the Hohokam had come to southern Arizona from an unknown location in Mexico as an already developed culture pattern. The early Hohokam met up with Mogollon people at Snaketown, where they began a time of coresidence that lasted through the Sacaton phase, which ended around A.D. 1100. The absence of Mogollon traits was never satisfactorily explained, though Gladwin suggested that the Mogollon were sufficiently impressed with the Hohokam to have adopted Hohokam practices.

The 1942 and 1948 revisions presented by Gladwin were irreconcilable, and one may justifiably ask how such contrasting opinions could be derived from the same body of evidence. Gladwin appears to have shifted the weight that he placed upon various facets of the evidence. In 1948 he accepted two facts as evidence for contemporaneity: first, that 2 sherds of Snaketown Red-on-buff, 945 sherds of Gila Butte Red-on-buff, and 1 sherd of Santa Cruz Red-on-buff were recovered from Section N-5 of Mound 29; and, second, that 9 sherds of Snaketown Red-on-buff, 611 sherds of Gila Butte Red-on-buff, and 1 sherd of Santa Cruz Red-on-buff were found in Section N-6 (Gladwin 1948:258). Haury, on the other hand, believed that these associations were probably due to differential deposition during the formation of the mound and that these associations were further complicated by subsequent natural and cultural disturbances and by the use of arbitrary units in excavation (Haury 1976:198–202). To subscribe to the Gladwin position would require one to overlook the substantial body of additional evidence at Snaketown, including the ceramic assemblages found on superimposed house floors and in the cremations.

DI PESO AND SCHROEDER: THE O'OTAM AND THE HAKATAYA

While Haury was inferring local Hohokam development, the work of others began to take different directions. Charles Di Peso had directed a number of research projects along the San Pedro and Santa Cruz rivers, while Albert Schroeder had been involved in research in the Verde Valley, Flagstaff, and western Arizona. Both Di Peso and Schroeder proposed reconstructions of Hohokam culture that deviated considerably from the views presented by Haury and echoed the thoughts of Gladwin.

Di Peso's reconstruction introduced still another modification of the original chronology, as well as a bold reinterpretation of the prehistory of the southern portion of Arizona. He proposed that most of southern Arizona had been occupied by the O'otam, an indigenous group of ceramic-producing descendants of the earlier Cochise culture. O'otam sites included Cave Creek and San Simon Village, the Gleeson Site in the San Pedro drainage, and several additional sites located in the Papagueria. The O'otam subsumed material previously associated with the Dragoon culture, the San Simon branch of the Mogollon, the desert branch of the Hohokam, and most of the Pioneer period at Snaketown. Basic traits included an extended family village pattern, round to square houses, community structures, semiflexed inhumation burials without offerings in pits and with rock cairn covers, randomly placed burials, sheet trash, and polished but unsmudged red ware and brown ware pottery. Subsistence activities emphasized hunting and gathering, but limited farming without the use of canals may have been practiced (Di Peso 1956:561–562; 1958:12–13).

Against this cultural background Di Peso introduced the Hohokam as immigrants from Mexico who occupied the southern Arizona region from A.D. 1000 until around A.D. 1250. He compressed the Hohokam presence to 250 years, based on his excavations at the Palo Parado Site, where he found a small quantity of the early red-on-gray and red-on-buff pottery mixed in with larger quantities of Santa Cruz and Sacaton phase pottery. These ceramic associations suggested to him that many of the Hohokam pottery types thought to be sequential were actually contemporary.

According to Di Peso's reconstruction, around A.D. 1000 the Hohokam appeared with large communities, stratified social organization, and extensive irrigation systems—all traits that contrasted sharply with the earlier O'otam pattern (Di Peso 1956:562–564). The Hohokam were seen as overlords who introduced many new features that resulted in a regional mosaic of cultural patterns throughout the desert area; their outposts were established in distant localities, such as Roosevelt 9:6. Thus, the period between A.D. 1000 and A.D. 1250 was a time of Hohokam domination over much of southern Arizona that continued until the indigenous O'otam gathered sufficient strength to break the oppressive hegemony.

Di Peso presented a novel reinterpretation of the history of Hohokam culture—one very close to the revisions that had been suggested by Gladwin (1948). Both Gladwin and Di Peso wanted to shorten the chronology; both withdrew the Pioneer period from the Hohokam sequence and attributed it to a different tradition, and both envisioned the Hohokam as late immigrants from Mesoamerica. In his later work

Di Peso (1974) placed even more emphasis upon Mesoamerican contacts as prime determinants of culture change in the prehistoric Southwest.

While Di Peso was concerned with the prehistory of southern and southeastern Arizona, Schroeder concentrated on the south-central and western portions of the state. Unlike Di Peso, Schroeder did not question the original Hohokam chronology; he reaffirmed 300 B.C. as the beginning of the Pioneer period at Snaketown. He was concerned with identifying the culture of the people and the processes of change represented at Snaketown. Like Gladwin and Di Peso, he proposed that the Pioneer period was not affiliated with the Hohokam, but with a group that he called the Hakataya (Schroeder 1957, 1960). This culture was introduced from southwestern Mexico or Guatemala, possibly by a group possessing a formative Mayan cultural pattern (Schroeder 1965:297, 307). These people introduced square houses, community lodges, the rectangular mano and trough metate, the effigy vessel and figurine complex, brown ware pottery, and cremation burial. In addition, they probably brought the first maize agriculture into the Southwest (Schroeder 1965:307). Schroeder argued that, since most of these traits were unknown to the Southwest at 300 B.C., their appearance could only be explained through a movement into the area. The Hakataya were seen to have radiated from the Gila and Salt rivers area to western Arizona.

According to Schroeder (1966:686), the Hakataya pattern was interrupted around A.D. 600 with the introduction of canal irrigation, ball courts, trash mounds, new pottery designs, new art and craft styles, and probably new forms of civil and ceremonial organization. These new traits were introduced by the Hohokam, a conquest culture that may have included *pochteca* traders (Schroeder 1966:687, 699). Schroeder felt that the presence of two distinct cultural patterns could be identified during the Colonial period at Snaketown by such contrasts as two- and four-beam house structures, in addition to many of the traits listed above. The Hohokam eventually assimilated the Hakataya.

Schroeder interpreted the Colonial and Sedentary periods of Hohokam culture as a time of social and political development: stratified social systems emerged, craft specialists and guilds appeared, and traders carried goods of Hohokam manufacture to the developing cultures to the north. The northern puebloan development may have been stimulated by contacts with the Hohokam (1966:700).

The Schroeder and Di Peso reconstructions were similar in that both viewed Pioneer period culture as non-Hohokam; they differed in regarding the origins of this culture. Schroeder saw Pioneer period culture as similar to the pattern found in western and north-central Arizona, while Di Peso interpreted it as belonging to the variable pattern that existed throughout the Papagueria and southeastern Arizona. Both researchers explained the appearance of the Hohokam as a migration from Mexico (at A.D. 1000 for Di Peso and at A.D. 600 for Schroeder, the latter date being comparable to the Gladwin revision). A common theme of these interpretations was to dispute the evolutionary sequence from Cochise to Hohokam that had long been championed by Haury.

By the 1960s Hohokam prehistory appeared to be in disarray. The cultural affiliation of the elusive Pioneer perod had been ascribed to the Hohokam, Mogollon, O'otam, and Hakataya; Hohokam origins were seen as being local and as a migration from Mexico; and at least three major versions of the chronology existed (see Haury 1976:326).

HAURY'S HOHOKAM REEVALUATION

Alternative reconstructions of the Hohokam obscured the resolution of fundamental issues. Indeed, answers to the basic questions of who the Hohokam were and how they fit into the larger picture of southwestern prehistory lacked agreement. With the Hohokam shrouded in controversy, Haury decided that new data were necessary before these basic questions could be answered. He returned to Snaketown during the winter of 1964–1965.

On the basis of a thorough evaluation of critical proveniences, as well as a well-reasoned questioning of Gladwin's methods, Haury concluded that the original sequence of periods and phases was accurate (Haury 1976:97–110, 325–340; see Chapter 17 for a more detailed discussion). On the other hand, the absolute dating of the periods was not so easily verified; serious problems were presented by conflicting dates, especially for the Pioneer period. Consideration of the evidence supplied by six different dating methods permitted Haury to propose his reevaluation of the Hohokam chronology (Haury 1976:338). Minor shifts of 50 to 150 years were suggested for several of the Pioneer period phases, and the troublesome Gila Butte phase was shortened from 200 to 150 years. The Santa Cruz and Sacaton phases remained intact.

Analysis of the large quantity of artifacts recovered from the excavations contributed to Haury's 1976 reevaluation of Hohokam origins. Many of the traits once thought to be culturally and temporally distinct were seen differently; this was especially true for the large sample of Pioneer-period material recovered. The discovery of a complex of contemporary traits in the earliest Vahki phase—a complex previously unknown to the Southwest—led Haury to conclude that Hohokam origins were not to be found in the Cochise culture. This trait complex included the application of water-management techniques to the cultivation of plants such as corn, beans, squash, and cotton; well digging; established village life; cremation burial; well-made, red slipped and plain brown pottery; human figurines made of fired clay; extensive use of marine shell; carved stone and bone industries; shaped trough metates; turquoise mosaics; and, inferentially, well-developed textile arts. Thus, Haury joined the position taken earlier by Gladwin, Di Peso, and Schroeder that the Hohokam were an immigrant group from Mexico, unrelated to the Cochise culture. However, he maintained his position that the Pioneer period began at 300 B.C., and that subsequent periods reflected the gradual unfolding of Hohokam culture, with additional infusions of Mesoamerican traits, especially after A.D. 500 (Haury 1976:355).

RESEARCH DIRECTIONS IN
THE 1970S AND 1980S

In 1956 Haury suggested a number of research directions and problems that came to dominate later research. He called for a shift from historical description to consideration of functional relationships with the environment, especially settlement pattern studies. Data derived from these studies were to lead to a better understanding of the relationships among environment, subsistence, and society. He also called for consideration of the non-material aspects of the societies under study. During the next three decades research in the Hohokam area could generally be seen to reflect these concerns. Settlement pattern studies, paleoenvironmental reconstruction, subsistence, exchange, and social organization dominated research.

Research in the Hohokam region in the 1970s and 1980s maintained a rapid pace, due almost exclusively to the tremendous increase in contract archaeology in response to rapid population growth in the Arizona desert. Over sixty significant research projects produced quality samples from both surveys and excavations in many different drainage areas (Doyel in press). These samples, while supporting some earlier models of Hohokam prehistory, were most significant for contributing an entirely new body of data to expand regional coverage. Although subject to continued healthy questioning, the sequence of phases suggested by Haury remained generally useful. The chronology of the Pioneer period received considerable reevaluation, with a number of investigators leaning toward a beginning date for the Vahki phase of around or after A.D. 200 (Wilcox and Shenk 1977; Plog 1980; LeBlanc 1982; McGuire and Schiffer 1982). Discussion continued regarding the origins of the Hohokam, with several scholars supporting the Cochise to Hohokam continuum originally suggested by Haury. It is ironic that after Haury concurred that the Hohokam were immigrants from Mesoamerica, others began to argue for his earlier Cochise-Hohokam continuum (Martin and Plog 1973; Wilcox and Shenk 1977; Wilcox and Sternberg 1983). Research also began to bridge the geographic gap between southern Arizona and Mesoamerica (Di Peso 1974; Doyel and Plog 1980; Wilcox and Sternberg 1983).

We can state more generally and with some certainty that three broad periods of Hohokam culture history can be identified. First, a Pioneer period began sometime between 300 B.C. and A.D. 200 and was characterized by the development of a settled, agriculturally based, ceramic-producing people. By the end of the Pioneer period, around A.D. 550, canal irrigation was well developed, large villages were present, contacts with Mesoamerica increased, and new levels of social interaction developed. Second, from A.D. 550 to A.D. 1150, contacts between the Hohokam and other southwestern people were apparent and exchange was active. Third, by A.D. 1150, a new tradition began with the appearance of massive platform mounds and adobe architecture, combined with large amounts of red ware pottery and variable mortuary patterns. This pattern, elaborated around A.D. 1300, with the appearance of multi-storied adobe architecture and polychrome pottery, came to an end in the A.D. 1400s. Many different interpretations have been presented to account for this sequence (Haury 1976; Doyel and Haury 1976; Doyel and Plog 1980; Wilcox and Sternberg 1983).

By the 1980s research determined that, while the Hohokam developed the largest irrigation networks in prehistoric North America, not all Hohokam folk practiced irrigation, even in the more fertile river valleys. Haury's model of a desert versus a riverine Hohokam oversimplified a complex mosaic of adaptations to Lower Sonoran Desert environments. In addition, later statements did not support Haury's notion of a Salado movement into the desert region during the Classic period. Continued research also suggested that Hohokam villages were characterized by more formal internal structure than the traditional "sprawling *ranchería*" model would allow.

Haury did not agree with some of these later interpretations; although he did enjoy the renewed interest in Hohokam studies, he always preferred the collection of new data to the rehashing of old material. In the final analysis, Haury's contribution to the original description and definition of Hohokam culture, his masterful detective work in unraveling Hohokam cultural history, his training of several generations of students, and his continued contribution to problems under investigation stand as testimony to his dedication to clarifying the prehistory of the desert people.

Roosevelt 9:6

A Hohokam Site of the
Colonial Period

Emil W. Haury

In earlier reports, several aspects of the Red-on-buff culture, here-inafter referred to as the culture of the Hohokam—the name by which the Pima refer to the "Ancient Ones"—have been dealt with. An analysis of the material remains in the Gila Basin provided the data for the first paper of the series (Gladwin and Gladwin 1929a). The southern, western, and northern ranges were subsequently defined with a view to determining, if possible, the origin of these people (Gladwin and Gladwin 1929b, 1930a, 1930b). The extension of the area beyond that already covered has taken the search northeastward, where the origin of the Hohokam complex was not to be expected in view of the presence, in that direction, of the better known Pueblo people, but where the extent was, nevertheless, to be ascertained.

During the progress of this work, George Dennis, a former resi-dent of Tonto Basin, pointed out to us that, at a site in the Basin, cre-mations and pottery had been exposed by the wash of the water as

Reprinted from *Medallion Papers* 11. Globe, Arizona: Gila Pueblo, 1932.

Figure 11.1. Roosevelt 9:6 (*left foreground*) showing its proximity to Salt River (*right*) and the floodplain bordering the river. This view, looking to the northwest, shows the Mazatzal Mountains in the far distance.

Roosevelt Lake receded. The site, Roosevelt 9:6 (Gladwin and Gladwin 1928), was examined, and the sherds, when compared with the sequence of red-on-buff pottery as drawn by Gladwin (1928:22–25), showed the period of occupation to be early in that scale. About 100 feet east there was a small stone-outlined village of pueblo form, accompanied by black-on-white and black-on-red wares, and, as far as could be told without excavation, no red-on-buff. On the basis of the pottery, there appeared to be a hiatus between the two sites, a fact which was further borne out by the evidence of houses in one case and their apparent lack in the other. In order to arrive at more positive conclusions concerning the relationship of these two dissimilar ruins and to gain additional knowledge of the little known early phases of the Hohokam culture from an area in which it supposedly did not exist, it was determined to explore the site.

LOCATION AND DESCRIPTION

Roosevelt 9:6 is located on the south bank of Salt River and about 25 yards from the 1932 channel (Figure 11.1), approximately one mile east of Grapevine Springs and 31 miles north of Globe, Arizona. The village occupied a low terrace rising but a few feet above the valley floor (Figure 11.2) which is now being dissected by several small

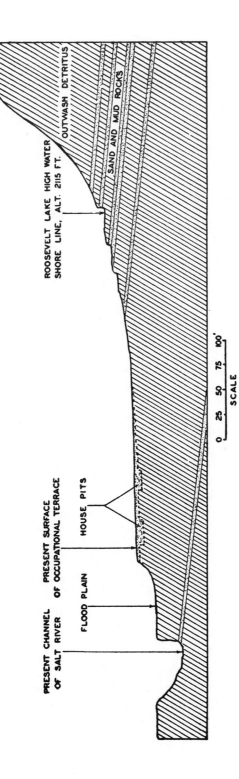

Figure 11.2. Section through Roosevelt 9:6 showing relationship of site to topographic features.

gullies that carry the water draining from the clay bluffs to the south. This location was advantageous to its occupants, in that water for domestic purposes could be obtained from the nearby river without great effort, and because of its proximity to arable land on the alluvial plain which borders the river channel. The site was selected without regard for defensive features, a characteristic of Hohokam communities.

As revealed by the excavations, Roosevelt 9:6 was composed of fourteen semi-subterranean houses, each being a separate unit of the settlement (Figure 11.3). There was also a room outlined by rocks which was undoubtedly related to the neighbouring pueblo and was not a part of the original red-on-buff village. Each of the other houses had been excavated to form a pit from 1 to 2 feet in depth, of rectangular form with rounded corners, and having an entrance passage leading to the room in one of the long sides. With the roofing-over of the pit by means of timbers, brush and dirt, the dwelling became, in all essentials, an earth lodge.

The pits of most of these lodges were buried from 1 to 5 feet beneath an accumulation of sand and silt, composed partly of material washed from the adjacent hills and partly of deposits put down during prehistoric river floods. Due to this collected mass of silt and to the inconspicuousness of the house remains, the exact extent of the village cannot be told, although it is believed that all of the dwellings were located.

All the lodges except one had been destroyed by fire, but not all simultaneously. House 5 succumbed to natural weathering and decay. The burning of an earth lodge, while destructive in itself, does much to preserve the details of construction. The collapse of the roof smothers the fire and preserves the incompletely burned timbers and brush in the form of charcoal. Once in this state, the evidence lasts indefinitely, as long as it is underground.

In addition to the dwellings, there were two shallow refuse mounds, two cremation areas, and a large outside hearth (see Figure 11.3). The houses are considered in the order of their excavation.

HOUSE REMAINS

House 1

This house, found while digging for cremations in the area immediately to the west (see Figure 11.3), was the first indication of the living quarters of the people who occupied the site. Its presence was in no way suggested by surface features. The dimensions of the room were: north-south, 22 feet; east-west, 10 feet 6 inches; depth, 18 inches.

In about the center of the east wall was the entrance passage (Figure 11.4A), 2 feet 6 inches wide and 4 feet long, terminating with a vertical step about 18 inches high. The top of this step marks the ground level which was in use during the occupation of the room. The floor in the entrance vestibule slopes gently downward from the base of the step towards the room.

About the circumference of the room and next to the earthen wall of the pit, were the charred remains of reeds set vertically in the floor. This feature suggests a wattle type of construction, but in the true sense of the word it cannot be considered as such as there was no evidence of a plaster coating. It seems, rather, that the reeds were placed about the room to prevent soil crumbling from the sides of the excavation. In the pit structures in the San Juan the same effect was achieved by lining the excavation with stone slabs; but the builders of Roosevelt 9:6, apparently preferred reeds, since stone slabs were available in an outcrop less than 100 yards from the site. The plant from which the reeds were obtained has been identified by Dr. J. J. Thornber of the University of Arizona, as *Baccharis glutinosa*. It grows, at the present time, in great thickets, sometimes attaining a height of 6 feet, on the flood plain just below the village site.

The floor of the dwelling was of clay, rather uneven, but hard packed and ash-covered. The firepit was set directly in front of, and less than 2 feet from the beginning of the entryway. It was circular, clay-lined, 10 inches in diameter and 5 inches deep, and surrounded by a low ridge or lip.

The postholes can be divided into two groups according to their size and position in the room. The two primary holes (see Figure 11.4C) into which the largest roof supports were set are located in the end centers of the house. They vary from 8 to 10 inches in diameter and are from 2 to 3 feet deep. The burnt end of an 8-inch mesquite beam was found in situ in the south hole. The secondary holes (see Figure 11.4D) were small, averaging 4 inches in diameter and 1 foot in depth. They were not placed with any great regularity, although a row at each end of the room about 2 feet from the wall was evident, providing some idea as to the mode of roofing. It seems not unlikely that these lighter support poles also extended the length of the room

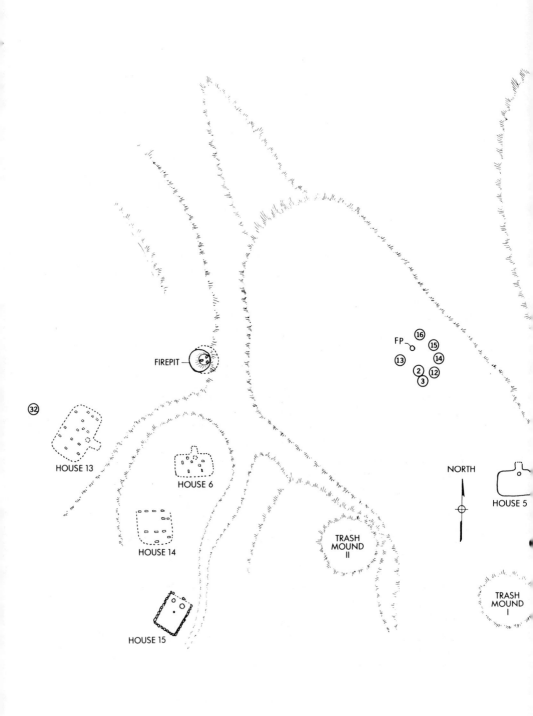

FP

⑯
⑮
⑬
⑭
②
⑫
③

FIREPIT

㉜

HOUSE 13

HOUSE 6

HOUSE 14

HOUSE 15

NORTH

HOUSE 5

TRASH
MOUND
II

TRASH
MOUND
I

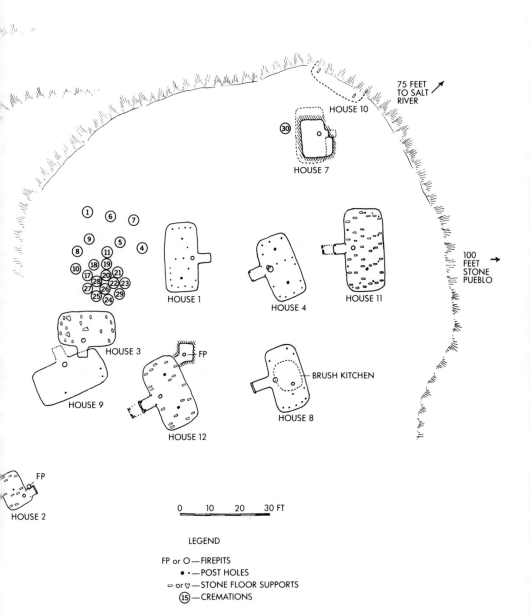

75 FEET
TO SALT
RIVER

HOUSE 10

HOUSE 7

HOUSE 1

HOUSE 4

HOUSE 11

100
FEET
STONE
PUEBLO

HOUSE 3

HOUSE 9

FP

BRUSH KITCHEN

HOUSE 8

HOUSE 12

FP

HOUSE 2

0   10   20   30 FT

LEGEND

FP or O — FIREPITS
● · — POST HOLES
▱ or ▽ — STONE FLOOR SUPPORTS
⑮ — CREMATIONS

Figure 11.3. Plan of Roosevelt 9:6.

217

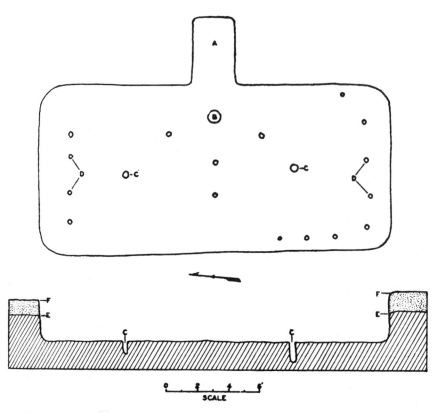

Figure 11.4. Plan of House 1: A, vestibule; B, firepit; C, holes for major roof posts; D, holes for lesser roof posts; E, surface level when house was built; F, existing surface.

near the wall, but these could not be determined except in the south-west corner. Four other holes, two in line west of the firepit and one at either side, were so symmetrically arranged that their function must have been a definite one.

The method of roofing the pit seems quite clear from the arrangement of the postholes, although many desired details are lacking. The two large supports (see Figure 11.4C) presumably carried a single large horizontal beam which formed the backbone of the roof. The smaller vertical poles (see Figure 11.4D) are likewise thought to have supported small horizontal beams in a complete circle about the room. Whether these were as high as the central beam is a matter of conjecture, but they were probably somewhat lower so as to give the roof a

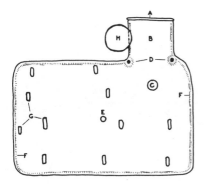

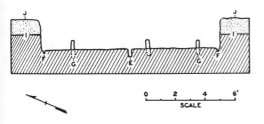

Figure 11.5. Plan of House 2: A, slab, lining step into vestibule; B, vestibule; C, firepit; D, clay cones plastered about base of poles supporting entrance cover; E, hole for roof support; F, floor groove which engaged ends of reed lining of room; G, notched stone floor supports; H, firepit of later level, partly superimposed over vestibule; I, surface level when house was built; J, existing surface.

sufficient pitch for the proper drainage of water. This framework then carried a pole, brush, and earth covering. The side walls sloped from the edge of the excavation to the cross beams above, and were also covered with brush and dirt.

House 2

In two respects, House 2 was different from the others uncovered in the village. First, it was considerably smaller—the smallest house, in fact, in the settlement. The north-south dimension was 12 feet, the east-west side measured 7 feet 6 inches, the depth 12 inches (Figure 11.5).

The second variation was found in the location of the entrance. Instead of being in the center of one of the long sides, as in all other houses, it was situated at the south end of the east wall. This has no other significance, perhaps, than to show that the position of the entrance, either as to direction or point of entry to the house pit, was not dictated by tradition. The entrance vestibule measured 3 feet in width and 2 feet 6 inches in length. At its end was a single stone slab 1 foot high which served as a threshold and a retainer for the soil at the step where it would be broken down by passing in and out of the room. On each side of the entrance where it joined the dwelling was a conical

Figure 11.6. House 2, showing the notched stones in the floor, firepit (*upper center*), and vertical slab forming step of entrance.

mass of clay rising 3 inches above the floor and having a hole in the center 4 inches in diameter which extended to, but not below, the floor. These clay hummocks appear to be reinforcements about the bases of poles supporting the entrance hood which were not solidly set into the ground. A single posthole was located in the center of the room. The firepit was directly in front of the passage and measured 9 inches in diameter and 4 inches in depth. When uncovered, it was found not to contain ashes, but a filling of earth and a flat river pebble in the bottom.

Extending about the periphery of the room, except at the base of the stone slab in the entrance, was found a groove in the floor about 2 inches wide and of the same depth. In several places the charred reeds, which lined the dwelling as in House 1, were directly above this groove, and it was inferred from this that the lower ends of the reeds were made secure by imbedding them in the floor. This belief was later confirmed in Houses 9 and 11 where the grooves still held the reed ends.

Imbedded in the clay floor in four more or less regular rows parallel to the long axis of the room, were found eleven stones bearing semicircular notches in the tops (Figure 11.6). They were made of a soft friable sandstone which outcrops in the nearby bluffs in the form

Figure 11.7. Firepit partly superimposed over entrance passage of House 2. The rocks were removed from the pit.

of thin strata. Their widths vary from 4 to 9 inches and they have an average thickness of 2 inches. The rocks extend from 6 to 8 inches above the floor, and the notches are about 4 inches wide and from 1/2 inch to 2 inches deep. The latter were cut into the rocks by a chipping and crumbling process.

The first row, a few inches inside of the east wall (see Figure 11.5) had but two stones about 4 feet apart; the second row also had two stones spaced at a little greater distance, both being north of the firepit. In the third row were four of the imbedded rocks, the first or northernmost one being somewhat out of line with the rest, but the series extended the length of the room; row four, along the west wall, was composed of three stones about equally spaced. The notches in these upright slabs were all arranged to face in the same direction, that is, at right angles to the length of the room. The alignment of these pillars in rows led to the belief that they were designed to support some sort of rack or floor. The presence of five large plain ware storage jars crushed on the floor implied that the room was used for storage purposes, as did the absence of ashes in the firepit and the small size of the room.

Outside of the entrance to House 2 on the north side and partly overlapping the entry passage about 6 inches above its floor, was a firepit belonging to a later level of occupation (Figure 11.7).

House 3

House 3 was important because of the time-relationship which it bore to House 9. Although two levels of occupation were evident in several of the other dwellings, these two furnished the only real case of superposition of rooms in the entire site.

Upon exploring for dwelling remains south of House 3, the floor of one was encountered 20 inches below that of the room in question. It was traced under the entry passage of House 3, but not under the floor of the house itself. There can be no question, however, that House 9 was long in disuse and filled with debris prior to the construction of House 3, as the floor of the entrance vestibule was hard packed and led out upon a level much higher than that of House 9 when inhabited.

The dimensions of House 3 were: east-west, 18 feet 6 inches; north-south, 10 feet 6 inches; depth, 1 foot (Figures 11.8 and 11.9).

As in House 2, there were found imbedded in the clay floor the notched stone piles which supported an elevated floor 6 to 8 inches above the earthen floor. It is apparent that these stones were set in four rows, and that the raised floor was carried well towards, if not touching, the sides of the pit. Some of the stones were obviously missing from their places, others were broken off at the floor level, while three were found resting on the floor as indicated in the diagram (see Figure 11.8). This gave rise to the belief that the room may have been abandoned and that the best of the stone supports were salvaged for use in another house.

House 4

This house may be regarded as the type example of those in Roosevelt 9:6 which lacked the supporting stones for the elevated floor. It was also particularly valuable as regards the position of structural supports, a point in which some of the other houses were lacking; openings in the floor, in some of which the decayed ends of posts which supported the roof were found, were of two sizes: those into which the large or primary posts were set, and those which held the lesser supports. Of the former there were two, one in each end center of the house, 3 feet in depth, 8 inches in diameter (Figure 11.10D). The smaller holes averaged 1 foot in depth, 5 inches in diameter, and were placed at a distance of one to two feet from the earthen walls, but no fixed distance apart (see Figure 11.10E).

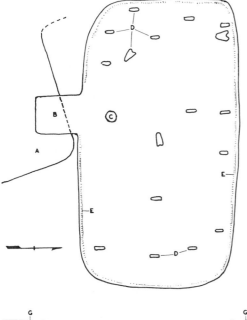

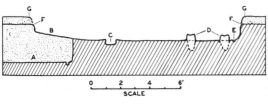

Figure 11.8. Plan of House 3: A, northeast corner of House 9; B, vestibule; C, firepit; D, stone floor supports; E, floor groove; F, surface level when house was built; G, existing surface.

Figure 11.9. Looking into the pit of House 3 toward the west. Note fire-pit (*extreme left*) and beginning of entrance, which extended over the floor of House 9.

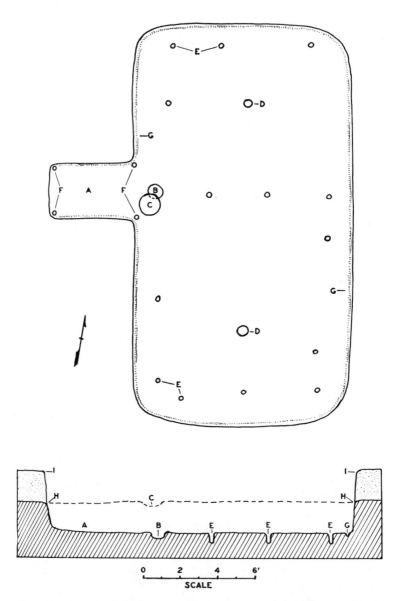

Figure 11.10. Plan of House 4: A, vestibule; B, firepit; C, firepit of a later level of occupation; D, holes for major roof supports; E, holes for lesser roof supports; F, holes for poles supporting entrance hood; G, floor groove; H, surface level when house was built; I, existing surface.

Figure 11.11. The entrance passage and firepit of House 4.

In the extreme west end of the entrance passage and again where it joined the room were paired holes which, without question, held the posts supporting a protective hood over the entrance (Figures 11.10F and 11.11).

The groove which held the reed lining of the house completely surrounded the floor and was carried to the step of the entrance (Figure 11.12).

The dimensions of this house were: east-west, 12 feet; north-south, 20 feet 6 inches; depth, 18 inches.

Further evidence to indicate that Roosevelt 9:6 was occupied during a sufficiently long period of time to allow for the formation of several distinct levels was found in this house. Almost directly above the firepit of House 4 at a distance of about 20 inches, a fire area was found, or what appeared to be the ashes of a fire mixed with burned stones. The ashes, in turn, rested upon an easily distinguishable level of occupation (Figure 11.13). The accumulation between the floors

Figure 11.12. Postholes and the marginal groove which held the ends of reeds in the floor of House 4.

Figure 11.13. The firepit of House 4 (*lower*) and a fire
area on a higher level of occupation (*upper*).

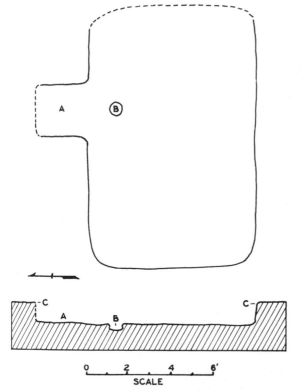

Figure 11.14. Plan of House 5: A, vestibule; B, firepit; C, existing surface.

Figure 11.15. Firepit and entrance of House 5. The manos at the edge of the pit were all found in the room and in the entrance passage.

contained culture throughout, hence it may be inferred that, upon the destruction of the dwelling by fire, the pit thus left was gradually filled up with debris until entirely obliterated, the fill then forming a part of the common plaza level.

House 5

So meager were the details of House 5 that it warrants little more than passing mention. Its dimensions were 8 feet by 12 feet, the long axis running east and west (Figure 11.14). The floor was only a foot below the present surface (Figure 11.15). Entry was on the north side, the passage being 2½ feet wide and of undetermined length. The firepit, 10 inches in diameter and 5 inches deep, was the only floor feature encountered.

A number of manos were found on the floor and in the entry passage.

House 6

Details of House 6 are also lacking. Its presence in the western part of the village was noted from the stone piles which projected above the surface of the ground because of soil erosion.

House 7

Due to the difficulty of accurately tracing the outlines of this house, it was not completely cleared. The firepit was found in its usual position in front of the entrance passage.

Brush Kitchen

Before proceeding with the consideration of House 8, it is necessary to describe what probably was an outside brush kitchen situated on a level above the floor of House 8. In a test pit a few feet south of House 4, at a depth of three feet, there appeared a floor bearing a hearth, metate, mano, and several other large rocks. At first it was thought that a house had been encountered, but, upon further tracing the floor, the customary dwelling features were not found. It was evident, after a considerable area had been uncovered, that the floor did not belong to a house. The floor became less distinct in proportion to the distance from the firepit, except to the north where the metate was located, beyond which it was difficult to follow. The area thus defined roughly measured 8 by 10 feet, plaza level lying beyond these bounds. On the west side of the firepit (Figure 11.16B) were

Figure 11.16. Plan of House 8 and brush kitchen: A–A', approximate outline of supposed brush-enclosed kitchen; B, firepit in kitchen; C, stone and clay wind-breaks for firepit; D, large flat rock; E, metate; F, stone slab lining step into vestibule; G, vestibule; H, firepit; I, hole for major roof support; J, holes for lesser roof supports; K, floor groove; L, surface level when house was built; M, surface level when brush kitchen was in use; N, existing surface.

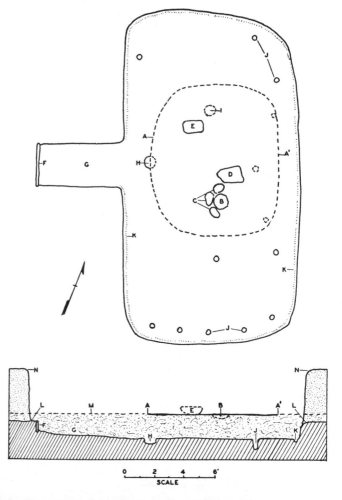

Figure 11.17. The floor of House 8. The metate rests in its original position on a pillar of earth to show the distance between the floors of the brush kitchen and the dwelling. The firepit (*right*) is partly covered with a fallen roof beam.

placed two rocks and a lump of burnt clay as though intended to form a windbreak, and a short distance to the north of the pit was a large flat rock suitable for a seat. The windbreak of the firepit, placed on that side exposed to the prevailing winds, suggested an outside kitchen. Since the floor could be traced approximately in the shape of an oval, as indicated in Figure 11.16, it was further supposed that the area was once enclosed on the sides with brush, similar to those still employed by the Pima Indians (Russell 1908:156–157). The hearth, it should be noted, was unlike those in the houses, in that it did not have a good clay lining and it lacked the bowl form, the sides rising gently to meet the floor. The diameter was somewhat more than one foot, and the depth was four inches.

Brush kitchens seem to be more or less distinctly related to the desert people in the Southwest, both past and present. While the Pueblo people may have prepared much of their food out-of-doors, it is doubtful whether their cooking areas were enclosed in the manner here suggested. It may be argued that the brush kitchen was merely an adaptation to the climate in which the Hohokam found themselves, but the absence of this feature in the later pueblos whose builders invaded the territory occupied by the Hohokam (Gladwin 1928:25, 27) stamps it as a non-Puebloan trait and a characteristic of the desert-dwelling people.

The fact that only red-on-buff sherds were found on this floor removes the possibility of its having been a hearth of the later Puebloan settlement. There does not appear to be any difference between the pottery from this floor and that of House 8 below.

House 8

The floor of House 8 was found about 20 inches below the floor of the cooking area (Figure 11.17), and the sides of the room extended beyond the limits of the latter on all sides. Distinctions between the potsherds gathered in the deposit separating the two floors and those from above the upper floor were not appreciable.

The dimensions were: north-south, 21 feet 6 inches; east-west, 11 feet 8 inches; depth, 15 inches (see Figure 11.16). In all the essential details of construction House 8 was identical with House 1.

On the floor of the southeast corner of the house were found the charred remnants of twilled matting. Its size could not be determined, but it covered several square feet of the floor and may have been used as a sleeping mat.

House 9

In a test pit a few feet south of the entrance of House 3 there were found repeated layers of ash and potsherds which extended below the floor level of House 3 and which ended with the floor of House 9. An attempt was made to segregate the sherds from the various strata, but it was found that the ashy layers were too confused to make this possible. A vertical section in the accumulation of House 9 clearly showed the irregularities of the layers of trash.

House 9 proved to be one of the largest dwellings in the community. Its length was 23 feet 6 inches, width, 13 feet, and depth, 1 foot 6 inches (Figure 11.18). The floor was very irregular and in spots showed silt deposits which were laid down before the house was destroyed. The entry passage was not uncovered, but it was situated in the north wall opposite the firepit which measured 4 inches in depth and 10 inches across. Floor features, as postholes and the marginal groove, were imperfectly shown.

House 10

This dwelling, the northeasternmost of the village, was almost entirely washed away by the wave action of Roosevelt Lake, and it contributed nothing further to the architectural knowledge previously obtained from the other houses. It is advisable, however, to mention all house evidences in order to gain a complete picture of the size of the village.

House 11

Aside from being the largest dwelling in the village, House 11 was also the most fruitful in yielding the structural details of the house itself, and particularly of the elevated floor which was again present. Up to the time of the excavation of this dwelling almost nothing was known of the nature of this raised floor, nor of the reason for its existence. Fortunately, the condition of the house was so good, even though burnt, that considerable information was obtained to shed light upon these questions.

The maximum dimensions of the pit of this dwelling were 14 feet east and west, and 26 feet 6 inches north and south (Figure 11.19). The size of this house and of several others which were nearly as large was one of the surprising features which developed during the excavation of the site. Houses with pits, in Chaco Canyon (Judd 1924:399–413; Roberts 1929), in the Piedra district, southwestern Colorado

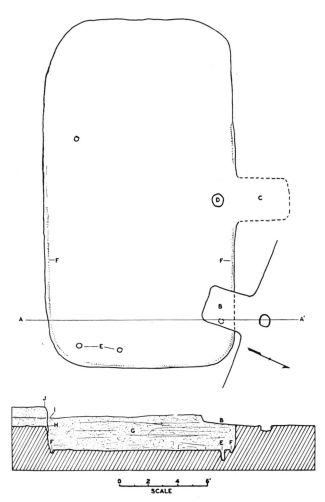

Figure 11.18. Plan of House 9: AA', section through House 9 and vestibule of House 3; B, vestibule of House 3; C, vestibule of House 9; D, firepit; E, holes for lesser roof supports; F, floor groove; G, lenticular debris fill of House 9; H, surface level when house was built; I, surface level when House 3 was built; J, existing surface.

(Roberts 1930), in northeastern Arizona, and pit houses in the vicinity of Flagstaff (Hargrave 1930), seldom approach the size of House 11. The dwellings recently uncovered near Casa Grande by the Van Bergen-Los Angeles Museum Expedition were also smaller than those in Roosevelt 9:6, although the sites, in some other respects, show similarity.

The original depth of the pit of House 11 was 18 inches below the plaza level; due to deposition since occupation, the floor now lies at a maximum of 5 feet 6 inches below the present surface. The arrangement of the floor postholes was essentially the same as that found in previous houses, although it is evident that not all of the holes were located. A new structural feature, however, must be added to those coming from this site. In all other houses it was clear that the sides of the superstructure, that is, the slanting poles which extended down-

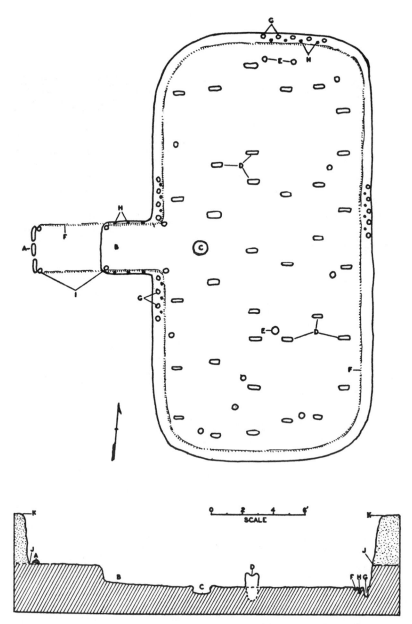

Figure 11.19. Plan of House 11: A, rock and clay sill at end of entrance passage; B, vestibule; C, firepit; D, stone floor supports; E, holes for roof supports; F, floor groove; G, side poles rising from floor to horizontal roof beams; H, small reinforcing poles; I, holes for entrance hood supports; J, surface when house was built; K, existing surface.

Figure 11.20. The charred lower ends of poles which extended from the floor upwards to form the sides of the superstructure of House 11. The trowel rests in the groove which held the ends of the reeds lining the room.

ward from the flat part of the roof, rested upon, or were set into, holes dug into the ground surface about the periphery of the pit; in House 11 it was found that these were planted in the floor at the base of the excavated earthen wall. The charred lower portions of these poles, varying in diameter from 1½ to 3 inches, were in evidence about the edge of the entire room (Figure 11.20). Most of these burnt beam remnants, some being juniper, others apparently willow, were inclined inwards slightly towards the center of the room. The holes into which they were set, averaging 8 inches in depth, could easily be determined. Spaced midway between these side poles and in front of them were burnt ends of smaller rods, (Figure 11.19H), not exceeding 1 inch in width. The only function which can be ascribed to them is that they helped to support and reinforce the reed-work which was set up immediately in front of them.

Figure 11.21. The entrance vestibule of House 11 showing holes for roof supports and relationship to firepit.

The groove which held the reeds, as in the other houses, was approximately 2 inches wide and 2 inches deep. By a careful examination of the burnt ends of the reeds still in position in the groove and in the few places where they extended upwards from 6 to 8 inches above the floor, it was possible to get a clearer idea of the nature of this feature. The reeds completely filled the width of the groove. They were held together by horizontal braces of the same material on both sides, the first being just above the floor, the second about 3 inches higher and the third, the last that could be traced, about 4 inches higher still. It will be seen in the diagram (see Figure 11.19) that the floor groove is located about 9 inches from the earth wall, thus reducing the inside measurements of the dwelling 18 inches each way.

The entrance passage (Figure 11.21) was situated in the center of the west wall, being somewhat shorter than in the other houses. Its length was 3 feet and the width 3 feet 4 inches. The floor in the vestibule sloped gently upward towards the step, reducing the step to a height of 14 inches. Four feet beyond the step were a rock and dirt sill

Figure 11.22. Reverse view of firepit of House 11 with three stone floor supports in view.

and a pair of postholes, indicating the length of the entrance hood. There were two other pairs of postholes in the corners of the vestibule. The reed-work was carried into the latter and out to the end of the hood, thus forming a rather long enclosed passage common to earth lodges. While there was ample evidence of a dirt covering for the roof, none was forthcoming to indicate that the vertical reeds of the entrance were once covered with clay or a coat of plaster. The roof of the entrance cover was probably capped with clay, but this treatment was apparently considered unnecessary for the sides. The low sill at the doorway served to prevent surface water from entering the house pit during rains.

The firepit was unusually well preserved (Figures 11.21 and 11.22). It was formed of puddled clay somewhat in the shape of a jar. The greatest diameter, attained below the floor, was 11 inches and the depth was 5 inches. It position was squarely in front of the entrance. The consistent occurrence of the firepits in this relationship throws doubt upon the presence of a smoke hole in the roof of the lodges.

Figure 11.23. House 11 showing the 35 stone pillars which
supported a platform floor.

The most prominent features of House 11 were the 35 notched
stones imbedded in the clay floor in 6 rows, lengthwise of the room
(Figure 11.23). While these have been noted from other houses, none
were so well formed as were those from House 11 and in none of the
other houses were these stone pillars so numerous. The longest in the
set, when removed from the floor, was 18 inches, having been imbedded to about one-half its length. The notches in the tops were either angular or crescent-shaped (Figure 11.24). The two stones on the
left in Figure 11.24 also show another feature which does not occur
on all stones, namely, the opposed notches in the sides a few inches
below the tops, apparently intended to aid in lashing down the floor
beams. One stone is pointed at the bottom, having been intentionally
made so by scraping with a sharp-edged tool. The average distance of
the upper ends of the stones above the floor when imbedded was 9
inches.

Figure 11.24. Four of the stone floor supports from House 11 removed to show details.

Structural details of the floor supported by the stone pillars were obtainable from a small floor section which fell to the dirt floor below during the fire, without disturbing the relative positions of the several elements. The main beams which rested in the notches of the piles were about 4 inches in diameter. Crosswise upon these, at from 4 to 6 inch intervals, were placed small rods about 1 inch in diameter, upon which, in turn, were placed a layer of brush and grass and a final covering of clay. Naturally, as the raised platform could not be built over the firepit which was in the earth floor below, allowance had to be made for sufficient clearance of the floor beams from the hearth in order that they would not catch fire. The set of five stone pillars nearest the firepit probably mark the approximate limits of the opening of the elevated floor. The dirt floor, from the hearth to these stones, was hard packed and had been much walked upon, whereas, beyond, it became indistinct.

The height of the stone supports plus the thickness of the raised floor, probably 6 inches, brought it nearly to the same level as the outside surface. Thus a paradox seems to be involved in the construction of this house: the floor was excavated below the ground surface only to be built up again. An explanation of this seeming contradiction is found in layers of silt on the earthen floor. During an abnormal flood period of Salt River which inundated the site or due to water draining from the bluffs to the southwest during torrential summer rains, moisture seeped into some of the pits, and floors were raised on stone stilts to make the houses habitable. This is indicated by the unbroken layers of silt which were deposited about the stone supports after they were placed in the floor. Furthermore, the deposition of silt was not all made during one flooding or wet period as several strata darkened by ash and charcoal followed by clean sediment indicate that the house was subject to repeated inundations.

The only other locality in which stones of this kind have been found is the Mimbres Valley, New Mexico. Mr. C. B. Cosgrove has informed the writer that he has found them in debris in clearing rooms, but never imbedded in the floors nor in large quantities.*

Replica of House 11

Upon the complete excavation of House 11, it was believed to be of sufficient interest for a reproduction to be made at Gila Pueblo in order to insure its preservation. This seemed particularly advisable as a future rise of the water in Roosevelt Lake would again submerge the site.

The stone pillars and the firepit were removed from the original structure and set in their relative positions in a pit which had been prepared at Gila Pueblo, exactly duplicating the original. The recon-

---

*The notched stones found in the house floors at Roosevelt 9:6 remained unique and enigmatic for several decades. Haury attributed the presence of the stones to local environmental factors, particularly flooding. Di Peso (1956) later found similar stones at the Palo Parado Site. The use of notched floor stones has been documented at the La Ciudad Site and at other sites in the Salt River Valley. Limited use of these features was also found at Snaketown in the Gila River Valley (Haury 1976). Haury's observation that notched wood could also have been employed for similar purposes suggests that the practice of constructing elevated floors in Hohokam pit houses may have been more common and widespread than suspected. The function of these raised floors, which now appear to date to the Colonial and Sedentary periods, remains unknown.

struction of the roof was based wholly upon the evidences as they were noted in the floor and the sides of the pit. As nearly as possible, the materials that went into the replica were the same as those that were used in the original building, and were obtained from the Tonto Basin not far from Roosevelt 9:6. The framework and its relation to the pit is shown in Figure 11.25; Figure 11.26 indicates the roofing method, and the reconstruction completed is shown in Figure 11.27.

The building of this replica has made real the great danger that must have existed from fire. A spark from an unguarded fire, lodging in the brush of the roof above, would almost instantly burst into a conflagration which would soon be beyond control. No doubt the destruction of some, if not all, of the houses in Roosevelt 9:6 can be attributed to this cause.

House 12

The floor of House 12 lay deeper under the present surface than that of any other house excavated in the village. The maximum depth was 6 feet, while the original pit was only 20 inches in depth. The north-south measurement of this house was 22 feet 6 inches; the east-west dimension was 12 feet 6 inches (Figures 11.28 and 11.29).

In all the essential details of construction House 12 was identical with House 11 with the exception that, where the vestibule joins the room, at either side were found bundles of reeds placed vertically and apparently taking the place of the posts. (For this and other details see Figure 11.30).

Over a large part of the floor, remains of brush and clay of the raised floor were in evidence. The floor of the dwelling was in very poor condition except within a two foot radius of the firepit (Figure 11.31) and in the entrance where it was much worn. The reason for this is obvious, as the raised floor prevented the packing of the underlying earthen floor. Along the east wall in the south end of the dwelling were found the charred remnants of a twilled mat (Figure 11.32; see also Figure 11.57). This had originally covered a part of the raised floor.

House 13 and House 14

These two houses were the westernmost in the village and contributed nothing towards the further knowledge of the site except to increase its size (Figure 11.33).

Figure 11.25. The framework of a reconstruction of House 11.

Figure 11.26. Interior view of House 11 reconstruction showing supposed roof treatment.

Figure 11.27. A view of the replica of House 11 after completion. The south end of the dwelling was left open in order to show structural features. Entrance was gained through the covered passage on the left.

House 15

House 15, located a few feet south of House 14, must be considered as foreign to the study of Roosevelt 9:6. This house was a rectangular, square-cornered, surface structure built of stone masonry, measuring 7 by 10 feet (Figure 11.34). It was, undoubtedly, an outlier from the stone pueblo situated about 100 feet east of the Hohokam village as indicated by their similarity in pottery and the dissimilarity between sherds from the stone house and those from the houses with pits.

Summary and Discussion of Architecture

From the foregoing description it will be seen that no single house gave all the details necessary for complete reconstruction; but, as all were approximately the same, those features lacking in one can be supplied from another to form a composite picture of the type of dwelling. Of such elements as the main and secondary roof support posts, the slanting side poles, and the reed-work about the margins of the rooms, there was sufficient evidence. But overhead features, such

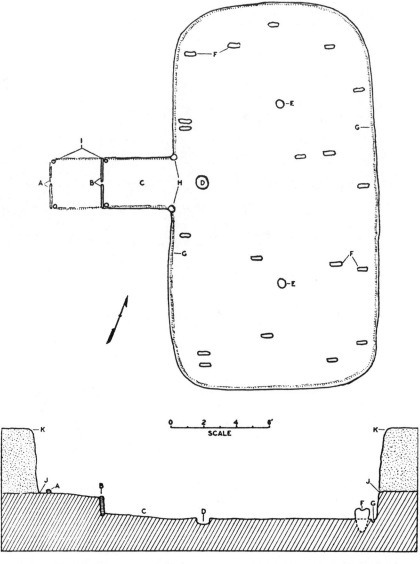

Figure 11.28. Plan of House 12: A, rock and clay sill at end of entrance; B, stone slabs lining steps into vestibule; C, vestibule; D, firepit; E, holes for major roof supports; F, stone floor supports; G, floor groove; H, bundles of vertical reeds substituted for posts; I, holes for entrance hood supports; J, surface when house was built; K, existing surface.

Figure 11.29. House 12 with entrance and firepit on left side.

Figure 11.30. A reconstruction showing details of the entrance hood and of the raised floor in House 12: A, sill at entrance; B, slab step-lining; C, vestibule; D, firepit; E, supports for entrance hood; F, main cross beams of hood; G, brush cover; H, reed bundles substituted for posts; I, reed-lining of room; J, notched stone floor support; K, large beams resting on notched stone; L, light cross-poles; M, brush; N, clay.

Figure 11.31. This picture shows the worn floor about the firepit of House 12 which was not covered with the supported floor. Arrow indicates direction of entrance.

Figure 11.32. The vertical black marks are the charred remains of reeds which lined House 12. On the floor may be seen a small fragment of charred twilled matting (*lower right*).

Figure 11.33. House 13. Erosion had practically obliterated the traces of this former pit dwelling.

Figure 11.34. Plan of House 15: AA′, section through firepit and floor hole; B, firepit; C, floor hole; D, posthole; E, stone masonry; F, surface level when house was built; G, existing surface.

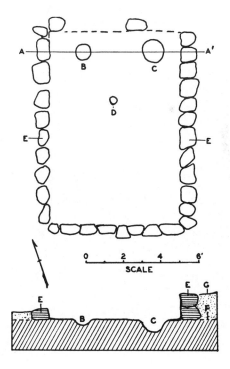

247

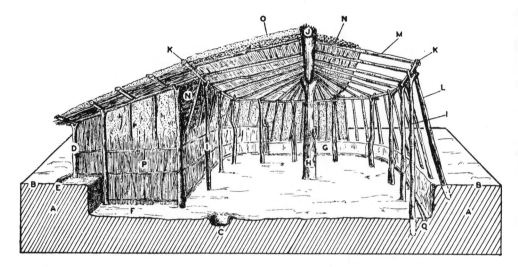

Figure 11.35. Postulated reconstruction of the type of earth lodge represented at Roosevelt 9:6: A, native soil; B, surface level; C, firepit; D, entrance; E, sill; F, vestibule; G, side of excavated pit; H, one of two major roof supports; I, small roof supports; J, ridge-pole; K, small horizontal beams placed on lesser roof supports; L, side poles; M, roof beams; N, brush covering roof and sides; O, clay; P, reed-lining; Q, floor groove which engaged ends of reeds.

as the height and the pitch of the roof, the exact method of placing and the frequency of the roof poles, the height to which reed-work was carried, and the exact nature of the outer covering must necessarily remain conjectural. However, as limitations in the mode of roof construction are indicated by the type of superstructure, there is little fear of being far in error. On these grounds a tentative reconstruction of the house type as seen in Roosevelt 9:6 has been drawn (Figure 11.35) as a supplement to the replica of House 11 already shown (see Figures 11.25, 11.26, and 11.27). The diagram is self-explanatory but emphasis should be placed upon those features which persistently occur, viz.: the floor holes into which were set the primary and secondary roof supports, the poles bearing the hood over the entry, and the marginal groove for the reed-work lining of the rooms. The elevated floor shown to be present in over one-half of the houses uncovered is not indicated, as a consideration of that feature has already been given elsewhere.

The Hohokam houses at Roosevelt 9:6 may be briefly characterized as earth lodges having shallow rectangular but round-cornered pits which were covered with a superstructure of poles, brush and clay. The roof was formed of a central ridge pole and rectangular plate, which carried the beams of the roof proper. The sides were formed by slanting poles extending from the edge of the pit to the plate. Ingress was gained by means of a side entrance leading from the plaza down a single step into the vestibule, a small passage extending out from the room placed without regard to direction. This feature was covered by a projection of the roof to which vertical sides were added and which was made to extend beyond the outer end of the vestibule to form a hood. The firepit was invariably placed immediately opposite the entrance passage. The presence or absence of smokeholes is conjectural. Plaster was nowhere found to have been used.

The persistence with which the several house elements occur is worthy of note as it points strongly to an inheritance from a well-established antecedent form which, as yet, has not been found. Explorations during the last ten years have brought to light numerous instances of semi-subterranean houses scattered over the Southwest. The indications are that, preceding the adobe-stone-house phase of architecture, there was a period of pit dwellings, those in the San Juan presumably developing from the Basketmaker storage cists, but those in the desert regions being without any known introductory forms. If the chronological correspondence of the Colonial Hohokam period with the Basketmaker-Puebloan development is correct, an outside source must be sought for the origin of the Hohokam house, as it was not directly developed from the pit dwellings of the San Juan, though fundamentally the two forms may be related. There is a growing tendency to regard the New World pit house as a derivative of Old World forerunners. Jochelson (1907) has pointed out certain existing connections between the two forms; more recently, the matter has been brought nearer home by Roberts (1929:85–87), who has drawn attention to similarities between houses uncovered by him in Shabik'eshchee Village, Chaco Canyon, with those used by certain Palae-Asiatic peoples. To this can be added a second parallel found between houses of the Hohokam from Roosevelt 9:6 and those excavated by Jochelson (1928:44–48) in Kamchatka. The shape, the presence of an entrance vestibule, and the position of the firepit of the Kamchatka houses are duplicated in those from the Tonto Basin Village. In the former, the vestibule is sometimes placed at the end of the pit rather than at the side, but the similarity of the entrance passage together with the other traits may eventually be shown to have a collateral relationship. Unfortunately, Jochelson does not report upon the details of the superstructure.

Based upon past work in villages of the Hohokam, a tentative evolution of house types can be drawn. The oldest house of the series, providing that the diagnostics for chronological determination be accepted, is that form represented by the dwellings in Roosevelt 9:6. Close parallels of these are seen in the habitations uncovered at the Grewe Site near Casa Grande by the Van Bergen-Los Angeles Museum Expedition, although the latter are somewhat smaller in average size, and the vestibules less conspicuous. The Grewe Site is typical of the Colonial-Sedentary phase, but, because of certain attributes which were present there and lacking in Roosevelt 9:6, the latter is regarded as the older, or better said, was not occupied as late as the Grewe Site. The chief characteristic of the Colonial house and a point in which it is distinguishable from all other southwestern pit dwellings, is the ridge pole of the roof held in horizontal position by two beams set in the end centers of the pit.

Houses of the Sedentary phase show a marked kinship with the former, although certain transitions have taken place. The Tanque Verde Site,* which is representative of this phase, produced houses of two forms: (a) those with rectangular pits, each forming a distinct unit of the community, and (b) rectangular, surface, adobe-walled dwellings which were contiguous, and postdated the former. The position of the entrance and the firepit in the first-type dwelling conform to those of Roosevelt 9:6, although there was no vestibule, as steps led directly out of the room. The ridge-pole type of superstructure was supplanted by a roof supported by four posts placed near the corners of the pit and to which slanting sides were added. Superimposed upon several Tanque Verde pits were found the rectangular surface rooms constructed of adobe and occasional rocks. The occupants of both house forms left behind them red-on-buff pottery typical of the Sedentary phase. The apparent rapid transition from an individual pit dwelling to contiguous, surface, adobe houses in this stage may be accounted for by the introduction of an external influence—by contact with the pueblo-building people who, in this case, were the nearest neighbors using this type of architecture.

---

*Located about 23 miles east of Tucson, Arizona, at the southern foot of the Tanque Verde Mountains, and partially excavated by the University of Arizona. The writer participated in the operation and reported upon it in "The Succession of House Types in the Pueblo Areas," MS, master's thesis, University of Arizona, Tucson, 1928.

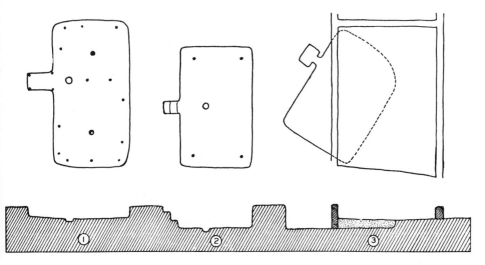

Figure 11.36. Composite diagram showing probable succession of early Hohokam houses: 1, typical house of Colonial phase represented in Roosevelt 9:6; 2, Sedentary pit house as shown in the Tanque Verde Village; 3, superposition of an adobe-walled surface house over a subsurface house, both of the Sedentary phase, Tanque Verde Village.

The house sequence from the Colonial into the Sedentary periods is shown diagramatically in Figure 11.36. Number 1 exemplifies the typical Colonial house from Roosevelt 9:6; Number 2, the Sedentary form from Tanque Verde; and Number 3, a similar house with an antechamber underlying a surface room, also found in Tanque Verde.

EXTERIOR REMAINS

Outdoor Firepits

Firepits not in houses fall into three classes according to size: (a) small, clay-lined, well-formed pits not exceeding one foot in diameter, usually situated near a house. These correspond with those situated in the houses and apparently were used in outdoor cooking. (b) Pits of the second group are usually larger than the first, although they seldom exceed 2 feet in diameter. They are shallow, not well made, and usually contain rocks which have been cracked and broken by heat. One of these may be seen in House 4 (see Figure 11.13), where it occurred in a later level of occupation than that represented by the dwelling in which it was located. (c) Pits of the third type are by far the most interesting because of their unusually large size and of their probable function. A single large pit was found in Roosevelt 9:6, but several have been unearthed near Casa Grande by the Van Bergen–Los Angeles Museum Expedition in a site of approximately the same cultural horizon, which seems to link this trait definitely with the Hohokam.

The pit under present consideration was located about thirty feet north of House 6 on the west side of a small gully (see Figure 11.3). A small area of burnt rock was the only clue to its presence. This hearth was composed of two parts: (a) an inner pit less than two feet deep and four feet in diameter having a concave bottom, and (b) a large flaring rim extending upwards and outwards from the inner pit, bringing the total depth to five feet and the diameter to eleven feet. The east side of the rim had been entirely washed away. The pit was lined with clay from two to three inches thick, burnt hard on the rim portion and excessively blackened by a penetration of a carbonaceous substance. In the bottom of the inner bowl were three large water-worn boulders set into the clay apparently to form a tripod rest.

The fill which hid the pit from view was composed first of a thin layer of top soil containing few rocks (Figure 11.37); next followed a three-foot layer of burnt rocks ranging in size from large fragments of metates to pieces the size of walnuts. These rocks all showed the effects of terrific heat, some being vitreous, while metate fragments were heat-cracked and warped out of shape. Below the burnt rocks and in the inner bowl were found wood ashes, some charcoal, and black soil.

Much speculation has arisen concerning the possible use of these large pits, since no concrete evidence has been found definitely to settle that problem. Two main hypotheses have been advanced: the first holding that they were cremation pits; the second, that they were used in connection with the preparation of some kind of food.

In support of the first theory is the fact that these pits have only been found in sites of the Hohokam—a people who practised cremation and in whose sites no other evidence of the burning process has been found. Further, the Maricopa Indians, who have been observed to cremate in recent times, constructed a large pit 4 to 5 feet deep in which the body was burned or over which a platform was built which fell during the fire into the pit. It also seems that the large flaring rim to the Roosevelt 9:6 pit would add to the difficulty of approaching and retrieving food stuffs left there to roast.

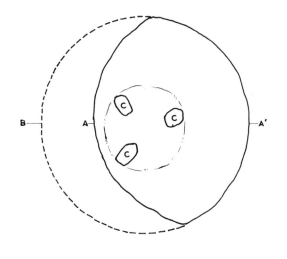

Figure 11.37. Plan and section of large outside firepit. AA', present outline of pit; BA', probable former outline; C, stones forming a rest in inner pit; D, clay lining of pit; E, ashes; F, burnt rock; G, top soil; H, existing surface.

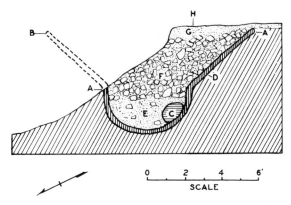

SCALE

On the other hand the belief that the pits were related to a food preparing custom is strengthened by the total absence of burnt human bone in the pits so far excavated; by the invariable presence of burnt rocks which it seems difficult to connect with an attempt to consume flesh and bone; by the fact that these rocks are found in the pit, whereas it would be necessary to remove them in order to collect all fragments of human bone after the final crematory fire; and, amongst the Pima and Papago, there are survivals of the pits in use today in the roasting of the cholla fruit. Further evidence is needed to form satisfactory conclusions regarding the use of these pits and future excavation of any that may be found should be done with the utmost care.

Refuse Mounds

Repeated tests in search for houses in the occupational area in Roosevelt 9:6 invariably produced debris which had accumulated over the common plaza level. This suggests that the Hohokam, in this site, followed a rather indiscriminate manner of disposing of the camp refuse. It also accounts for the shallowness and the smallness of the two trash mounds connected with the village. The mounds were close together in the southern part of the area and of about equal size. In efforts to make stratigraphic tests in the deepest parts of these mounds, native soil was encountered at from 12 to 18 inches, thus providing little material for stratigraphic studies.

MATERIAL CULTURE

When considering the minor antiquities of Roosevelt 9:6, it should be borne in mind that the materials here listed do not comprise the entire category of objects made by the occupants of the village. Only those lasting artifacts, as pottery, stone, bone, and shell, can be described. A discussion of the more perishable objects as textiles, basketry, and wooden implements must await a time when they are found preserved under more favorable circumstances. Their presence, however, is indicated from time to time by impressions left in clay or by charred remnants, but at best these do not give much information.

Food

The most important food of the Hohokam was probably corn, although evidence to support this is chiefly based on the presence of milling stones and the location of the village with respect to arable land. Direct evidence, however, was found in fragments of charred corn cobs, one trodden into the floor of House 9 and another from the floor of House 8. The cobs were too incomplete to permit a counting of the number of rows of kernels.

Animal bones were few in the rooms and in the trash mounds.

Pottery

The pottery-making industry of the Hohokam has only recently taken on an important aspect in the study of southwestern ceramic development. It has, in the past, been subordinated to a minor position, first, because red-on-buff pottery as made by the Hohokam was practically absent from museum shelves, and secondly, because it was regarded as a variation of a Puebloan subculture. Evidence is rapidly accumulating to show that, in addition to the true Pueblo pottery which is considered to be an indigenous product, there is also present in southern Arizona a second, non-Puebloan pottery which, in some respects, assumes a role of greater importance than that of the northern areas.

To appreciate fully the significance of red-on-buff pottery, particularly that of the Colonial period, emphasis must be placed upon the technological difference which separates it and Pueblo pottery. A fundamental difference in the method of making earthen vessels as practised by two peoples can only mean a lack of relationship. The first fired pottery from the north, dating from late Basketmaker times, was made by a process of moulding. Later, the technique was improved by the development of the coiling process, which became the dominant and characteristic fashion of making earthenware vessels. The earmarks of this method are seen in the culinary jars and pots on which the coils were not obliterated on the outside.

Red-on-buff vessels, with their associated plain ware, on the contrary, show that a paddle and anvil method was used. This is particularly noticeable in larger jars, the interiors of which were not smoothed after being completed. The method is clearly shown on vessel interiors by concave depressions which are the impressions of the anvil or stone where it was held to receive the impact of the paddle applied against the vessel wall from the outside. As further evidence, anvils have been found, rounded stones of specialized form as described herein under the heading of stone artifacts. Paddles, it may be assumed, were made of wood in accordance with the custom among the Pima and Papago who use this method at the present time; their absence at the site being explained by the perishable quality of the material.

Two main groups of pottery were manufactured by the occupants of Roosevelt 9:6. They are: plain ware and a ware carrying a red decoration on a buff background. Plain ware greatly outnumbers the decorated variety as it was used for cooking, while painted pottery is apparently of the nonculinary group.

Before taking up the plain ware in detail certain points of unity can be stressed. The color of the paste varies from a brick red through browns and greys to nearly black. Not infrequently all these shades are found in the same vessel due to unequal firing or to its later use over fire, but in many cases the vessels have a uniform color. Firing clouds, caused by permitting the vessels to come into contact with the fuel during the firing process, are common, and their haphazard occurrence would show them to be accidental rather than intentional. The tempering material of the paste is coarse, angular and abundant.

The coarseness of the temper seems to depend somewhat upon the size of the vessel, as the large storage jars often have fragments which are nearly as large as the vessel walls are thick. It is surprising that the adhesiveness of the clay was not entirely destroyed by the quantity of the temper as seen in some of the vessels. The tempering material itself is normally a mixture of quartz, feldspar and mica. The mica content in many cases appears to have been derived from a micaceous schist, and was probably not added as pure mica. Mica schist, however, lacks feldspar, which introduces the possibility that the latter was added as a separate ingredient. On the other hand, it is possible that all ingredients were obtained by pulverizing a certain form of granite whose mineral constituents are feldspar, quartz and mica. The minute membranes of mica, freed from the matrix, form the most conspicuous surface feature of plain ware. Iron pyrites or "fool's gold" does not commonly occur.

Plain ware containers do not show a slip; they were apparently smoothed with the hand, thus bringing the finer clay particles and small mica plates to the surface and obscuring the coarser material. The striae of the polishing stone are broad and indiscriminate except for their direction which apparently depended upon the vessel shape. On bowls, the polishing marks are parallel to the rim, or horizontal; on jars, they are vertical, or at right angles to the rim. The striations are seldom if ever brought down to cover the bottom of vessels. In the plain ware of this stage is seen the prototype of Gila Red ware (Gladwin and Gladwin 1930c) of later horizons with its singular development in the polishing marks. Jar interiors show no modification after the vessels were formed, as the anvil imprints in most cases are clearly visible.

PLAIN WARE VESSEL FORMS*

Plain ware vessel shapes can be broadly divided into three groups: bowls, jars, scoops. A great diversity of forms cannot be claimed, although there are modifications within the groups.

The largest bowls of the first group belong to that class referred to as shallow bowls (Figure 11.38A). These were found only in fragmentary form in Roosevelt 9:6, and, judging from the amount of sherds, they were not particularly abundant.

---

*Description of vessel forms is based on the "Glossary of Vessel Forms," submitted by Mr. Arthur Woodward and adapted at the conference at Gila Pueblo, April 1931.

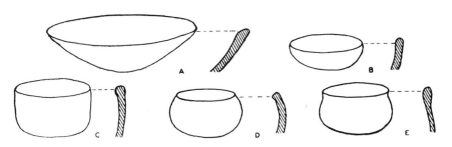

Figure 11.38. Plain ware bowl shapes.

Straight-sided bowls (Figure 11.38C) are not common. Lips are rounded and may be thickened on the inside of the vessels. The diameter of the largest bowl of this form is 6 inches.

Incurved bowls (Figure 11.38D) are abundant. Diameters range mostly between 6 to 8 inches and the depths are equal to about one-half the diameter. This vessel form shades almost imperceptibly into jars.

Recurved bowls (Figure 11.38E) are not plentiful, only one having been found. The recurve of the rim is slight and the vessel wall shows a moderate thickening at the lip.

Globular jars having short necks and slightly outcurving rims (Figure 11.39A) are the commonest variety and range widely in size from 6-inch cooking jars to storage vessels up to 25 inches in diameter.

On one smaller jar of this class was found the only attempt to place handles on a vessel. On opposing sides just below the rim are paired vertical protuberances about one inch apart. Each of the projections shows broken surfaces indicating that clay loops or some other feature have been broken away.

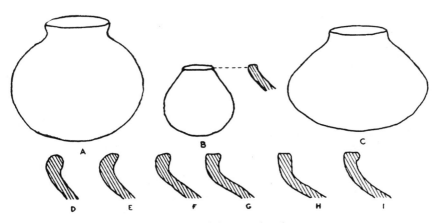

Figure 11.39. Plain ware jar shapes.

The necks of the large jars seldom extend above the body more than one inch, and the openings generally equal about one-half the diameter. Lip treatments vary as indicated in Figure 11.39D to I.

Egg-shaped jars are small vessels with full, rounded under-bodies and high, sloping upper-bodies. The rims are low and direct, ending in a flat lip (Figure 11.39B). Measurements of a typical specimen are: diameter, 6 inches; height, 5 inches; diameter of opening, 3½ inches.

Semi-globular jars are represented by fragments only (Figure 11.39C).

Scoops are oval shaped, the dipping and handle ends rising higher than the sides, thus forming a concave top. The dipping end is rounded and often expanded, while the end held in the hand usually tapers, sometimes to a blunt point (Figure 11.40A).

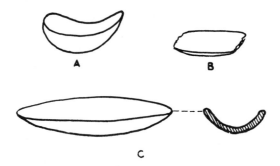

Figure 11.40. Plain ware scoops.

A single large flat scoop about 6 inches long is contained in the collection (Figure 11.40B). It is oval shaped, the ends slightly battered and showing much use.

Not infrequently scoops were fashioned from large jar sherds, preferably those from the sides where the shoulders make the sharpest bend. One scoop of this type is 10¼ inches long, 4¾ inches wide, and 1½ inches deep (Figure 11.40C).

Concluding the description of plain ware from Roosevelt 9:6 it may be said that no aberrant forms were found; the few standard shapes that existed appear to have been rigidly copied.

RED-ON-BUFF WARE

Decoration consists of painted designs and incising. Models and figures, such as were found by the Van Bergen–Los Angeles Museum Expedition near Casa Grande, are not represented.

The base clay of the red-on-buff ware shades from a brick red to a lighter color except where stained by improper firing. Angular particles of quartz, feldspar and mica comprise the temper, but smaller quantities were added in painted ware than in plain ware and the ingredients were ground finer. In most cases the clay was thoroughly fired, as the vessel walls show little variation in color from inside to outside.

Shaping of the painted vessels was accomplished in the same manner as described for the plain ware: by the aid of concentric coils and the paddle and anvil. It is doubtful whether the rubbing stone was used on painted ware; if so, it was applied prior to the application of the slip which completely hid the polishing striations.

The slip is very thin, being apparently a light clay wash. Its color is cream to buff, seldom marred by firing clouds but often showing tiny flecks of mica. Faint and minute striations on the surface, such as would be left by the strokes of the fingers, suggest that the liquid was applied with the hand. On bowls, both inner and outer surfaces were treated; the entire outer surface of jars was covered as well as the inside of the neck. The thinness of the wash and the fact that the polisher was not used resulted in a rather soft coating which readily took the pigment of the design, but, because of its softness, the designs are often partly obliterated.

The red-brown paint of this ware is basically iron. The remarkable feature about it is the lack of variation in color. Vessel after vessel shows practically the same shade, unless changed by a secondary firing, and the comparison can be carried to vessels coming from widely separated sites. This striking uniformity of color can only be explained by standardized constituents, mixed according to a definite formula.

Incising on the pottery from Roosevelt 9:6 is confined to painted bowl exteriors. This type of ornamentation usually starts with a spiral on the outside bottom of the bowl and is continued upwards to the rim. Often, after a few turns of the spiral were made, the continuity was broken but the effect continued by making a series of quick strokes

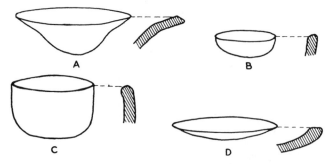

Figure 11.41. Bowl forms in red-on-buff pottery.

parallel to the rim over about one-quarter of the surface. The position of the bowl was then shifted and the strokes repeated, but not necessarily joining those of the previous operation, until the entire surface was thus treated. Several sherds, however, indicate a greater care in the incised treatment, as the lines are deeply cut and carefully spaced. Painted decoration was often applied over the incised area.*

DECORATED (RED-ON-BUFF) VESSEL FORMS

Flare-rimmed bowls (Figure 11.41A) range in diameter from 4 to 13 inches, but fragments of several were found that must have been even larger. This type of bowl, as remarked by Kidder (1924:110–111) has no counterpart anywhere in pre-Spanish southwestern pottery. It is without doubt one of the most reliable determinants of the Colonial period. The chief decoration is on the inside (Figure 11.42A) consisting usually of an all-over pattern. Exteriors (Figure 11.42B) may be treated with the incising already described and with painted lines which trail from the rim towards the center, without converging, in an oblique curve, thus giving the effect of a spiral (Gladwin and Gladwin 1929a).

Bowls also occur which are hemispherical in form and quite shallow (Figure 11.41B). Those in the collection are small, measuring up to 6 inches in diameter, and they are decorated in the manner described for the flaring bowls, both inside and out. The lips are rounded or trimmed in the characteristic pie-crust fashion.

---

*The incising of decorated vessel exteriors is found on Hohokam pottery from the Pioneer and Colonial periods, but, apparently, it was de-emphasized during the Colonial period and was generally absent by the Santa Cruz phase (A.D. 700 to A.D. 900). The presence of incised pottery at Roosevelt 9:6 may indicate that a portion of the occupation could date to the Gila Butte phase (A.D. 550 to A.D. 700), a phase unrecognized at the time of excavation.

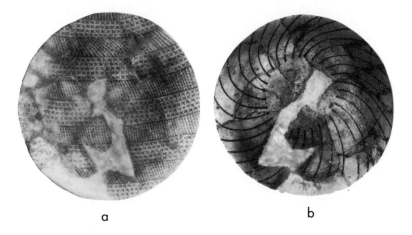

a   b

Figure 11.42. Decoration of a flaring rim, red-on-buff bowl (Diameter 13 inches): A, Inside decoration; B, Exterior decoration.

Two straight-sided bowls were recovered during the present operation. The larger of the two measures 7 inches in diameter and 4½ inches in depth (Figure 11.41C). Decoration is on the exterior surface, consisting of four horizontal bands of oblique hatching (see Figure 11.47A). The inner surface shows the anvil marks left during the process of manufacture but bears no painted decoration. The smaller is 3¾ inches in width and 1¼ inches in depth. Decoration is again on the outside in the form of a horizontal band (see Figure 11.47B).

Shallow plates also found in Colonial sites, grade into true bowl forms. A single plate was recovered in Roosevelt 9:6, measuring 8¾ inches in width and 1½ inches in depth (Figure 11.41D). The decoration, both inside and out, resembles that found on flare-rimmed bowls.

Incurved bowls (Figure 11.43A) are small, not exceeding 6 inches in diameter, and appear to be comparatively common.

Recurved jars are represented in the collection of small jars; one with a spherical body elongated vertically has a rather large unrestricted mouth (Figure 11.43B).

Semi-globular jars are the more prevalent forms; these have vertically compressed bodies with large flaring rims as in Figure 11.43C, or with smaller openings and less conspicuous rims as in Figure 11.43D. In the specimens pictured in Figure 11.44 the compression of the bodies has been carried to an extreme.

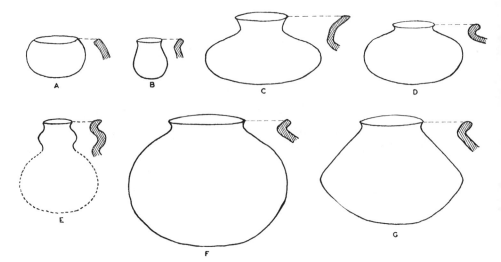

Figure 11.43. Red-on-buff jar shapes.

Figure 11.44. Red-on-buff jars from Roosevelt 9:6. 1, diameter 7.25 inches; height 5 inches; 2, diameter 7.75 inches; height 4.50 inches.

Gourd-shaped jars are represented by the single rim sherd of a vessel with an expanded neck shown in Figure 11.43E. The reconstruction of the lower part is based upon several specimens of similar forms found in Hohokam sites.

The large painted jars, used perhaps to store water or food, sometimes reach a diameter of 20 inches. While no complete ones were found, their shapes can be determined from large sherds.

Figure 11.45. Rectangular, flat-bottomed vessels from Colonial Hohokam sites: *upper figure*, Roosevelt 9:6, length 9 inches; *lower figure*, the Grewe Site, length 7 inches.

a

b

Globular jars consist of nearly spherical vessels which have low necks and out-curving rims (Figure 11.43F). In the second form, the bottoms are somewhat flattened and bend back at the maximum diameter in a sharp curve to form the straight and steeply rising sides. At the mouth, the sides are turned vertically or outwardly to form a very low rim (Figure 11.43G).

Of the large jars it may be said that the diameters exceed the heights practically without exception. The Gila shoulder, a sharp angle formed by the junction of the upper with the lower part, usually below the vertical center of the vessel, was not found in painted jars. The sharp returning of the rims is a feature common to nearly all jars.

A single painted scoop came from Roosevelt 9:6. Its form is practically the same as the plain ware scoops except that the sides are not so pronouncedly concave. Decoration is confined to the interior.

Rectangular vessels as shown in Figure 11.45 are examples of a type in spite of the eccentricity of form. The upper vessel, found in a cremation at Roosevelt 9:6, is duplicated by the lower one, found at the Grewe Site by the Van Bergen–Los Angeles Museum Expedition.*

---

*This specimen was contained in a collection of pottery presented to Gila Pueblo by the Los Angeles Museum.

On the Roosevelt specimen the bottom is entirely flat and the sides are vertical, bearing on the outside a continuous series of interlocking scrolls in red paint. Its length is 9 inches, width 4⅞ inches, and depth 1¼ inches.

DESIGN TREATMENT OF PAINTED POTTERY

Concerning the designs of red-on-buff pottery, Dr. Kidder (1924: 111) has said that "they represent the impressionist school in ancient Southwestern art, and break very radically from the rigid formality that in general characterizes it." The treatment of this ware has thus been considered as a departure from the normal development of Puebloan pottery; it should, however, be looked upon as something quite apart and independent. Rather than being a departure, it was a distinct entity, lacking affinity with that which was being evolved in the area to the north.

As previously mentioned, the patterns of the flare-rimmed bowls were applied to the interior surfaces. The field of decoration completely covers the inside without leaving any unpainted zones. Diversity, however, is noted in the division of the decorative area. The several treatments may be grouped as follows: parallel divisions, concentric circles and spirals, quadrate and fold, all over.

The first of these treatments is adequately depicted by the bowl in Figure 11.43 and by Figure 11.46A. This form seems to be the most elemental in the series, certainly it took less judgment than the equating of the decorative area of the following methods.

The style occurring with greatest frequency is the quadrate division of the field. In this the field was either divided into quadruplicate sectors (Figure 11.46B and C) or the design was based on a square in the center of the bowl, of which each side was extended in one direction to the rim (Figure 11.46D).

Next follows a treatment in which small repeated elements were arranged in concentric circles, filling the area from the rim to the center. The example illustrated in Figure 11.46E is reconstructed from a large sherd in which the center is not shown, hence the incompleteness of the pattern. In Figure 11.46F, the same principle has been applied but a more delicate adjustment has been attained by making the elements smaller, placing them closely together and obliquely to the rim.

Two examples of the more involved type of pattern are shown in Figure 11.46G and H. In the former, a star-shaped effect is produced by straight and wavy lines pivoting about a "sunburst" center and the

Figure 11.46. Design treatments on flaring bowl interiors.

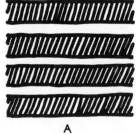

Figure 11.47. Designs from straight-sided bowl exteriors.

A

B

interstices between the many points are filled in with a conventional use of the scroll. The bowl on which this design is found measured 12½ inches in diameter. Figure 11.46H is probably the most complicated of the entire series. The motive is the interlocking scroll, but it is combined in a form which is difficult to duplicate. The dotted line in the center indicates the loss of the design due to the fact that the bottom sherds of the bowl were not recovered.

In all the foregoing examples it will be seen that an unbroken line at the rim was used only twice, while all the others show breaks, the number apparently depending upon the character of the pattern. Another common form is illustrated in Figure 11.47B, in which the rim was embellished with short oblique lines. Thus it may be said that a standard rim decoration is lacking.

Figure 11.48. Designs on small red-on-buff jars.

A

B

The hemispherical bowls and the plates are treated in the manner described above for the flaring bowls. Straight-sided bowls, however, are ornamented on the exterior only. Patterns on the two bowls of this type which were found are reproduced in Figure 11.47. The hatching (A) occurred in four horizontal bands on the larger bowl; the interlocking elements (B) in a single zone which covered the entire side of the smaller vessel.

Decorative treatments on small jars may be of two forms: (a) a single broad horizontal band extending from the neck to below the greatest diameter (Figure 11.48A and B), leaving an unpainted area on the bottom; (b) narrow horizontal bands of repeated small elements usually alternated with bands of oblique hatching (see Figure 11.44). This latter form is very characteristic of the Colonial Red-on-buff wherever found.

Large jars, judging from the sherds, are also covered with patterns from the returned rim to below the maximum diameter. The decoration invariably begins with a wavy line around the neck to which are appended short oblique lines to form what has been called a fringe (Figure 11.49A). This may then be followed by a continuous stream of life forms, either human or animal (Figure 11.49B and C), completely around the vessel, or by broader zones which are treated in a variety of ways (Figure 11.49D, E, and F). Where the jar rims are decidedly flaring, a fringe is often on the inside, beginning at the lip.

Figure 11.49. Forms of decorations on large red-on-buff jars.

The foregoing description of designs is based wholly upon pottery from Roosevelt 9:6, and it is presented with the hope that sooner or later diagnostics will be found which can be utilized either in segregating local types or determining design sequences in pottery of the Colonial period.

A beginning towards the building up of a series of criteria for distinctions within the culture is seen in the relative numbers of painted bowls and jars. It has been suspected by Mr. Gladwin from surface sherd analyses that there was a time in the Colonial period when decorated jars were few and bowls abundant. With the lapse of time, a stage was reached when jars were practically as abundant as bowls. About this latter stage there remained little doubt, but the former needed confirmation which the excavations at Roosevelt 9:6 provided.

The superposition of one house over another and the presence of firepits and plaza levels over abandoned houses, makes it possible to place all but three of the dwellings as either early or late in the occupation of the village. By analyzing the sherds from each house on a percentage basis, the frequency of decorated bowl and jar sherds becomes evident. It can be shown that the fill in the oldest houses contained a higher proportion of painted bowl fragments and fewer jar sherds than the houses of later date. Following is the list of oldest houses giving the percentages of decorated bowl and jar sherds of the entire content, plain ware fragments making up the balance:

House 2	4% bowls	2% jars
House 4	13% bowls	2% jars
House 8	1% bowls	0% jars
House 9 (floor)	16% bowls	4% jars
House 11 (floor)	10% bowls	4% jars

In the above instances the jar percentages are out-numbered on an average of 4 to 1. The case is further strengthened by an examination of the proportions in the houses known to be late:

House 3	3% bowls	5% jars
Brush kitchen above House 8	1% bowls	0% jars
House 11 (upper level)	4% bowls	4% jars

The increase of jars is thus shown in House 3 and the upper level of House 11. The percentage from the upper level of House 8 remained constant with the figures given for the floor of that house. Houses which could not be definitely identified as early or late give the following percentages:

House	1	15% bowls	4% jars
House	5	5% bowls	0% jars
House	7	3% bowls	3% jars

By applying the above criterion it would seem that Houses 1 and 5 were earlier than House 7. It should be possible to carry this further to individual ruins in any attempt to define the minor changes of a given phase of development.

In addition to the plain and decorated ware from Roosevelt 9:6 a few sherds of unpainted bowls with smudged interiors and several with black burnished interiors were also found. On technical grounds these wares cannot be considered as intrusive, but rather as early expressions of a technique, the burnishing of bowl interiors, which was to reach its culmination in a later stage.

Potsherds that can be regarded as intrusive in Roosevelt are all of the black-on-white genus, but they are readily classifiable into two groups. The first of these are believed to have been scattered over the red-on-buff site by people who built the stone village east of Roosevelt 9:6, who probably were not aware of the existence of demolished semi-subterranean houses below their very feet. Red-on-buff sherds do not occur in the trash of the Pueblo and no black-on-white sherds of the Pueblo horizon have been found in the rubbish of the Hohokam village. Thus the relationship of the pottery to the Hohokam wares is purely accidental in that it arrived long after the pit-house village was abandoned.

The second class of black-on-white sherds (Figure 11.50) is recognized as of greater importance because of their direct association with red-on-buff pottery. It is believed that the black-on-white vessels represented by these fragments reached the village during its occupation and that contact had therefore been established with the northern culture. The black-on-white sherds are readily identified as of Basketmaker III and Pueblo I origin, and they may be looked upon as indicants to show that the above stages and the Colonial period of the Hohokam were broadly coeval.

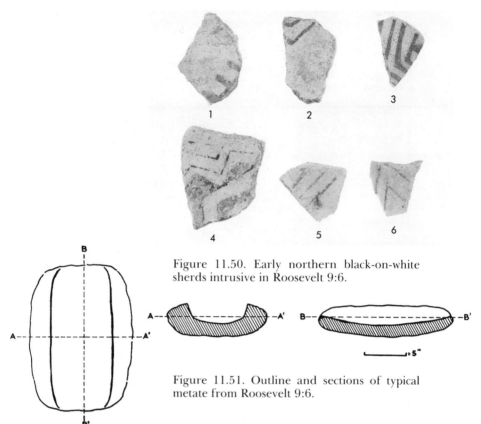

Figure 11.50. Early northern black-on-white sherds intrusive in Roosevelt 9:6.

Figure 11.51. Outline and sections of typical metate from Roosevelt 9:6.

Objects of Stone, Bone, and Shell

Next to pottery, stone artifacts were the most prevalent remains found in Roosevelt 9:6. Milling stones and hammerstones are abundantly represented in the collection and appear to be more or less generalized as to types. Specialization in the stone culture is noted mainly in the so-called slate tablet or paint palette which may be considered as a specialized trait of the Hohokam culture in stone work. Chipped implements are few but of good workmanship.

METATES AND MANOS

Only one complete metate was recovered during the entire operation, although fragments were sufficiently common to permit a description of the type. Suitable river boulders of granite were selected as the raw material. On the flattest surface of these the grinding groove, extending the full length of the stone, was started (Figure 11.51). It is deepest in the center and curves upwards at the ends (section BB', Figure 11.51). Section AA' through the short dimension shows a concave trough. Neither the complete specimen nor the discards show any evidence of shaping.

Figure 11.52. Types of manos and handstones
from Roosevelt 9:6. Length of 7, 9 inches.

Minor distinctions can be made in the manos. First are those which
are more or less discoidal in shape having either one or two grinding
facets (Figure 11.52, 1 and 2). Originally, they were river pebbles, selected because of their convenient form. Specimens 3 and 4 (Figure

11.52) were also gathered from the stream bed and have but one grinding surface each. The irregular obverse side in most cases was retouched. Numbers 5 and 6 have grinding faces on both sides but lack symmetry of outline. The material in the foregoing examples is an indurated sandstone and they vary from 4 to 9 inches in length. Number 7 (Figure 11.52) is formed of lava, shows two grinding faces and edges that have been modified to give the object a uniform shape. It bears more resemblance to Pueblo manos than any of the preceding forms. Only two of this type were found.

Pitted surfaces on both metates and manos were apparently attempts to sharpen the tools. This was necessary in order to overcome the smooth surface which would eventually result from long wear on the type of stone employed.

MORTAR AND PESTLE

This grinding combination is represented by a single fragmentary mortar and by a broken pestle. The mortar is formed in an unshaped boulder of metamorphosed sandstone and the pear-shaped pestle is of the same material. The depth and the width of the grinding hole is 5 inches.

HAMMERSTONES

The most elemental of this group of objects is a spherical stream pebble, unmodified except for the concussion marks received during its use. A discoidal tool of diorite shows battered edges. A small hammerstone was intended, apparently, for delicate work; it is a flat pebble of fossiliferous limestone 2⅜ inches long and ¾ inch thick. The centers of the flat side are pitted opposite each other to render secure finger grips, and the entire circumference of the tool is battered from the work that was performed with it.

A tool tentatively identified as belonging in this class is an uncommon form in that it has been carefully shaped, particularly the edge which is brought to a sharpened ridge at the greatest diameter. The artifact is made of diorite; its maximum diameter is 3¼ inches and its thickness is 2 inches.

POTTERY ANVILS

It has already been shown that, in the making of pottery, the paddle and anvil method was used. In all probability the anvils were rounded stream pebbles which could readily be adapted to that use. Numerous stones of this type were found in the rooms, some of which may have been used as anvils. Their diameters apparently depended somewhat upon the size of the vessels in which they were used. One is 4½ inches in diameter. Its identification is fairly certain because of a high polish due to much use which could not have been obtained through water action alone, and because of faint striations such as would be caused by the angular fragments of quartz tempering in the paste.

A specialized type of pottery anvil was also used. At first it was thought to be made of clay, but upon washing and more careful examination it was found to be made in two pieces and of two types of rock. The head, or that part which came into contact with the clay, is 2⅜ inches in diameter, of convex form and made of fine-grained sandstone (Figure 11.53A). Its underside was partly cut out in order to receive the small end of the handle. This latter part has a porphyritic texture and is slightly expanded at the bottom (Figure 11.53B). A concavity ½ inch deep has been carved into the flat base. The union of the components was probably made with clay which held even in spite of the fact that the object went through a crematory fire. It was found as an offering with Cremation 15.

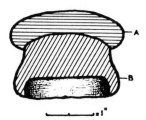

Figure 11.53. Cross section of stone pottery anvil: A, sandstone; B, porphyry.

The identification of this implement as a pottery anvil is confirmed by its likeness to tools which have been observed in use among present-day Indians in the process of pottery making (Gifford 1928:362). Archaeological occurrences of pottery anvils have been noted in Wisconsin, Missouri, Kentucky, Tennessee, and Alabama (Gifford 1928:361–362). The eastern anvils are made of clay, formed in the shape of mushrooms, frequently with concavities in the ends of the handles. They resemble the example from Roosevelt 9:6 in every way except the material of which they are fashioned.

STONE AXE

A single stone axe was recovered from the site. It is of the three-quarter or interrupted groove type and made of diorite. On the underside is a slight groove running lengthwise which may have been designed to receive a wedge. The cutting edge has been broken off and the implement was apparently used as a hammer in its last stage.

The three-quarter grooved axe is the characteristic type in the ruins of the Gila drainage and in the Tonto Basin. In workmanship they are superior to the small full grooved axes from the northern Pueblo territory, and they compare equally well with those found elsewhere in North America. The occurrence of the three-quarter grooved axe in three Colonial sites (Roosevelt 9:6; Sacaton 9:4; and Sacaton 9:6) places them undeniably as early arrivals in the Hohokam area.

DIGGING TOOLS

For the excavation of house pits, for disposing of the cremated dead, etc., it was necessary to have some form of tool to loosen the soil. Wooden implements may have assisted in this task but it is more likely that the major work was done with flat stone objects. These vary from thin plates of stone ¼ inch thick on which the edges have been sharpened, to heavier and more unwieldy tools struck off a boulder with a single blow.

PAINT MORTARS

Three mortars are probably paint mortars, although the identification is not definite since paint stains are not evident on the grinding surfaces. A small lump of paint was found with one of these, however. Another is unfinished, the grinding surface being just started in a flat waterworn rock. The third is about 4½ inches long, 2 inches wide and ¾ inch thick, and the depression is shallow.

PLUMMET-SHAPED STONES

Plummet stones from 1 to 3 inches long, having a groove a short distance from the large end, are frequently found in ruins of various horizons from Flagstaff south. Four of these were recovered in Roosevelt 9:6. The larger specimen is 2½ inches in length, and the material, regardless of where they are found, is almost always a scoriaceous lava.

POINTED STONE OBJECT

Among the offerings that were placed with Cremation Number 20 there was a stone dagger-like blade about 5½ inches long. The rock of which it is made has a fine-grained texture and is much too soft for use as a tool.

OBSIDIAN NODULES AND WORKED STEATITE

Small rounded nodules of obsidian seem to have held some peculiar charm for the occupants of the ruined villages as they are very abundant. Perhaps the larger ones were sought out and the material utilized in the manufacture of projectile points.

The presence of worked steatite at Roosevelt 9:6 implies the early recognition of its tractability.

POTTERY POLISHER

The polishing of pottery with small stone pebbles is almost a universal trait among non-wheel-using potters. The pottery of the Hohokam, particularly the plain ware, shows the striations of this process, the tool used being a small pebble.

REEL-SHAPED STONE

With Cremation 11 was found a piece of worked sandstone 3½ inches long and 2½ inches wide, the ends of which had been made slightly concave. Its use is not known.

BOILING STONES (?)

Not infrequently there were found in the houses flat oval-shaped stream pebbles which invariably showed fire marks. At first their presence was thought to be accidental, but their continued appearance suggested the possibility that they served some purpose, perhaps as boiling stones. Typical examples are about 4 inches long and ½ inch thick.

SLATE TABLETS

Slate tablets or paint palettes are characteristic of the Hohokam culture, and they are already present in specialized form in the earliest known phase. Their actual use as paint mixing tablets cannot be doubted as specimens have been found with paint stains and shallow central depressions which have resulted from long use. With the exception of two or three, the tablets recovered from Roosevelt 9:6 were found with cremations as mortuary offerings to the exclusion of everything else except pottery. The heat of the crematory fire through which the tablets passed completely vitrified a substance on their surfaces which is said to be paint material.

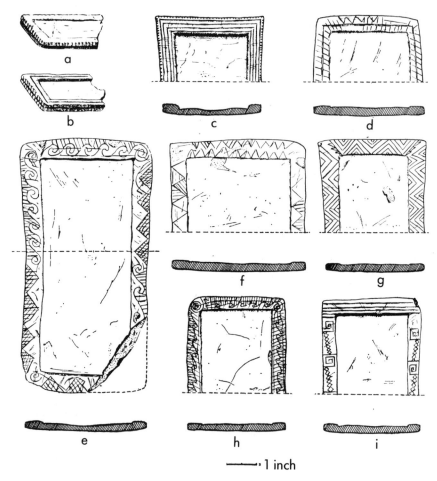

Figure 11.54. Partial sketches and sections of slate
tablets or paint palettes from Roosevelt 9:6.

The material of which these palettes are made is a soft schistose
rock having a slaty cleavage which breaks readily into thin plates. By
rubbing these over an abrasive surface and using flint flakes for carving, the desired shapes and ornamentation were obtained. The slates
in the collection from Roosevelt 9:6 vary in size from 2 inches by 3½
inches to 4 inches by 8 inches, the length being about twice the width.
The average thickness is ¼ inch.

The upper surface has two parts: the frame or border, and the
palette surface which is usually somewhat sunken below the frame.
The former is ornamented with incised lines in various patterns as

Figure 11.55. A slate tablet or paint palette from Roosevelt 9:6. Note incrustation. Length 6.1 inches.

shown by the representative series in Figure 11.54. On fragments A and B, the incisions have been carried to the sides, but in the majority of cases this is not seen. Carved patterns are mostly rectilinear, but in examples E and H, curvilinear figures were also attempted. Occasionally small sculptured figures were added to the border as shown by the specimen in Figure 11.55.

The slate tablet cannot be regarded as an independent invention of the Hohokam, since they occur with greater abundance in the earliest recognized stage of that culture than in later stages. The origin of the trait, together with painted paddle and anvil pottery, must be sought in a horizon still more remote than that represented by the Colonial period.

As to the duration and diffusion of the slate tablet, it decreased in numbers in periods following the Colonial horizon and died out by the time the Classic period was reached, about A.D. 1200. Turning to the diffusion, we find that to the east, south and west it does not pass beyond the bounds of the Hohokam culture itself, but to the north it found its way well into Pueblo territory, approximately as far as the three-quarter grooved axe. A number of paint palettes were found in Turkey Hill Pueblo several miles east of Flagstaff, Arizona, excavated during the summers of 1928 and 1929 by the University of Arizona under the direction of Dr. Cummings. In every respect these are like the Hohokam slates. A recent tree-ring date of A.D. 1278, has been assigned to Turkey Hill Pueblo (Douglass 1929:743), which would make its occupation broadly contemporaneous with ruins of the Classic period of the Hohokam. It is evident, therefore, that slate tablets survived later in the northern limits of their distribution than in the region from which they spread.

CHIPPED IMPLEMENTS

Chipped stone artifacts were very rare. Only four complete and two fragmentary arrowpoints and one knife or scraper were found. The process of chipping, however, was well understood as revealed by the specimens at hand, and their scarcity cannot yet be explained.

Two complete arrowpoints (not illustrated), were found on the floor of the vestibule of House 12. They are 1¾ inches in length and made of a light brown colored chert. The greatest width is reached at the bases which are straight and which were formed by the opposed notches placed ³⁄₁₆ inch from the basal ends. The points are long and keen and the edges are without serrations.

The other two complete arrowpoints (not illustrated) are also duplicates as to type, but they were not found together. Each was included as an offering with a cremation. Their lengths are practically the same as the preceding pair and the material is gray chert. They belong to the shouldered and barbed class of points as described by Wilson (1899:925–934). One of the incomplete arrowpoints displays a feature which is seldom seen in stone implements, i.e.: the forming of barbs along the sides. They undoubtedly are serrations carried one degree in advance and resemble very strongly the barbed harpoons of the northwest coast. This fragmentary specimen was found with Cremation Number 20; its length is 1 inch, maximum width, ⁷⁄₁₆ inch, and the material a gray chert. The knife was retouched from a flake of fossiliferous chert. Its length is 3 inches.

BONE OBJECTS

Bone artifacts were surprisingly scarce at Roosevelt 9:6. All of those recovered were found in houses, none with cremations, and all are in an advanced stage of decay. Only two types can be listed: awls and tubes. Awls are without exception fragmentary and the majority of them are points.

One complete and one fragmentary bone tube came from House 11 and from House 12, respectively. They are both formed of mammal leg bones, removed from the major part of the bone by cutting deep incisions and breaking. The rough ends were later ground down. The one from House 11 is 3½ inches long and 1 inch in diameter; the other one is 2¼ inches long and ⅞ inch in diameter. The latter has been completely and the former partly burned. Their use is not known. Similar tubes have been reported (Abbot and Putnam 1879: 228–229) from the vicinity of Santa Barbara, California (Dos Pueblos).

ORNAMENTS

Ornaments at Roosevelt 9:6 were scarce as compared to their abundance at other Hohokam sites of the same general period. Shell bracelets worked from the *Glycymeris* were common, although none were found in a complete state. Fragments indicate that they were ground thin, more than was customary in later times, and that the beaks were treated in several ways. In one the beak was carved to give the impression of a setting which is here further accentuated by a natural coloring of this part of the shell. A single gastropod (*Turritella*), was found having a hole broken through the wall for suspension. A squared and probably unfinished fragment of *Cardium* was also found.

Figure 11.56. A shell pendant carved in the image of a pelican.

The most striking shell work is seen in the pendant pictured in Figure 11.56, carved in the image of a pelican. The acquaintance of the Hohokam with the pelican is due to the fact, no doubt, that they were valley dwellers, building their villages along the banks of the larger streams in the southern part of Arizona. At the present time, this bird is an all-year resident on Roosevelt Lake and early settlers state that these birds were seen along Salt River prior to the construction of the dam. Pelicans were often painted on pottery or carved in shell, in unmistakable likeness, and the motive was one of apparent importance and wide distribution during the Colonial period.

Fresh water mussel shells from Salt River were also used, but not as commonly as salt water shells, as they were less adaptable to the manufacture of ornaments. Fragments of these were found in nearly every room, but only one showed artificial working in a simple drilled hole.

Small stone ornaments consist first of a bird-head fashioned from turquoise which was found on the floor of House 1. The object is ½ inch long and incomplete.

A small roughly made pendant of turquoise was found in trash mound 1 in the upper six inches of the deposit. This, together with the bird head, were the only turquoise objects recovered. Both were found under such circumstances as to link them definitely with the occupants of Roosevelt 9:6. Hence it may be claimed that this stone was recognized for its decorative value by the Hohokam of the earliest known horizon.

The only bead of the entire operation was found on the surface. It is of steatite and unfinished. A fragmentary ring or pierced disc of calcareous rock was also found.

Perishable Materials

MATTING

Bits of charred matting and the impress of the same in clay were found on the floors of Houses 8 and 12. In both cases the unsplit leaf of the *Yucca glauca* was used. The leaves were twilled diagonally in an over-two and under-two weave (Figure 11.57).

COILED BASKET

The sole evidence of sewed or coiled baskets was found on the interior of a plain jar, the bottom of which showed that it had been formed over a basket. While the impression is faint, there is no doubt as to its form. The basket measured 6¾ inches in diameter and was

Figure 11.57. Drawing of twilled matting found on floor of House 8.

about 1½ inches in depth. The coils appear to have numbered about eight to the inch but the fineness of the stitches cannot be determined.

CREMATIONS

Disposition of the dead at Roosevelt 9:6, as elsewhere among the Hohokam, was by cremation. Since the funeral pyres, whether built upon the ground or in pits, have not been definitely identified, nothing can be said as to the process.

In all, 32 cremations were located during the present work. With the exception of three scattered instances, all were concentrated in two plots: the first, immediately west of House 1, contained 22 burials; the second, on a ridge about 75 feet west of the first area, contained seven burials. The latter were in a fill above what appeared to be a former plaza level with a firepit (Figure 11.3) and therefore may be late in the occupation of the village. No earth burials were found.

The cremations of Roosevelt 9:6 were all of the pit type recently discovered by Woodward (1930:10–11, 27–28) and shown by him to be the characteristic form in the Colonial period. At Roosevelt 9:6, disposition of the unconsumed bones was made, first, by digging a hole in the subsoil from 1 to 3 feet deep in which they were placed without a container. Then broken fragments of earthen vessels which endured the crematory fire, together with slate tablets or other offerings, were placed over the bones before the earth was thrown back into the pit (Figure 11.58). There were seldom more than two vessels with one cremation and, in several cases, no offerings of any sort.

Figure 11.58. Broken earthen vessels and a fragmentary slate tablet which were found as offerings with Cremation 10.

CONCLUSIONS

Up to the present time only two sites of the Colonial period have been thoroughly examined, the Grewe Site (Sacaton 9:4) near Casa Grande and Roosevelt 9:6. A comparison of the culture from these two sites leads us to believe that Roosevelt 9:6 is slightly earlier than Sacaton 9:4 since Roosevelt 9:6 was totally lacking in many objects of specialized work which were present in quantity at Sacaton 9:4, namely: thick-walled vessels to which legs and effigy heads had been added, tripod trays, figurines, mirrors, exquisite work in bone and shell, and a great profusion of large red-on-buff storage jars which, at Roosevelt 9:6, were scarce. A point worthy of note in this discussion is that those traits of the Grewe Site not evident in Roosevelt 9:6 have been said to suggest southern affinity, but the nucleus of the culture, that is, rectangular earth lodges, paddle and anvil pottery, and universal cremation are not known to be attributes of any southern culture. Thus, while it is possible that southern contacts once existed, actual facts concerning the origin of the Hohokam are not yet forthcoming. Let it be said, however, that, in the territory in which the Hohokam sites are concentrated, there have been found no remains that can be interpreted as being introductory to the present earliest recognized phase, a prerequisite if an autochthonous development is to be assumed.

Turning now to other aspects of the Hohokam culture which arise in view of the past discussion, it is necessary first, to point out their endowments; second, to show the unity of these over the entire known range; third, to dissociate the Hohokam from the Pueblo or Plateau people; and last, to attempt to correlate the two groups as to their relative ages.

In order to sum up the attributes of a people, the consideration should be based upon the examination of remains representative of that group at a time when they were little affected by external forces. The Colonial period of the Hohokam satisfies this qualification as the sites of this horizon indicate that few outside influences were at work. A characteristic of first importance is the physiographic factor; the Hohokam were, without exception, valley or desert dwellers. Their villages were situated in the broad semi-arid valleys of southern Arizona. This, no doubt, was largely dictated by the demands of agriculture for arable land and water. Defensive features apparently did not enter into the selection of a village site.

Accurate information concerning the physical characteristics of the Hohokam is lacking. Due to the fact that the dead were cremated, the only evidence at hand to point towards the cranial type comes from chance finds of bodies which were not cremated. One authentic discovery of this kind was made by Dr. Cummings in a Hohokam village on the outskirts of Tucson some years ago. The body was found below the floor of a pit house and the skull measurements showed it to be dolichocephalic. Other instances have been reported but lack authenticity.

Other distinguishing features briefly enumerated are: extensive agriculture accompanied by irrigation; single-story, subsurface houses of rectangular form having entrance vestibules, each dwelling forming a unit of the community; brush-enclosed outside kitchens; cremation of the dead; red-on-buff painted pottery, made with paddle and anvil; large outside firepits; the three-quarter grooved axe; slate tablets; and shell carvings.

A characteristic of Colonial sites is the unity or standardization of the artifacts found in them, a feature not evident in either the Sedentary or Classic periods. The present range of Colonial sites can be bounded by Bouse on the northwest, Congress Junction on the north, the Tonto Basin and San Carlos on the east, south to Nogales, and southwest to Crater Mountains.

The paste, paint, vessel shapes, treatment of decorative area, and the design motives are remarkably constant for a culture so widely distributed.

Analogies in the manner of treating the field of decoration are almost without end. Believing that the case will be further strengthened by a listing of the minutiae of design, the following motifs have been selected and their recurrence in various sites has been recorded below (in this comparative study, sherd collections and complete vessels, now deposited in Gila Pueblo, were studied from over 200 sites):

1. Small repeated elements fringed on one or both sides with oblique parallel lines were found to occur in one or all of the forms given below in the following sites:

Arizona A	11:6	Gila Butte	5:14
Arizona A	11:9	Mesa	4:3
Arizona A	11:11	Phoenix	3:1
Arizona A	11:12	Roosevelt	9:6
Arizona A	14:7	Sacaton	4:6
Arizona J	12:1	Sacaton	9:1
Casa Grande	2:1	Sacaton	9:4
Ft. McDowell	7:1	Signal Peak	9:1
Gila Butte	5:11	Tucson	7:1

2. The so-called "bird symbol" is almost universal. In bands between fringes or in solid arrangement, it has been noted in the following:

Arizona A	9:3	Gila Butte	5:27
Arizona A	11:10	Gila Butte	5:28
Arizona A	11:12	Gila Butte	5:29
Arizona A	14:1	Gila Butte	5:30
Arizona A	14:5	Gila Butte	5:33
Arizona A	14:9	Gila Butte	5:36
Arizona C	5:2	Gila Butte	5:39
Arizona C	5:4	Gila Butte	5:40
Arizona J	5:1	Mesa	1:8
Casa Grande	2:1	Mesa	2:3
Desert Well	8:12	Mesa	4:3
Florence	1:5	Phoenix	3:1
Florence	4:4	Phoenix	1:3
Florence	5:2	Phoenix	2:1
Florence	5:3	Phoenix	2:6
Ft. McDowell	7:1	Roosevelt	9:6
Gila Butte	5:1	Sacaton	2:1
Gila Butte	5:4	Sacaton	2:4
Gila Butte	5:5	Sacaton	2:7
Gila Butte	5:7	Sacaton	4:2
Gila Butte	5:9	Sacaton	9:4
Gila Butte	5:10	Sacaton	9:12
Gila Butte	5:12	Sacaton	9:42
Gila Butte	5:16	Signal Peak	9:1
Gila Butte	5:17		

3. Mammal, reptile, bird and human forms are common as band decorations, usually on jars. Below are given typical examples and the close duplication of some in widely separated sites:

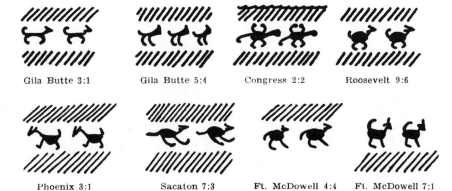

Gila Butte 3:1   Gila Butte 5:4   Congress 2:2   Roosevelt 9:6

Phoenix 3:1   Sacaton 7:3   Ft. McDowell 4:4   Ft. McDowell 7:1

Sacaton 9:4

Roosevelt 9:6

Mesa 2:5

Sacaton 9:4

Roosevelt 9:6

Phoenix 3:1

Sacaton 2:7

Ft. McDowell 7:1

Roosevelt 9:6

Phoenix 3:1

Gila Butte 5:9

Sacaton 2:6

Roosevelt 9:6

Sacaton 9:4

Phoenix 3:1

4. Small elements within frames or solids as below, used as parts of designs or filling in corners, appear in:

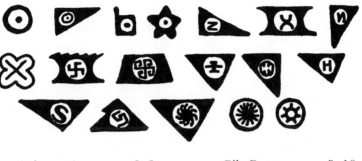

Arizona A	8 : 2	Gila Butte	5 : 10
Arizona A	11 : 10	Gila Butte	5 : 16
Arizona A	11 : 13	Gila Butte	5 : 27
Arizona A	11 : 18	Gila Butte	5 : 28
Arizona A	14 : 11	Gila Butte	5 : 29
Arizona I	2 : 1	Gila Butte	5 : 33
Arizona I	2 : 3	Gila Butte	5 : 37
Camelback	9 : 3	Gila Butte	5 : 40
Casa Grande	3 : 1	Phoenix	3 : 1
Desert Well	8 : 13	Phoenix	3 : 2
Florence	7 : 6	Phoenix	3 : 5
Florence	1 : 2	Roosevelt	9 : 6
Ft. McDowell	4 : 3	Sacaton	2 : 1
Ft. McDowell	4 : 4	Sacaton	2 : 6
Ft. McDowell	8 : 1	Sacaton	2 : 7
Gila Butte	3 : 3	Sacaton	4 : 3
Gila Butte	3 : 5	Sacaton	9 : 4
Gila Butte	5 : 1	Sacaton	9 : 42

5. Hatch-filled circles occur in:

Arizona A	14 : 1	Phoenix	3 : 1
Gila Butte	5 : 14	Roosevelt	9 : 6
Gila Butte	5 : 36	Sacaton	2 : 4
Mesa	2 : 5	Sacaton	2 : 7

6. A combination of straight and wavy lines as filling elements has been found in the following sites:

Arizona A	11:6	Gila Butte	5:10
Arizona A	11:9	Gila Butte	5:11
Arizona A	11:10	Gila Butte	5:13
Arizona A	11:12	Gila Butte	5:16
Arizona A	11:13	Gila Butte	5:28
Arizona A	11:16	Gila Butte	5:29
Arizona A	13:1	Maricopa	6:1
Arizona A	14:1	Mesa	2:6
Arizona A	14:10	Mesa	5:2
Arizona I	2:3	Phoenix	4:1
Arizona J	11:10	Roosevelt	9:6
Camelback	9:3	Sacaton	2:7
Florence	1:3	Sacaton	9:4
Florence	4:4	Sacaton	9:41
Gila Butte	5:1	Sacaton	9:42
Gila Butte	5:4	Signal Peak	9:1
Gila Butte	5:5	Tucson	4:6
Gila Butte	5:8		

7. Stepped lines as below, while not so regularly used, are characteristic nevertheless:

Arizona A	11:13	Gila Butte	5:17
Arizona A	11:18	Maricopa	6:1
Arizona A	14:2	Roosevelt	9:6
Gila Butte	5:16		

8. Interlocked scrolls in narrow bands have been noted in:

Arizona A	11:6	Gila Butte	5:28
Arizona A	11:9	Maricopa	2:1
Arizona A	11:11	Phoenix	2:3
Arizona A	11:17	Phoenix	4:1
Arizona I	2:3	Roosevelt	9:6
Arizona J	16:3	Sacaton	2:1
Camelback	9:3	Sacaton	2:7
Desert Well	8:4	Sacaton	9:2
Gila Butte	5:1	Sacaton	9:4
Gila Butte	5:5	Sacaton	9:42
Gila Butte	5:9	Tucson	4:6
Gila Butte	5:11	Tucson	7:4
Gila Butte	5:17	Verde	14:6
Gila Butte	5:18		

9. Interlocked scrolls with pendant or serrated edges, often forming units in themselves occur commonly:

Arizona A	11:11	Gila Butte	5:10
Arizona A	11:13	Gila Butte	5:14
Arizona A	11:17	Gila Butte	5:28
Arizona A	11:18	Gila Butte	5:30
Arizona A	13:1	Gila Butte	5:41
Arizona A	14:1	Phoenix	3:1
Arizona I	2:3	Roosevelt	9:6
Arizona J	5:1	Sacaton	2:1
Arizona J	12:3	Sacaton	4:2
Desert Well	8:3	Sacaton	9:4
Florence	1:3	Sacaton	9:11
Ft. McDowell	4:4	Sacaton	9:41
Gila Butte	5:1	Tucson	4:12
Gila Butte	5:7	Tucson	7:2
Gila Butte	5:8		

10. The multiple or quadruple scroll with modifications is found in the following:

Arizona A	13 : 1	Gila Butte	5 : 1
Arizona A	14 : 11	Mesa	4 : 3
Gila Butte	5 : 5	Roosevelt	9 : 6

11. As a final comparison, note the similarity in treatment of the reptile pattern below taken from a scoop from Sacaton 2 : 7, with the bowl shown in Figure 11.46D from Roosevelt 9 : 6.

Other Hohokam traits lend themselves to the same treatment, but it is believed that the examples just given and pertaining only to pottery designs, will suffice to show the homogeneity of the Colonial period. It should be remembered that the pottery examined in the above study was not the output of a central factory but rather the product of many hundreds of individuals living in widely scattered villages. A common origin must be called upon to explain the ceramic and cultural unity. The sudden efflorescence of the Hohokam, as expressed in the Colonial period, apparently without initiatory steps, shows a colonizing period in which the red-on-buff traditions were deeply rooted. Later, however, after local adjustments had been made and contacts with the Plateau culture established, regional types both in pottery and in other traits make their appearance.

To show wherein the Hohokam and the Pueblo people differ, a list of contrasting elements is shown below. The comparison is made at a general period of A.D. 1000, as after that time the coalescence of the two groups makes the line of division less sharp:

HOHOKAM	PUEBLO
Valley Dwellers	Plateau and Canyon Dwellers
Rectangular, semi-subterranean earth lodges with entrance vestibule	Multi-storied stone communal houses
Cremation	Inhumation
Dolichocephalic, not deformed (?)	Brachycephalic, posterior deformation
Agriculture with extensive irrigation	Intensive agriculture
Paddle and anvil-made pottery	Coiled pottery
Three-quarter groove, long-bitted axe	Full-groove, short-bitted axe
Slate tablets	Slate tablets absent
Shell carving	Shell carving rare
Apparently did not have turkey	Turkey domesticated

Variation in such basic elements as the choice of environment, the probable difference in head form, the mode of disposing of the dead, and the technological difference in the manufacture of pottery, can only be the result of two independent lines of growth.

Last is the major problem of correlating the periods of the Hohokam with the better-known horizons of the north, some of which have been accurately dated (Douglass 1929:737–770). Unfortunately, the structural wood employed by the pueblo-building people from which this data has been procured is lacking from Hohokam sites which occupy the broad semi-arid valleys where types of wood usable in dendrochronological studies did not grow. (The woods employed at the present time in dating ruins, listed in the order of their preference, are: Douglas Fir, Western Yellow Pine, and Pinyon.) This is not intended, however, to discourage the preservation of wood, whether decayed or charred, from Hohokam villages, as what appears to be worthless now may ultimately be of great importance in the reconstruction of the history of that culture.

Any attempt, therefore, to correlate the Hohokam with the Pueblo culture, prior to their commingling, must of necessity be made by the aid of cross-finds of objective material. This means that pottery, stone objects, or other artifacts of undisputed northern origin which can be allocated to a definite horizon, if found in Hohokam sites, will show the time relationship of the latter to the former.

To bring the matter to the case in point: Among the wealth of sherd material from Roosevelt 9:6 are six fragments of black-on-white ware which is entirely foreign to local culture. Three of these fragments (Figure 11.50, Numbers 1, 2, and 3) were recovered from the surface. The first two, although somewhat small for accurate identification, date almost certainly from Basketmaker III times; the third is suggestive of the Pueblo I period. Numbers 4, 5, and 6 were found underground directly associated with red-on-buff pottery, at depths varying from 2 to 4 feet. All of these are unquestionably of Pueblo I origin. The nearest sites yet recorded of these horizons are located in the San Francisco Mountain region (Hargrave 1930) whence the sherds in question may well have come. The implication of this association is that the Hohokam culture as represented in Roosevelt 9:6 and the Basketmaker III-Pueblo I stages of the north were synchronous. But before entering into further discussion concerning this point, it is well to look at another possible origin for the black-on-white sherds.

One hundred feet to the east of the village of semi-subterranean houses and separated from them by a small gully, is a small, stone-outlined site of perhaps a half dozen contiguous and rectangular rooms. Due to the entire difference in architecture and the lack of red-on-buff pottery among types of late black-on-white, decorated red ware, and Salado Red ware (Gladwin and Gladwin 1930c:10–11) found here, it is assumed that no relationship whatever existed between the two occupations; that the peoples of the two sites were basically distinct; and that the interim was of long duration. A relative date can be assigned to the masonry pueblo by virtue of pottery types occuring therein which have also been found in dated cliff ruins in the Sierra Ancha. Its occupation probably does not persist far into the fourteenth century, being mainly in the thirteenth century.

The mere presence, however, of this later community introduces the possibility that the early black-on-white sherds in question were dropped by some of its occupants together with a few of their own. This seems unlikely for two reasons: first, the long span of time existing between the Basketmaker III–Pueblo I periods and the thirteenth century occupation would make it extremely difficult if not impossible for the early black-on-white wares still to be in circulation; and second, the absence of early Pueblo sites in the Tonto Basin precludes any chance introduction of the black-on-white sherds in Roosevelt 9:6. (In sherd collections from 180 sites in the Tonto Basin showing Pueblo culture, no Basketmaker III, Pueblo I, or Pueblo II sherds have yet been found.)

In view of the unlikelihood, therefore, that the foreign ceramic types reached the red-on-buff settlement after its abandonment, there is only one other alternative, namely, that the Hohokam of this village were in contact with the northern culture and procured from them, either directly or indirectly, black-on-white vessels now represented by the few fragments. This opinion gains strength from the following cases of association: at the Grewe Site, the Van Bergen–Los Angeles Museum Expedition recovered half of a Pueblo I black-on-white bowl on the floor of a house, and in the sherd collections of Gila Pueblo. Pueblo I sherds occur with Colonial Red-on-buff in the following sites:

Arizona A	11:4	Congress	5:2
Arizona A	11:6	Diamond Creek	13:1
Arizona A	11:11	Diamond Creek	14:1
Arizona A	14:1	Florence	1:3
Arizona A	14:7	Jerome	8:1
Arizona A	14:9	Maricopa	9:3
Arizona A	14:11	Sacaton	2:7
Congress	2:2	Verde	6:1

The astonishing fact that now arises in the light of this correlation is that the pottery of the Hohokam as illustrated here, evidences a complexity of design which is not seen in the contemporary pottery of the north, and furthermore, that certain treatments and elements of design seen in the Hohokam painted ware of the Colonial period later become dominant in Pueblo wares. Likewise, other traits, such as Gila Red ware, the three-quarter groove axe, and paint palettes make their appearance in southern pueblos as adoptions. This introduces quite another aspect to the whole study—to what extent did the Hohokam influence Puebloan development—a line of investigation which must be relegated to future consideration.

Acknowledgments

On behalf of Gila Pueblo, the writer wishes to express keen appreciation of the willingness of the Salt River Valley Water Users' Association to permit the archaeological investigation of a ruin described herein, which lies under the high water mark of Roosevelt Lake. To the staff of Gila Pueblo much credit is due for ideas and opinions embodied in this chapter which arose from discussions afield and in the laboratory; particular mention is made of Mr. George Dennis, who was constantly on the ground during the course of excavations, and of Mr. O. C. Havens, who has supplied many of the photographs.

PART FIVE

Mogollon

People of the Mountains

◄ 12 ►

Development of Archaeological Thought on the Mimbres Mogollon

Steven A. LeBlanc

The Mimbres region of the Mogollon encompasses most of southwestern New Mexico and centers on the Mimbres River and its tributaries. The area also includes the upper portion of the Gila River and a lower portion of the tributary San Francisco River. Emil Haury's research in this area provided the excavation material for the definition of Mogollon culture. As such, it laid the foundation for a coherent picture of the cultural history of the Mimbres region, although it was overshadowed by his later work in Arizona at Forestdale and Point of Pines, which figured more prominently in the broad debate over the validity of the Mogollon concept.

Prior to Haury's work, the area was primarily known for its famous Mimbres Classic Black-on-white pottery, which was recovered from cobble-walled pueblos. Research activity, initiated by Hough (1907) and Fewkes (1914), included major expeditions by the Cosgroves (1932) at the Swarts Ruin, by Nesbitt (1931) at the Mattocks Ruin, by Bradfield (1931) at Cameron Creek, and by the Southwest Museum (Bryan 1927) and the University of Minnesota (Jenks 1928) at Galaz. By 1930 this research had resulted in as much concentrated archaeology in the Mimbres region as in any comparable area of the American Southwest outside of the San Juan Basin.

In excavating surface pueblos, the early workers encountered numerous underlying pit houses as well as ceramics that were distinctly different from Mimbres Classic Black-on-white. None of these investigators, however, drew attention to the differences between the pit house material and what was then called Basketmaker-Pueblo (Anasazi), nor did they propose a temporal framework for architectural or ceramic developments. It took Haury's work at Mogollon Village and the Harris Village to produce the first synthesis of the pit house occupation of the Mimbres region. While such a contribution would seemingly be of interest primarily for its historical importance, both the ceramic and architectural frameworks were as valid in the mid-1980s as when they were proposed in 1936. Anyon's (1980) synthesis of 33 excavated Mimbres sites that contain several hundred pit houses amply verified Haury's original framework. In fact, probably nowhere else in the American Southwest has the initial cultural framework been so accurate.

With hindsight, one can perceive what led to Haury's success. Previous workers had concentrated on single sites, and, thus, were never certain of how broadly their conclusions could be applied. In addition they worked on sites with surface pueblos whose inhabitants had disturbed the underlying pit house occupation. Haury's strategy circumvented both these problems. He began in 1933 by excavating Mogollon Village, a site on the San Francisco drainage at the extreme western margin of the Mimbres area. This village contained only pit houses, which spanned the period from about A.D. 550 to A.D. 900. In 1934 he went to the heart of the Mimbres Valley to excavate the Harris Village, which again had no surface pueblo remains. This site essentially duplicated the time range found at Mogollon Village. With the same sequences present at both sites, he was able to conclude that they were regional patterns. Not only did Haury accurately work out much of the local sequence, he recognized that it was fundamentally different from the Basketmaker-Pueblo (Anasazi) sequence to the north. On the basis of this difference, he defined the Mogollon—a concept with major implications for the development of southwestern archaeology.

Haury's work in New Mexico was followed by Paul Martin's 1939 excavations at the SU Site near Reserve. The SU Site clearly fell within Haury's concept of the Mogollon as being distinct from the Anasazi, and it substantiated and extended the original concept. Haury began work that same year in the Forestdale Valley of Arizona. Here, again he found remains that fit within the Mogollon concept. Although a debate existed for a number of years over the validity of the Mogollon concept, by the mid-1950s further work by Haury and Martin had clearly demonstrated its distinctiveness from the Anasazi. In addition, dates from the Bluff Site (Haury and Sayles 1947) showed that this material predated developments in the plateau area to the north, thus strengthening the case for the analytic usefulness of the Mogollon concept. Historically, the Mogollon concept helped to eliminate the use of Basketmaker-Pueblo as a monolithic and valid concept for the entire Southwest and to set the stage for the study of regional diversity and the development of a more precise view of prehistory. Later the Mogollon concept expanded to encompass questions of cultural process: archaeologists became concerned with how cultural differences inherent in the concepts of Mogollon, Anasazi, or Hohokam came to exist and with the degree to which they were the result of historic "accident" or of adaptation to different environments.

Even though in later years it seemed easy to use the term Mogollon and, with hindsight, to see its necessity, it must be remembered that in the mid-1980s the term was still used ambiguously both as a spatial and temporal designation, and there was little more agreement on its proper usage than there was in the 1930s regarding the value of the concept itself.

While a full critique of the nature and usage of the Mogollon concept is beyond the present scope, some points can be made. Haury restricted his definition to the pit house builders (prior to A.D. 1000–1100), while most archaeologists today employ the term for later occupations as well. In this case, I believe Haury was more correct than many scholars realize. As discussed below, I think a strong case can be made that the post-A.D. 1000 occupation in the Mimbres area (the Classic Mimbres) was fully Mogollon. Haury never argued specifically against this idea; he worked on sites that did not have a Classic Mimbres occupation, and he never focused on the continuity problem in the Mimbres region. However, in the northern section of the Mogollon area, at Forestdale and Point of Pines, Haury did excavate post-A.D. 1000 sites to which he was unwilling to apply the term Mogollon. While the cultural mechanisms are unclear, although I suspect a role for the Chaco system, Haury was seeing a very real difference between the pit house and pueblo occupation in the northern Mogollon area. I agree that the post-A.D. 1000 sites in the northern Mogollon area reflect something different from the Mimbres. This does not automatically imply new people, but it may very well mean a new organizational pattern. If we remember that Haury's original use of the term Mogollon was to define a part of a previously perceived monolithic whole in order to conceptualize and study the differences, we can then see his reluctance to use the term Mogollon post-A.D. 1000 as part of the same logic and concern. By being unwilling to extend the use of the concept, he forces us to define a new analytic unit, thereby setting the stage for our understanding of the relationships and processes involved in differences between the two.

Turning again to southwestern New Mexico, it is enlightening to review Haury's original Mimbres research from the perspective of recent work on the Mimbres Mogollon sequence.

EARLY PIT HOUSE PERIOD: A.D. 200 TO A.D. 550

Today we see the Mimbres sequence beginning around A.D. 200 with the appearance of plain and some red slipped pottery and of deep, well-made pit houses with lateral entrance ways clustered into villages. These small pit house villages were located on high isolated knolls or ridges usually overlooking perennially watered river valleys.

Haury did not excavate any pit houses of this period, nor did he include it in his developmental scheme, although these early villages are clearly ancestral to Harris Village and Mogollon Village. Not long after Haury's work in the Mimbres, however, he excavated the Bluff Site (Haury and Sayles 1947) in the Forestdale Valley, a settlement contemporary with the earliest Mimbres villages. Haury correctly perceived its ancestral nature and that it provided the strongest evidence for the distinctiveness of the Mogollon from the Anasazi.

In fact no pit houses of this early period were excavated in the Mimbres region until Fitting's (1973) work on the Winn Canyon Site along the Gila River, and none were excavated in the Mimbres Valley until 1974 (LeBlanc 1975, 1980a). It is unclear why these early sites went unrecognized for so long. One reason may be that few people, other than Haury, looked on the high knolls where these sites are located, sometimes 700 feet above the nearby Mimbres Valley.

The Early Pit House period was labeled the Hilltop phase in the Forestdale Valley (Haury and Sayles 1947), the Pinelawn phase in the Reserve region (Martin 1943), and the Cumbre phase in the Mimbres Valley. It is clear that the later pit house material is a direct outgrowth of these early manifestations. Haury's concept of an independent development for the Mogollon is substantiated by these early sites.

LATE PIT HOUSE PERIOD: A.D. 550 TO A.D. 1000

It is the Mogollon of the Late Pit House period that Haury first defined and described. There are broad similarities found in settlements of this period; they appear stable and reflect similar adaptations. After A.D. 550 knolls were abandoned for locations on river terraces. The location of Mogollon Village on a high mesa is a rare exception. Pit houses continued to be used until about A.D. 1000. Haury's work at Mogollon Village and the Harris Village provided the framework for this 450-year period of Mogollon development.

Haury discovered that the pottery on these later sites formed a distinct developmental sequence. At first both a plain ware (Alma Plain) and a highly polished red ware (San Francisco Red) were produced. The red ware evolved into decorated pottery with red paint on a brown background (Mogollon Red-on-brown), which, in turn, evolved into the short-lived Three Circle Red-on-white pottery and subsequently into Bold Face Black-on-white. Using stratigraphic and stylistic relationships, Haury was able to demonstrate this developmental sequence.

Haury's ceramic sequence permitted the temporal placement of excavated pit houses, which revealed the architectural sequence of round structures developing into rectangular ones with curved sides, and later into fully rectangular pit houses. By excavating large communal-ceremonial structures or Great Kivas, he laid the foundation for identifying the sequence of communal architecture for the Mimbres (Anyon and LeBlanc 1980). Interestingly, while Haury did not propose a Great Kiva sequence for the Mimbres area, he did for eastern Arizona (Haury 1950b). Similarities in these two sequences support Haury's Forestdale reconstruction and suggest close relationships among the Mogollon of the mountain regions. Briefly, the Great Kiva sequence in the Mimbres region also goes from round structures to rectangular ones, but shape changes lag behind those of the domestic structures, and there is an increase in size and elaboration over time. Mogollon Village and the Harris Village provide important examples in the development of communal-ceremonial architecture.

Using the ceramic and architectural sequence, Haury (1936) proposed the Georgetown, San Francisco, and Three Circle phases for the period A.D. 550 to A.D. 1000. A hypothesized San Lorenzo phase had not been substantiated by 1985. Several formulations of the actual dating of Haury's three phases were proposed later, including that of Anyon, Gilman and LeBlanc (1981), but the dates proposed by Haury form much of the basis for others' chronologies. In the mid-1980s both the Georgetown and San Francisco phases were viewed as being relatively short, with each lasting about 100 years, and the Three Circle phase was considered to be quite long, running from around A.D. 750 to A.D. 1000.

CLASSIC MIMBRES PERIOD: A.D. 1000 to A.D. 1130

The Late Pit House period came to a close around A.D. 1000 with the shift to surface architecture. Since Haury did not excavate sites with surface architecture, he did not include sites of this time period in his formulation. In retrospect this was unfortunate, because misinformation and misinterpretation have plagued understanding of Classic Mimbres from the beginning. Much of this confusion might have been avoided had Haury investigated settlements of this later period as well.

Today we see the Classic Mimbres period occurring at sites that had previously been composed of pit houses. Virtually every major Classic pueblo has an underlying pit house component, so the shift to surface rooms did not result in any appreciable changes in settlement pattern or site location. Surface room blocks began as small clusters of 2 to 6 rooms, and for 100 years grew by haphazard accretion to form room blocks of up to 50 rooms each. A typical large site had 4 to 6 room blocks and consisted of 100 to 150 rooms total. Great kivas gradually ceased being built and were probably replaced by open plazas, but smaller kivas came into existence (Anyon and LeBlanc 1980).

Misconceptions have existed over the transition from pit houses to surface pueblos. On the one hand this change was seen as a result of Anasazi influence or cultural "swamping." In reality, there was continuity between the pit house and pueblo occupations in both painted and utility ceramics, burial patterns, site locations, and, essentially, in all other forms of material culture. In particular, the design style of the painted pottery shows a very clear evolution from Bold Face Black-on-white through an intermediate style to Mimbres Classic Black-on-white. The steps are so minor and gradual and so many intermediate examples exist that it is difficult not to accept the continuity of this change.

Furthermore, there are more architectural parallels than generally thought. Roofing patterns are quite similar between the latest pit houses and surface rooms, and cobble walls were used in many late pit houses. In the case of the Three Circle phase pit houses, the cobble masonry was laid against sterile soil while in the pueblo period the walls were free standing. Regardless of this difference, there was an established pattern of masonry construction preceding the actual building of free-standing rooms. Thus, no major cultural break came until after A.D. 1130, the end of the Classic Mimbres.

A second misconception has been the idea of a Mangas phase, which was hypothesized to have fit between the Three Circle phase and the Classic Mimbres phase. The Mangas phase was presumably characterized by small surface pueblos which preceded the large villages like Swarts, Galaz, and Mattocks. This phase was a result of trying to fit the Mimbres sequence into an Anasazi model (Gladwin and Gladwin 1934) and was no longer considered to be valid in 1985.

While it is true that the large, Classic period pueblo room blocks grew by accretion from smaller ones, there is not a separate class of sites comprising small pueblos and another set of later, larger ones. Evidence shows that there was a steady growth in population at the larger sites and not a retrograde phase of movement into smaller communities (Anyon and others 1981).

Little research was conducted on Classic Mimbres villages after the development of tree-ring dating, so it was not until the 1970s that a firm understanding of the chronology was achieved. By 1985 there was overwhelming evidence that the Classic Mimbres period came to an end between A.D. 1130 and A.D. 1150—much earlier than previously perceived. Moreover, the occupation that followed was so unlike the earlier sequence in terms of ceramics, architecture, settlement patterns, and ceremonial structures that it would be inappropriate to label it Mogollon.

In the 1980s our understanding of the termination of the Mimbres sequence was still limited, but two aspects were of interest. First, there was good evidence that the Mimbres population grew some tenfold from its beginning in A.D. 200 to its peak in the 1100s (Anyon and others 1981). As a consequence, significant difficulties in food provisioning arose (Minnis 1981) and probably played a role in the Mimbres demise. Secondly, the timing of the Mimbres collapse is coeval with the collapse of Chaco (between A.D. 1130 and A.D. 1150) and with the initial development of the Casas Grandes interaction sphere (LeBlanc 1980b). It would seem highly unlikely that these three events were unrelated, but to what degree they were all related to general climatologic events or to the sociopolitical interaction between the areas had not been determined by 1985. However, it did seem clear that after A.D. 1150, most of the previous Mimbres area was integrated at some level into the Casas Grandes sphere.

In the 1980s archaeologists perceived a long sequence of cultural development from A.D. 200 through A.D. 1130 in the Mimbres region. Haury's work at Mogollon Village and the Harris Village provided the basis for defining the Mogollon and their cultural history from A.D. 550 to A.D. 1000 and played a major role in the development of a larger framework in the 1970s, when Haury's pioneering efforts were incorporated into a detailed cultural history for the Mimbres Valley.

13

The Mogollon Culture of Southwestern New Mexico

Emil W. Haury

This chapter is concerned with the excavations in two pit-house villages of southwestern New Mexico; the first is the Mogollon Village, situated on the east bank of the San Francisco River about ten miles north of Glenwood, in Catron County; and the second, the Harris Village, is located on the east bank of the Mimbres River opposite the Mimbres Post Office, in Grant County.

The work in the Mogollon Village was conducted in the summer of 1933 under a permit granted Gila Pueblo by the United States Department of Agriculture. The ruin was first visited by us in July, 1931, during the course of an archaeological reconnaissance in west-central New Mexico, when an effort was being made to define the eastern boundary of the Hohokam culture. On this initial visit the site yielded pottery which it was thought might be related to the Hohokam, at the same time exhibiting a sharp contrast with that seen in many nearby ruins. It appeared to be either something basically new or a stage of Hohokam development which had not been defined. With these factors as inducements, the work was undertaken. During the excavation

Reprinted from *Medallion Papers* 20. Globe, Arizona: Gila Pueblo, 1936.

of this village, eleven pit houses and a number of storage pits were cleared. The nature of the material remains led to the conclusion that something new and practically unknown was being dealt with, and that the culture was not a product of the Hohokam.

The need for further studies in this same culture led to the excavation, in the summer of 1934, of the Harris Village, which had also been visited during the general survey in 1931. The pottery collected from the surface promised greater cultural depth than was found at the Mogollon Village, with the additional likelihood of determining phases. This goal was eventually realized and, from the combined results of the two villages, a new conception of the cultural history of southwestern New Mexico was developed.

In recent years several excellent reports on studies in the Mimbres have appeared. The remains of the Classic period have formed the major theme, although nearly all reports also recognized traces, both architectural and ceramic, which came before the peak of Mimbres development. Yet little light was shed on the origin of the Mimbres culture, and the early stages in its history. It has generally been felt that the Mimbreños represented a southern development of the Pueblo Indians, directly linked with, and derived from, the San Juan area. Furthermore, just how the Mimbreños came by their distinctive pottery has always been a moot point. This report on the investigations of these two villages will be found to have a direct bearing on some of these questions.

The identification of the two villages with the Basketmaker-Pueblo, on the one hand, and the Hohokam, on the other, would have been impossible without unduly stretching the definitions of those cultures. The material at hand is therefore regarded as the manifestation of a third and fundamental group which has been called the Mogollon culture (Gladwin and Gladwin 1935:221–225).

This report has been divided into three parts: the first two are concerned with the architecture and material remains of the Mogollon and Harris villages respectively; the third and final part is devoted to correlation and discussion. Since mention is made of the growth stages found in these villages before the evidence has been examined to justify them, it will be advantageous to enumerate them, so that the reader will feel some acquaintance with the names. These stages, worked out on the phase system as adopted by Gila Pueblo (Gladwin and Gladwin 1934), beginning with the earliest now known, are as follows: Georgetown phase, San Francisco phase, Three Circle phase, Mimbres (classic) phase.

THE MOGOLLON VILLAGE

The Mogollon Village (Mogollon 1:15) is situated in Catron County, New Mexico, in Section 20, Township 10 South, Range 20 West, on the east bank of the San Francisco River, about ten miles north of Glenwood (Figure 13.1). The site lies on a small mesa approximately sixty meters above the river (Figure 13.2), and is accessible only from the northeastern side where the surrounding cliff merges into broken country. The mesa is about 1700 meters above sea level.

Protected by steep cliffs on all sides but one, the village was ideally situated for defense, and commanded an unobstructed view of the surrounding territory. To the north, the valley of the San Francisco extends for several miles before becoming hemmed in by mountains; towards the east rise the Mogollon Mountains. Open country lies to the south; to the west and northwest, ridges and low mountains divide the drainage of the San Francisco River from that of the Blue River in Arizona.

Agricultural lands, doubtless once cultivated by the occupants of the village, are situated on the valley floor to the west and north in plain sight from the mesa (Figure 13.3). At the present time approximately one hundred and thirty acres are under cultivation here. Water from the river is used for irrigation to bring the crops to maturity. The only vegetal products recovered during the excavations were charred and very fragmentary cobs of corn, and walnuts (*Juglans major*), the latter native to the region.

The region is one in which game is still abundant. That the occupants of the village relied heavily upon game is attested by the abundance of animal bones scattered throughout the rubbish. The species represented are listed below:

Badger (*Taxidea taxus*)
Racoon (*Procyon lotor*)
Coyote (*Canis* cf. *latrans*)
Gray fox (*Urocyon cinereoargenteus*)
Red fox (*Vulpes*)
Mountain lion (*Felis* cf. *concolor*)
Bob-cat (*Lynx rufus*)
Ground squirrel (*Citellus*)
Wood rat (*Neotoma*)
Jack rabbit (*Lepus* cf. *townsendii*)
Cotton-tail rabbit (*Sylvilagus* cf. *floridanus*)
Mule deer (*Odocoileus* cf. *hemionus*)

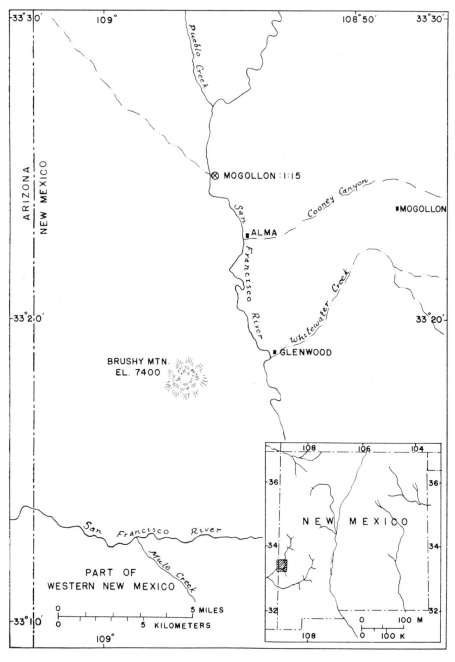

Figure 13.1. Map showing the location of Mogollon Village (Mogollon 1:15).

308

Figure 13.2. Location of Mogollon Village: *top*, mesa seen from the southeast along the San Francisco River; *bottom*, mesa seen from the northeast, showing the accessible side.

Figure 13.3. Overlooking the valley of the San Francisco River northwest of Mogollon Village.

Prong-horned antelope (*Antilocapra americana*)
Bison (*Bison*)
Turkey (*Meleagris*)
Great horned owl (*Bubo virginianus*)
Hawk (*Buteo*)
Duck sp.

The mesa itself was covered with a low growth of grass and a few junipers along the edges. The adjoining territory supports a scattered growth of juniper and pinyon, forming the lower fringe of the timbered belt. Mesquite and oak occur infrequently, and the river is edged with large cottonwoods. Smaller vegetation consists of narrow-leaf yucca, cholla, prickly pear, and beeweed.

From the climatic standpoint, the site was ideally located. It was high enough to escape oppressive summer heat, and low enough to miss the severe winter temperatures of the nearby mountains. First frosts may be expected late in September or early in October, thus giving ample time for the ripening of corn.

The top of the mesa measures approximately 110 meters on an east-west line, and 160 meters on a north-south axis. The broadest part lies at the north end where the mesa joins broken country, while the south end tapers to a point at the foot of which flows the San Francisco River (Figure 13.4). Before excavations were begun, the sole indications of occupation were found in scattered sherds, arrowheads, flint chips, and shallow depressions, marking the locations of pit houses.

HOUSE REMAINS AT MOGOLLON VILLAGE*

Eleven houses were cleared in the Mogollon Village (Figure 13.4). Each one of these formed a distinct unit in the community and was placed without regard for a plan. All houses, irrespective of form, share the pit character, a graded entrance passage, and a uniform position of the hearth about midway between the entrance and the center of the room.

For convenience, the house types of both villages have been grouped on the basis of form, function, and phase. The house numbers listed below apply to the Mogollon Village, where Types I, II, and

---

*See editors' note at end of this section on house remains for revised dating of pit houses.

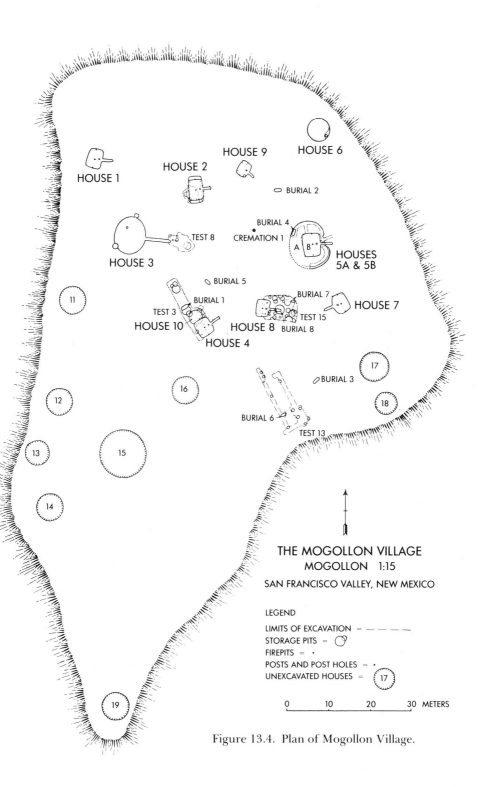

HOUSE 1

HOUSE 2

HOUSE 9

HOUSE 6

BURIAL 2

TEST 8

HOUSE 3

BURIAL 4

CREMATION 1

A   B

HOUSES
5A & 5B

BURIAL 5

11

BURIAL 1

TEST 3

BURIAL 7

HOUSE 7

HOUSE 10

HOUSE 8   TEST 15

BURIAL 8

HOUSE 4

17

16

BURIAL 3

12

18

13

15

BURIAL 6

TEST 13

14

19

THE MOGOLLON VILLAGE

MOGOLLON   1:15

SAN FRANCISCO VALLEY, NEW MEXICO

LEGEND

LIMITS OF EXCAVATION = — — — —
STORAGE PITS =
FIREPITS = ·
POSTS AND POST HOLES = ·
UNEXCAVATED HOUSES = 17

0   10   20   30 METERS

Figure 13.4. Plan of Mogollon Village.

III only were found; Types I to VI were represented at the Harris Village. Pottery determinations are based on the sherds found on or within 10 centimeters of the floors of houses. In most cases it is believed that these samples provide a sound criterion for dating.

Round Structures:
    Type I, Domestic: House 10. Georgetown phase.
    Type II, Ceremonial (?): Houses 3 and 5A. San Francisco phase.
Rectangular Structures:
    Type III, Domestic: Houses 1, 2, 4, 5B, 7, 8, 9. San Francisco phase.
    Type IV, Domestic. Three Circle phase.
    Type V, Domestic. Three Circle phase.
    Type VI, Ceremonial (?). Three Circle phase.

Round Structures

Type I. Domestic (n = 2).
House 10 (Figures 13.5 and 13.6).
Lies partly below House 4 under deep rubbish; was built through early storage pits and cut by later ones. Central postholes only were found; hearth very shallow and not well defined, occupies position midway between center and edge; entrance passage was probably directed south of hearth, but could not be determined owing to destruction of this part of house by later dwelling. The second round house of this type (Number 6) was never completed, hence offered no significant features.
Pottery: San Francisco Red, Alma Plain.
Phase: Georgetown.

Type II. Ceremonial (?) (n = 2).
House 3 (Figures 13.7 and 13.8).
Cut well into native soil; floor rough, giving no indication of prolonged use; postholes and hearth lacking; a shallow floor pit occurs in the north half of the structure. Long entrance passage leads to east, floor is irregular and does not rise uniformly as in other houses, ends at well defined level carrying hearths and storage pits. House wall broken by two oval recesses on north and southwest sides; both contained ashy soil and animal bones.
Pottery: Mogollon Red-on-brown, San Francisco Red, Alma Plain, Alma Scored, and Alma Neck Banded.
Phase: San Francisco.

House 5A (Figures 13.9 and 13.10).
Large bean-shaped structure with a later dwelling (5B) built inside. Southeast quarter has bench along wall formed of native soil, narrows and ends at entrance. Other floor features not determined owing to incomplete

Figure 13.5. Plan and sections of Houses 4 and 10: C, primary roof support; D, secondary roof supports; E, charred juniper beam incorporated in wall; F, beams for supporting hood over entrance; G, entrance passage; H, hearth; I, floor pit; J, hearth; K, floor pit; L, primary roof supports; M, posthole(?) in pit; N, Burial 1; O, plaster on rubbish; P, rubbish; Q, native soil; Numbers 2 to 8, storage pits.

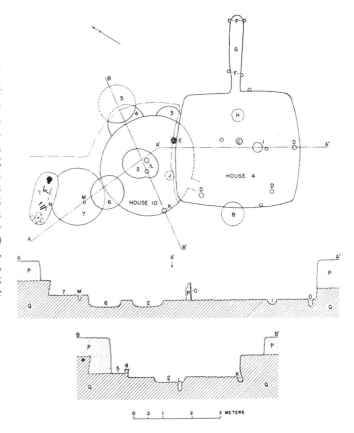

Figure 13.6. The round house on the left (House 10, Type I) was partly destroyed when the later rectangular dwelling (House 4, Type III) was built over it. Diameter of House 10, about 3.5 meters. Arrow at center of photo, pointing to the north, is 24 inches long.

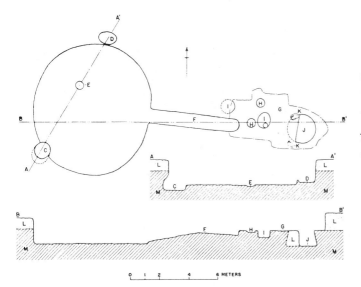

Figure 13.7. Plan and sections of House 3: C, D, recesses; E, floor pit; F, entrance; G, occupation area; H, hearths; I, J, storage pits; K, metates; L, rubbish; M, native soil.

Figure 13.8. House 3, a large round structure, probably for ceremonial use. Looking east. Diameter, about 9 meters.

excavation and destruction of same by House 5B. Entrance on east side starting from short straight set-in portion of wall; stone forms step at beginning of entrance.

Pottery: Mogollon Red-on-brown, San Francisco Red, Alma Plain, Alma Scored.

Phase: San Francisco. House 5B produced a tree-ring date of A.D. 897, hence 5A is somewhat earlier to allow for its complete filling with rubbish before construction of the later house. (Key samples were submitted to Dr. A. E. Douglass who arrived at the same dates put upon them by the writer.)

Figure 13.9. House 5A (partly outlined by trenches) and 5B, both representing the San Francisco phase. Diameter of House 5A, 11.5 meters.

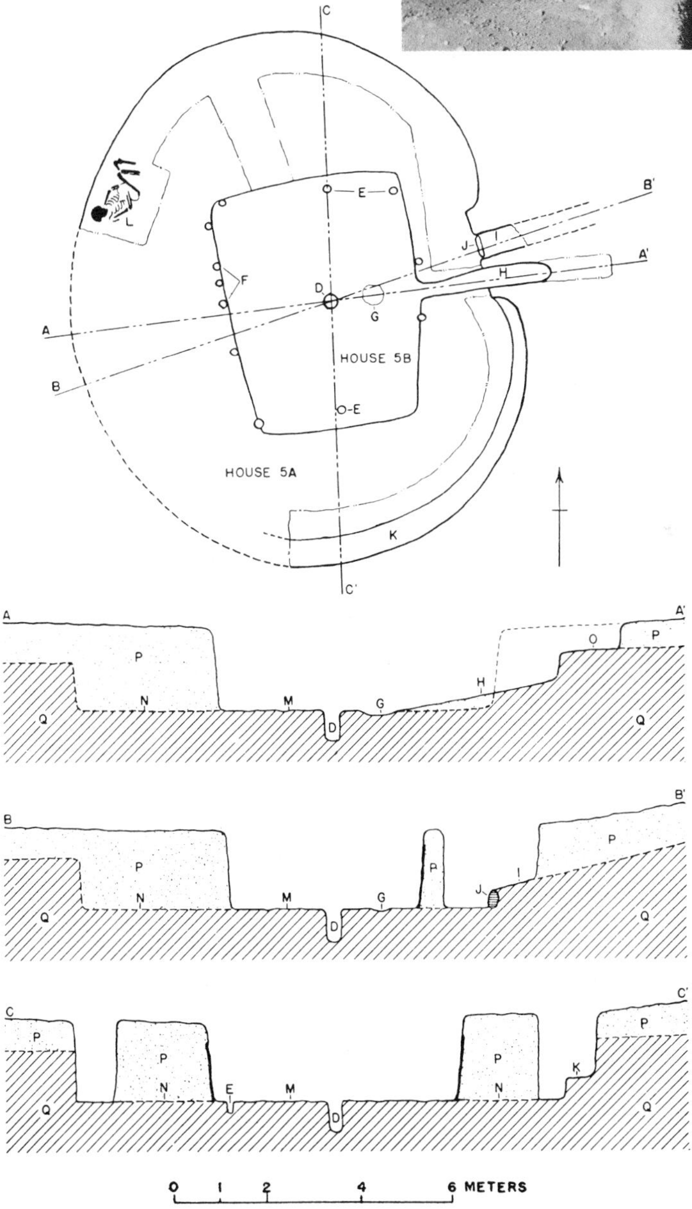

Figure 13.10. Plan and sections of Houses 5A and 5B: D, primary roof support; E, secondary roof supports; F, beams built into wall; G, hearth; H, entrance of House 5B; I, entrance of House 5A; J, stone step; K, bench; L, Burial 4 in fill of House 5A; M, N, floors of House 5B and House 5A; O, old surface level; P, rubbish; Q, native soil.

0   1   2   4   6 METERS

Figure 13.11. House 4, a typical rectangular dwelling of the San Francisco phase. Dimensions, about 4 meters × 4.5 meters.

Rectangular Structures

Type III. Domestic (n = 7).
   House 4 (Figures 13.5 and 13.11).
   Sides bowed outward slightly and corners rounded; pit excavated through rubbish and shallowly into subsoil as indicated by plaster occurring on both, which rises to within 30 centimeters of surface. Floor well smoothed, native soil coated with clay; hearth is shallow depression in front of entrance; major postholes arranged through long axis of house suggesting low gable-type of roof; entrance covered with hood extended from roof; structural wood predominantly juniper. Floor of entrance is level; may have had notched beam or ladder in extreme outer end to reach old surface. House destroyed by fire.
   Pottery: Mogollon Red-on-brown, San Francisco Red, Alma Plain, Alma Scored, and Alma Neck Banded.
   Phase: San Francisco.
   Dates: Three logs gave A.D. 896 as bark dates. House relatively late in occupation through being superimposed over an older structure.

House 5B (Figures 13.9 and 13.10).
   Built entirely in rubbish fill of House 5A; plaster applied to rubbish, reaching almost to present surface; west wall has closely set poles whose purpose may have been to strengthen wall; hearth shallow; roof support

arrangement as in House 4. Structural wood predominantly juniper; house destroyed by fire.

Pottery: Mogollon Red-on-brown, San Francisco Red, Alma Plain, Alma Scored, and Alma Neck Banded.

Phase: San Francisco.

Date: A.D. 897, based on one log.

House 2 (Figures 13.12 and 13.13).

Notable chiefly for benches in short sides of house, apparently connected with construction of roof. Arrangement of charred logs on floor suggests following type of roof: uprights D, E, and F (Figure 13.13) supported a long horizontal beam forming gable, secondary posts set into or near wall also carried horizontal beams to support rafters from gable; front and back walls were apparently vertical whereas roof sloped down to benches on sides. House walls heavily plastered on native soil and rubbish alike. Entrance ends with series of steps; hearth bowl-shaped, clay-lined. Structural wood almost exclusively pinyon.

Pottery: Mogollon Red-on-brown, San Francisco Red, Alma Plain, Alma Scored, and Alma Neck Banded. Four fragmentary Mimbres Bold Face Black-on-white vessels were found on the floor.

Phase: San Francisco.

Dates*: Every datable piece of wood, representing 24 logs out of 27 recovered, gave A.D. 898 as the bark date. Hence this may be unquestionably taken as the construction date.

---

*Editors' note: Tree-ring samples from Mogollon Village were reevaluated by Bannister et al. (1970:48−49), with the following results:

House 1		GP-510	809p−898r
GP-495	669fp−755vv	GP-512	841p−898r
House 2		GP-513	823p−898r
GP-505	655p−786r	GP-514-1	833p−898r
GP-506	804p−858vv	GP-522	815p−898r
GP-501	812p−882vv	GP-523	798±p−898r
GP-507	819p−886vv	GP-524	834p−898r
GP-497	815p−892vv	GP-526	787p−898r
GP-527	848p−895vv	*House 4*	
GP-518	812p−897+r	GP-551	676±p−728vv
GP-516	823p−897r	GP-553	673p−733vv
GP-499	782p−898v	GP-552	645p−736v
GP-514-2	834p−898v	GP-511	661p−736r
GP-498	843 −898r	*House 5B*	
GP-500	831p−898r	GP-557	669p−736vv
GP-502	795p−898r	*House 8*	
GP-503	782p−898r	GP-5817	666 −712vv
GP-504	825±p−898r	GP-5816	676p−743+v
GP-508	848p−898r	GP-555	679p−746r
GP-509	823p−898r	GP-554	691p−748r

House 2, well dated at A.D. 898, contained four partial Mimbres Bold Face Black-on-white vessels and must be the latest structure at the site. The other dated structures of the San Francisco phase tend to fall in the middle of the eighth century, although none are very well dated.

Figure 13.12. House 2, San Francisco phase, showing benches in the sides. Length, including benches, 7 meters.

Storage Pits

Size and Shape.

Encountered wherever tests were made; form round, sides undercut so that maximum diameter was reached at floor level. Range in diameter .5 to .2 meters; range in depth, slightly less than 1 to 2 meters. Pits were never lined with stone slabs; lined with applied clay in one instance only. Contents were uniformly soil, ash, and abundant bones of animals used as food; pottery was lacking with one exception; none of the pits were found burned.

The cross-cutting of one pit by another was a recurring feature (Figures 13.14 and 13.15), indicating frequent renewal. Where pits were found during the excavation of houses, the former were always cut through by the latter (Figures 13.5, 13.13, and 13.14). Pits in houses were very rare.

DISPOSAL OF THE DEAD AT MOGOLLON VILLAGE

Inhumation (n = 8).

Bodies apparently not confined to specific burial grounds but scattered throughout village, disposed in abandoned houses, storage pits, and especially dug graves. Position of body: prone, on back (1), loosely or tightly flexed, generally on back or in semi-sitting posture (7). Orientation: gener-

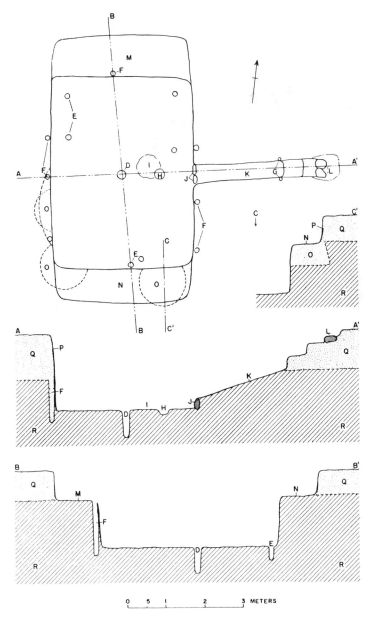

Figure 13.13. Plan and sections of House 2: D, primary roof support; E, secondary roof posts imbedded in floor; F, secondary roof supports built into wall; G, uprights for entrance hood; H, hearth; I, ashy area; J, stone step; K, entrance; L, stones at outer end of entrance; M, N, benches; O, storage pits antedating house; P, plaster; Q, rubbish; R, native soil.

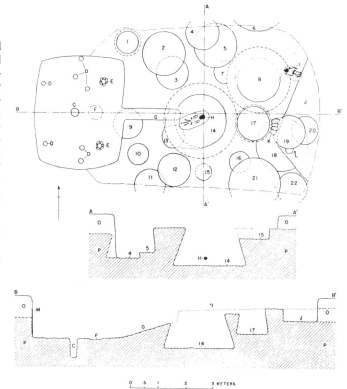

Figure 13.14. Plan and sections of House 8 and adjoining area of storage pits: C, primary roof support; D, secondary roof supports; E, stone-lined postholes; F, hearth; G, entrance; H, Burial 8; I, Burial 7; J, old floor level; K, stonework between two pits; L, hearth; M, plaster on native soil and rubbish; N, surface at time House 8 was occupied; O, rubbish; P, native soil. Numbers 1 to 22, storage pits.

Figure 13.15. House 8, characteristic of the San Francisco phase, and adjoining area of storage pits. Most, if not all, of these pits had been abandoned when the dwelling was occupied. One log from the house gave A.D. 908 as the date. Length of house, about 4 meters.

Figure 13.16. Typical burial, an adult female. Arrow, pointing north, is 6 inches long.

Figure 13.17. Pit with cremated human bones and offerings.

ally east, but may be in any direction. Offerings: with four burials, including a "killed" metate, projectile points, bone tool, shell bracelet, clay vessel, and concretion. A typical burial is shown in Figure 13.16.

Cremation (n = 1).

Burnt human bones deposited in prepared pit about .5 meters in diameter at a depth of 1.5 meters. Offerings: shell ornament, *Vermetus* beads, yellow paint, galena, arrow point. A pit with cremated human bones and offerings is shown in Figure 13.17.

MOGOLLON VILLAGE MATERIAL CULTURE

Pottery

Local.

Types named and described in detail in Haury (1936d). The three major types and percentages of each based on a sample of 13,000 sherds accruing from the excavations are as follows:

Alma Plain 75%
San Francisco Red 20%
Mogollon Red-on-brown 5%

Three minor types, all related to Alma Plain, form less than 1% of the ceramic output. In order of their abundance, these are: Alma Scored, Alma Neck Banded, and Alma Incised. Nearly all sherds recovered date from the San Francisco phase, a meager representation belonging to the preceding Georgetown phase. Pottery from the four houses giving tree-ring dates ranging from A.D. 896 to A.D. 908, was uniformly the same. Only one whole and one restorable vessel were found during the entire season's work.

Intrusive.

Total number of foreign sherds and fragmentary vessels, 24; of these, 8 are Mimbres Bold Face Black-on-white (Cosgrove and Cosgrove 1932:76), and 16 are northern Basketmaker III–Pueblo I. Details of the more significant finds, illustrated in Figure 13.18, are as follows:

White Mound Black-on-white (Gladwin and Gladwin 1935), House 3 (San Francisco phase), fill.
White Mound Black-on-white, House 2 (San Francisco phase), fill.
White Mound Black-on-white, House 5B (San Francisco phase), fill.
White Mound Black-on-white, House 7 (San Francisco phase), fill.
Kiatuthlanna Black-on-white, House 4 (San Francisco phase), fill. Kiatuthlanna Black-on-white was described by Roberts (1931:114), referring particularly to that from the pit houses; the name was first used by Gladwin and Gladwin (1934: Figure 4.)
Mimbres Bold Face Black-on-white, House 2 (San Francisco phase), floor. These are two of four fragmentary vessels of this type from House 2.

Miscellaneous Clay Objects

Potsherd discs (n = 10).

2 to 6 centimeters in diameters, only one is perforated.

Pottery smoothers (n = 4).

All fragmentary, made of potsherds; variable as to size and form. Used on most coiled pottery to scrape interiors. See Figure 13.57b, for specimen from the Harris Village.

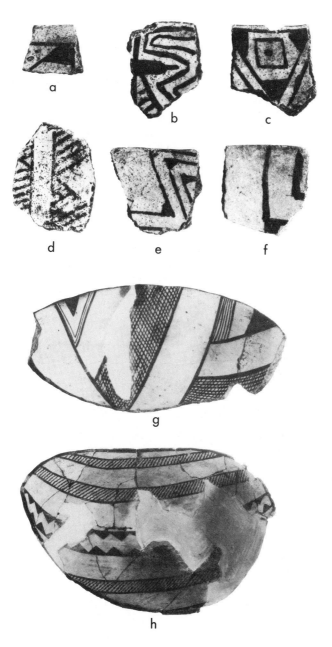

Figure 13.18. Intrusive pottery found in the Mogollon Village: a–e, White Mound Black-on-white; f, Kiatuthlanna Black-on-white; g–h, Mimbres Bold Face Black-on-white.

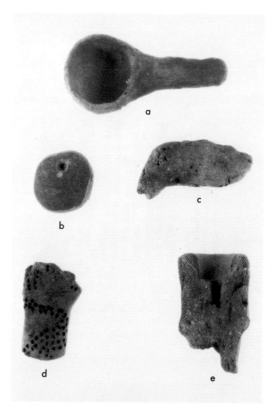

Figure 13.19. Miscellaneous clay objects
from the Mogollon Village. Length of a,
7 centimeters.

Miniature ladle (Figure 13.19a).

Fired, brown color; bowl-and-handle variety represented. Sherds of large ladles were not found.

Pendant (Figure 13.19b).

Plain sherd ground to oval form; perforation begun from both sides, but not finished.

Animal effigy (Figure 13.19c).

Fired, brown color; probably had twig forelegs, hind legs not shown.

Cornucopia-like object (Figure 13.19d).

Fired, brown color; decorated with incised lines and punctuations.

Pipe (Figure 13.19e).

Fired, brown color; stem broken; had a marked shoulder separating bowl from stem; a painted triangle in red occurs at the rim.

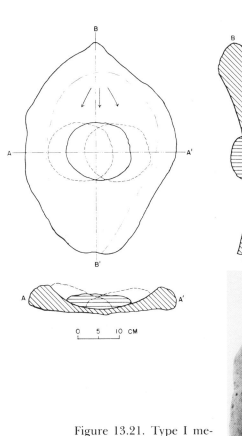

Figure 13.20. Outline and sections of Type I metate showing unrestricted position of mano.

Figure 13.21. Type I metate showing basin-shaped grinding surface. The above example was found with a burial, hence the "killing." Length, 50 centimeters.

Stonework

Metates.

Type I (n = 2) (Figures 13.20 and 13.21).

Unshaped blocks of vesicular lava and rhyolite; average size 35 × 50 × 15 centimeters; grinding surface oblong, somewhat basin-shaped, reaching edge at far end of stone (Far and near ends of the metate are determined by its position in relation to the person grinding; the closed part of the metate, in this case, would be near, and the open end away from the grinder.); grinding stroke not confined to one channel, as in trough type, but followed several directions. Type I manos fit metates of this form, although none were found in position.

Phase: Insufficient data.

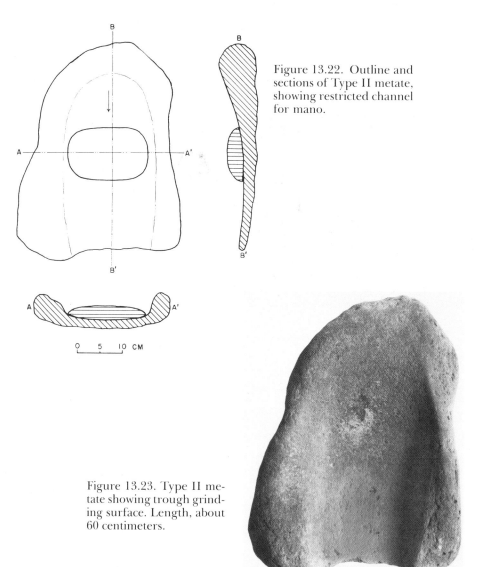

Figure 13.22. Outline and sections of Type II metate, showing restricted channel for mano.

Figure 13.23. Type II metate showing trough grinding surface. Length, about 60 centimeters.

Type II (n = 9) (Figures 13.22 and 13.23).

Unshaped blocks of vesicular lava and indurated sandstone; sizes variable; range in length from 35 to 60 centimeters, and in width from 30 to 50 centimeters; average thickness 12 centimeters; grinding surface trough-shaped, open at far end and sloping up steeply at near end; greatest concavity of trough is reached about two-thirds from near edge; grinding stroke confined to one axis, hence sides are more or less parallel. One example has short extension from near end with smoothed and slightly depressed surface, possibly a resting place for mano when not in use. Type II manos are associated with this form of metate.

Phase: San Francisco.

Figure 13.24. A metate in situ, braced with small stones.

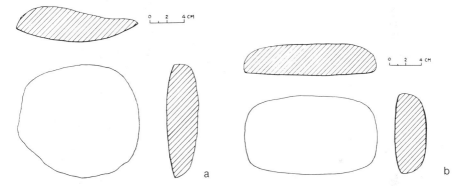

Figure 13.25. Outline and sections of Type I mano (a) and Type II mano (b).

Placement of metates.

When found in original position, metates were located in front half of house, placed so that the person milling would be facing the entrance; bins were never used; metates were placed directly on floor, held steady and at proper angle by small stones; in two metates thus found, the angle of grinding plane in relation to the floor was about 15°, and the near end of the stone was not more than 20 centimeters above the floor. A metate in situ, braced with small stones, is shown in Figure 13.24.

Manos.

Type I (n = 7) (Figure 13.25a).

Vesicular lava and basalt; unshaped, oval in form, measuring up to 20 centimeters in diameter and 8 centimeters in thickness; worn on one side only; wearing surface strongly convex; adapted for use in Type I metates (Cosgrove's [1923:37] turtle-back, rocker-bottom type).

Type II (n = ± 20) (Figure 13.25b).

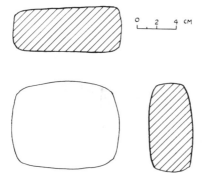

Figure 13.26. Outline and sections of rubbing stone.

Vesicular lava, basalt, rhyolite; sides nearly parallel, ends rounded, all but two have been shaped; average size 18 × 12 × 4 centimeters; frequently worn on both sides, although unequally; wearing surface slightly convex and does not extend over ends, as is the case with manos fitting tightly in troughed metates. Associated with Type II metate.

Rubbing stones (n = 14) (Figure 13.26).

Basalt, indurated sandstone, granite; average size 12 × 9 × 4 centimeters; irregular, rectangular, and rounded in form, the rectangular type predominating; worn on both sides and a few show wearing on ends. None of these fit Type I metates, but they could be used in Type II although they would fall short of reaching the full width of the trough.

Hammerstones (n = ±12).

Diorite and basalt; 4 to 10 centimeters in diameter; both angular and smooth types represented, all generally spheroidal.

Chopper.

Rhyolite; diameter 10 centimeters; originally a core for supplying flakes, secondarily used as a crushing tool.

Abrading stones (n = 3).

Sandstone; show narrow grooves for sharpening such tools as bone awls, and irregular wearing surfaces for grinding down such articles as stone pipes, etc.

Pitted stones (n = 2) (Figure 13.27a).

Andesite tuff (?); spheroidal and egg-shaped in form; pitted at one end only.

Hoes (n = 2) (Figure 13.27b).

Thin natural flakes of andesite, roughly shaped and one edge sharpened.

Mauls.

Vesicular lava, basalt, limestone, granite.

Type I. Full-grooved.

A. Spheroidal (n = 3) (Figure 13.27c).

Shaped, round cross section; average diameter 10 centimeters.

B. Elongated (n = 8) (Figure 13.27e).

Little or no shaping, elliptical cross section; average length 15 centimeters. One example (Figure 13.27d) is shouldered at groove.

Type II. Three-quarter grooved (n = 1) (Figure 13.27f).

Porous lava, oval cross section.

Figure 13.27. Pitted stone (a), hoe (b), and mauls (c–f) from Mogollon Village. Width of b, 12 centimeters.

Pipes:

Type I (n = 1).

Soft, fine-grained rock; short; bowl blackened.

Type II (n = 5) (Figure 13.28a–b).

Rhyolite, porous lava; generally long; shorter examples average 8 centimeters in length, but fragments of long pipes are also represented, probably running up to 20 centimeters in length; bowl usually small in relation to the pipe.

Type III (n = 1) (Figure 13.28c).

Tuff; spheroidal, bowl tapers to small hole, probably for insertion of bone mouthpiece.

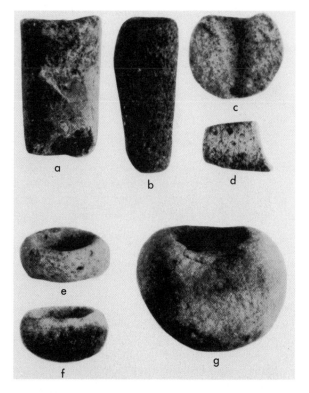

Figure 13.28. Stone objects from Mogollon Village:
a–c, stone pipes; d, atlatl stone; e–g, stone vessels.
Length of b, 8 centimeters.

Atlatl stone (Figure 13.28d).

A fragmentary pillow-shaped piece of soft white stone; present length 3 centimeters (estimated length 5 centimeters); weight complete, about 1 ounce; ends squared; upper surface convex, under side smooth and flat; upper surface scored laterally, evidently to prevent binding elements from slipping off.

Stone bowls (n = 8) (Figure 13.28e–g).

Andesite tuff and sandstone; outside diameters from 10 to 20 centimeters; average inside diameter 8 centimeters; depth variable; vessel walls uneven, thickest at bottom; only one (f) carries decoration, a simple incised pattern.

Chipped stone.

Preferred materials: obsidian, chalcedony, chert, felsite.

Blades (n = 5) (Figure 13.29a–c).

Core implements exhibiting percussion flaking only.

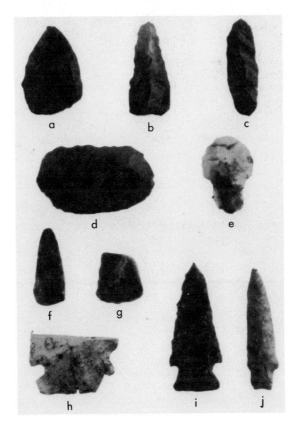

Figure 13.29. Chipped implements from Mogollon Village. Length of i, 8 centimeters.

Knives:
    Type I. Flake (n = 1) (Figure 13.29d).
        A random felsite flake retouched along thin edge.
    Type II. Chipped:
        A. Notched (n = 5) (Figure 13.29h–j).
            All examples stemmed, but notch form varies; base straight; 5 to 8
            centimeters long; example h probably over 10 centimeters long.
        B. Triangular (n = 4) (Figure 13.29f–g).
            Average length about 6 centimeters.
Scraper (Figure 13.29e):
    Spoon-shaped; bulb of percussion near scraping end; retouching confined to one side except on handle.
Projectile points.

Figure 13.30. Projectile points from Mogollon Village. Length of i, 4.5 centimeters.

Type I. Expanding stem, deep notches (n = 59) (Figure 13.30a–f).

Notches diagonal; point broad in relation to length; edges tend to be slightly covex; length ranges from 2.5 to 4 centimeters; average 3 centimeters; weight 0.64 to 3.83 grams; average 1.91 grams.

Type II. Slightly expanding or straight stem, shallow notches (n = 16) (Figure 13.30g–i).

Barbs rudimentary; points narrow in relation to length; length from 2 to 4.5 centimeters; average 3 centimeters; weight 1.60 to 4.47 grams; average 2.23 grams.

Type III. Stemmed, shallow side notch (n = 5) (Figure 13.30j–l).

Stem broad, edges and base slightly convex; length from 2 to 4 cen-

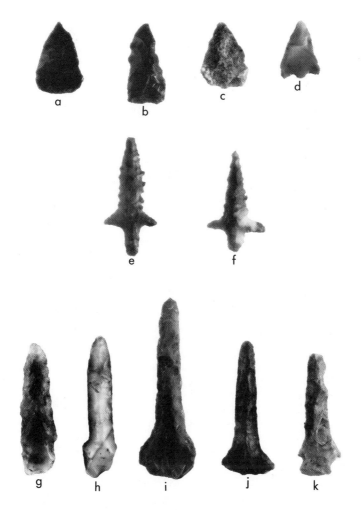

Figure 13.31. Projectile points and drills from Mogollon Village. Length of i, 6 centimeters.

timeters; average 2.5 centimeters; weight 0.89 to 1.60 grams; average 1.28 grams.

Type IV. Stemmed tapering (n = 1) (Figure 13.31e).

Brown chert; laterally projecting barbs, edges serrated; length 3.5 centimeters; weight 1.15 grams.

Type V. Triangular (n = 7) (Figure 13.31a–d).

Edges and base slightly convex, d being exception; length from 2 to 3 centimeters; average weight 1.28 grams.

Drills.

Chalcedony or chert, none of obsidian; length from 3 to 6 centimeters.

Type I. Plain-shafted (n = 3) (Figure 13.31g).

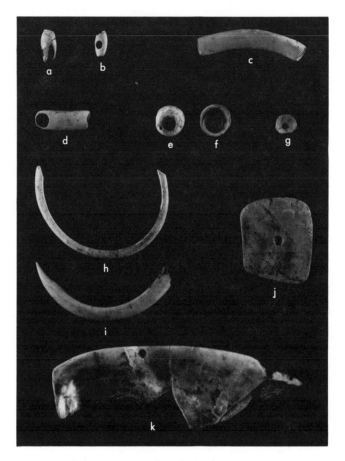

Figure 13.32. Shell ornaments from Mogollon Village. Length of k, 12 centimeters.

Type II. Thickened base (n = 3) (Figure 13.31h).
Type III. Flanged base (n = 5) (Figure 13.31i–j).
Type IV. Stemmed (n = 1) (Figure 13.31k).
Pigments.
   Red, yellow, green; prepared by mixing pulverized minerals with clay.
Minerals.
   Found in houses and with burials; azurite, malachite, galena, limonite, hematite.

Shellwork

Beads.
Raw shells slightly modified:
Type I. *Olivella* (n = 6) (Figure 13.32a).
Spires broken off, not ground as is usually the case; one has perforated side wall (Figure 13.32b).
Type II. *Vermetus* (n = 3) (Figure 13.32c–d).
Tubular marine worm casing, broken into segments measuring up to 4 centimeters in length.
Shells greatly modified:
Type I. Made from spire of *Conus* (?) (n = 5) (Figure 13.32e–f).
Discoidal, but strongly concavo-convex with whorls clearly marked on inside; perforation at apex of spire by grinding.
Type II. Saucer-shaped (n = 1) (Figure 13.32g).
Bracelets (n = 9) (Figure 13.32h–i).
All fragmentary; thin, fragile type; made of *Glycymeris.*
Ornament (Figure 13.32j).
Squared plate, pierced centrally.
Gorget (?) (Figure 13.32k).
Haliotis, has two perforations on long sides, as judged from fragments; roughly rectangular in form; length about 12 centimeters.

Bonework

Awls.
Type I. Head split, but other wise unworked (n = 7).
Made from distal ends of deer metapodials split down the middle; 8 to 18 centimeters long.
A. With side notch (n = 6) (Figure 13.33 a–c).
About 5 centimeters from head is a short lateral notch or offset, slanting towards the point; always occurs on posterior side whether right or left half of bone was used. Four awls in this group are made of left half of bone; notch probably made to assist in cutting away superfluous bone, appears to have had no functional value.
B. Without side notch (n = 1) (Figure 13.33d).
Otherwise the same as above.
Type II. Head partly worked down (n = 7) (Figure 13.33e–f).
Made of unidentifiable bone, but probably deer leg, by longitudinally sawing out suitable pieces and grinding them down for nearly their full length.
Type III. Splinter (n = 7) (Figure 13.33g).
A convenient splinter, unworked except for sharpening of point.
Tubes (n = 7) (Figure 13.33h–j).
Made of both bird and animal bones; length from 3 to 12 centimeters.
Antler object (Figure 13.33k).
Cylinder-like, ends rounded.

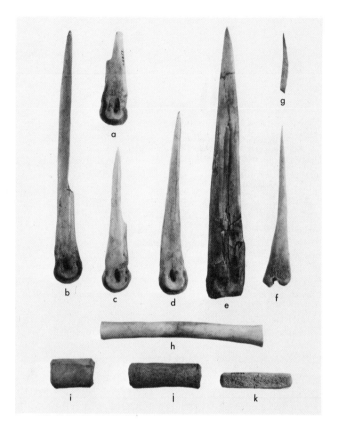

Figure 13.33. Bone artifacts from Mogollon Village. Length of e, 20 centimeters.

THE HARRIS VILLAGE

About 75 miles southeast of the Mogollon Village lies the second village of pit houses with which this paper is concerned. It is to be found on the east bank of the Mimbres River, a quarter of a mile east of the Mimbres Post Office (Figure 13.34 *top* and 13.35), and is located on the property of Mrs. John N. Harris after whom it is named (designated as New Mexico Q:1:14 in the classification employed by Gila Pueblo). The Harris Village occupies a portion of a large flat terrace which rises abruptly above the river for a height of about 20 meters. The openness of the terrace and the ease with which it may be approached from all sides would indicate in this instance that defense was not a consideration (Figure 13.34 *bottom*). The topography of the

Figure 13.34. Location of Harris Village: *top*, the Mimbres Valley at Mimbres (*right center*), looking east. The Harris Village lies on the open ground beyond the large trees in the left center of the photograph; *bottom*, terrace of open ground from the east.

337

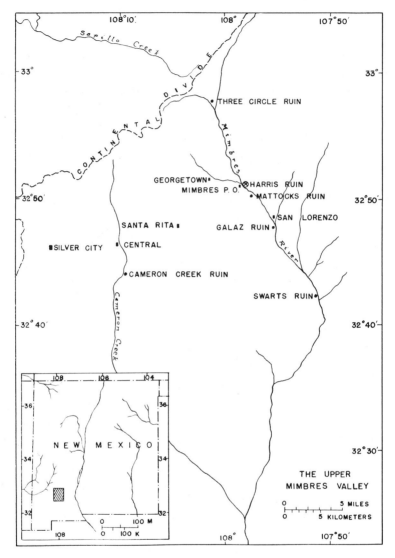

Figure 13.35. Map showing the location of Harris Village (New Mexico Q:1:14) and others in the Mimbres Valley, New Mexico.

surrounding area is rugged, the hills bordering the valley rising on almost all sides to meet conspicuous mountain ranges (see Cosgrove and Cosgrove 1932:1–5). As almost everywhere in this region, farming lands are located along the streams and, although the fields are small, abundant crops may be raised with the aid of irrigation.

The altitude above sea level at this point is about 1850 meters, which brings the village into the lower fringe of the juniper-pinyon belt. At the present time, only a few isolated junipers stand on the site, but a denser growth is indicated by numerous stumps. Heavy groves of cottonwood, poplar, and walnut thrive in the floor of the valley.

Among the food items, ten-row corn cobs were recovered, and the seeds of the alligator bark juniper (*Juniperus pachyphlaea*). Bones of animals were very abundant. The animals represented were essentially the same as those of the Mogollon Village with the following additions: pocket gopher (*Thomomys*), Indian dog (*Canis*), bear (*Ursus*), tortoise sp.

Although house remains extend over several acres, evidence of occupation was not obvious to the untrained eye (Figure 13.36). Two large depressions and several smaller, less distinguishable hollows were the chief clues to architectural units. At one point, a concentration of boulders suggested the presence of a badly demolished stone structure of limited size. But the remains of large stone pueblos, such as occur in abundance up and down the valley, were absent. For this reason, and because villages of this type are not profitable hunting grounds, the site was not well known to local collectors, and fortunately was dug over but very little.

The Harris Village lies in the heart of an area which has been extensively investigated by excavation. Within a radius of 15 miles lie the following ruins on which a great deal of work has been done: Three Circle, Mattocks (Nesbitt 1931), Galaz, Swarts (Cosgrove and Cosgrove 1932), and Cameron Creek (Bradfield 1931). Opportunities for comparative studies are therefore nearly ideal. This, coupled with the further advantage that occupation in the Harris Village did not extend into the Mimbres phase, enables a more convincing segregation of the early and late culture elements than would otherwise be possible.

HOUSE REMAINS AT HARRIS VILLAGE*

Figure 13.36 shows the distribution of the thirty-four houses partially or wholly uncovered. As only about one-fourth of the occupied area was dug, it may be stated that the village was comprised of well

---

*See editors' note at end of this section on house remains for revised dating of pit houses.

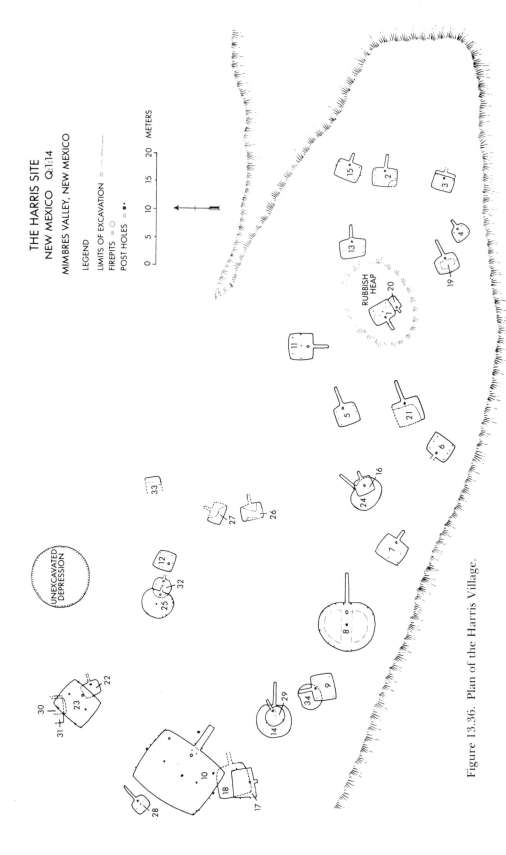

Figure 13.36. Plan of the Harris Village.

over a hundred houses. As in the Mogollon Village, all houses are of pit character but a wider range in types is distinguishable. Form differences are due chiefly to natural changes in architecture resulting from a long occupation. The houses have been grouped according to types as follows:

Round Structures:
　　Type I, Domestic: Houses 24, 25, 29, 32, 34. Georgetown phase.
　　Type II, Ceremonial (?): Houses 8 and 14. Georgetown and San Francisco phases.
Rectangular Structures:
　　Type III, Domestic: Houses, 1, 11, 18, 20, 22, 28. San Francisco phase.
　　Type IV, Domestic: Houses 2, 3, 4, 5, 6, 7, 9, 13, 15, 16, 19, 21. Three Circle phase.
　　Type V, Domestic: House 17. Three Circle phase.
　　Type VI, Ceremonial(?): Houses 10 and 23. Three Circle phase.

Round Structures

Type I. Domestic (n = 5).
　House 24 (Figures 13.37 and 13.39).
　　Lies underneath rectangular House 16; entrance with graded floor leads off flat side; other features not determinable.
　　Pottery: San Francisco Red, Alma Plain, Alma Scored.
　　Phase: Georgetown; priority of round structures indicated by this case of superposition.
　House 25 (Figures 13.38 and 13.40; also see Figures 13.41 and 13.43 for House 29, another dwelling of this type).
　　Overlaps House 32 which is smaller, but of the same general form and phase; front wall straight, the center of which gave rise to entrance (not evident in photograph); main posthole in center with secondary postholes along margin; firepit partially stone-lined, situated midway between center post and entrance; plaster did not rise above native soil.
　　Pottery: San Francisco Red, Alma Plain.
　　Phase: Georgetown.
Type II. Ceremonial(?) (n = 2).
　House 8 (Figure 13.42).
　　Form characterized by flattening in front part of house where entry begins; posthole arrangement appears to be same as in round domestic structures; hearth supplied with single stone on entrance side, extending about 5 centimeters above floor; flat stones on each side of entrance may have special significance or may have been foundations for posts supporting the entrance roof.

Figure 13.37. House 24, typical of the Georgetown phase, and House 16, Three Circle phase; the latter is superimposed over the former. Diameter of House 24, slightly over 4 meters.

Figure 13.38. House 25 and House 32, typical of the Georgetown phase; the smaller structure being built partially over the larger. Diameter of House 25 (*foreground*) about 5.5 meters.

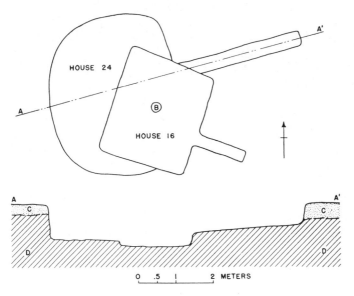

Figure 13.39. Plan and section of Houses 16
and 24: B, hearth; C, rubbish; D, native soil.

Pottery: Mimbres Bold Face Black-on-white, Mogollon Red-on-brown, Three Circle Red-on-white, San Francisco Red, Alma Plain, Alma Neck Banded, Three Circle Neck Corrugated, Alma Scored. The great mixture of pottery in this house suggests an intentional rubbish fill, and pottery is therefore less useful in dating than is the architectural type which, in the Mogollon Village, was allocated to the San Francisco phase.

Phase: San Francisco.

House 14 (Figures 13.41 and 13.43).

Of same character as Number 8, but exhibits a straight front wall and relatively longer entrance passage; small house built within shows difference in size between domestic houses and structures probably used religiously.

Pottery: San Francisco Red, Alma Plain.

Phase: Georgetown.

Rectangular Structures

Type III. Domestic (n = 6).

Houses 1 and 28 (Figures 13.44, 13.45, 13.46, and 13.48).

Form characterized by rounded corners and moderately curving sides; original depth of both houses over 1 meter; present depth of nearly 2 meters due to accumulation of rubbish since houses were abandoned; plaster

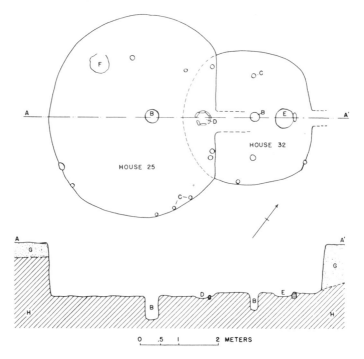

Figure 13.40. Plan and section of Houses 25 and 32: B, primary support posts; C, secondary support posts; D, stone-lined hearth; E, hearth with stone on entrance side; F, floor pit; G, rubbish; H, native soil.

Figure 13.41. House 14, a large unit of the Georgetown phase, with the smaller House 29 of the same phase built within. Maximum diameter, 7.5 meters.

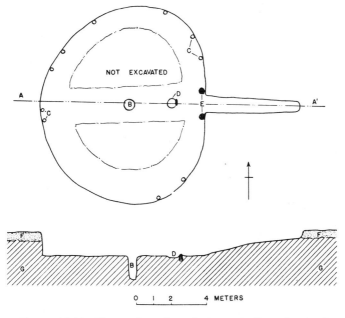

NOT EXCAVATED

Figure 13.42. Plan and section of House 8: B, major roof support; C, secondary roof supports; D, hearth with stone; E, flat rocks; F, rubbish; G, native soil.

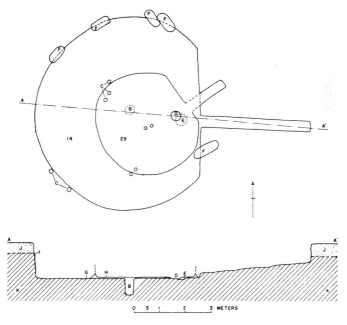

Figure 13.43. Plan and section of Houses 14 and 29: B, major roof support; C, secondary roof supports; D, hearth of House 29; E, hearth of House 14; F, burials; G, floor of House 14; H, floor of House 29; I, height of plaster; J, rubbish; K, native soil.

Figure 13.44. House 1 (Type III), San Francisco phase, showing posthole alignment on long axis of room. Length, 4 meters.

Figure 13.45. House 28 (Type III), San Francisco phase. Note metate in situ. Length, 3.5 meters.

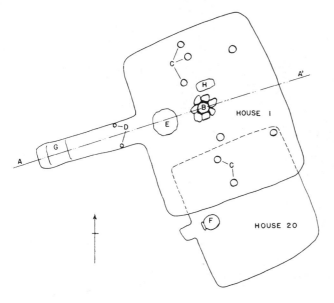

Figure 13.46. Plan and section of Houses 1 and 20: B, position of major post, supported around base with rocks; C, secondary roof supports; D, support posts for entrance hood; E, F, hearths; G, steps; H, infant burial on floor; I, rubbish; J, native soil.

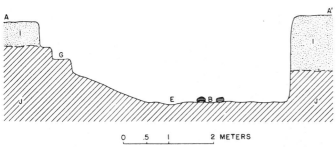

does not rise above native soil; chief postholes follow long axis with major posts in center; subsidiary posts may occur near corners; especially those farthest from entrance; hearth shallow, basin-like, situated in front of entry; outer end of entrance of House 1 terminated with steps; masonry absent.

Pottery: Mogollon Red-on-brown, San Francisco Red, Alma Plain, Alma Neck Banded, and Alma Scored.

Phase: San Francisco. House 1 was covered with a low rubbish accumulation, the upper layers of which produced Mimbres Bold Face Black-on-white of the Three Circle phase.

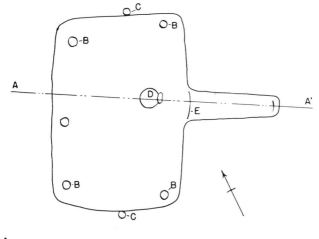

Figure 13.47. Plan and section of House 15: B, major support posts; C, secondary posts built into wall; D, hearth with stone; E, step; F, rubbish; G, native soil.

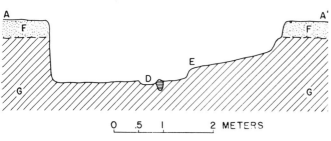

0 .5 1   2 METERS

Type IV. Domestic (n = 12).
House 15 (Figures 13.47 and 13.49).

Corners generally squarer and sides straighter than in Type III houses; may be built into native soil, sometimes largely into rubbish; plaster occurs on native soil and rubbish alike; posthole characterized by corner posts and intermediate supports placed where needed; center post absent; hearth and entrance as in Type III; rough masonry occurs at spots where soil was not resistant.

Pottery: Mimbres Bold Face Black-on-white, San Francisco Red, Alma Plain, Three Circle Neck Corrugated.

Phase: Three Circle.

Type V. Domestic (n = 1).
House 17 (Figures 13.48 and 13.50).

Masonry-lined pit house, built entirely into rubbish; corners square, walls straight; roof support posts incorporated into walls; entrance very short, and hearth in usual position; original excavation for house pit shallow as compared with earlier types.

Pottery: Mimbres Bold Face Black-on-white, San Francisco Red, Alma Plain, Three Circle Neck Corrugated.

Phase: Three Circle.

Type VI. Ceremonial(?) (n = 2).
House 10 (Figures 13.48, 13.51, and 13.52).

Much larger than domestic houses but of same general form; massive posts imbedded in wall and placed in floor on long axis supported roof with auxiliary posts also built into wall; main hearth occupies normal position, having inner pit and stone lining on entrance side; supplementary hearths occur near north and south corners; masonry of waterworn boulders laid up roughly where needed to retain soft soil; entrance passage begins with step and has transverse gutter about midway with stone sill on high side. House 10 was built through rubbish into subsoil overlapping House 18 of the San Francisco phase. Ventilator absent.

Pottery: Mimbres Bold Face Black-on-white, Mogollon Red-on-brown, San Francisco Red, Alma Plain, Three Circle Neck Corrugated.

Phase: Three Circle.

House 23 (Figures 13.53 and 13.54).

Built entirely into rubbish, overlapping older houses (Number 22 San Francisco phase, Numbers 30, 31, unplaced); masonry of waterworn boulders laid up roughly wherever needed to retain soft soil; ventilator absent.

Pottery: As House 10.

Phase: Three Circle.

Dates.*

---

*Editors' note: Tree-ring samples from Harris Village were reevaluated by Bannister and others (1970:63–64), with the following results:

House 4				*House 17*	
GP-601	729–801vv	GP-660	816p–877v	GP-653	814p–856vv
House 10		GP-679	805p–877r	*House 18*	
GP-647	655p–736+vv	GP-666	807p–877r	GP-687	657p–708vv
GP-673	803p–843vv	GP-672	815p–877r	*House 22*	
GP-645	821p–846vv	GP-677	816–877r	GP-643	562p–635vv
GP-646	805p–854vv	GP-681	816p–877r	*House 23*	
GP-651	817–858vv	GP-665	822–877r	GP-644	782p–836vv
GP-667	766p–860++vv	GP-663	823–877r	GP-649	802p–838vv
GP-676	836p–861vv	GP-664	835p–877r	*House 25*	
GP-657	817p–869vv	GP-632	835–877r	GP-654	531p–593vv
GP-678	810p–870vv	GP-671	836fp–877r	GP-688	567–624v
GP-641	819p–870vv	*House 13*		*House 26*	
GP-675	832±p–873vv	GP-629	818p–858vv	GP-650	649p–716vv
GP-640	800±p–874vv	*House 14*		*House 28*	
GP-661	837fp–875vv	GP-655	532–582vv	GP-690	570–608vv
GP-680	804p–876vv	*House 15*		GP-656	541p–624v
GP-631	821p–876vv	GP-637	531p–593vv	*House 33*	
GP-657-1	840p–876vv	GP-633	772p–834vv	GP-691	691–759vv
GP-626	849–877vv	GP-636	771p–857++r	*Rubbish Mound*	
GP-682	799p–877v	GP-635	790p–859vv	GP-684	621–686vv
GP-658	807p–877v	GP-634	817p–861r		

House 10, Three Circle phase, is confidently dated at A.D. 877 with a good group of cutting dates. House 15 has the only other terminal cutting date and may date at A.D. 861. Although none of the other structures may be surely placed, the dates follow the sequence well with Georgetown structures dating before A.D. 624, San Francisco between A.D. 624 and about A.D. 850, and Three Circle after A.D. 850.

GP-654, from House 25, and GP-637, from House 15, both date 593vv and are parts of the same log. With one house of the Georgetown phase and one Three Circle, this phenomenon may reflect cultural reality or clerical confusion.

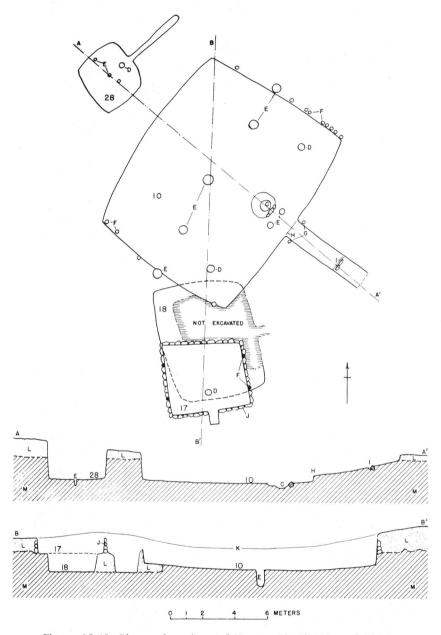

Figure 13.48. Plan and sections of Houses 10, 17, 18, and 28: C, large hearth with inner pit and stones on entrance side; D, hearths; E, major roof supports; F, secondary roof supports rising either from floor or built into walls; G, supports for entrance hood; H, step; I, transverse gutter; J, masonry; K, surface line before excavation; L, rubbish; M, native soil.

Figure 13.49. House 15 (Type IV), Three Circle phase, showing position of posts near corners and absence of center posts. Length, 4 meters.

Figure 13.50. House 17 (Type V), Three Circle phase, a masonry-lined pit house. Maximum width, 5 meters.

Figure 13.51. House 10 (Type VI), a ceremonial structure (?) of the Three Circle phase, in process of excavation with House 17 in foreground.

Figure 13.52. House 10 excavation completed. Greatest length, about 12 meters.

Figure 13.53. House 23 (*left*, Type VI) of the Three Circle phase built over House 22 (*right*, Type III) of the San Francisco phase. Greatest length, 7 meters.

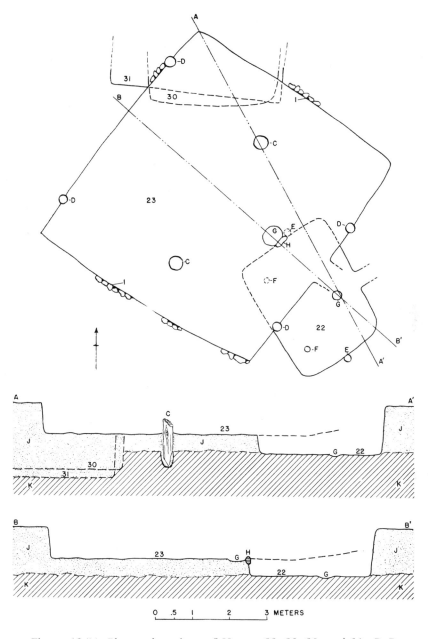

Figure 13.54. Plan and sections of Houses 22, 23, 30, and 31: C, D, major roof supports for House 23; E, F, primary and secondary roof supports for House 22; G, hearths; H, stone on entrance side of hearth; I, masonry; J, rubbish; K, native soil.

Storage Pits

Size and Shape.
    Much less common and not so carefully constructed as those in the
Mogollon Village; sides normally straight with rounded bottoms; diameter
from 1 to 2 meters; depth seldom over 1 meter. Contents rubbish with
abundant pottery, occasionally used as burial place.

DISPOSAL OF THE DEAD AT HARRIS VILLAGE

Inhumation (n = 48).
    Burials were indiscriminately scattered over inhabited area, but con-
centration occurred in and about Houses 12, 14, and 25, where all were
made in rubbish; one burial occurred in abandoned storage pit, two under
floors of houses of the Three Circle phase. Bodies tightly or loosely flexed,
and placed on back or in sitting posture in a grave just large enough to accommodate; head generally in easterly direction but may be oriented to any
point; one burial prone, on back, head east; fractional burials frequent,
skull missing in 8 cases. All skeletal remains very poorly preserved. Offerings occurred in 30% of burials, including pottery, seed beads, bracelets,
small carved bone talisman, and shell beads. A burial is shown in Figure
13.55.
Cremation (n = 2).
    Number 1 in abandoned storage pit; Number 2 in rubbish fill of House
14; adults represented in both cases; bones placed in pit, not in urn. Offerings: obsidian projectile point (see Figure 13.60b) with Number 1.

HARRIS VILLAGE MATERIAL CULTURE

Pottery

Local (see Haury 1936d for a description of ceramic types).
    The principal pottery types ranked according to frequency in a sample of
45,000 sherds, are as follows:

> Alma Plain 75%
> San Francisco Red 11%
> Mimbres Bold Face Black-on-white 6%
> Mogollon Red-on-brown 3%

Six minor types combined form only 5% of the above sample. In order of
their abundance, these are: Three Circle Neck Corrugated, Three Circle
Red-on-white, Alma Neck Banded, Alma Scored, Alma Punched, Alma
Incised.
    Complete and restorable vessels found are distributed as follows:

> Mimbres Bold Face Black-on-white 7

Figure 13.55. Burial of adult female, Harris Village.

Mogollon Red-on-brown 7
Alma Plain 7
San Francisco Red 4
Three Circle Neck Corrugated 8
Alma Neck Banded 3
Alma Punched 2

This pottery is representative of three phases; for assignment of pottery to phases, comparative and chronological deductions, see final section herein.

Mimbres (Classic) Black-on-white pottery is represented by fragments of six bowls, all coming from near the surface.

Intrusive (Figure 13.56).

Lino Black-on-gray (Hargrave 1932:11–12), House 9 (Three Circle phase), floor.

Lino Gray (Hargrave 1932:11–12), House 1 (San Francisco phase), fill.

Kana-a Gray (Hargrave 1932:11–12), same position as above.

Red Mesa Black-on-white (Gladwin and Gladwin 1934: Figures 3 and 4), Houses 2 and 9 (Three Circle phase).

Reserve Black-on-white (Gladwin and Gladwin 1934: Figures 3 and 4), ten fragments, all from fill of House 10 (Three Circle phase).

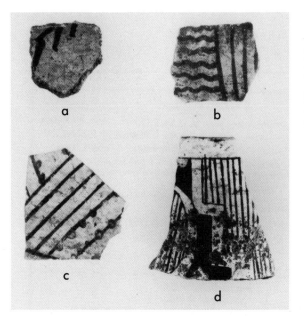

Figure 13.56. Intrusive pottery at the Harris Village: a, Lino Black-on-gray; b–c, Red Mesa Black-on-white; d, Reserve Black-on-white.

Miscellaneous Clay Objects

Potsherd discs (n = 25).

Made from all basic types of pottery; 3 to 6 centimeters in diameter; 14 are unperforated; 1 has radial scratches on both sides (Figure 13.57a).

Pottery smoothers (n = 7) (Figure 13.57b).

Miniature vessels (n = 11).

All plain except one which is Mimbres Bold Face Black-on-white; diameters from 3.5 to 6 centimeters; forms as follows:

> Bowls 4
> Jars 4
> Seed jars 3
> Ladle (bowl and handle) 1

Animal effigy (Figure 13.57e).

Head fragment, of burnt clay.

Pipes (n = 2) (Figure 13.57).

13.57c) Slipped red, and highly polished; designed to receive tubular mouthpiece; some of cementing material still adhering to inner wall.

13.57d) Brown, unslipped; bowl and stem in one piece.

Cornucopia-like objects (n = 2) (Figure 13.57).

13.57f) Baked clay, brown; decorated with punctuations on exterior.

13.57g) Fired, rough brown ware; flared part oval in form; tapers to solid handle-like projection; several red painted lines extend from rim downward both inside and outside.

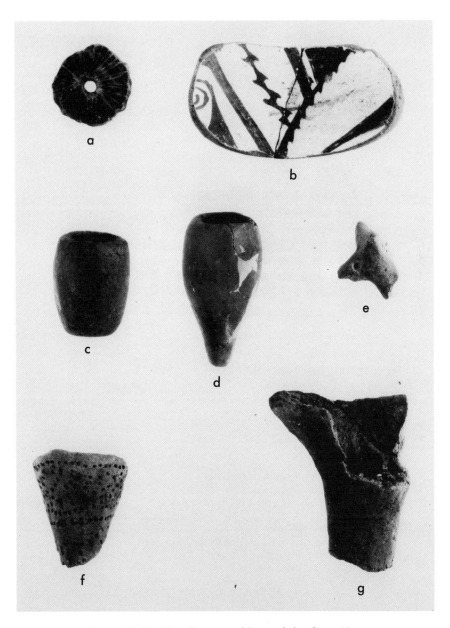

Figure 13.57. Miscellaneous objects of clay from Harris Village. Length of d, 6 centimeters.

Figure 13.58. Primitive axes and sculptured stone from Harris Village. Length of b, 15 centimeters.

Stonework

Metates.

Types I and II (see descriptions under Mogollon Village) both occurred, about equally represented. Type I assignable to Georgetown phase, although surviving later, and Type II associated with San Francisco and Three Circle phase houses.

Manos and rubbing stones.

See descriptions under Mogollon Village.

Mortars and pestles (n = 4).

Mortars unshaped lava blocks; grinding pit conical with rounded bottom; pestles convenient long stones, not especially shaped.

Hammerstones (n = 10).

Rounded, angular, and pitted types represented.

Mauls (n = 10).

Type I (full-grooved) and Type II (three-quarter-grooved) are equally represented; all but one of Type I and all of Type II fall into the elongated subtype (see descriptions under Mogollon Village).

Axes (n = 2) (Figure 13.58a–b).

Found together near surface outside of House 11; made of angular pieces of diorite slightly waterworn by percussion flaking; large areas of original surface remain; edges near broad end notched, and high ridges grooved by pecking for haft.

Sculptured stone (Figure 13.58c).

Specimen incomplete; made of soft tuff, breast-like form; painted red.

Pipes (n = 5).

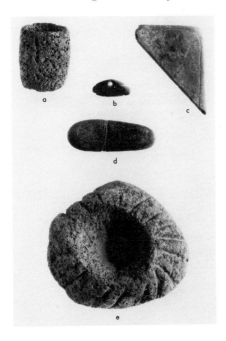

Figure 13.59. Stone objects from Harris Village. Diameter of e, 11 centimeters.

Types I and II (see descriptions under Mogollon Village) represented, the latter predominating. The only Type I (Figure 13.59a), made of porous lava, is designed for insertion of tube mouth piece.

Paint palettes (n = 2) (Figure 13.59c).

Both fragmentary; material schist and fine grained stone; both display features found in Hohokam palettes, i.e., incised borders on faces and medial grooves about edges. One example has traces of white paint.

Grooved pebbles (n = 2) (Figure 13.59d).

Stream pebbles grooved at middle; length 3 and 6 centimeters respectively.

Stone bowls (n = 5).

Identical with those of the Mogollon Village; one decorated by incising (Figure 13.59e).

Ornaments.

Turquoise: one bead from House 4 and one pear-shaped pendant from House 19, both Three Circle phase; several worked fragments from surface.

Redstone: Pendant (Figure 13.59b) of Hohokam type, surface.

Stone ring.

Fragmentary; tuff, perforation bi-conical; diameter 6 centimeters.

Miscellaneous.

Concretions, quartz crystals; fossil *Spirifer* and coral.

Chipped Stone.

Knives:

Type I. Flake (n = 3).

c

a

b

d

e

Rare; mainly random flakes adapted for use.
   Type II. Chipped:
      A. Notched (n = 2).
         Figure 13.60d made of hard crystalline stone, fashioned by primary flaking only; cutting edge strongly convex; Figure 13.60e, chert, convex sides and base, notches slightly directed towards point.
      B. Triangular (n = 1).
Projectile points.
   Type I. Expanding stem, deep notches (n = 11).
   Type II. Slightly expanding or straight stem, shallow notches (n = 5).
   Type III. Stemmed, shallow side notches (n = 2).
   Type IV. Narrow stem, tapering point (n = 3) (Figure 13.60a–b).
All obsidian; one edge deeply serrated towards base.
   Type V. Broad stem, lateral projections from edges (Figure 13.60c); obsidian (n = 1).
Drills (n = 3).
   All flanged, Type III (see Figure 13.31i–j).

Figure 13.61. Objects of bone from Harris Village. Length of b, 18 centimeters.

Bonework

Awls (n = 39).

Type I. Head split, but otherwise unworked; all deer metapodials (n = 9).
 A. With side notch (n = 6).
 B. Without side notch (n = 3).
Type II. Head partly worked down (n = 29).
Type III. Head left intact (ulnae Figure 13.61a) (n = 1).

Spatulate implements (n = 4) (Figure 13.61i).

Made of ribs and flat sections of large bones; two complete specimens measure 10 centimeters in length.

Pin or skewer (Figure 13.61d).
    A carefully finished splinter.
Unidentified tools (n = 2) (Figure 13.61b, c).
    Split bone with head partly worked down, pointed end blunt and some-
what cylindrical (Figure 13.61b).
    A pointed, crescentic implement (Figure 13.61c).
Scraper (Figure 13.61e).
    Segment of turtle carapace.
Die (Figure 13.61f).
    A thin, highly polished, discoidal piece of bone, one side roughened.
Talisman (n = 3) (Figure 13.61g–h).
    Small flat pieces of bone, variable as to shape, bear incised patterns; all
found with burials.
Antler flakers (n = 3).

Shellwork

Beads.
    Raw shells slightly modified:
        Type I. *Olivella* (n = 9).
        Type II. *Olivia* (n = 108).
    Shells greatly modified:
        Type I. Discoidal (n = 164).
        Type II. Bi-lobed (n = 1).
    One lobe perforated; 7 millimeters long.
        Type III. Hemispherical (n = 1).
    Hollow; diameter 1 centimeter.
Bracelets (n = 23).
    All found with burials; twenty-one on one individual; twelve on left
humerus, seven lying loose over lumbar vertebrae, two on right wrist;
bracelets were graded and worn with concave side of shell towards hand; all
of thin type.

Perishable Materials

Basketry.
    Small charred fragment from floor of House 9; two-rod-and-bundle
foundation; stitches interlocking and not split.
Fabric.
    Heavily matted, impossible to determine weave; fiber not cotton, possibly
apocynum.
Beads.
    Several hundred; with infant burial (Number 2, Three Circle phase);
made of hackberry seeds. (See Bradfield 1931; Plate 103, Number 514 for
illustration of similar beads.)

DISCUSSION

The foregoing sections make it clear that the two villages excavated were broadly comparable in age and in the character of the material products. For the Mogollon Village, the history begins with the Georgetown phase, although weakly represented, and carries into the San Francisco phase, while, for the Harris Village, there is ample evidence for extensive occupation through the Georgetown, San Francisco, and Three Circle phases. It is now necessary to test the stratigraphic evidence and other conditions on which the order of phases has been built to see if they can be made to stand. Further, the placing of the material traits in the phase, the tracing of changes within a trait through the phases, and, finally, the position held by the culture in the area at large must be considered.

Architecture

The derivation of a sequence of architecture has been based primarily on stratigraphy and ceramics. The absence of tree-ring data from all but four houses in the Mogollon Village, has forced the use of other criteria. In dating a house ceramically, only the sherds on or within 10 centimeters of the floor have been used. With the pottery sequence established through stratigraphy, this was not difficult. However, since it is entirely possible that late sherds may drift downward into early rubbish and early sherds persist upward into later deposits to introduce extraneous material, it is necessary to disregard these in favor of the predominating type or types. Whole vessels on the floor are naturally very desirable for dating. In addition to stratigraphy and ceramic analysis, which are of next importance to tree-rings, several lesser and independent lines of evidence have also been used to determine the sequence. These are: form of house, arrangement of postholes, character of entrance, presence or absence of masonry, plaster and subfloor and intrusive burials. The results of this study as based on the houses of the Harris Village are given in Table 13.1, where it will readily be seen that some traits are limited to certain house types.

Houses have been classified as follows:

Type I	Georgetown Phase
Type II	Georgetown and San Francisco Phases

Table 13.1
House Features in Harris Village

		Houses																												
Trait		1	2	3	4	5	6	7	8	9	10	11	12	13	14	15	16	17	18	19	20	21	22	23	24	25	28	29	32	34
Type		III	IV	IV	IV	IV	IV	IV	II	IV	VI	III	?	IV	II	IV	IV	V	III	IV	III	IV	III	VI	I	I	III	I	I	I
Shape	Rounded	x	x		x				x						x										x	x		x		x
	Rectangular with Rounded Corners											x	x	x					x	x	x	x	x				x			
	Rectangular with Square Corners			x		x	x	x		x	x					x	x	x						x						
Arrangement of Major Roof Supports	Center and Marginal								x																					
	Center and Long Axis	x	x	x		x					x	x													x	x	x	x	x	
	Near Corners	x	x	x			x	x	x	x				x	x	x								x						
	In Wall									x	x						x	x	x					x						
Entrance	Long	x	x			x	x	x	x	x	x	x	x	x	x	x	x		x	x	x	x	x	x	x	x	x			
	More Than ½ Room Width	x										x			x	x												x		
	Short				x												x	x												
	Less Than ½ Room Width																			x										
	Inclined	x	x		x		x	x	x	x	x		x	x	x	x	x	x	x	x	x	x	x		x	x	x	x		
	Starting with Step	x						x	x	x	x		x	x	x	x	x	x	x	x	x	x	x		x	x	x	x		
Hearth	Stone on Entrance Side	x							x				x	x	x	x	x	x	x	x	x	x	x	x	x				x	
	Stone Lined				x											x	x	x							x	x				
	Clay, Shallow	x	x	x		x	x	x		x	x	x	x									x				x	x	x		

Plaster	On Rubbish Above Native Soil	
	On Rubbish in Old Rooms	
	Not Above Native Soil	
	On Masonry	
Stone Work	In Patches	
	All Around	
Super-Position	In or Over Old Houses	
	Overlapped by Late Structures	
	Through or Over Late Structures	
Floor Pottery	Mogollon Red-on-Brown	
	Three Circle Red-on-White	
	Mimbres Bold Face Black-on-White	
	San Francisco Red	
	Alma Plain	
	Alma Neck Banded	
	Three Circle Neck Corrugated	
	Alma Scored	
	Alma Punched	
Burials	In House Fill	
	Sub-Floor	

*Starred columns under Floor Pottery indicate that the floor and fill sherds were not segregated.

Type III   San Francisco Phase
Type IV   Three Circle Phase
Type V   Three Circle Phase
Type VI   Three Circle Phase

The sequence of the phases was first determined by stratigraphy of pottery types, and the association of these types with houses. This order was confirmed at the Mogollon Village where Type III (House 4) was built over Type I (House 10, see Figure 13.6), and again at the Harris Village where, in two instances, Type I houses were found under Types IV and V (House 9 on 34; 16 on 24; see Figure 13.37). The relative age of Types III, IV, and V was shown in two instances where Type IV and V overlay Type III (House 17 on 18; 23 on 22; see Figures 13.48 and 13.53).

The main changes in form and structural details of the three principal dwelling houses are shown in Figure 13.62. The Three Circle phase house as illustrated (Type IV) leads directly into Type V, still of the same phase, but forecasting the pueblo type of structures of the Mimbres phase. The changes are logical and not very great except between the Georgetown and San Francisco phases; it is not improbable that our excavations failed to give us a house form which would bridge this abrupt change. A similar break in the established order of pottery types coming at precisely the same place makes the omission of a phase almost a certainty.*

Turning now to local ruins as a starting point in a comparative study of houses, we may begin with the Swarts Ruin—located about fifteen miles south of the Harris Village—which was excavated by Mr. and Mrs. C. B. Cosgrove (1932:113) for Peabody Museum. Several houses were found here underlying the masonry pueblo which suggested the houses of the Three Circle phase. Since nothing was found in them to indicate an earlier stage, it was concluded that the underlying houses showed no great antecedence over the stone building. Hence a rapid architectural change was inferred. The validity of this view is upheld at Harris Village, which carried the sequence just to the Mimbres phase (Classic), but which lacked the surface stone houses. The transition from a full subsurface dwelling in the Three Circle phase to the complex surface houses of the Mimbres phase was

---

*Editors' note: Recent work by Anyon (1980; see also Bullard [1962]) reveals no intervening phase.

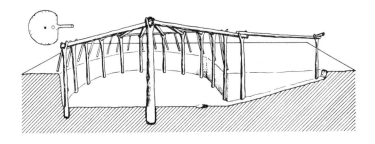

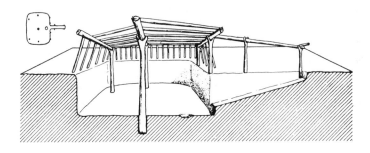

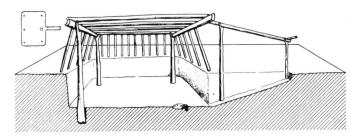

Figure 13.62. Postulated reconstructions of dwelling units of the three phases represented by the houses in Harris Village: *upper*, Georgetown phase (Type I); *middle*, San Francisco phase (Type III); *lower*, Three Circle phase (Type IV).

apparently accomplished through several short-lived house forms. House 17 in the Harris Village would be one in this class, and a further stage would be contiguous masonry-lined pit houses as seen in the Galaz Site, excavated by Dr. Jenks of the University of Minnesota.* In the Mattocks Ruin—only a little more than a stone's throw from the Harris Village—Nesbitt (1931:33–39) reports pit houses, semi-subterranean rooms, and surface dwellings, believing that a very long period of occupancy is represented. Since the pit houses described are those of the Three Circle phase as found in the Harris Village, and since an examination of the pottery from the Mattocks Ruin shows a predominance of Mimbres Black-on-white and only a minor representation of Mimbres Bold Face Black-on-white, a further indication is provided for the rapid change in architecture at this particular stage. The actual time involved is probably not much over a century, although in the case of the Mattocks Ruin occupation may have somewhat exceeded this period.

Pit houses therefore persisted to the very threshold of the peak of this culture, reached in Pueblo III, when suddenly the many-roomed pueblos were adopted. Pottery, like architecture, at this point shows some significant changes, and it is believed that the apparent acceleration in the rise of the Mimbreños was due to a stimulation from the northern Pueblos and a second thrust from the western Hohokam. Pit houses in the Mimbres—since they were used approximately until A.D. 1000—do not in themselves indicate great age; their chronological place can be determined only by an analysis of their form and contents.

But, looking backward, while we do not have firmly fixed dates, greater stability in architecture seems to have existed. Cross-finds of Pueblo I pottery, in the San Francisco phase houses which were both succeeded and preceded by phases when pit houses were used, implies that here this type of structure may well have lasted from Basketmaker III to Pueblo II of the north.

---

*Editors' note: Roger Anyon has informed us that these contiguous, masonry-lined pit houses at the Galaz Site were not recorded by Jenks himself. An isolated pit house with four masonry-lined walls much like House 17 at the Harris Village, has, however, been excavated at Galaz (Anyon and LeBlanc 1984).

In previous excavations, findings not in agreement with the architectural stages presented in this paper were made by the late Wesley Bradfield in the Cameron Creek Village. Bradfield (1931:13–14) writes:

> The earliest evidence of occupation was found in a few shallow floor areas that were leveled off on the surface of the cemented gravels, prior to the accumulation of much, or any, of the later used soil. . . . These floor areas cannot be called pit rooms, but were occupied immediately preceding the construction of the earliest types of shallow pit rooms.

Evidence to support the above situation was not found in either of the two villages studied, nor were the oldest houses in the Harris Village shallow as those of the Cameron Creek Village. While Bradfield uncovered some houses suggestive of those of the Georgetown phase but did not isolate them on the basis of pottery, one cannot be absolutely sure that the oldest remains in both villages were comparable. Hence the writer is inclined to regard the unalterable stratigraphic evidence in the Harris Village as more nearly reflecting the true conditions. But, for all that, future excavators should be on guard for additional data concerning this point. Unfortunately, Bradfield's death prevented the production of a report on his diggings in the Three Circle Ruin, located about seven miles north of the Harris Village, which might have shed some light on the question involved.

Turning to the west beyond the limits of the Mimbres area, one encounters the Hohokam territory with its shallow pit houses. While there is a general difference in the depth of the house pit in the two areas—those in the Mimbres area being the deeper—certain other comparisons can be made. Having in mind particularly the San Francisco phase dwelling and the house of the Colonial period (Santa Cruz phase) (Haury 1932:8–55) the form, the gable type of roof, the position of the firepit, and entrance through the side, are parallel. The entrance passage in the Hohokam area, however, shows a great reduction in length and is equipped with a step rather than a graded floor, this feature being obviated by the shallowness of the house pit. Insofar as the present evidence suggests, these two regional types were broadly coeval, and may therefore imply a connection. But, upon examination of the trend of development in Hohokam architec-

ture which passes slowly from large, nearly square, structures in the
earliest stages (Gladwin and others, 1937) through rectangular to
round dwellings in the latest phases, a direct reversal is to be seen over
the trend outlined here (Gladwin and others, 1937). It may be a coincidence that the resemblance of San Francisco to Santa Cruz phase
houses occurred in the two cultures whose later development trends
moved in counter directions. There is very little evidence of actual
contact between the two regions at this time, although somewhat later
Hohokam elements were being adopted in the Mimbres. It is therefore too early as yet to draw specific conclusions as to the relative status of the house in these two territories, but the existence of certain
basic similarities must be recognized.

As we move northward, Hough's (1919) pit house village at Luna is
the first to be encountered. Here an inexplicable situation arises, for
the houses are reported as being round and entered through the
roof, while the pottery would indicate a later stage than either the
Georgetown or San Francisco phases. Contradictions of this sort de-
mand further work. Perhaps no area calls more urgently for additional studies than west-central New Mexico where pit house remains
are very abundant. Here the possibilities for obtaining tree-ring dates
are as good as in the Flagstaff area; this region, lying between the
north and the south, would inevitably supply useful material, leading
to the clarification of the relationship that existed between the Basketmaker-Pueblo and the Mogollon peoples.

At Kiatuthlanna in eastern Arizona, Dr. F. H. H. Roberts, Jr. (1931:
15–86), unearthed a series of Pueblo I pit houses which have almost
nothing in common with those to the south. Since there is fairly good
evidence that Pueblo I at Kiatuthlanna was broadly contemporaneous
with the San Francisco phase in the Mogollon area, a comparison can
be made with the houses of this stage. The Kiatuthlanna houses were
round, possessing a four-post roof support plan, a bench, roof entrance, and deflectors, features not duplicated in the San Francisco
phase houses except House 2 in the Mogollon Village which had
benches in the ends of the room. This is rather surprising, since some
of the material culture of Kiatuthlanna would indicate cultural connections with the southern area. Considering other ruins, as Shabik'eshchee Village in Chaco Canyon (Roberts 1929), the pit houses
excavated in the same area by Judd (1924), those in the La Plata (Mor-

ris 1939), and others in the San Francisco Mountain section about Flag-staff (Hargrave 1933:26–46) of a somewhat later date, one finds that these combine in a general way to emphasize the differences existing between the Kiatuthlanna and San Francisco phase houses. Hence it would appear that the northern and southern house-building concepts were somewhat different. While, during Basketmaker III, both side and roof entrances were used, Pueblo I structures—and where pit houses persisted into Pueblo II—were almost universally entered through the roof. This contrasts directly with the side entrance uni-versally used by the Mogollon and Hohokam cultures in all stages of development now known. Further, northern houses show interior furnishings not seen in those of the south,—deflectors, ventilating flues, benches, antechambers, *sipapus*, and a dividing partition usually in the southern part of the house extending from the hearth to the sides. Remote analogies are to be found in the D-shaped Georgetown phase house and a few houses in Shabik'eshchee and Kiatuthlanna, and the stone on the entrance side of the hearth in some southern houses may be ultimately related to the northern deflector, but it served no apparently useful purpose, as it never projected more than a few centimeters above the floor.

As we go farther afield, we find that houses in Nebraska offer gen-eral similarities to those of southwestern New Mexico. Gilder (1909:68) reports a pit house with a graded entrance, and Strong (1935) and Wedel (1935) both illustrate round and rectangular earth lodges with side entrances which basically would appear to bear some relationship to those of the southern part of the Southwest. These are placed in the Upper Republican culture, defined by Strong (1933:278–281; 1935:245–250), which, according to best judgments, gave rise to the later Caddoan Pawnee.

As for the probable ceremonial structures of the Mogollon and Harris villages (see also Bradfield 1931:22–28), both round and rect-angular forms occurred. Placed as to phase on stratigraphic and ce-ramic grounds, the round structures can be assigned to the George-town and San Francisco phases, the rectangular to the Three Circle phase, and, while our excavations did not extend into the Mimbres phase remains, the type carries through into this final stage. The change in form took place between the San Francisco and the Three Circle phase, while, for domestic structures, this transition occurred between the Georgetown and the San Francisco phase. Thus a lag is indicated in the trend of development for ceremonial buildings, doubtless attributable to the conservatism seen in most ecclesiastical architecture.*

The houses uncovered in this category yielded meager indications both as to the type of roof and the interior furnishings. Although a bench was found in House 5A of the Mogollon Village, in no instance were other kiva features preserved. Ventilators were apparently not used until very late (Cosgrove and Cosgrove 1932:22–23).† Functionally these were probably related to the northern kivas but, in the strict sense of the word, they cannot be given that name.

Storage Pits

The two villages demonstrate a marked difference in storage pits. For the Mogollon Village it has been pointed out that they were very abundant, stratigraphically early, and, with one exception, contained no pottery, although quantities of ash and bone refuse were always present. Since in the Harris Village the pits were comparatively rare, never so well made, and filled with rubbish containing mixed pottery types, the question must be raised whether or not the pits in the Mogollon Village represent a pre-pottery horizon. That they are earlier than the Harris Village pits would appear certain, and it would be very difficult to interpret the absence of pottery in any other way.

---

*Editors' note: Roger Anyon has informed us that the lag in the change in shape of ceremonial structures between the San Francisco and Three Circle phases noted by Haury was an astute observation verified by recent analyses. Anyon observed a succession of communal structures from the Early Pit House period through the Mimbres Classic period. In general, these structures increase in size through time and become more elaborate. Lobes next to the ramp entryway occur as earthen columns in the Georgetown phase, becomes stylized during the San Francisco phase, and dies out in the Three Circle phase and Mimbres Classic period. Partial masonry walls first appear during the Three Circle phase and becomes complete masonry walling in the Mimbres Classic period. Almost all the Three Circle phase communal structures appear to have been deliberately burned. There is some evidence to suggest that the size of the communal structures correlates directly with site size (Anyon and LeBlanc 1980; Anyon 1984).

†Editors' note: Roger Anyon has emphasized that Haury was discussing two different types of structures here. Structure 5A represents a type of communal structure, much larger than any contemporaneous domestic structure, that occurred from the Early Pit House period through the Mimbres Classic period. The kivas with ventilators, discussed by the Cosgroves, are small semisubterranean structures that occur only during the Mimbres Classic period. Both kivas and large communal structures occur in Mimbres Classic pueblos (Anyon and LeBlanc 1980; Anyon 1984).

However, I am unable to offer proof, and the matter must rest in the form of a question.

As a culture trait, storage pits appear quite widespread. They are to be noted especially in the northern and eastern part of the Southwest and in the Plains among people who combined hunting and agriculture. In the Hohokam area, subterranean pits are also found, but they served quite another purpose than that of storage. There they represent quarry pits from which caliche and clay were taken for house material, and they were subsequently used as rubbish dumps.

Disposal of the Dead

In both villages, the graves were scattered among the houses. Little effort is shown to keep them confined to certain areas, nor is there evidence of any particular care in the treatment of the body. This is especially true for San Francisco phase and for most Three Circle phase burials. However, in the latter phase, a change is perceptible, since house-burial first appears. While only two subfloor interments were found, this practice marks the beginning of the change in burial custom which ultimately, in the Mimbres phase, became the common method. Cosgrove and Cosgrove (1932:23–24) report that over 80% of 1009 burials, not all of the same age, were intra-mural in the Swarts Ruin. Throughout all stages, however, flexure of the body was normal, and orientation was not dictated by custom. Offerings, at first infrequent and poor in early phase burials, increase in frequency and improve in quality in the burials of the Mimbres phase. First evidence of ceremonial "killing" appeared in the San Francisco phase when the vessels were entirely broken and the pieces scattered in the grave.*

---

*Editors' note: The work of Anyon and LeBlanc (Anyon 1980; Anyon and LeBlanc 1984) has supported Haury's statements concerning change in the location of burials and the killing of ceramic grave goods. Anyon informs us that only one intramural subfloor burial in a San Francisco phase pit house is recorded in the Mimbres area; all others are Three Circle phase or Mimbres Classic period burials. Three Circle phase intramural subfloor burials commonly occur on sites that later become the locations of large Mimbres Classic pueblos. Furthermore, ceramic grave goods exhibit development in killing technique. The practice of smashing the vessel and scattering the pieces occurs with Bold Face Black-on-white. Killing by punching a hole in the base of the bowl, and inverting the bowl over the skull of the deceased, begins by A.D. 900, with late Bold Face Black-on-white and early Mimbres Classic Black-on-white and continues with the use of Mimbres Classic Black-on-white during the Mimbres Classic period. Killing by punching a hole in the base of the bowl does not occur with Bold Face Black-on-white bowls.

The practice of cremation, while never common in the Mimbres, extended through the last three of our four phases, and may even have been employed in the earliest. The fact that all the early cremations were of the pit type is significant; later the bones were placed in urns, or bowls were inverted over them (Nesbitt 1931:44; Cosgrove and Cosgrove 1932:25–26), following the same order of pit-to-urn deposition which was practiced by the Hohokam, among whom cremation was habitual. Because of this parallel and the earlier use of urn cremation by the Hohokam than by the Mimbreños, one is inclined to regard cremation in the Mimbres as something derived from their western neighbors.

Food

Charred corn cobs and milling stones are ample evidence that agriculture must be included in the Mogollon culture, beginning with the Georgetown phase. Beans and squash were not found. Even though agriculture was practiced, a rich fauna suggests a heavy reliance on game as well, possibly more than was the case with the northern Pueblos, and certainly more so than with the Hohokam whose specialty was farming. Only vigorous hunters could have brought in the abundance of game indicated, or dared to tackle the bear and the bison. Turkey bones, while comparatively common, do not necessarily indicate domestication of this bird, for they abound in this region and would be hunted equally with other animals. Perhaps the only domesticated animal known to these people was the dog.

Pottery

Since the pottery types occurring in the Mogollon and Harris villages have already been described individually (Haury 1936d), attention can be directed to the tests by means of which the Georgetown, San Francisco, and Three Circle phases have been defined.

In the Harris Village, opportunities for stratigraphic tests were limited to shallow rubbish deposits and the trash accumulations in houses. A low mound in the southern part of the village proved to be a deposit of rubbish which had been begun by filling in the pit of an abandoned house, a fortunate circumstance which provided more than the usual depth of debris. After the boundaries of the house were defined by trenching, the remaining pier in the center was removed in four layers, each of the first three being 0.5 meters in thickness, while the fourth and lowest was 0.33 meters. The test yielded about 1700 sherds for analysis (see Table 13.2), and the results, in percentage form, are given in Figure 13.63. All pottery types have been treated individually except those which showed embellished surfaces, as Alma Neck Banded, Alma Scored, and Incised, and Three Circle Neck Corrugated, which form one group labelled textured types. Too few sherds of these types occurred to warrant individual treatment, hence the chart gives only the trend of texturing as a technique.

Inspection of the chart shows that, a) Mogollon Red-on-brown reached its greatest density in the second level, decreasing in the first and falling off in rapidly decreasing volume in the lowest layers; b) Three Circle Red-on-white follows the same course; c) Mimbres Bold Face Black-on-white, with a very strong showing in the uppermost layer, is reduced to zero in the bottom stratum; d) San Francisco Red and Alma Plain remain fairly constant in all strata; and e) the textured types decrease rapidly towards the bottom. From these conditions one may infer that Mimbres Bold Face Black-on-white was the latest painted type, coming into existence only after the rubbish began to accumulate; that it was preceded by Mogollon Red-on-brown and Three Circle Red-on-white, two obviously related types although the latter was secondary as shown by a comparison of the sherd frequencies; that San Francisco Red and Alma Plain as companion wares revealed very little change, being less subject to development than painted types; and lastly, that texturing was rising in favor from early to late.

As a substantiation of the trend indicated in this situation, further tests in houses of the Harris Village produced essentially the same results. The houses, ranked chronologically by superposition, represent the Georgetown, San Francisco, and Three Circle phases. Since ceramic changes progressed more or less synchronously with the house forms, the task of placing the pottery in the respective phases was not difficult. For this analysis, five houses of each of Types I, III, and IV were used (see Table 13.3; since only one Type V house was found, and since the pottery it contained did not differ from that of the Type IV houses, it has not been included in this analysis). The results are given in Figure 13.64, which, when compared with Figure 13.63, brings out

Table 13.2
Distribution of Pottery Types (in Sherds) According to Strata of
Stratigraphic Test in House 1, Harris Village

Stratum	Mogollon Red-on- brown	Three Circle Red-on- white	Mimbres Bold Face Black-on- white	San Fran- cisco Red	Alma Plan	Textured Types
1	26(24.3%)	3(23.1%)	23(74.2%)	70(23.7%)	344(28.7%)	30(44.1%)
2	59(55.1%)	6(46.1%)	6(19.3%)	96(32.5%)	378(31.6%)	24(35.3%)
3	16(15.0%)	3(23.1%)	2(6.5%)	66(22.4%)	269(22.5%)	9(13.2%)
4	6(5.6%)	1(7.7%)	—	63(21.4%)	206(17.2%)	5(7.4%)
	107(100%)	13(100%)	31(100%)	295(100%)	1197(100%)	68(100%)

some significant points. Mogollon Red-on-brown and Three Circle Red-on-white occur as companion types chiefly in the San Francisco phase houses, again demonstrating the close affinity between the two. Their decline in the upper layer of the rubbish test and in Three Circle phase houses is made clear by the tremendous increase in a new type, Mimbres Bold Face Black-on-white. It is new, however, only in the sense that it evolved from the preceding two types with the adoption of some outside elements, as typologically it carries forward an established tradition. Small percentages of Mimbres Bold Face Black-on-white are indicated for Georgetown and San Francisco phase houses, based on four sherds distributed between Houses 25 and 29 (Type I) and five sherds distributed between Houses 11 and 18 (Type III). These are so small and the pottery on which they are based so out of place where they were found that they are regarded as intrusive from later deposits, hence discredited in value as indicative of the beginnings of the type. Likewise, the showing of Mogollon Red-on-brown in Three Circle phase houses and in the upper layers of the test is undoubtedly an intrusion of sherds already abundantly spread over the site. That Mogollon Red-on-brown and Mimbres Bold Face Black-on-white were not companion wares is shown by the mutual exclusion in some San Francisco and Georgetown phase houses, and by the failure of the two types to appear in association with burials.

Little change is again to be noted in San Francisco Red, except a rather marked reduction in the latest stage. In this respect Alma Plain is comparable. While I do not have figures to quote, my impression is that, if carried into the Mimbres phase, a still further decrease in

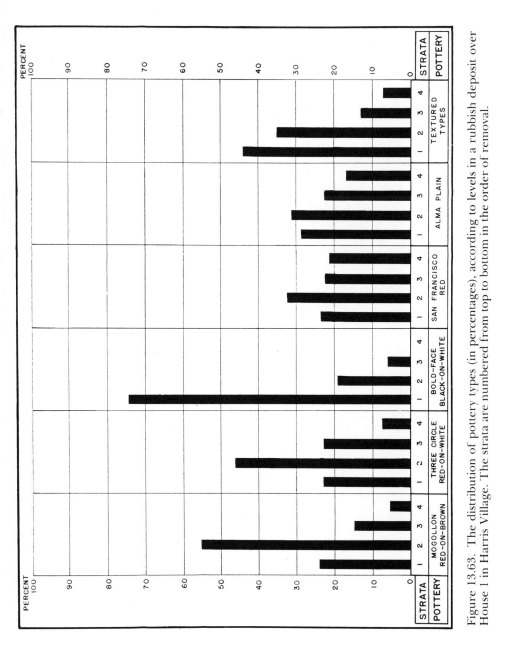

Figure 13.63. The distribution of pottery types (in percentages), according to levels in a rubbish deposit over House 1 in Harris Village. The strata are numbered from top to bottom in the order of removal.

Table 13.3
Distribution of Pottery Types (in Sherds) as to
Phases and House Types in Harris Village

House	Mogollon Red-on-brown	Three Circle Red-on-white	Mimbres Bold Face Black-on-white	San Francisco Red	Alma Plain	Textured Types
Georgetown Phase (Type I)						
24	—	—	—	18	808	6
25	—	—	1	20	98	1
29	—	—	2	44	679	3
32	—	—	—	5	46	1
34	—	—	1	26	124	8
	0 (0%)	0 (0%)	4 (4.6%)	113 (29.9%)	1755 (57.8%)	19 (18.7%)
San Francisco Phase (Type III)						
1	6	1	—	63	206	5
11	14	5	1	39	205	6
18	24	18	4	24	61	8
20	7	4	—	9	56	—
28	4	—	—	63	320	15
	55 (93.2%)	28 (84.8%)	5 (5.6%)	198 (52.4%)	848 (27.9%)	34 (33.7%)
Three Circle Phase (Type IV)						
2	1	3	25	14	102	17
7	—	—	28	21	117	12
9	2	1	14	10	81	14
13	—	—	6	11	59	2
16	1	1	6	11	75	3
	4 (6.8%)	5 (15.2%)	79 (89.8%)	67 (17.7%)	434 (14.3%)	48 (47.6%)
Grand Totals	59 (100%)	33 (100%)	88 (100%)	378 (100%)	3037 (100%)	101 (100%)

these types takes place. This may be partly due to a relatively greater production in painted types in the later phases; conversely, the increase in Alma Plain in the Georgetown phase is explained by the almost complete lack of painted pottery. (In five houses of this phase, only four painted sherds of apparently the same horizon were found. Basically the pottery is Alma Plain, bearing faint broad-lined decoration in red. The type (if one) has not been named, nor is its status known.)

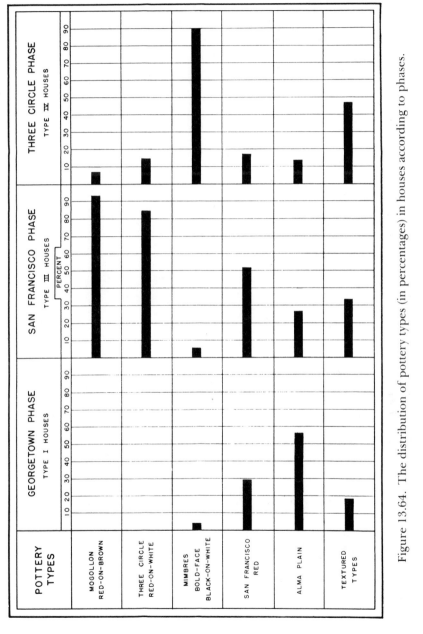

Figure 13.64. The distribution of pottery types (in percentages) in houses according to phases.

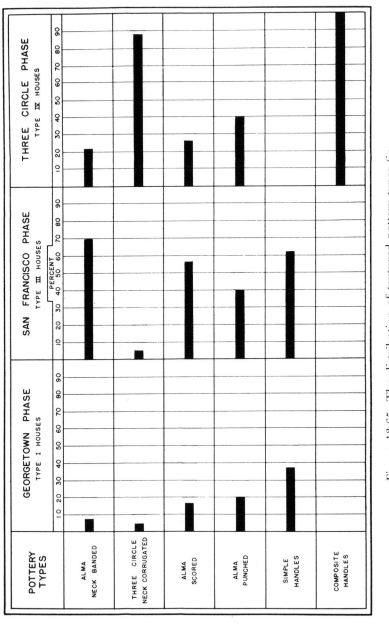

Figure 13.65. The distribution of textured pottery types (in percentages) in houses according to phases.

Table 13.4
Distribution of Textured Pottery (in Sherds)
in Five Houses of Each Phase in Harris Village

	Alma Neck Banded	Three Circle Neck Corrugated	Alma Scored	Alma Punched	Simple Handles	Composite Handles
Georgetown Phase (Type I)	3(8.3%)	3(5.1%)	5(16.7%)	3(20.0%)	3(37.5%)	—
San Francisco Phase (Type III)	25(69.5%)	4(6.8%)	17(56.7%)	6(40.0%)	5(62.5%)	—
Three Circle Phase (Type IV)	8(22.2%)	52(88.1%)	8(26.6%)	6(40.0%)	—	9(100%)
	36(100%)	59(100%)	30(100%)	15(100%)	8(100%)	9(100%)

The trends of the various subtypes in the textured group are illustrated in Figure 13.65 (see also Table 13.4), based on the same houses employed in the previous analysis. Alma Neck Banded, while starting in the earliest house type, is really a criterion for the San Francisco phase after which it declines in favor of its derivative, Three Circle Neck Corrugated. Although the chart shows that Three Circle Neck Corrugated occurred in the Georgetown phase, it is quite clear that this type was out of place, the sherds having drifted down from later deposits. Its absence even in San Francisco phase houses in the Mogollon Village substantiates this interpretation. Alma Scored appears strongest in the San Francisco phase, although well represented in all, as is Alma Punched. Scoring becomes quite rare after the Three Circle phase, while the various methods of punching persist. Alma Incised is too rare to be of any real value.

Handle forms throughout the span of time represented in the two villages have a distinct chronological significance. Simple handles made of a single rod of clay without decoration belong to the two underlying phases, while the composite type (twisted, braided, more than one element) occurs only in the Three Circle phase.

Returning to the stratigraphic test in House 1, in the light of what was found in the analysis of house material, it may be concluded that the deposit collected during the San Francisco and Three Circle phases. More important, however, is the fact that the two approaches

Table 13.5
**Comparison of Sherd Frequencies From Selected Houses
at Mogollon Village and Harris Village**

House	Mogollon Red-on-brown	Three Circle Red-on-white	Mimbres Bold Face Black-on-white	San Francisco Red	Alma Plain	Textured Types
			Mogollon Village			
1	5	—	—	27	144	1
2	5	—	4	18	74	2
4	3	—	—	17	122	2
5B	3	—	—	40	96	—
7	9	—	—	163	448	17
	25(31.3%)	0(0%)	4(44.5%)	265(57.3%)	884(51.1%)	22(39.3%)
			Harris Village			
1	6	1	—	63	206	5
11	14	5	1	39	205	6
18	24	18	4	24	61	8
20	7	4	—	9	56	—
28	4	—	—	63	320	15
	55(68.7%)	28(100%)	5(55.5%)	198(42.7%)	848(48.9%)	34(60.7%)
Totals	80(100%)	28(100%)	9(100%)	463(100%)	1732(100%)	56(100%)

to the problem of pottery sequence have given identical results, at the same time confirming the architectural evolution as previously outlined. The phases, then, may be considered as firmly established.

Since the houses of the Mogollon Village were predominantly of the San Francisco phase, a comparison has been made between them and those of the same phase in the Harris Village. The sherd frequencies and percentages of five houses from each village are given in Table 13.5.

It will be seen that Mogollon Red-on-brown was considerably less abundant in the Mogollon Village than in the Harris Village. A possible reason for this is that, although the same phase is represented, a slight difference in time must be recognized. Since we know that the Georgetown phase, almost wholly lacking in painted pottery, preceded the San Francisco phase, it is justifiable to assume that the figure given for the Mogollon Village would place it somewhat nearer the beginning of the phase, for the amount of painted pottery in the total output diminished as one proceeds from the more recent to the older phases. Two additional points may indicate lateness for the San Francisco phase houses of the Harris Village: a) the abundance of Three Circle Red-on-white and its very meager representation in the Mogollon Village; b) the greater emphasis on the methods of texturing in the Harris Village. (It should be explained that Three Circle Red-on-white is a short-lived type occurring between the peaks of production of Mogollon Red-on-brown and Mimbres Bold Face Black-on-white. At the time the Mogollon Village sherds were analyzed, the type had not been recognized, hence no figures are available, but a re-examination of the material showed very little of it to be present.) In connection with the latter, it will be recalled that texturing increased in the later phases. These two factors also have one further implication, namely, that the pottery of the Mogollon culture in the San Francisco drainage did not develop along exactly the same lines as it did in the Mimbres area proper. To be specific, Bold Face Black-on-white, genetically related to Mogollon Red-on-brown through Three Circle Red-on-white, is a type belonging strictly to the Mimbres area. While a few pieces of it were found in the Mogollon Village, it was clearly intrusive and late. There seems to be no real successor to Mogollon Red-on-brown in the San Francisco drainage, it being replaced by black-on-white types drifting down from the north. Alma Plain, or derived forms, on the other hand, certainly survived in the region for some time. Neck corrugating, incising, punching, etc., markedly stronger in the Harris Village, find their culmination in the Mimbres during the Classic stage, while in the San Francisco area this turn in ceramics seems to be preserved in the incised-over-corrugations of the Reserve phase, and possibly later in the fillet rim bowls common in the Upper Gila (see Haury 1936d, for further discussion of pottery).*

Miscellaneous Clay Objects

Noteworthy are the three cornucopia-shaped objects represented in both villages. In form and decoration these show a detailed resemblance to similar articles possessed by the Basketmakers (Morris 1927: 156–158; Guernsey 1931:87–88; Morss 1931:50; Steward 1933:9). All specimens were associated with material of the San Francisco

---

*Editors' note: Anyon and LeBlanc (1984) supported the essential correctness of the ceramic sequence outlined by Haury and provided adjustments based on later information.

phase which places the element as early. These objects were made of clay native to the region and it is therefore to be inferred that as a trait they were shared by the Basketmaker and Mogollon peoples.

Both single-piece and two-piece clay pipes were used. Two of the former are distinctly early, i.e., Georgetown and San Francisco phases, while the two-piece pipe from the Harris Village was found with a burial in rubbish and therefore possibly late. The pipe illustrated in Figure 13.19e bears no close likeness to other pipes from early sites described in the literature. The shoulder takes it out of the cone-like class so generally used by the Basketmakers and the painted exterior is also unique. With the exception of a black-on-white pipe stem from Pueblo Bonito figured by Pepper (1920:51), I have been unable to find reference to this trait in the Southwest. Painted stone pipes have been reported (Cosgrove and Cosgrove 1932:51). Harrington (1920: 196) notes that a certain type of Caddo clay pipe was often painted. The painting of pipes, whether clay or stone, was apparently pretty well confined to the southeastern part of the Pueblo region.

Stonework

The stone tools of the two villages excavated are approximately the same as to type and variety. In the Harris Village certain artifacts were found not represented in the Mogollon Village.

In metates and manos a change was perceptible between the Georgetown and the two succeeding phases. The change was brought about chiefly by limiting the grinding axis in the earlier form. From the Three Circle phase on into the Mimbres phase another change took place, seen in the shaping of the stone and in the grinding trough which more nearly approaches a plane in both directions (Cosgrove and Cosgrove 1932:35–37). The basin-shaped metates (Type I) are by no means confined in distribution to the San Francisco-Mimbres area, for they occur from Flagstaff eastward into the Plains, in early horizons from early Basketmaker to Pueblo II, and survive to the present day among some of the living Indians. (For a summary of distribution, see Bartlett 1933:20–21.)

The troughed metate (Type II), appearing mainly in the San Francisco and Three Circle phases, was also widespread. It corresponds with those employed in Basketmaker III and Pueblo I of the northern sector (Guernsey 1931:83; Roberts 1929:132–134, 1931:154). Most northern metates of these periods are made of sandstone, while those in the south are mainly of lava.

The metates of the Mogollon area had little in common with those of the Hohokam, for to the west a full-troughed, carefully shaped type was already well established.

As a general statement, it may be said that the northern and southern parts of the Southwest differed as to the tools used in the cultivation of maize. In the north, the digging stick was dominant; in the south, the stone hoe. (A certain amount of overlap may be indicated by the hornstone blades of the San Juan [Kidder and Guernsey 1919: Pl. 52, l, m] which, when mounted on a shaft, would serve as useful cultivating tools, and by the finding of occasional digging sticks in the south. C. B. Cosgrove discovered one in a cave in southern New Mexico [now in Peabody Museum], and Russell [1908:97] reports their use until recently among the Pima.) While the hoe was used by the Mogollon people—at first (San Francisco phase) a broad, unspecialized tool—it became abundant only in the Mimbres phase when it assumed a slender blade-like form (Nesbitt 1931:80–82; Cosgrove and Cosgrove 1932:45–46). Whether or not the Mogollon culture derived its hoe from the Hohokam remains to be shown, although it is quite possible.

The lack of axes but the abundance of grooved mauls in the two villages is a curious paradox. Mauls, both full- and three-quarter grooved, are represented in all phases, including the Mimbres. It is a fair assumption, however, that three-quarter grooving is in general somewhat later than full grooving. A small type, illustrated by Cosgrove (1932: Plate 42) from the Swarts Ruin, occurred in neither of our two sites.

The two crude axes illustrated in Figure 13.58 from the Harris Village could, with some degree of certainty, be placed in the Three Circle phase. They are so unlike anything from the immediate area or even adjoining regions that they are considered aberrant; and all the more so since, in the Mimbres phase, numerous well-formed axes of the three-quarter grooved type suddenly appear. Since it is not likely that the two crude Harris Village axes could have been so abruptly transformed to a skillfully made axe by indigenous development, there remains little doubt that the conception of the Mimbres phase axe—if not many of the axes themselves—is a direct importation. Among the Hohokam, the three-quarter grooved axe had long been established. As a strong group who were instrumental in producing other changes in the Mimbres, the Hohokam are the only logical donors. The Mimbres phase axe could certainly not have come from the north, characterized by a short-bitted, full-grooved type (for hafted example, see Fewkes 1911: Plate 20), or from the upper Rio Grande where the curious spirally grooved axe is at home (Kidder 1932:45–54).

The stone pipes are all of the tubular type, excepting one of unusual spherical form. The short pipes have much in common with those of the northern Basketmaker-Pueblos, although the long examples, sometimes painted (Cosgrove and Cosgrove 1932:50–51), appear to be centered well to the south. The long pipes are apparently late (Three Circle to Mimbres phases). By way of contrast, it should be stated that the Hohokam at no time employed pipes of either clay or stone.

Stone vessels in the form of small bowls carry through the San Francisco and Three Circle phases in our series in rather simplified form, sometimes having scratched patterns. In the Mimbres phase, however, zoömorphic types and painted vessels are found (Cosgrove and Cosgrove 1932:32–33). The latter bear more than a chance resemblance to the carved stone vessels of the Hohokam who made them not only in great abundance, but used them over a long range of time. Although stone vessels have been reported widely,* they center in the south in the Hohokam and Mogollon areas where the carved forms are found almost exclusively.

Among the chipped stone objects, the large notched blades are assuredly bound up with hunting activities and in their character are somewhat more suggestive of tools found in the Plains than in the Southwest. In both villages these are to be assigned to the Georgetown and San Francisco phases. The deep notched, expanding stemmed projectile points were likewise associated in deposits dating from these two phases. From the standpoint of size and type, they have been regarded by several people who have seen them as having been used in atlatl darts, and the finding of a fragmentary atlatl stone in the Mogollon Village helps to sustain this view. Strong (1935: Plate 24, Number 2, e) illustrated a similar type as occurring in the Signal Butte II horizon of western Nebraska, evidence of an early hunting group.

The long, slender points, illustrated in Figure 13.60a–b, sometimes having serrated edges, were not represented in the Mogollon

---

*Flagstaff area (Pueblo II), Bartlett (1934:26–27); Kiatuthlanna (Pueblo I), Roberts (1931:156); Upper Gila area (chronological position unknown), Hough (1914: Figure 49); southeastern Arizona (Colonial-Sedentary), Trisckha (1933:426); Chihuahua (Pueblo IV), Sayles (1935).

Village, and they can therefore be placed as late for the Harris Village. They became the prevailing form in the Mimbres phase (Cosgrove and Cosgrove 1932: Plate 50).

What may be considered as an intrusive type, probably from the east, is the point illustrated in Figure 13.31e, in comparison with a point from Sierra Blanca:4:1 in Texas. Roberts (1931: Plate 39f) shows a point of similar character from Kiatuthlanna pit houses which, along side of the prevailing type from the same site, looks quite out of place. Because points of this character have not been definitely placed as to horizon in Texas where they are widely spread, nothing can be directly inferred from the association.

Drills were mainly of the flanged type, occurring principally in the Georgetown and San Francisco phases. Judging from those found in Classic or Mimbres phase sites (Cosgrove and Cosgrove 1932: Plate 52), they underwent a decline in standardization and workmanship. Only one stemmed drill was found but it, like other items in the culture, has an eastern flavor.

Fragments of paint palettes and a broken stone ring found in the Harris Village date from the Three Circle phase. For analogies and a possible source of these traits of late origin in the Mimbres, it is necessary to turn to the Hohokam.

As a generalization, it may be stated that the stonework of the late Basketmaker and early Pueblo peoples and the people of the Mogollon area was about on the same level. Both used chipping and polishing for the same objects with about the same degree of skill. The full-grooved maul, short pipes, troughed metates open only at one end, large chipped knives, and the absence of grooved axes, are points in which the two groups agree; they disagree in that the Mogollon people possessed the hoe, stone bowls, long stone pipes, a slightly differing projectile point. Absent in both are the three-quarter grooved axe and the slate palette, two characteristics of the Hohokam, whose stonework at an early date excelled in kind and form that ever produced by either the Basketmaker-Pueblo or the Mogollon people.*

---

*Editors' note: Anyon has informed us that hoes, which occur primarily in the Mimbres Classic period, are found almost exclusively in caches. Both full and three-quarter grooved axes appear throughout the Late Pit House and Mimbres Classic periods in the Mimbres area. Palettes and carved stone bowls are primarily associated with Three Circle phase contexts and look very similar to pieces in the Hohokam area (Anyon and LeBlanc 1984).

Shellwork

One or two general trends may be noted: In the San Francisco phase (there are no data for the Georgetown phase) shellwork was not abundant, and the number of species represented were few; but in the Mimbres phase the amount of shell itself increased, the objects made became more diversified, and the number of species increased. It is not unlikely that most of the shell used in the Mimbres found its way along a trade route that roughly followed the Gila from the Gulf of California. Hence it is not surprising to find, in the Gila Basin, that the same conditions relative to the use of shell pertained, although there the stage of greatest richness and multiplicity of objects produced was somewhat ahead of that in the Mimbres.

As for specific objects, beads of the *Olivella* shell were used, perhaps, more widely and over a longer period of time in the Southwest than any other shell; *Oliva* beads are early in the Basketmaker territory, and they are early here also; bracelets are of the thin fragile type in early horizons generally, the broad heavy type apparently appearing for the first time in the Mimbres phase (Cosgrove and Cosgrove 1932: Plate 72f), and it is likewise late in the series in the Hohokam area. The shell gorget (?) from the Mogollon Village is quite unlike the normal shell objects produced in the Southwest, the type generally running to the east. (Strong 1935, Plate 11, Number 1, g, shows an almost identical specimen from an Upper Republican culture site in Nebraska.)

Bonework

The chief item of interest is the notched awl which carries through from the San Francisco to the Mimbres phase. The notch, cut into the awl a few centimeters from the head, was probably only a means for assisting in the removal of surplus bone from the shaft, but it is so unique a feature and occurs in so limited an area that some cultural significance may be assigned to it. Large collections of bone tools from late sites, as Hawikuh (Hodge 1920) and Pecos (Kidder 1932) do not contain specimens of this sort, nor can they be traced in either early or late sites of the San Juan. That they should occur in the pit house horizon at Kiatuthlanna (Roberts 1931: Plate 25a) is not surprising, since a number of other Mogollon traits have already been noted from there. They reach their greatest density in the Mimbres proper, then die out again going south into Chihuahua. It is certainly one of the distinctive features of the Mogollon culture, being common in all phases except Georgetown, from which there is no information.

Table 13.6 is included at this point as a synthesis of the material already given, and to aid in the quick comprehension of the changes that took place from phase to phase. Owing to the incompleteness of the data in the Georgetown phase, it would appear that this member in the series might not be well established. However, I believe that the weight of the architectural and ceramic differences alone are sufficient to create it. Cognizance has not been taken of the possibility of an additional phase between the Georgetown and San Francisco phases.

The Physical Type

Up to this point nothing has been said about the physical characteristics of the Mogollon people, but herein lies one of the strongest arguments for the distinctness of the culture. In the Mogollon Village the skeletal material was both meager and poorly preserved. Judgment of the racial type was therefore limited to a single measurable skull and a fragmentary skeleton until a larger series from the Harris Village provided strengthening evidence. Dr. George Woodbury studied the skeletal remains from both sites and I shall therefore quote liberally from his reports (Woodbury, G., 1934, MS. Preliminary Report on the Mogollon Skeletal Material; a copy of this and the other reports referred to are in Gila Pueblo files). Concerning the Mogollon specimen, he writes:

> In general appearance, the skeleton is that of a small person of slight physique whose skull is small and delicate and whose long bones are straight with feebly developed muscular rugosities. The skeleton is that of a woman of about middle age.
>
> The skull is definitely brachycephalic (Index 90.06) and the cranial vault is low (123), a combination typical of some of the non-pueblo tribes of the Southwest. Due probably to improper cradling in infancy, there is a slight flattening of the left occipital region, a condition frequently met with in Indian crania. The forehead of this individual is protruding and typically feminine in contour.
>
> The most conspicuous feature of the face is its length (112) which is noticeable because the facial width (132) is rather narrow for an Indian. The orbits are round in contour (Index

| Phase | Physical Type | Burial Custom | Architecture | | Pottery | Stone Metates & Manos |
			Domestic	Ceremonial (?)		
Mimbres	"Pueblo" type combining a high vault with deformed brachycephaly.	Normally under house floors; occasionally extramural; bodies flexed and usually accompanied by "killed" offerings. Cremation rare.	One-story masonry pueblos.	Large, rectangular, semi-subterranean; entered by long inclined passage; ventilator shaft present.	Mimbres Black-on-white, San Francisco Red, Alma Plain, Mimbres Corrugated.	Full-troughed type, often shaped. Manos four-sided, shaped.
Three Circle	"Pueblo" type and "Caddoan" type combining a low vault with undeformed brachycephaly.	In old storage pits, in deep rubbish, or in graves dug into native soil; burials occasionally made below house floors, especially infants; bodies flexed; offerings rare. Cremation rare.	Plaster-on-soil (Type IV) and stone-lined rectangular pit houses (Type V) with lateral inclined entrance passage. Roof supported by four main posts placed near corners of house.	As above (Type IV) but without ventilator.	Mimbres Bold Face Black-on-white, Three Circle Red-on-white, San Francisco Red, Three Circle Neck Corrugated, Alma Plain, Alma Punched.	Troughed, closed at one end (Type II), unshaped. Grinding axis limited. Manos as above.
San Francisco A.D. 900*	"Caddoan" type.	Burials scattered indiscriminately between houses; never intramural; offerings very rare, bodies flexed. Cremation rare.	Plaster-on-soil rectangular pit houses (Type III) with lateral inclined entrance passage. Masonry absent. Roof supported mainly by center post and auxiliary posts in line with long axis of house.	Type II. Sides at entrance drawn in giving structure kidney shape. Ventilator absent.	Mogollon Red-on-brown, San Lorenzo Red-on-brown, Three Circle Red-on-white, San Francisco Red, Alma Plain, Alma Neck Banded, Alma Punched, Alma Scored.	Type II as above and Type I having basin-shaped milling surface. Grinding axis not limited. Manos rounded in form and grinding surface strongly convex; not shaped.
Georgetown	No data.	No data.	Pit houses (Type I), roughly circular with flat side which gave rise to inclined entrance passage. Major roof support in center, secondary posts about periphery.	Same as domestic units but larger (Type II). Ventilator absent.	San Francisco Red, Alma Plain, Alma Neck Banded, Alma Scored. Painted pottery represented by only four fragments of crude broad-line red-on-gray.	Type I only.

*Based on tree-rings

| | Stone | | | | Shell | Bone | Miscellaneous |
Hoes	Mauls & Axes	Stone Vessels	Chipped Stone	Miscellaneous			
Long, narrow blades.	Full- and three-quarter-grooved mauls and axes. Three-quarter-grooved axes predominate.	Simple, but sometimes carved in life forms and painted.	Long, narrow-stemmed projectile points, plain or serrated edges, often on one side only. Large blades rare and crude.	Notched floor stones. Slate palettes. Long stone pipes.	Abundant; diverse objects including life-form carvings.	Plain and notched awls, heads sometimes carved. "Dice."	One-piece, short, clay pipes. Copper bells.
No data.	Full-and three-quarter grooved mauls. Axes crude, notched for hafting.	Simple, occasionally with scratched patterns.	As above, projectile points serrated on both edges. No data for blades.	Slate palettes. Long and short stone pipes.	Abundant but relatively few species used. Bi-lobed beads.	Plain and notched awls. "Dice." Burial talisman.	Short, clay pipes fitted with stem. Two-rod-and-bundle coiled basketry. Ten-row corn.
Broad blades.	Full- and three-quarter grooved mauls. Axes absent.	Simple and roughly cut, patterns of any sort rare.	Short, broad-stemmed projectile points with deep diagonal notches and stemmed points shallow notches. Large, chipped blades, stemmed. Stemmed drills.	Atlatl weights. Pipes as above.	Rare. Olivella and Vermetus beads, saucer-shaped beads, bracelets of Glycymeris.	Plain and notched awls. Tubes.	Cornucopia-like clay objects. Worked copper. Six-row corn (data incomplete).
No data.	No data.	No data.	Projectile points and blades as above.		No data.	No data.	Short, one-piece, clay pipes.

93.30) and the nasal aperture is low and wide (Index 57.14) with clearly defined nasal gutters. The palate is broad (Index 105.77) and the teeth are well aligned although much worn as a result of a gritty diet. . . . The angles of the lower jaw are wide (100) and the chin is well developed.

The general appearance of the skull is definitely Indian and typically feminine.

Dr. Woodbury first compared this skull with a series of female Apache crania resulting in some rather striking similarities. He then used a series of female Caddoan (Caddo and Wichita; Hrdlicka 1927) finding an even greater likeness. (Dr. Woodbury stated that the Caddo and Wichita were selected because the Pawnee, although also Caddoan people, are characterized by a much higher skull vault.) Quoting Dr. Woodbury again:

> Points of close similarity between the Mogollon and the Caddoan are apparent in the mutual brachycephaly combined with a low skull vault. The facial diameters are also similar. . . . These measurements have been compared in graph form (Figure 13.66) where both the Mogollon and the Caddoan values have been plotted against a base line (Pecos, Total Series A) and the similarity between them is even more striking. . . .
>
> This leads us to conclude for the moment or until we have more data for comparison that the Mogollon specimen . . . is probably allied to the Caddoan stock as shown by a comparison of the crania of these two series. That is to say that both, Mogollon and Caddoan, are brachycephalic and low vaulted with similar facial proportions.

This was the state of affairs up to the time when work was first begun in the Harris Village. Forty-eight burials from this ruin yielded a sufficient amount of material further to substantiate the physical type constructed from the single Mogollon Village skull. The fragmentary nature of the material made statistical calculations impossible and Dr. Woodbury was forced to rely largely on observational data. On purely morphological grounds three physical types were segregated, and it is noted that, while the three types are not new to the Southwest, they are seldom all found in the same site. To quote further from Dr. Woodbury's report:

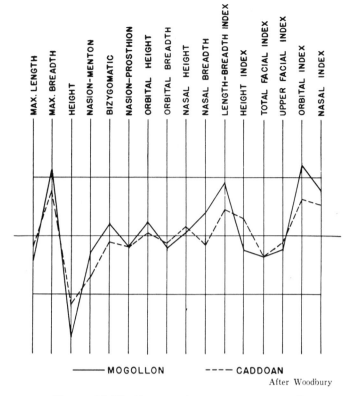

Figure 13.66. Comparative measurements of the Mogollon skull and a female of the Caddoan (Caddo and Wichita) series.

The majority (16) of the crania from this site combine undeformed brachycephaly with a conspicuously low cranial vault, features which appear among the Caddo and Wichita tribes of the Caddoan stock. The prehistoric people of the Mogollon site also conform to this type, which, for purposes of convenience, has been called the "Caddoan" type. . . .

One specimen, which differs markedly from the others of the series, is small, undeformed, and dolichocephalic. It has become conventional to term crania of this variety "Basketmaker" when found in the Southwest, . . . For this reason and for want of a better term this skull is described as of "Basketmaker" type.

The third variety, represented by two female crania, has been called the "Pueblo" type because the skulls show excessive deformation combined with natural brachycephaly and a high cranial vault so characteristic of many of the Pueblo Indian tribes, both prehistoric and present. . . .

The evidence for placing the foregoing types in phases, while not altogether satisfactory, is capable of interpretation. Individuals of the "Caddoan" type run almost the entire range of burial conditions, from graves made entirely in native soil or rubbish, to graves from filled-in houses and rubbish pits. In only two of the sixteen cases were there offerings, dating from the Three Circle phase in one case, and possibly earlier in the second. The abundance of this physical type here and its presence in the Mogollon Village indicates that it was basic in both—that the first and chief occupants belonged to it. The type may therefore be regarded as the main physical component of the Mogollon culture. The single "Basketmaker" type individual was found under conditions that would place him early rather than late, while the two "Pueblo" type individuals were both late, having been buried in rubbish; with one were found four pieces of pottery referable to the Three Circle phase. This becomes even more significant when we learn that the crania from the Swarts Ruin, chiefly of the Mimbres phase, were "homogeneous and all of the 'Pueblo' type." Regardless of the scarcity of metrical data supporting the "Caddoan" type, the sharp difference in later times points to a change in physical type interpreted best by the infusion of new blood. The "Pueblo" type appears late in the Mimbres—not until the Three Circle phase— when black-on-white pottery and pueblo architecture also first put in an appearance, thus doubly distinguishing the later remains from the earlier. Contact between the Mogollon culture in the earliest phases with the Basketmakers is suggested both by the physical characteristics of one skeleton (female) and by some material traits, as the atlatl and cornucopia-shaped objects. Some of the more general implications occasioned by the "Caddoan" type will be discussed in later pages.

Dating

Unfortunately the wood recovered in the Harris Village was largely juniper and a small series of pinyon. The former is still of little use in tree-ring dating, and the latter, while useful, could not be dated into the present calendar. For the Mogollon Village, which lies west of the Continental Divide, and on the west side of the Mogollon Mountains where the weather conditions were apparently more comparable to those of northeastern Arizona and northwestern New Mexico, a few tree-ring dates are available. These come from four houses of the same type and ceramic content representing the San Francisco phase, falling in the short space of time from A.D. 896 to A.D. 908. It is impossible, of course, to state positively just where in the phase—whether early or late—these dates fall; but, from one or two minor conditions, I infer that the dates, or A.D. 900 as a round figure, would mark the end of the phase rather than the beginning. The Three Circle phase would then be consigned to the tenth century, which I believe is about right, since Classic Mimbres pottery certainly comes in soon after A.D. 1000. A conservative estimate for the Georgetown phase would place it before A.D. 800, but if, as seems possible, another phase should be inserted before the San Francisco, the Georgetown phase would be pushed even earlier.

In the final analysis, cross-finds are little more than suggestive clues. Much depends upon the identification of foreign specimens. There is always the possibility of error in the association, and this is especially true where sherds only are available. An examination of the intrusives in the two villages demonstrated that, for example, both Lino Black-on-gray and Red Mesa Black-on-white were found on floors of Three Circle phase houses, yet the two types can be reasonably dated on tree-rings as having been separated by not less than a century, while both were certainly earlier than the Three Circle phase in the Mimbres. Nevertheless, intrusive sherds do carry some significance when considered as a group in relation to the ruin where found. The Mogollon Village, for example, produced upwards of a dozen black-on-white sherds which came from the north: none of these were later than Pueblo I, several being late Basketmaker III. Negative evidence—the absence of later northern black-on-white types—is important, because such do occur in other later sites in the southern area. This leads to the conclusion that the Mogollon Village was not occupied later than a Pueblo I stage. With this tenet, the tree-ring dates are in accord, for the latest northern intrusive type, Kiatuthlanna Black-on-white, occurs in an identifiable Pueblo I horizon at Allantown, excavated by Roberts, with dates ranging from A.D. 844 to A.D. 918 (Miller 1934:15–16; 1935:31). A closer correspondence in dates could not be desired. We may thus conclude, for the present, that the San Francisco phase was generally coeval with Pueblo I, that the Georgetown phase may well extend into Basketmaker III, that the Three Circle phase is broadly identifiable with Pueblo II (eastern), and that the Mimbres phase can be equated with early Pueblo III in the northern series. A correlation with the Hohokam is somewhat more difficult, but, relying solely on the nature of the objects in the Mimbres exhibiting Hohokam influence, the Sedentary period

(Sacaton phase) had been reached in the west before a full-fledged Mimbres phase came into existence.

Further justification of the age assigned to the Mogollon culture has been found in the recent excavations at Snaketown, west of Sacaton, Arizona. The only foreign sherds dating from early periods were those of the Mogollon culture, occurring, in several instances, in earlier Hohokam levels than the northern sherds. This emphasizes the fact that, at or before A.D. 700, three broad types of pottery were being made, the black-on-white of the late Basketmakers, the ancestral forms of the red-on-buff of the Hohokam, and the red-on-brown of the Mogollon. Thus it would appear that three major groups shared in the structure of the rather complex southwestern picture. Of these three, the Pima are believed to represent the modern survivors of the Hohokam, the living Pueblo Indians the descendants of the ancient Pueblos who were, in some sense, to be linked with the Basketmakers, but no sure group can be identified as the living remnants of the Mogollon. In the Mimbres area, their identity was lost by a replacement of Hohokam and Pueblo characters. If present representatives exist, they doubtless occur in Mexico where some cultural connections with the Mogollon are manifest.

THE MOGOLLON CULTURE

All the essential facts regarding the Mogollon culture have now been given, and an effort must be made to fit the complex into the background of the Southwest. Speculation naturally enters into anything that may be said, especially since the work in this culture is still in its primary stages. What follows should therefore be read with this point clearly in mind.

At the close of the first field season in the Mogollon Village, an initial difficulty was experienced in attempting to relate the remains to either of the two currently recognized culture groups in the Southwest, the Hohokam, on the one hand, and the Basketmaker-Pueblo on the other. The difficulty was not lessened after excavating in the Harris Village. The problem of relationship resolved itself into three questions: Were the remains to be regarded as a peripheral variation of the Basketmaker-Pueblo complex of the north; of the Hohokam to the west; or was a third basic group represented which, up to this stage in the investigations, had not been recognized?

Before endeavoring to answer this query, it will be well now to present, in summary, those elements, placed in the Georgetown and San Francisco phases, which characterize the culture type possessed by the occupants of the Mogollon and Harris villages. For subsistence, hunting and agriculture seem to have been relied upon equally, with corn providing the main—if not the only—food in the rural economy. The physical type has been described by Dr. Woodbury as "combining undeformed brachycephaly with a conspicuously low cranial vault." Interments were made indiscriminately between houses, never within them, the bodies being flexed but not uniformly oriented; burial offerings were rare. Cremation was known, but seldom practiced. Dwellings consisted of deep pit houses, first rounded and later rectangular in form, entered by long inclined passages.

Large structures, used possibly for ceremonial purposes, were analogous to houses in form, but the change from round to rectangular lagged. Undercut storage pits were abundant, occurring mainly outside of the dwellings. The evidence suggests that both the atlatl and the bow were used as weapons. Pottery was of several types: painted with red on brown decoration (Mogollon Red-on-brown); a slipped and highly polished red ware (San Francisco Red); and a plain ware ranging from gray to nearly black in color (Alma Plain), frequently heavily scored as if with a bundle of grass, and occasionally neck banded. All types were made by coiling and were extensively polished. The painted and red types frequently display a dented exterior which, in its effect, suggests hammered metal, the result of pressing the successive coils of clay together with the finger.

Metates were troughed and closed at one end; the milling surface in the oldest was basin-shaped, the later ones had a grinding surface with parallel sides. The earliest manos were round in form and the grinding surfaces were strongly convex; later examples were oblong and possessed a fairly flat grinding face. Mortars, full-grooved mauls, stone vessels, short and long straight stone pipes, hoes, large chipped blades usually stemmed, broad projectile points with deep diagonal notches, and flanged and stemmed drills constitute the major items in the stone industry. Grooved stone axes were absent. Shell objects were limited to simple beads, bracelets, and a gorget-like ornament. In bone, the notched awls and tubes were important.

The Hohokam offer comparatively few basic similarities with this type of culture pattern. Hohokam economy was mainly agricultural, as shown by the canal systems and the scarcity of animal bones in the refuse. Disposal of the dead was by cremation and, because of this fact, nothing sure is known of the physical type. In architecture, the underlying principle of disengaged units was the same in both groups and the houses were entered from the side, the entrance of the Hohokam house being short with a step, that of the Mogollon being long and inclined. The evolutionary sequence in each area, however, was the reverse of the other. Identifiable ceremonial structures among the Hohokam were lacking. In pottery, some superficial likenesses, as in color, occur, but the pottery was made differently, and identities are difficult to ascertain. In stone, bone, and shell, the Hohokam outstripped their eastern neighbors. Absent in the Mogollon culture were paint palettes, three-quarter grooved axes, elaborate bone and shell carving, figurines, mosaic plaques, and carved stone vessels; while such items as the full-grooved maul, stone pipes, atlatl dart points, and weights were not found with the Hohokam remains. Apart from superficial contacts, the two groups, at this stage, were not directly related.

With the Basketmakers, a somewhat closer relationship is apparent. The economy of the two groups was about the same, but the physical type of the Basketmaker was quite different. In inhumation, metate forms, full-grooved mauls, pipes, cornucopia-shaped objects, atlatl, and some vessel forms, there are parallels. Rather elementary differences are to be noted, however, in architecture, in the stone culture, and especially in pottery.

The manifestations of the culture, both racial and material, are neither Basketmaker nor Hohokam as now defined, and it cannot be equated with either without many qualifications. It is therefore felt that a logical solution lies in the recognition of a third group—The Mogollon Culture.

Previous reports (Gladwin and Gladwin 1934: Final chart; Gladwin and Gladwin 1935:221–233; see also Haury 1936d) have pointed out the wide sphere of influence exerted by the Mogollon culture. Practically all villages of the eleventh to fifteenth centuries which lay to the west, south, and east of the Mimbres area proper were founded on the Mogollon complex. This is particularly seen in the pottery and other material traits. In all of southeastern Arizona red-on-brown pottery was predominant. Some of this bears strong Hohokam features, but most of it is distinctly Mogollon in character, particularly that from the earlier ruins, as the Fulton Site in the Dragoon Moun-

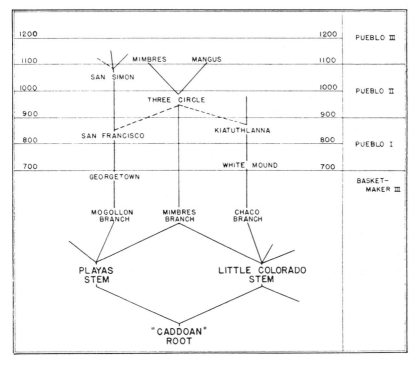

Figure 13.67. A portion of the phase chart given in Medallion 15 (Gladwin and Gladwin 1934) revised on the basis of new data.

tains (Fulton 1934a; Fulton 1934b). A northwestern extension was San Carlos Red-on-brown, occurring chiefly on the Gila west of Bylas and in the vicinity of Globe. It is notable for its burnished black interiors, exterior decoration on bowls, and excellence of manufacture. Far to the southwest in Sonora, is found another related type—Sonora Red-on-brown—as yet little known. In Chihuahua, practically the entire ceramic complex of painted, red, plain, and textured wares reverts directly back to the Mogollon substructure (Sayles 1936), while east of the Rio Grande, as a component of the San Andreas phase, is Three Rivers Red-on-terra cotta, also attributed to the same source.

As a result of this work, several minor changes can be made in the phase chart given in Medallion XV (Gladwin and Gladwin 1934: Figure 9), pertaining especially to the Mogollon branch of the Playas stem, and the Mimbres branch of the Little Colorado stem. These modifications are shown in Figure 13.67. As before, the Mogollon culture, as expressed by the Caddoan Root, and the Basketmakers are believed to have merged to produce the Little Colorado stem. (The term Caddoan Root refers to a generalized horizon of hunting-agriculturists of the Middle West, out of which it is believed the later groups of the Caddoan family developed on the one hand, and the Mogollon culture on the other.) In the accompanying chart, the Mimbres branch draws from both the Playas and the Little Colorado stems because, even in the late phases, many Mogollon traits persisted. In the Mogollon branch, the Georgetown phase, the earliest in the series, has been added, as has also the White Mound phase of late Basketmaker III times in the Chaco branch, which gave rise to the Kiatuthlanna phase. The Three Circle phase of the Mimbres branch draws from both the San Francisco and Kiatuthlanna phases to give us the beginning of the Pueblo domination in the Mimbres drainage. The Mimbres and Mangus phases are indicated as collateral developments rather than as a unilateral evolution as originally shown.

Still another angle remains which gives the Mogollon culture individuality. This is a number of traits eastern in complexion, some exclusively so, some being shared in a limited way by southwestern groups. The items which appear most significant are: equal dependence upon hunting and agriculture; pit houses with graded side entrances; storage pits; a low vaulted, undeformed, brachycephalic physical type; a painted ware with red decoration on a neutral brown background; the association of a red ware and a dark plain ware; a scoring technique on pottery; vessel forms (see Haury 1936d, for further details); to some extent, the painting of clay pipes; stone hoes; full-grooved mauls; large chipped blades; stemmed drills; and shell gorgets.

Considered individually, these traits would be meaningless, but collectively they build up into a substantial case. The suggestion of affiliation with the east is made only in a general way; no individual eastern group can be singled out as direct relatives. If the connection exists, it must be with a generalized hunting-agricultural stage of about the type represented by Strong's Upper Republican culture, or Signal Butte III (Strong 1933:278; 1935:228–239, 245–250).

A few additional points may now be mentioned concerning the racial aspect of the Mogollon culture. The low vaulted, undeformed, brachycephalic type represented in the two villages excavated seems to be distinct from the high vaulted, deformed, brachycephalic Pueblo type predominant in the north and, at a later time, in the Mimbres. It therefore seems likely that two waves of round-heads should be recognized. It has long been acknowledged that a brachycephalic strain (northern type) entered the Southwest between Basketmaker III and Pueblo I, and that it superseded the native long-heads, resulting in what we know as the Pueblos. The southern type of round-head may indeed have been in the area before this, since it was dominant at a time comparable to Pueblo I (San Francisco phase) and probably was the type represented in the Georgetown phase. It is believed that, in the north, the round-heads introduced the cradle board (hence head deformation), full-grooved axes, and the bow. With the first two items, the Mogollon folk were not acquainted, although they probably knew the bow. There is thus slight additional indication of a difference between the two groups.

In Kiatuthlanna, the burials related to the pit house horizon (Pueblo I) showed a mixture of long and round heads, both with and without deformation (Roberts 1931:171). This led Roberts to state that a mixture of stocks was represented. While the data on the Kiatuthlanna skulls has not been released, it is not unlikely that the round-headed strain there came from the Mogollon area to the south. This proposed diffusion is further borne out by the community of possessions in material culture of Kiatuthlanna, and the southern villages, while this condition is not seen in the early villages in the San Juan. As for the wider influence of the southern round-heads, nothing further can be said.

On the whole, it would appear that the Mogollon physical type is to be derived (prior to A.D. 700) from the east—from a Plains group in a hunting-agricultural stage—and confined, at first, to the southern part of the Southwest. Contact with the Basketmakers, already at hand, was responsible for certain parallels that have been pointed out. After A.D. 900, Hohokam and Pueblo influences suppressed the basic Mogollon type of culture and their resulting blend was what we know as the Mimbreños.

SUMMARY OF MIMBRES PREHISTORY

Turning now to the Mimbres drainage proper, it will not be out of place to add a few comments on the prehistory of that area in the light of these excavations.

To my knowledge, Basketmaker I remains, as elsewhere in the Southwest, have not been found. Cave material representing a possible Basketmaker II stage does occur (Cosgrove 1947). This suggests a closer relationship with the Texas Cave Dwellers (Sayles 1935:63) than with the northern Basketmakers. Nothing is known of the physical character of the bearers of this culture. San Juan Basketmaker III is represented by sporadic sherds only.

The first local pottery-makers belonged to the Mogollon culture. This was firmly rooted in the region by A.D. 700, and its history may go back some centuries earlier. Several growth stages are recognizable before about A.D. 900, when a process of cultural accretion set in which completely altered the complexion of the group. These transforming influences can be attributed to the Basketmaker-Pueblo complex on the one hand, and to the Hohokam on the other. Profoundest changes took place in architecture and in pottery. The principle of underground disconnected houses gave way to surface connected rooms of normal pueblo type, which were seldom, if ever, more than one storey high, and the masonry and the details of construction were undeveloped. Thus, architecture per se impresses one here as being borrowed. Once acquired, nothing of merit was added to give it distinction. A date of A.D. 900 in the Mogollon Village for pit houses throws some light on the rapidity accompanying the change, for certainly, in the early decades of the 1000s, pueblos were already being built. Pit houses, therefore, survived late in this region, and need not be assigned the great age customarily associated with dwellings of this type.

The pottery passed from a tradition of rectilinear painting in red on a brownish background to black-on-white types of decided Pueblo flavor, but also embodying design elements derived from the Hohokam (Haury 1936d).

In this same formative period, a physical type of Pueblo origin also appears.

Not until these changes take effect does the Mimbres culture, as it has been generally known, emerge, and it is even then still in a nascent stage. In terms of the northern chronology, the basic Mogollon culture was dominant, possibly, in Basketmaker III, certainly in Pueblo I (Georgetown and San Francisco phases). Pueblo II can be recognized as a period of change and assimilation (Three Circle phase), rising, in Pueblo III, to full force as the Mimbres culture (Mimbres phase). In the Mimbres Valley these people apparently withdrew by A.D. 1150 or soon after, while in the far south the culture may have survived later. The region then seems to have been deserted, but not for long. A new and mixed group appears, also pueblo-building, for their remains are to be found in some cases almost a stone's throw from the former Mimbreños' houses. Judging by the pottery introduced by these people (Gila Polychrome, Ramos Polychrome, Chupadero Black-on-white, El Paso Polychrome), they can be placed in Pueblo IV and, in terms of our calendar, roughly between A.D. 1250 and A.D. 1400 (the Animas phase of Gladwin and Gladwin 1934).

Much has been written and more said concerning the disappearance of the Mimbreños. Their great achievement in pottery has doubtless drawn undue attention to this fact, for, after all, the problem of disappearance here is not unique. Fertile valleys, the Southwest over, tell the same story of intensive aboriginal occupation, then desertion. The factors involved in the solution of this problem are larger and more comprehensive than any isolated drainage can give; they require a study of the region as a whole, then part by part, in a manner such as that being undertaken by Gila Pueblo. While we may not yet be able to say specifically that abandonment of the Mimbres was due to hostile neighbors, to climate, to this or to that cause, a few observations may be made.

If one examines the distribution of Mimbres ruins yielding both early and late pottery, it is clear that the center of production of the two does not coincide. The focus for Mimbres Bold Face Black-on-white would lie somewhere well up in the Mimbres Valley, while Mimbres Black-on-white (Classic) would be well out in the more arid sections to the south. This suggests a gradual north-to-south movement, and theoretically one would expect to find the most recent Mimbres remains on the southern fringe of their distribution. Some ruins east of the Rio Grande consistently yield an association of Mimbres and Chupadero Black-on-white, and El Paso Polychrome, suggesting a probable over-lap, and thus necessitating a later date, say A.D. 1250, for the Mimbres culture in this outlying district. On this southern margin of the Mimbres culture existed another group, the people of Chihuahua, virile potters, in whose pottery may be recognized certain elements probably contributed by the Mimbreños. With the position of these groups which reached ascendancy in Pueblo IV all along the southern frontier of the Mimbres area, there is but one logical solution—absorption, loss of identity through the constant change which is evident everywhere among the former peoples of the Southwest. In fact, we have seen that this force was in operation earlier in the Mimbres itself when the Mogollon culture was submerged and altered in the growth of the Mimbres culture.

Acknowledgments

Permission to dig in the Harris Village was freely given by Mrs. John N. Harris, the owner. To her, on behalf of Gila Pueblo, I express my gratitude for this privilege. I am also personally indebted to her for many courtesies extended to the staff during the course of the work. The working force consisted mainly of the holders of scholarships for Training in Anthropological Field Methods, granted by the Laboratory of Anthropology, Santa Fe, New Mexico. The personnel of this group and the institutions represented were: Gordon C. Baldwin, University of Arizona; Francis M. Cresson, Jr., University of Pennsylvania; Gordon F. Ekholm, University of Minnesota; Ralph T. Esterquest, Columbia University; Hans E. Fischel, University of California; and Norman E. Gabel, Harvard University. Deric Nusbaum, of Santa Fe, New Mexico, and Erik K. Reed, of Washington, D.C., also assisted. To all of these men I feel a sense of obligation for their sustained interest in the work and participation in the discussion of problems.

The task of identification and analysis of the material has been shared by the entire staff of Gila Pueblo, and I wish especially to acknowledge the assistance of Russell Hastings during the excavation of the Mogollon Village and subsequently in the laboratory. Erik K. Reed likewise assisted in the study of the material from the Harris Village. W. H. Burt, of the California Institute of Technology, Pasadena, California, kindly identified the animal bones.

PART SIX

Anasazi

People of the Plateaus

ᐊ 14 ᐅ

Delineating the Anasazi

Jeffrey S. Dean

By the 1930s the emerging complexities of southwestern prehistory had begun to undermine the simple, unitary conceptual schemes that had been devised to systematize prevailing archaeological knowledge. Conceptions based on assumptions of southwestern cultural uniformity and on a Puebloan archetype of southwestern culture were crumbling under the weight of accumulating evidence for a hitherto unimagined measure of diversity in the southwestern archaeological record. The Pecos Classification (Kidder 1927), not yet five years old, no longer was capable of encompassing the variety of remains that were being exhumed in an unprecedented burst of archaeological activity that spanned the entire region.

In response to this crisis of concept, southwestern archaeologists began paring newly defined "cultural" entities away from the Puebloan core of the Pecos Classification. First to be differentiated was material found in the Sonoran Desert during extensive surveys by the Gila Pueblo Archaeological Foundation. Begun in the late 1920s, these surveys showed the desert material to differ radically from archetypical Basketmaker-Pueblo. Resurrecting a term proposed by Russell (1908:24), Gladwin and Gladwin (1934:3) dubbed the desert materials "Hohokam." Next to be excised from the Basketmaker-Pueblo concept was the Mogollon, which, like Hohokam, was delineated by the survey work of Gila Pueblo and which first appeared as a "Branch" of the "Playas Stem" in the writings of Gladwin and Gladwin (1934:31, 1935:221–233). In 1936, Haury (1936a:118–130), in his report on the Harris Village and Mogollon Village, described the Mogollon manifestation in detail and launched the Mogollon concept on its long and stormy course toward acceptance as one of the major adaptive traditions of the prehistoric Southwest. Not to be outdone in the prehistoric culture christening derby, Colton (1938, 1939) completed the dissection of Basketmaker-Pueblo by applying the term Patayan to materials from the lower Colorado River valley that Gila Pueblo surveys had shown to be non-Puebloan.

The general acceptance by the middle 1930s of the Hohokam designation for the archaeological remains of the Sonoran Desert adumbrated the demise of the concept of a pan-southwestern culture of a Puebloan configuration. The dean of southwestern archaeologists, A. V. Kidder, perceived a need for a term to denote non-Hohokam materials of the mountains and plateaus. He also felt that the prevailing usage, Basketmaker-Pueblo, perpetuated a false dichotomy between Basketmaker and Pueblo and that it should be replaced by a more inclusive term that reflected the continuity of the Basketmaker and Pueblo manifestations. Consequently, in 1936 Kidder (1936:589–590) proposed the use of the Navajo word "Anasazi" to designate the non-Hohokam archaeological materials of the southwestern mountains and plateaus. Despite a few demurrals (McGregor 1941:249), Anasazi was rapidly assimilated into the lexicon of southwestern archaeology (Colton 1938, 1939; Roberts 1939:4–17). Over the years, and not without contention, the term was gradually disencumbered of other non-Hohokam manifestations, such as Mogollon, and by the 1950s was widely accepted as one of at least four major adaptive traditions in southwestern prehistory. Stripped of extraneous connotations, "Anasazi" survived to designate the irreduceable minimum of ancestral Puebloan archaeological remains of the Colorado Plateau and the Rio Grande Valley.

Emil Haury's involvement with the archaeology of the Anasazi was far more extensive than has been generally supposed. His initial contact with prehistoric Puebloan archaeology came through Byron Cummings, the indefatigable explorer of the plateau country of northern Arizona. Haury's first fieldwork in the Anasazi area occurred in the summer of 1927, when Cummings sent him and a small party to investigate Basketmaker sites along the western flanks of the Lukachukai Mountains (Haury 1936b, 1945a:9–11). This expedition accomplished the excavation of Vandal Cave and the cursory examination of Painted Cave, a nearby cliff dwelling that had been dug earlier that summer by the Amerind Foundation. The following summer he was involved in archaeological explorations in the Tsegi Canyon area far to the west of the Lukachukais. Excavation of a burial in the canyon produced a distinctive black-on-white double ceramic vessel—one half decorated with a Pueblo I design, the other in a Pueblo II fashion—that has enlivened the oral examinations of generations of archaeology students as the University of Arizona.

This early fieldwork involved little excavation and produced few published reports; however, it did provide Haury with invaluable first-hand experience with the Colorado Plateau and its abundant archaeological remains. Although a report on the Vandal Cave work was never published, much information on this important site has entered the oral tradition of Anasazi archaeology. Years after the fieldwork was finished, the Amerind Foundation did publish Haury's (1945a) report on the work at Painted Cave, a site notable for its yield of Anasazi textiles. Haury's master's thesis, which was completed in 1928 and which summarized much of the Anasazi research undertaken between 1904 and 1928 by Cummings and his students, concluded the initial phase of his involvement with the Anasazi. Haury's participation in the summer of 1929 in the Third Beam Expedition excavation at the Show Low (Whipple) and Pinedale ruins began a brief period of intense immersion in archaeological tree-ring dating, a subject that he continued to emphasize throughout his career.

Haury's acceptance of the position of assistant director of Gila Pueblo in 1930 began a period in which his direct concern with Anasazi archaeology diminished but did not cease. In general, Gila Pueblo's interests lay south of the Colorado Plateau with the Mogollon and Hohokam manifestations of the mountains and desert. Nonetheless, the fertile mind of Harold Gladwin was not bound by geography, and Gila Pueblo did not neglect the Anasazi altogether. Inevitably, Haury was involved in some of this work, which further broadened his experience in Anasazi archaeology. As a matter of fact, his first assignment for Gila Pueblo was the excavation of two kivas at the Tusayan Ruin, a small, peripheral Kayenta Anasazi pueblo near the south rim of the Grand Canyon (Haury 1931).

Even more important was the excavation in 1936 by Haury and Ted Sayles of a late eighth-century (Basketmaker III), pit-house village in the Rio Puerco drainage. The work at White Mound Village (Gladwin 1945:11–40) introduced Haury to yet another regional variant of the Anasazi tradition, this time one located on the Anasazi-Mogollon frontier, not too distant from the Mogollon sites that later claimed his attention. Subsequently, Haury's dendrochronological dating of both the Tusayan Ruin and White Mound Village became issues in Gladwin's attack on archaeological tree-ring dating in general (Gladwin 1945:28–34, 1946). Quite apart from the fact that reanalysis of the Gila Pueblo tree-ring collections vindicated Haury's dating of both sites (Bannister, Hannah, and Robinson 1966:21–23; Bannister, Dean, and Robinson 1968:11), the controversy could hardly have failed to sharpen his perceptions of Anasazi chronology and its relationship to the Mogollon sequence.

Haury's move from Gila Pueblo back to the University of Arizona in 1937 marked his withdrawal from archaeological fieldwork in the Anasazi area, as the Hohokam and Mogollon claimed his attention. He did not, however, abandon his research interest in the Anasazi. One major theme dominated Haury's involvement with Anasazi archaeology during this period: the temporal, spatial, and interactional relationships between Anasazi and Mogollon. This emphasis on Mogollon-Anasazi relationships was understandable in view of the dispute over the legitimacy of the Mogollon concept that waxed and waned between 1936 and 1960. The basic issue of this polemic was whether these two archaeological manifestations represented a single population—characterized by considerable geographical variability caused by differential contact with the Hohokam (Daifuku 1952, 1961; Kidder 1939)—or whether they represented two different, interacting populations. Obviously, resolution of these issues rested first on the archaeological differences between the two. Haury and his allies devoted considerable effort to documenting the configurational, spatial, and temporal differences between Mogollon and Anasazi architecture, artifacts, and ceramics. Of nearly equal importance to this problem was the nature of the interactions between Mogollon and Anasazi populations. The idea of Mogollon independence from Anasazi could be strengthened measurably by demonstrating that groups of people distinct enough to be identified as Anasazi and Mogollon interacted with one another in consistent and systematic ways.

Haury's concern with Anasazi-Mogollon relationships was manifested in several ways. His idea of a wave of Anasazi influence overwhelming the Mogollon after A.D. 1000 was only one expression of his continued interest in the Anasazi. The establishment in 1939 of the University of Arizona Archaeological Field School in the Forestdale Valley was another. Forestdale, located on the Mogollon-Anasazi frontier, was selected for study partly for the information on Anasazi-Mogollon connections it was expected to yield (Haury 1940:7–8). Furthermore, a locale in which Anasazi-Mogollon relationships might be isolated might also provide conclusive evidence of the basic independence of the two. In this latter expectation Haury was not disappointed: the combination of tree-ring dates and other archaeological evidence from the Bluff Site clearly established the existence of a "pure" Mogollon configuration, complete with characteristic Mogollon pottery that predated by nearly three hundred years the first appearance of ceramics among the Anasazi (Haury and Sayles 1947)—strong evidence, indeed, that Mogollon and Anasazi were not the same thing. Work in later sites in the Forestdale Valley fulfilled Haury's expectations of acquiring information on Mogollon-Anasazi interactions. The seventh-century Bear Ruin yielded pit houses with mixtures of discrete architectural features attributable to both groups, along with Anasazi and Mogollon pottery. Later sites in the valley, such as Tla Kii and Tundastusa, were characteristic of the post-A.D. 1000 period, when the Mogollon had, by and large, taken up residence in true pueblos.

Removal of the Field School to Point of Pines in 1946 extended Haury's interest in the relationships between Mogollon and Anasazi populations. At Point of Pines, however, much of the evidence relevant to this issue concerned a period of time later than that exemplified at Forestdale, specifically developments postdating A.D. 1000. Haury's involvement with this problem at Point of Pines culminated in his brilliant demonstration of a late thirteenth-century immigration into the area by a group of Anasazi from the Kayenta or Tusayan areas far to the north. These "foreigners" were accommodated by the local inhabitants to the extent of permitting the newcomers to incorporate their own rooms into the existing Mogollon pueblo and to construct a distinctly Anasazi D-shaped kiva nearby. The facts that the relationships apparently soured and the immigrants were burned out and forced to move do not gainsay Haury's conclusive documentation of a singular episode in Anasazi-Mogollon relations. Reed (1958) drew the obvious conclusions that the Anasazi emigrants set out with a clear idea of where they were going and that the incident testifies to a high level of premigration contact between the two populations. The extraordinarily well documented details of the Anasazi immigration into Point of Pines provide strong support for Haury's thesis of the independence of the two groups, even after A.D. 1000 when, it was thought, the Anasazi predominated over the Mogollon.

Haury's syntheses of southwestern archaeology constitute yet another important contribution to Anasazi studies. As one of a handful of archaeologists to possess first-hand field and analytical experience with all three major adaptive traditions—Anasazi, Mogollon, and Hohokam—he demonstrated an exceptional ability to systematize the raw data of southwestern archaeology into cogent syntheses of the general patterns of prehistoric cultural development in the region. Notable among his efforts of this kind are his report on contacts between the prehistoric peoples of Mexico and the Southwest (Haury 1945b), his "speculations" on regional settlement patterns (see Chapter 16), and his general synthesis of southwestern prehistory (see Chapter 2). These integrative works elucidate the similarities, differences, and relationships among the prehistoric populations of the region and, in so doing, illuminate the place of the Anasazi in the broad sweep of southwestern prehistory.

Despite the magnitude of the analytical and synthetic accomplishments enumerated above, Haury's greatest contribution to Anasazi archaeology was theoretical in nature and lay in his creation of the Mogollon concept. To the extent that the definition of Mogollon prescribed the concept of Anasazi, Emil Haury was in large measure responsible for the modern definition of Anasazi. The history of the Anasazi concept became one of decreasing generality and growing specificity as accumulating knowledge of the diversity of southwestern archaeological remains required the excision of various archaeological manifestations from the Puebloan nucleus of what originally had been thought to be *the* basic southwestern culture. Hohokam cleaved easily from Basketmaker-Pueblo. Mogollon did not, because of intrinsic similarities between Mogollon and Anasazi and because of correspondences generated by interactions among Anasazi and Mogollon populations. Haury's definition of the Mogollon culture and the perseverance he and his colleagues exhibited in establishing its independence from Basketmaker-Pueblo simplified and clarified Anasazi archaeology. The paring of Mogollon from Basketmaker-Pueblo freed archaeologists from having to treat two quite different cultural adaptive systems as manifestations of the same phenomenon and from the concomitant necessity of creating convoluted explanations for the patent differences between the two. The separation of Mogollon from Anasazi sharpened the conceptual focus on both and thereby contributed significantly to a refinement of archaeological effort that advanced the study of the prehistoric Puebloan populations of the Colorado Plateau.

Evidence at Point of Pines for a Prehistoric Migration From Northern Arizona

Emil W. Haury

A review of the ethnological and the archaeological records makes it clear that population movements have played a major role in spreading human knowledge and experience from one area to another for a long time. Where documentary or remembered information is obtainable, as among contemporary societies, the investigator begins with migration as a fact and searches for causes and effects. In archaeology, however, the first task is to establish migration as a fact, and only then may questions of cause and the changes produced on both the stationary and the migrating groups be assessed. The key problem, therefore, is to identify the phenomenon of migration in that small portion of the cultural record which is available. The archaeologist must, in the course of his analysis, sort out the clues which truly reflect population movement from those which may be due to other mechanisms of cultural transmission and change. This kind of evaluation requires the formulation of an operating base, a statement of principles and assumptions, against which the evidence must be weighed.

Reprinted by permission from "Migrations in New World Culture History," edited by Raymond H. Thompson. *University of Arizona Bulletin* 29:2, *Social Science Bulletin* 27:1–8. Tucson: University of Arizona Press, 1958. Contribution to Point of Pines Archaeology Number 12.

In reaching the conclusions expressed in this chapter, I have drawn upon the following minimum set of conditions:

A migration is the probable, though not the only, explanation in the archaeological record of past people if:
1) there suddenly appears in a cultural continuum a constellation of traits readily identifiable as new, and without local prototypes, and
2) the products of the immigrant group not only reflect borrowed elements from the host group, but also, as a lingering effect, preserve unmistakable elements from their own pattern.

The probability that the phenomena outlined above do indeed represent a migration, rather than some other force that induces culture change, is increased if:
1) identification of an area is possible in which this constellation of traits was the normal pattern, and
2) a rough time equivalency between the "at home" and the displaced expressions of the similar complexes can be established.

For a number of years (1946–1960), the University of Arizona excavated a large pueblo ruin at Point of Pines on the San Carlos Apache Indian Reservation. In its present form, this demolished town consists of a solid block of rooms some 275 meters in length and 100 meters in greatest width, aggregating an estimated minimum of 800 rooms. This settlement was not constructed as a single premeditated unit as we see it today, but its history encompasses several building phases. This history began about A.D. 1200 with a cluster of pit houses and a contemporaneous adjacent pueblo structure of undetermined size. This was followed by a building spurt during the last decades of the 1200s, which resulted in a village of large, closely knit, solidly built masonry rooms. Then came a sharp and extensive building expansion in the 1300s, which was terminated by the abandonment of the town but not of the area at about A.D. 1400. This abandonment resulted in the establishment of a number of small settlements several of which were built upon the ruins of the old town. The latter event and the final abandonment of the area by pueblo peoples probably took place by the mid-fifteenth century.

It is with the block of large, expertly built rooms of the thirteenth century, predating the major population expansion, that we are here concerned. Although the full form of this room block has not been established, the directional limits are known. The unit consists of a probable 70 rooms, of which 21 have been cleared. Arranged in an L-shape, it was built on a low ridge free of older occupational refuse or structures, but near a pueblo of contemporary date. Only the wall footings of the latter now remain, deeply buried by later architectural debris, while the walls of the unit in question stand 2 meters when excavated. Much of this unit was two stories high and the rooms were rectangular and large with average dimensions of 4 meters by 6 meters, contrasting in this respect with rooms in contemporary buildings of the area which tend to be smaller and squarer with dimensions of about 4 meters by 4 meters. The rooms in question generally lack formal stone-lined fireboxes, mealing-bin assemblages, and built-in masonry storage cubicles, further contrasting with what appears to have been the contemporary local house-building fashion. By architectural style alone these rooms constitute something of a puzzle because they depart from the indigenous room pattern. Without further evidence, this situation might well have been explained as a normal change in architectural evolution. But if we now compare these rooms with those later built against them or in them after they were abandoned, we see retained the tradition of the small room tending to squareness with fireboxes and other fixtures. In other words, the large rectangular room form did not survive as the norm, thereby leading to the suspicion that the building style itself may have been an intrusion.

At this point it should be noted that 18 of 21 excavated rooms were destroyed by fire during occupancy. This catastrophe came at the time of the year when some of the rooms were bulging with the harvest fruits. One room alone yielded in the order of 25 bushels of charred corn. Of approximately 100 rooms excavated in the town, both older and younger than those in the block in question, only one has shown destruction by fire.

The burning of these rooms paradoxically preserved through charring many things which otherwise would have wasted away. Since the rooms were destroyed during occupancy, an extraordinarily full complement of material culture is present. Pottery, the most abundant item, often numbers scores of vessels from a single domicile. The pottery is easily divisible into two broad categories: 1) the culinary and storage pots of types distinctly native to the area and 2) painted vessels. The latter may be grouped into three classes: a) a minority representing the local types, those normally associated with the culinary vessels; b) a second minority represented by vessels foreign to the area and traceable to the Kayenta-Hopi region 200 miles to the north (Tsegi Orange Ware: Ware 5B, Types 5 to 13; Colton 1956); and c) a majority of vessels made of local clays, easily identified by the highly specific mineral leucite derived from the local tuff, manufactured in forms and painted in patterns foreign to the local traditions but consistent with those of the northern area from which the trade pieces came. Several artistic devices, fashionable on the pottery native to the Point of Pines region, occur in these vessels. Except for the appearance of potsherds in trash, whole or restorable vessels of the locally made but foreign-in-style types originated predominantly in the burned rooms. A few were found in the burial area. Furthermore, these types did not survive, even as modified versions in the time period post-dating the burning. In summary, the ceramic evidence, like the architectural evidence, suggests an intrusion, and the direct association of these two elements begins to take on meaning.

By chance, test excavations exposed a D-shaped kiva at a distance of 65 meters to the south of the burned rooms. Although some 15 kivas have been cleared at Point of Pines, ranging over a probable thousand years of time, none were of this form. D-shaped kivas are, however, known in the tradition of religious architecture of northern Arizona. As a further clue of its identity, the ceramic complex from this structure matched that of the burned rooms.

Fragments of charred wooden tools, also from the burned rooms, reveal tree growth peculiarities which are foreign to the trees of the Point of Pines region (identification by T. L. Smiley). It is a reasonable supposition that the artifacts were brought in from another locality, though this source has not been identified.

Among the surviving domestic botanical remains, Hugh Cutler found seeds of the squash *Cucurbita mixta* (personal communication). Heretofore in the Southwest this species has been recovered predominantly in the cliff ruins of the San Juan Basin where, by A.D. 1250, it was a common plant. Cutler has informed me that although *Cucurbita mixta* is a central Mexican species, occurring in Tamaulipas at about A.D. 750 (Whitaker and others 1957), its wide use from at least the thirteenth century to the present by both Western and Rio Grande pueblos, leads him to think the species was brought directly from Mexico to the San Juan Basin, whence it was later moved south to the Point of Pines region. In view of the constellation of northern elements we see emerging at Point of Pines, *Cucurbita mixta* may well have been introduced as a part of that complex.

A study of corn provides even more specific botanical evidence of an intrusion. We now have large samples of this grain from two sources: the first lot comes from the burned rooms and the second from Red Bow Cliff Dwelling situated in the Nantack Ridge only a few air miles from the Point of Pines Ruin (Gifford 1957). The latter corn was grown perhaps 50 years later than that represented in the carbonized sample, by people who were native to the area. A review of both samples by Cutler and colleagues reveals the fact that the burned Point of Pines Ruin sample ". . . is more like the corn of the same period from the Kayenta Tsegi Canyon area than that from Red Bow Cliff Dwelling which has many resemblances to Papago corn" (personal communication). The inference to be drawn from this is that a northern type of corn was introduced into the Point of Pines region, that it was successfully grown for a while, but that it did not replace the strains grown locally over a long period of time.

In October, 1957 the Arizona State Museum came into possession of an interesting cache of ceremonial paraphernalia which bears further upon the thesis around which this discussion revolves. The discovery was made by S. R. Claridge of Safford in a small cave on Bonita Creek about 25 air miles southeast of Point of Pines (Wasley, 1962). It consists of a polychrome jar manufactured of materials native to Point of Pines but painted in the northern tradition. Although the jar was broken when found, circumstantial evidence indicates that it contained the following items: two strings of miniature baskets, five composite flower clusters the petals of which were made of thin triangular plates of soft wood skillfully sewn together and colored green, blue, and black; eight wooden cones, a "tablita," miniature bow, and several fragments of cotton cloth. A stylized, cross-shaped, green-painted bird, miniature and full-sized arrows, and additional "tablitas" were recovered in the deeper recesses of the cave on an inspection visit in March, 1958. The cave's small size and the absence of camp refuse indicate it to have been a depository for ceremonial gear.

This material is reminiscent of the famous sunflower cache reported by Kidder and Guernsey (1919:145–147) from Sunflower Cave on Laguna Creek near Kayenta. Although differing in details, in both occurrences there were flowers, cones, and a bird, constituting what appear to be direct parallels. The pottery type of the container further aids in fixing the relationship. The time periods of the two caches, assignable to the terminal decades of the thirteenth century, are approximately contemporaneous. It is not difficult to imagine that the religious leaders of the colonizers at Point of Pines safeguarded this prized ritual gear by hiding it in a distant cave.

So far reference has been made several times to the probable source area for the elements which have been listed. Correspondences in the particular combination of traits which have been observed occur only in northern Arizona, more specifically in the Kayenta-Hopi region. The detailed documentation of the analogies is possible but not feasible in the space available here.

The final and fundamental question concerns the age of the evidence cited. A wealth of charred architectural timbers provides the answer. The Laboratory of Tree-Ring Research at the University of Arizona has dated 120 ceiling beams from 11 of the 16 rooms which produced dating material (data supplied by T. L. Smiley and colleagues). Of this number of dated specimens 48, or 40 per cent, yield bark or cutting dates. These range from A.D. 1262 to A.D. 1293. But inspection of the range reveals a clustering of 38 dates, or about 80 per cent, in the period from A.D. 1280 to A.D. 1285. Only three dates follow and seven precede this concentration. Of the remaining 72 dated specimens on which the true outer rings are not preserved due to fragmentation 64, or about 90 per cent, register years of A.D. 1284 or earlier. While the number of rings lost on these pieces is not directly calculable, it is probable, in view of the clustering of specimens with bark dates, that many of the fragments are from trees felled in the period from A.D. 1280 to A.D. 1285. Since bark dates may be regarded as cutting dates and cutting dates mark construction activity, the conclusion follows that most of the burned rooms were built between A.D. 1280 and A.D. 1285. Taking into account a few scattered dates which are later than A.D. 1285, it may be concluded that all building activity ceased by the early 1290s. Other archaeological evidence permits the inference that the destruction of the rooms by fire took place within a decade, or at the most two, thereafter.

The age thus derived for these rooms coincides with the period of stress, perhaps climatically related, in northern Arizona. In the closing decades of the thirteenth century, densely inhabited areas, such as Tsegi Canyon, were depopulated (Haury 1934a). Movement out of one area and into another therefore becomes a logical succession of events.

From the foregoing observations, we may draw the following conclusions: both secular and religious architecture, a number of highly specific details in the ceramic tradition, and, secondarily, the growth

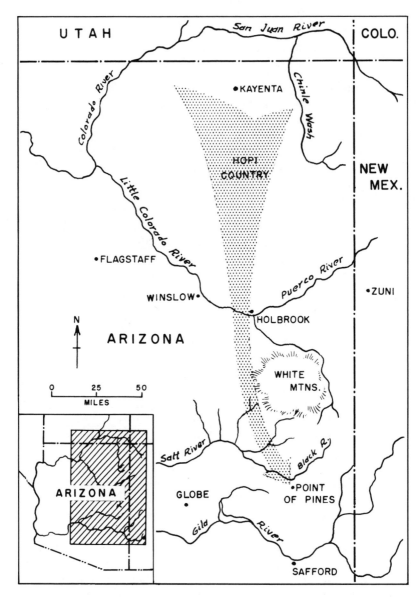

Figure 15.1. The probable route and extent of a
thirteenth-century migration in Arizona.

pattern in wooden artifacts and the botanical evidence indicate that a
new complex of elements was abruptly introduced into the local culture pattern, thereby satisfying the first of the conditions set forth in

this chapter. It is conceivable that all of this might have taken place by mechanisms of cultural transmission other than migration. But the survival of a foreign art style, expressed on locally made pottery and exhibiting a tendency to assimilate native motifs at the same time, and the maintenance of a distinct kiva form are here considered as lingering effects and indicative of a migratory group. The second condition is thereby met.

The two remaining qualifications are also satisfied because the source area in northern Arizona is easily demonstrable, and the time of the general areal shrinkage of the inhabited northern region, in the final decades of the thirteenth century, agrees remarkably well with the advent of the new group in the Point of Pines Village.

Two other phenomena establish this as a migration beyond any reasonable doubt. The first was the burning of the rooms inhabited by the migrants. This was more than an accidental destruction of homes. The distribution of the burned versus unburned rooms indicates intentional setting, most likely by hostile neighbors. This possibility is strengthened by the timing of the conflagration, for it came when the storehouses were full and the loss was a double one of homes and foodstuffs. The second point is that, with the burning, the immigrants withdrew abruptly, for no vestige of their goods survived in the rooms that postdate the fire. Their sojourn left no recognizable imprint on the host group except perhaps for a great defensive wall circling the village, which was built about A.D. 1300 possibly in response to fear of reprisal.

As one who has always viewed archaeological evidence for migration skeptically, I find myself now in a situation where suspended judgment is no longer rational. The data we have, drawn chiefly from domestic structures rather than from ceremonial caches or burials, support the thesis that from 50 to 60 families, a large enough group to maintain religious practices and to function as a social unit, moved a distance of approximately 200 miles from northern Arizona to the Point of Pines region in the closing decades of the thirteenth century (Figure 15.1). Their stay was short, perhaps no longer than 20 years and, having fallen on evil days, they departed their adopted home as a group. The total evidence stands, in my opinion, as a model example of a small scale, short distance, short-term migration, about as clearly demonstrable as we can ever hope to gain from the archaeological record.

◄ 16 ►

Speculations on Prehistoric Settlement Patterns in the Southwest

Emil W. Haury

The archaeological literature of the Southwest of the United States is astonishingly unproductive on the general problem of settlement patterns and interpretations of settlement data in cultural terms. This is all the more surprising for an area that has been studied so intensively for so many years and where existing groups provide living models of what went before. The main efforts at extracting socio-political factors from archaeological data have been made by ethnologists, though there are a few notable exceptions (Martin and Rinaldo 1950). Obviously, what is needed is the formulation of problems and the invention of procedures for gathering and studying comparable data. This will mean a shift in emphasis from historical to functional research and a more intensive dependence upon the work of the ethnologist, at least for the interpretive basis of certain aspects of southwestern prehistory. The works of V. Mindeleff (1891), Fewkes (1900), C. Mindeleff (1900), Kroeber (1917), Strong (1927), Hawley

(1937), Steward (1937), Parsons (1939), Eggan (1950), and others could be consulted with profit by the archaeologist as a point of departure in the development of this problem.

Specifically oriented studies of two categories might be undertaken. First, environmental research, focusing on the forces at work, land forms, changes through recent times, the nature and amount of resources, etc. Hack's analysis (1942) of Hopi Indian physical environment has superbly demonstrated what can be done along this line, how an exposed, wind-swept desert actually is superior to other nearby areas for primitive agriculture because of a permanent groundwater supply and its greater resistance to the effect of climatic change resulting from a peculiar combination of exposure, duning of sand, and little arroyo-cutting. Second, parts of the Southwest must be understood by intensive investigation of the human adaptation to the land on the order of Willey's (1953) Virú Valley studies. Two threads in such studies must be interwoven—the historical and the functional—as either one by itself will not do. After these regional studies are viewed against one another, generalities may emerge. The trend in southwestern research, happily, is in this direction, as witness Peabody Museum's early work at Awatovi and later in western New Mexico, the Chicago Natural History Museum's endeavors near Reserve, New Mexico, and the University of Arizona's excavations on the San Carlos Indian Reservation.

We are, as yet, ignorant about the nature of settlements of early man. The existence of the elephant hunters (Clovis) and bison hunters (Folsom) is known chiefly, though not exclusively, through widely scattered "kill" sites. Mobility, demanded by a hunting economy, suggests small, loosely knit family, or at the most, band units. Formal structures of a shallow-pit nature are known within the first millennium B.C., possibly coincident with the advent of agriculture, but before the arrival of pottery in the Southwest. The archaeological record shows that this stationary existence, related to an improved food supply, was also characterized by larger and more population groups than was the case earlier. Fixed village life, with some grouping of families and possibly a kin-determined headman implied, probably came into being no more than four thousand years ago among the people of the Cochise culture.

We have, of course, numerous site reports encompassing the last two thousand years which show the nature of the individual houses, their arrangement with respect to one another, and their relation to buildings other than domestic units for the three of the Southwest's chief physiographic provinces, namely, the northern plateau, the central mountains, and the southern desert. With these as a starting point, a few problems can be formulated. The physiographic differences themselves, impressive to the modern traveler, have frequently been cited as the prime reason for cultural differences. This has led to the correlation of the Anasazi with the plateau province on an early time level, later extending over into the mountain zone; Mogollon with the mountain region; and the Hohokam with the desert. But no one, to my knowledge, has attempted seriously to single out the factors, ecological or cultural, which explain why this is so. By size, by climatic and altitudinal extremes, by accessibility, and by archaeological resources, the Southwest would appear to be an ideal test area for some "grass-roots" studies along this line. In this connection a desirable starting point would be a study of the distribution of species of wild food and the influence of spotty rainfall on food supplies, apart from those produced by agriculture, following Steward's analysis (1938) of the Basin-Plateau region.

The dispersal of sedentary people over the ground in the Southwest, regardless of the physiographic province, was determined, first of all, by water. This, of course, is generally true, but the aridity of the area concerned imposed greater limits on the location of settlements than was the case in better-watered regions. In other words, habitation depended acutely on the conditions of physiography, exemplified especially by the Hopi (Hack 1942). It stands to reason that limited water sources or those with a slow recharge would allow a wide dispersal of small groups; but, with town development, larger water reserves were necessary, and the number of possibilities was at once limited to settlement along living streams, near permanent springs, and where the water table could be tapped by shallow wells. Mesa Verde, Chaco Canyon, the Hopi country, the Rio Grande, the Gila River and its upper tributaries, and the White Mountains were such areas.

The second requisite for an agricultural people was land, present in the instances mentioned, but each area required special agricultural techniques to make the land produce. This is a problem which has not been adequately explored.

Both these factors—water and land—tended to anchor people to one spot. It should be observed that land as such need not keep an agricultural people rooted, as is illustrated by the Papago. The degree of permanence appears to be dependent on the extent to which natural foods supplemented the foods grown. An awareness of this element is essential in assessing settlement patterns archaeologically. On the whole, however, southwestern societies maintained a high degree of permanence, which shaped the effects of both internal and external cultural forces.

Before about A.D. 700 the villages of the Anasazi, Mogollon, and Hohokam were not greatly different, being composed of independent dwelling units arranged in clusters without formal order, strategically located with respect to water and arable land, and usually on high ground. When seen in plan only and without consideration of differences in structural details and materials, the village pattern was essentially uniform in spite of sharp environmental differences. The subsequent divergences, culminating in such concentrations as in Chaco Canyon, Mesa Verde, and the Gila Valley, came within documented archaeological time, and these trends are traceable in some cases to existing people. Hence the opportunity to recapture social, political, and religious elements would appear to exist. What factors there were or by what strange coincidence a common force was operative up to a certain time, less so afterward, has no immediate answer, though I suspect it lies in the non-material aspects of the societies.

In my opinion one of the greatest achievements of the Indians of the Southwest was the development of the pueblo type of domestic architecture. This employed the principles of joining room to room, of one wall serving two rooms, and of going upward more than one story, with the roofs supported by the walls, and the houses often arranged around plazas. Early explanations held that the limited environment of cliff recesses and caves caused buildings to be put hard by one another and one on top of another so as to accommodate the maximum number of people. This supposition will not stand much scrutiny. It would not be difficult to show that the cliff house was the exception, that infinitely more compact buildings were in the open, where the same restrictions did not hold. Furthermore, the best evidence for the origin of pueblo architecture exists in open sites rather than in caves. Some other explanation must be sought.

Obviously, two conditions were needed for this achievement. The first was environmental: the existence of building stone, clay, and structural wood. All these were to be had in unlimited quantities in almost all parts of the plateau and mountain zones. But abundance did not assure use. Another condition had to be operative, and that was internal or within the social environment. The explanation, perhaps naively sought by a "dirt" archaeologist, lies in the kinship organization of the modern western pueblos.

Using Eggan's study (1950) of western pueblos as the starting point, we see that the Hopi, Zuni, Acoma, and Laguna present a remarkably uniform architectural adjustment to the environment and that the territory encompassed by these villages lies close to the heart of the area where, long ago, pueblo architecture arose. In the modern villages the outward appearance often reflects the internal organization of the occupants (Eggan 1950:3). For our purposes it is important to note that among the Hopi, as an example, the primary local organization is the extended family, based on matrilocal residence, the members occupying a series of *adjoining* rooms, which are used in common. These groups Eggan refers to as the "household" (1950:29–30), and the unity of the group is retained in the face of divisive forces. This pattern, with minor variations, holds for the other western pueblos also.

Since the household, determined by kinship and marriage, is an economic unit and group welfare is dependent upon cooperative effort, living in close geographic proximity had its practical advantages. In basic plan, contiguous rooms could be added to accommodate new families as needed. So the requirements of the social structure to maintain cohesion along lineages or segments of them and for expansion are met architecturally by the agglutinated dwellings. We may rightfully ask that, if this is a widespread and firmly fixed pattern today, was it not also true for the large pueblos of Pueblo III times? And if we are entitled to assume this, as I think we must, some inkling of the beginning, at least of the formalization, of the extended-family type of housing may be found in the architectural record of Pueblo II or, in round terms, about A.D. 1000.

Many, though not all (Brew 1946:224), of the Pueblo II settlements were small, architecturally representing a metamorphosis from the earlier pit houses to the predominantly large pueblos of later times. They undoubtedly were extended-family dwelling units situated in the midst of or near the fields; or, to put this in another way, during Pueblo II it would appear that more extended-family groups were living as independent units than was the case both in Basketmaker III and in Pueblo III. Later the agglutination of numbers of these units, together with normal population increase, resulted in the large towns of Pueblo III and IV. Eggan (1950:130) believes that the "matrilineal lineage principle was utilized in organizing the large pueblos on the Hopi mesas." Once again it would be my contention that this was also true on earlier time levels. It remains for the archaeologist to adduce supporting evidence. This move must also have been accompanied by the development of new political controls. What it was that brought people together in towns has been expressed in the pueblo formula of a community stronghold near water. The concept of banding together for mutual defense has much to recommend it, but there may also be other factors, one being the requirements of the religious system in promoting rain-producing ceremonies.

Still another effect on the settlement plan arising from the concentration of people concerned the maintenance of the agricultural activities. Previously, it would appear that household groups, living as small independent communities, were close to their fields. Nucleation meant that some fields were far away. This demanded more time in transit to and from field work and greater risk of loss of crops to marauders. The distant farmhouse, strategically located with respect to the fields, was the solution. This served jointly as a temporary home, as an observation post, and for crop storage at harvest time. On the whole, archaeologists have not paid much attention to these units, but, generalizing on my own experience, it would appear that the farmhouse was a function of urbanization and that few, if any, will be found dating from before about A.D. 1000. The inference may be drawn that the distant deployment of farmhouses was associated with times of peace, which, if correct, considerably reduces the force of the argument that towns arose in response to a need for mutual protection.

Numerous aspects, such as the clan and ceremonial systems, the effects of population influxes and diffusion, regional and temporal differences, the influence of natural events like volcanic eruptions (Colton 1932, 1936) and droughts, and other problems, would need to be considered for a thorough-going interpretation of the pre-Spanish pueblo settlements in terms of socio-political factors. It is a task well worth the effort.

The Hohokam settlements of the Gila Basin present a strikingly different picture from that of the Pueblos, and the data are far more difficult to assess, first, because the connection between the Hohokam and existing groups has not been clearly demonstrated and, second, because there is far less archaeological information than exists for the Pueblos. Except for the fourteenth-century intrusion of pueblo architectural principles into the Hohokam territory, the village types remained almost unchanged from the beginning of Hohokam history at about the time of Christ to A.D. 1300. The same compelling conditions of water and soil determined the location of their abodes, but villages were even more localized to main valleys than among the Pueblos and Basketmakers because of the larger unwatered and inhospitable areas of the desert. Even so, this did not result in the compact, concentrated house clusters seen to the north. Village size appears to have been the product more of the magnitude of the population and local ecological factors than of social or political forces or the necessity of defense, which may have merged earlier independent units in some places. The organization of Snaketown, judged on the basis of rubbish mounds (only about 5 per cent of the site has been excavated), would appear to indicate random house clusters, dispersed over a large area. To a greater or lesser degree this applies to other Hohokam villages, too. What this means in terms of societal arrangement can only be surmised—possibly some segregation by kin. But other than DiPeso's recent work in the Santa Cruz Valley on a late (post-1000) time level, Hohokam archaeology has revealed little to suggest the existence of sharply defined social units or a rule of residence.

The presence of ball courts does, however, reflect an overriding binding force, undoubtedly primarily religious, though the competitive aspect of the games (inferred) was probably determined by the social organization of the group. Among the Anasazi and Mogollon, the Great Kiva was firmly intrenched. The location of this structure was generally central, or nearly so, with respect to the domestic structures. The ball courts among the Hohokam, on the contrary, were frequently marginal, at the edges of the living areas. What conclusions may be drawn from this I do not know, but it could be a hint of inter-village competition of the kind still existing in the kick-ball races of the Papago.

We know that the ball courts do not occur in all Hohokam villages, from which we may gather that differences of importance between them did exist. Those villages with courts may have had a moiety or phratry division from which competing "teams" could be drawn and also the necessary leadership, whether religious or secular, to determine the time and the conduct of the games.

The outstanding achievement of the Hohokam with political consequences and implications was the development of their irrigation system. It was only by intervillage cooperation that individual ditches, 20 or more miles in length, up to 60 feet in width, and 10 feet in depth, could have been constructed. Aggregate canal mileage in the Salt River Valley alone has been calculated to be in excess of 200 miles (Turney 1929), which, even in our present mechanized society, would be regarded as a large-scale operation. In some instances several villages drew benefits from the same canal. The planning, construction, and maintenance of these ditches reflect some degree of centralized authority, possibly in the nature of an intervillage council. At the same time, the inference can be drawn that villages were under strong political leadership, for labor recruitment would have been at this level.

Other important effects on the society deriving from public waterworks programs would have been new concepts regarding water rights and possibly landownership. The nature of these is not recoverable. Elongated river cobbles have been found by present-day farmers in the Salt River Valley, set vertically in the ground, sometimes in alignment, suggesting field or "property" boundaries, but modern reclamation blotted out the field systems before this was called to archaeologists' attention.

Wittfogel and Goldfrank (1943) have noted the influence of waterworks and irrigation in shaping agrarian societies, with special reference to the eastern Pueblos. They point out: "If the Pueblos represent a waterwork society in miniature, then we should look for certain authoritative forms of civil and magic leadership, for institutionalized discipline, and a specific social and ceremonial organization." If this is true for the Pueblos, it may have been infinitely more so among the Hohokam, who had superior technological mastery of irrigation.

Another consequence of Hohokam canal-building which materially affected their dispersal has, I think, been overlooked. For all arid-country dwellers, water determines the site of residence. Given the proper topography, ditches could be built to lead water for miles away from the river which supplied it. This permitted settlements to spring up far from natural water sources in the midst of the preferred fertile plains. A notable example of this was Los Muertos in the Salt River Valley, which flourished in the fourteenth century as one of the Southwest's larger population centers, 6 miles from Salt River. At least three small ditches directed water from the main canal to reservoirs conveniently placed in a cluster of two-score domestic compounds (Haury 1945c:30–42).

This emancipation from naturally occurring water was one of the unique advances of prehistoric community life in the Southwest. Under this system, village well-being was in delicate balance, for the water flow had to be kept up. Once again from this we infer the existence of a central authority and organized activities connected with the repair, cleaning, head-gate tending, and protection of the canal systems. It passed out of existence as a pattern, however, with the decline of the desert people after A.D. 1400 and was not revived until the last century, with the digging of wells.

Before leaving the Hohokam area, mention should be made of several characteristics which have never been adequately explained. The basal platforms for houses, or platform mounds, of the Salt, Gila, and Santa Cruz River valleys surely mean something in settlement terms. Historically late and dating from a time of considerable cultural mixture, they exist as architectural anomalies in the Southwest. Also the fortified hills and strongholds of Papagueria (Hoover 1941) with their related villages have not been fully assessed as to the implication of warfare affecting the desert Hohokam in late prehistory. The defense villages of the Papago should shed light on this.

By way of recapitulation, Pueblo and Hohokam development can be briefly summarized as follows: Both have similar beginnings in so far as village plan is concerned, the groups having been given permanence by ecological factors and economic pursuits. In time (Pueblo II), among the Anasazi, pueblo architecture grew out of an increasingly sharpened feeling of kinship bonds and a rule of residence. After A.D. 1000, lineages were drawn together in towns. This was accompanied by new ideas pertaining to farming, to civil and religious conduct, and to the achievement of political autonomy. The Hohokam villages, on the other hand, show a weakness in all the elements which characterize the Pueblos throughout their history. House organization suggests no strong lines of descent or the dictates of a residence rule. We may infer that their strength lay along political lines, geared to an agricultural economy by irrigation. Diffusion tinged this culture with Mesoamerican elements, far more so than among the Pueblos. But, in spite of this evident contact, social classes, cities, emphasis on warfare, the religious architecture and ceremonial centers of the South did not take hold, which argues against their migration out of the South as a full-blown group. I mention this seemingly unrelated fact to emphasize that both Anasazi and Hohokam were in the Southwest at the time of Christ, that their proximity to each other, yet divergent development observable over many centuries, provides us with cultural phenomena of exceptional interest.

As noted before, most of the efforts to project social structures backward into the archaeological past based on the settlement patterns have come from the pens of the ethnologists, not from the archaeologists. I do not intend this to be a rebuff of my colleagues—we have had our own time getting our archaeological house in order through intensive historic and taxonomic studies. But it does appear now, with the trend toward broadened horizons, that inference as to the non-material aspects of archaeological groups must be as much a part of our reports as is the description of architecture and pottery.

The crux of the matter is, of course, how far we can go in making such inferences and interpretations. The ball courts, irrigation canals, and symbolic art of the Hohokam tell us that their society must have been structured; but how do we arrive at its precise nature? Obviously, this accomplishment is an impossibility. The limits to which we can go are set in part by the nature of archaeological data; beyond this the frontiers will be established only by our own ability or inability to evaluate the information available to us.

PART SEVEN
Retrospection

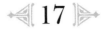

17

Thoughts After
Sixty Years
As a
Southwestern Archaeologist

Emil W. Haury

In the mid-1980s a former student reminded me that I had once said that a "new" trend in archaeology was discernible about every ten years. While I have no clear recollection of the circumstances that prompted the statement, it must have been one of those times when the pronouncements of the "new" archaeology were particularly annoying. The intent of the remark was, of course, to show the myopia of the fervor that was submerging us at the time by drawing attention to the fact that even in the late 1920s and in the 1930s and 1940s, the then-budding archaeologists were also trying "new" approaches. In other words, the workers in the 1960s and 1970s did not have a monopoly on what was good in archaeology and their work did not render sterile all that had been done before. Fortunately, the methodologies and the immediate aims of science are ever changing, though philosophical premises are not.

A candid appraisal is needed of what we, the older generation of archaeologists, would revise of our earlier work. The truth is, of course, that out of it all, progress has been and is being made and that our understanding of the past is continually being sharpened. As is usually the case when new ventures and ideas are being touted, the pendulum's swing at first outreaches itself, only to settle back to record a higher midpoint, a comfortable gain. I delight in seeing that process take place, in recognizing that solid advances have been made and that unreachable goals are being seen for what they are.

The transient nature of some of what one has written is dramatically driven home upon rereading earlier writings. Committing ideas to the permanence of type is a necessary form of communication, but it carries with it certain disadvantages, for revisions in thinking inspired by new discoveries are not correctable once those pages are broadly circulated. The stage is thereby set for the continued citation of views which have long since been revised; the consequence is an unnecessary prolongation of the process of change. This chapter elaborates on a few points of substance where I believe amendments or restatements of previously expressed views are called for.

In the 1970s and early 1980s certain revisions seemed appropriate to me on some of the major topics that I have investigated. These revisions—on the Clovis and Cochise cultures, the rise of agriculture, Hohokam culture and chronology, and the Mogollon and Anasazi—are quoted below from works written or published in that time period. These amended thoughts are then followed by further minor revisions and comments on work in the 1980s in order to bring sixty years of thinking about southwestern prehistory up to date.

CLOVIS AND COCHISE

Beginning in the 1950s one of the most important discussions concerning the Clovis and Cochise cultures was whether the Clovis hunter economy lineally preceded the Sulphur Spring gathering and food-grinding economy:

> Were they the same people, who changed their economic base when the big game was lost due to climatic change? Or were hunting and food processing facies of a single people, the "kill" sites and the food-processing sites being contemporaneous special activity areas?
>
> Let me digress for a moment to recognize what I believe to have been an undesirable side-effect of our taxonomic system. In our attempts to classify people, the dominant activity or pursuit is often selected as the basis for the identifying label. Hence,

the big game kill sites led to the rubric Clovis hunter. Similarly, the great abundance of grinding tools in early as well as later stages of Cochise was responsible for seeing them essentially as food gatherers. These labels have been cast in a kind of puristic context suggesting that the two economies were mutually exclusive, thereby warping our understanding of what people really did.

Within the time range of concern here, the last dozen millennia, surely the Clovis hunter did not spurn plant foods and the Cochise gatherer depended on game that he himself took for his protein intake. Certainly the emphasis on these pursuits fluctuated within any calendar year in response to seasonal availability of the resources. In short, hunting did not preclude gathering, and plant food dependence did not preclude hunting. A kill site, either where a single animal was dispatched as a chance encounter of hunter and prey, or the repetitive killing of game animals around a water source, as at Lehner and Murray Springs, would not likely provide much evidence of plant food processing. At the same time, camps established near plant food resources might not show much, if any, large game hunting gear.

Nevertheless, if this hypothetical situation had been a reality, it would appear that by now some evidence of coexistence of the two pursuits would have emerged in southeastern Arizona. Since it has not, a firm decision must be held in abeyance. We must either believe the negative evidence reflects separateness or that at best it is misleading.

The radiocarbon dates we now have support the idea of a shift from animal to plant dependence but the stratigraphic record does not yet fully support this view. A tenuous hint of this succession is seen in the Lehner Site where hearthstones and crude broken rock, but no grinding tools, occurred on top of the black mat that lay stratigraphically over the Clovis Complex layer (Haynes 1982) but the lithic materials were both so few in number and so undiagnostic in form that no definitive inferences may be drawn.

The absence of stone projectile points in the known sites of the Sulphur Spring stage cannot be taken at face value. The Clovis Complex with highly sophisticated projectiles has been repeatedly documented as having existed at about 11,000 B.P. The somewhat younger age, an estimated 10,000 B.P. for Sulphur Spring, without projectiles, appears at the present time to be acceptable. Then, in the Cazador assemblage, at about

8000–9000 B.P., stratigraphically later than Sulphur Spring and associated with modern fauna, projectile points once again are present.

It is highly unlikely that any people, exploiting the animal resources of the southwestern United States, or anywhere for that matter, should not have had some form of projectile point. This is all the likelier since stone-tipped weapons were known immediately earlier and later than Sulphur Spring time. The use of wood- or bone-tipped projectiles was also a possibility.

In principle, therefore, I favor tempering the negative evidence, or the lack of projectiles in the Sulphur Spring stage, as a manifestation of a specialized activity site, namely, plant processing, by people who had a well-rounded tool kit suitable to meet their dependency on plants and animals. The inference from this statement is that at no time in the cultural stages under discussion was the projectile point a foreign element. The stratigraphic records in Ventana Cave support this contention. Sayles recognized this possibility, but held to the position that the problem had not been solved.

It seems to me that the vexing question of the contemporaneity of grinding stones and hunting tools at the earliest time level, the 11,000 to 12,000 year range, could be settled by dedicated work in the Willcox Playa area. Here would be the place where both tool kits might have been simultaneously employed—the Clovis hunter stalking game and the Cochise gatherer reaping the plant foods at the lake edge or along the lagoons at the same time. The projectile points and grinding tools in the same beach context of Arizona CC:13:5 is a signal that this idea has merit.

If this association can be verified by other instances, and if the dating can be established as coincident with the last maximum lake level in the order of 11,000 years B.P., then contemporaneity would appear to be clear. We would then need to ascertain whether we are dealing with subsistence economies followed by two different people or whether the two economies were the ways a single people met food needs. What I have seen reflects the latter probability (Haury 1983:161–162, 165–166).

From the vantage point of the mid-1980s, it seems clear that the work of Michael Waters (1983) in the Cochise culture remains of southeastern Arizona has clarified a few issues basic to that complex.

The Cazador stage, viewed by Sayles (1983) as sequel to the Sulphur Spring stage, has been joined with the Sulphur Spring stage on what appear to be sound stratigraphic grounds determined by extensive testing in the alluvial deposits of Whitewater Draw. My arguments to the contrary must, therefore, be modified. On principle, merging the two lots of cultural materials expands the Sulphur Spring tool inventory in a way which makes it more easily understood as the accessories of a people who both hunted and gathered, as the requirements of life demanded, rather than being dependent on only one economic pursuit. That view never made much sense anyway. What this merging actually does, however, is to widen the gap in evidence between Sulphur Spring and Chiricahua. The interval for which we now have no clear cultural evidence comes after 10,000 B.P. and before about 8000 B.P., at the time of environmental changes involving shifts from megafauna to modern fauna and from cooler-moister to drier-warmer climates. Since those transitions were not catastrophic, I doubt that environmental circumstances militated against preservation of the human record; it seems more likely that the evidence of the continuity of life between Sulphur Spring and Chiricahua is yet to be found.

Regarding the even more pressing problem of the Clovis-Cochise connection—or lack of it, it seems to me that Waters (1983) clarified the matter a bit by suggesting that the radiocarbon dating of the Sulphur Spring stage be moved backward in time to 10,500 years ago. This change reduces the gap in chronology between Sulphur Spring and Clovis to only a few hundred years. The probability is, therefore, substantially increased that a continuity existed, that we are seeing the kill sites of Clovis-Cochise the Hunter and the gathering sites of Cochise-Clovis the Gatherer under the stressful conditions of a changing climate; the likelihood that one culture replaced the other is greatly reduced. The desire to see Cochise following Clovis in an unconnected fashion—the popular view—is, I fear, an artificial influence of the taxonomic units, which are neatly separated functionally.

Indeed, the question has been raised as to whether or not the usefulness of the label Cochise has passed. Huckell (1984) asked whether regional names, like Cochise, continued to be helpful in the understanding of a broadly based Archaic tradition characterized by more similarities than differences. It would appear that differential emphasis on grinding tools versus chipped stone implements is more the response to regional resources, or the lack of them, than evidence of deeply rooted cultural contrasts. I must agree that reassessing our system of labeling the remains we deal with and expanding the reasons for doing so are steps that should be taken periodically, lest the nomenclature in which we take a certain pride of authorship becloud the cultural vestiges we are expected to elucidate.

Those problems of process aside, it is clear to me that in the American Southwest we are coming closer to bridging the connection between the Paleoindian and the initial bearers of what we call Archaic than elsewhere in the continent. When the gap is bridged to the satisfaction of the majority, we will once again face the question of whether or not to recognize a continuous phenomenon by two labels.

THE RISE OF AGRICULTURE

At one time I regarded the corn found at Bat Cave, dated at 2500 B.C., and the maize pollen found in the Cienega Site at Point of Pines as evidence of an incidental addition to native food plants. These items did not seem to have had any measurable impact on the people who had lived there. It did not seem evident that any significant behavioral change had taken place in this area until shortly before the time of Christ, when improved varieties of maize were acquired. A question, however, lingered in my mind:

What is the probability that intensive plant cultivation was earlier than can now be demonstrated? The Chenopod-Amaranthus complex of plants was native to the region. Pollen records suggest these plants were nurtured by man millennia ago as they also were in more recent times. Other native food plants may also have been helped along by tending them. The following points would seem to support early plant culture.

First, the apparent quick and widespread acceptance of the maize complex, that is, the plant itself, the basic techniques of cultivation, methods for its preparation before consumption, the tools needed to grow and process it, the recipes of its use and related ceremonialism, suggest prior experience in these activities and tool uses.

Second, the frequency of grinding tools, particularly in the Sulphur Spring and Chiricahua stages of the Cochise culture, is impressively high. Scores of handstones may be picked up in a freshly eroding site of these culture horizons, far too many, it would seem, where processing of naturally dispersed plants only took place. Either natural plant stands were revisited over long periods of time to account for the vast number of grinding tools, or plant processing was heightened by the intentional growing of foodstuffs in the same locality. Expansion of the typological range of grinding tools possibly hints at a move toward plant-tending.

Third, the implement frequency noted above is due to either continuous or repetitive use of the locality. I have the impression that the sites might represent an incipient village existence, and that we are seeing a developmental stage of stable community residence. If this idea has merit, then an early effort at food production might be postulated. The Cochise people may, in fact, have reached the level of native plant cultivation demonstrated for the Paiute of Owens Valley, California (Lawton and others 1976:19–20). Otherwise, immediately local resources would have quickly been used up, forcing the group to move on. This idea will fall by the wayside if seasonality of use can be demonstrated. Formal house-living and the presence of storage pits in San Pedro stage times are reflective of an increasingly stable existence.

In 1962, I postulated that long after podcorn had reached Bat Cave in 2500 B.C., improved races of maize flowed northward through the Sierra Madre corridor to initially stimulate the resident food gatherers to adopt settled living and become the incipient farming Mogollon people. That took place in the centuries immediately before the time of Christ. From the mountain environment, maize then was dispersed northward to the Anasazi and westward to the Hohokam where cultivation skills geared to local environmental dictates were learned (Haury 1962a:113–118). Not until then did stable farming communities become a reality.

Now, about two decades later, my position must be altered. The first part of the script is still viable. Podcorn in the highlands of New Mexico at 2500 B.C. seems certain. But its acquisition there, and doubtless elsewhere, by the Cochise foragers left no appreciable stamp on their life style. For a little more than 2000 years life continued much as before. Then, evolutionary improvement in Mesoamerica led to new races of maize. These, adapted to highland cultivation, moved north through the mountain corridor, and were the prime moving force in the establishment of the oldest Mogollon communities. At this point I now see a change in the events.

Highland maize in Mexico was matched by evolving races suited for lowland cultivation. I would assume this took place somewhere in western Mexico where a great cultural time depth is now being demonstrated (Kelly 1980). From there,

within the first millennium B.C., both maize and the technology
to grow it under arid conditions by irrigation, moved into the
northwestern frontiers of the higher Mesoamerican societies.
From this reservoir we must draw the immigrant Hohokam
who introduced not only maize, but the hydraulic controls
to produce it, into the Sonoran Desert as a quick and near-
instantaneous take-over of an arid country (Haury 1976). The
experimentation to develop successful farming techniques in
the desert did not take place there. And while late Cochise foragers were in the region, they played no role in the initial transformation. Their territory was along the mountain threshold
better suited to their exploitive skills. They were not to taste the
full fruits of planting until somewhat later.

So, a two-pronged introduction of agriculture from the
south is envisioned. One arm, through the mountains shortly
before the time of Christ, needed the older substratum of
plant-oriented people, the Cochise, as a seed bed; these became
the Mogollon. The other arm was a transit by people through
the desert west of the Sierras in search of the right combination
of land and water where their learned skills and an already established agrarian system could be transplanted; these people
were the Hohokam. This also took place by about 300 B.C.

Not until the time of Christ or later did the Cochise of
southeastern Arizona feel the effects of Hohokam planting.
These Cochise survivors, as incipient mountain farmers, acquired Mogollon and Hohokam attributes to form a cultural
amalgam, as seen in the San Simon Village.

The role of the Cochise people was thus an important one
but they must be seen as willing recipients of cultural advances
made elsewhere. They were not innovators. Their acceptance
of agriculture was made easy by a long acquaintance with the
basic milling and handstone tools, which became the metate
and mano, needed to convert maize into its most useful form as
a human food (Haury 1983:163–164).

In the mid-1980s we have seen a major overhauling of our notions
of the introduction of maize into the Southwest. The podcorn of Bat
Cave, New Mexico—first thought to date from 3000 B.C., and later revised to 2500 B.C.—is now thought not to be podcorn at all, but cobs
of immature ears dating not much older than the beginning of the
Christian Era (Richard Ford, personal communication, 1984). Further, Austin Long's persistent search for old maize has failed to turn
up anything older than a few centuries before A.D. 1. Significant fresh

and seemingly indisputable evidence that maize was grown by Archaic people at Matty Canyon in the Empire Valley, fifty miles southeast of Tucson, by the first century B.C. has come to light. The deeply buried (five meters) cultural remains are linked to the San Pedro stage of the Cochise. Corroborative evidence has been recovered by Paul Fish of the Arizona State Museum, and, on the basis of one date of 2600 years ago, culturally related occupants of Tumamoc Hill (near Tucson in the Santa Cruz Valley) already had maize.

The importance of the last two occurrences is that while maize was present, pottery was absent. The communities appear to have been stable as evidenced by architecture, the accumulation of considerable trash, and the burial of the deceased. Apart from a host of interesting questions that these remains raise, the evidence does ask whether or not a reassessment of my view of pottery and maize in Snaketown at 300 B.C. is in order.

My notion of Hohokam beginnings held that a people well adapted to dry-land conditions on the northwestern frontier of Mesoamerican high cultures migrated northward about 300 B.C. and settled in the Gila River Valley below Florence, and perhaps elsewhere, where they could best pursue irrigated agriculture, a knowledge they brought with them. They also brought with them a race of maize more advanced than any possible previously introduced varieties adapted to arid-land cultivation. According to this interpretation, irrigation and maize were parts of the same complex. How, then, can we have maize without pottery at Matty Canyon a few hundred years later?

Such apparent contradictions force one to make adjustments in the elements of a reconstruction that best suit his preference and yet fit available information. If the goal of the migrants was to find the best desert land suitable for agriculture by irrigation, then they were on target by selecting the flattest part of the Gila Valley, with its fertile soil and adjacent live river. Similar opportunities existed along the lower Salt River and, to a more limited extent, along the Santa Cruz River. But the Empire Valley, although well watered, had a considerably higher altitude and had little land to offer that was suitable for irrigation.

My view, therefore, is that pottery may have existed in the Gila Valley several centuries earlier than elsewhere in southern Arizona and that it took some time for the knowledge of pottery production and use to spread outward from that source. This lag is not at all surprising when one considers that the Anasazi, next-door neighbors to the

Hohokam and Mogollon, had ample opportunity to acquire pottery from them. By the most conservative estimates both the Hohokam and Mogollon had pottery by the time of Christ, but the Anasazi did not begin to produce it until about A.D. 400. In short, I do not find the absence of pottery in the Empire Valley at the time of Christ and the presence of maize to be inconsistent with the hypothesis of Hohokam possession of maize and ceramics at the time of their *entrada* a few centuries B.C.

The reasonable certainty that maize was already on hand in the Southwest early in the first millennium B.C. (see Chapter 9) does not negate the thought that the Hohokam also brought with them a variety or varieties of the cereal well suited to a desert environment, as initially claimed. The test of the soundness of this idea will be the determination of the races or varieties of maize among the Matty Canyon and Tumamoc Hill samples. The fascinating element in this story is the fact that we are looking at the threshold moment in prehistory when sedentism and all that went with it was coming into full flower.

HOHOKAM CHRONOLOGY AND CULTURE

The Snaketown Project (Haury 1976) was designed to gather data that would enable a reassessment of Hohokam chronology, clarify Hohokam origins and Mesoamerican influences, and illuminate the cultural history of these people.

Chronology

Two important points on Hohokam chronology resulted from the excavation at Snaketown in 1964–1965 (Haury 1976):

First, the order of phases as determined in 1934–1935 was upheld. I am not concerned here with differences of opinion as to our use of the phase concept or as to where the division between two phases has been drawn. What does matter is the nature of the evolutionary thread that was identified. This is known reasonably well, even though all the related factors which determined Hohokam destiny are not well understood. The orderly nature, magnitude, and direction of the development can be described, and the basis for the succession of events is what appears to be an unimpeachable stratigraphic record.

Second, the importance of year-values in making all manner of archaeological assessments needs no justification. For Snaketown, to know when Hohokam evolution took place in relation to the Christian calendar is essential if measurements are to be made of cultural longevity, vitality, and its place in a regional and indeed, continental, context. By using the stratigraphic record, and somewhat subjective estimates of the speed of cultural unfolding drawn from well-dated segments of their history, and by merging the best data available derived from tree-ring dated intrusive pottery, from radiocarbon analyses, from archaeomagnetic and alpha-recoil track studies, an initial value of 300 B.C. has been derived. I will not be overly disturbed by opposition to this value, provided that it departs only nominally from that figure and that the objections voiced adequately explain possible errors in the data at hand, nor will I be too worried over juggling of phase durations. What does count is the proposition that Hohokam prehistory had a respectable longevity and that a 300 B.C. beginning date, and A.D. 1450 date of the phasing-out from a stage of cultural supremacy but not a terminal date for the culture, are acceptable. These anchor points in the Christian calendar are justifiable on the basis of the data at hand, and I subscribe to them (Haury 1976:3510.)

In the mid-1980s Hohokam chronology is still being debated. All revisions have one characteristic in common: the time has been shortened. But at that point, similarities end. While I am impressed by the fact that a shorter chronology is uniformly favored, it seems to me that there still are some questions that must be resolved, value judgments of the validity of dates aside. I see certain parallels between the Mogollon and Hohokam sequences. Martin's dates for Tularosa Cave (Martin and others 1952), with Mogollon pottery at 250 B.C., is not out of line with a 300 B.C. date for Hohokam. Further, Hohokam pottery in Mogollon sites in the Forestdale Valley in the third and fourth centuries A.D. cannot be ignored. Those wandering potsherds were not the earliest in the Hohokam ceramic history. More than that, a compression of the Hohokam sequence to the fifth and sixth or even seventh centuries cannot be made to fit reasonably well-dated sequences for the Anasazi and Mogollon, or, for that matter, the chronologies of Mexico, a dimension not to be ignored. Other factors that may have an effect on the accuracy of chronometric measurements are: charcoal derived from old wood, technical difficulties in laboratory analyses, and the question of relating dates to cultural events.

Hints of earliness, rather than lateness, for Pioneer Hohokam are beginning to surface, such as in the work of David Doyel and John Cable in Phoenix, and I am confident that, as time goes on, we will have further support for the long chronology, though some modification may be in order.

At the recent end of the Hohokam time scale, after A.D. 1450, we are still floundering in our efforts to close the gap from about A.D. 1450 to A.D. 1700. If we believe in the continuity of life in the Gila and Salt River valleys, as I do, then the disintegration of the large urban centers of late prehistory—Casa Grande, Los Muertos, Pueblo Grande, Las Colinas, and a host of others—eliminated the monumental architecture we enjoy digging in and replaced it with the fragile brush and mud homes known to the Pimas when they were first seen by Father Kino in the late seventeenth century. Changes and losses in other cultural elements have further complicated the issue, but not beyond the point of recovery. Willingness to look for the less obvious and learning to recognize undramatic remains will surely bring the two ends of the story together. I suspect that the data may already be on hand, buried in survey materials, and that intensive studies, as at Las Colinas, may well provide remains that bring the record closer to the present.

Origins

The clarification of Hohokam origins required a sharp delineation of the Vahki phase. Due to new information resulting from the 1964–1965 excavations at Snaketown, I completely revised my ideas. Instead of viewing the San Pedro stage of the Cochise culture as the basis that gave rise to Mesoamerican ideas out of which the Hohokam grew, in the 1970s I saw them as immigrants from the South:

> The idea that the Hohokam were a migratory people, coming out of Mexico into what is now Arizona, is not new. Gladwin proposed this in 1948(232) and categorically supported the view again in 1957(81–94). Sauer implied as much (1954), and further endorsement came from Ferdon (1955:29), Jennings (1956:92–93), Di Peso (1956:259–264, 562–564), and Schroeder (1960; 1965:302). This is a formidably held position, and I seem to have been the only one who believed otherwise. My early opinion was that the late Cochise Gatherers, people of the San Pedro stage, having been inoculated with a host of new cul-

tural factors flowing from Mesoamerica, became the Hohokam with the adoption of the same, leading to the eventual efficient exploitation of their arid environment. This view I now reject in favor of the migration hypothesis, putting me in the Gladwin—Di Peso camp. However, there is a fundamental and important difference in our positions which I do not wish to have misunderstood.

In Di Peso's reconstruction, the Hohokam arrived after A.D. 900, in Gladwin's about A.D. 700, after which the irrigation system was put into use. Gladwin recognizes nothing as introductory to Colonial Hohokam, which leads to the query as to what is to be done with all the pre-Colonial remains known to have existed at Snaketown. They cannot be ignored. Di Peso, on the other hand, does recognize cultural time depth, but the pre-Colonial remains are put into a different category, the O'otam. In simple terms, I see the pre-Colonial evidences as directly and lineally antecedent to the Colonial period and therefore prefer to call the whole continuum Hohokam. My reconstruction proposes that a group of people came from Mexico probably as early as 300 B.C. and that after having "settled-in" the society enjoyed a long local development, though nudged to greater cultural heights from time to time by infusions from Mesoamerica.

As part of the process of growing roots, the transplanted people began the inevitable development of a life style that befitted the setting. This required a merging, mostly undirected, of their responses to the environment, of the ways in which they saw themselves meeting the needs of survival, and of their own Weltanshauung. Out of these thrusts the Hohokam character was shaped. To identify the distinguishing qualities is not an easy task. In spite of the risks in drawing on a modern ethnological model to explain the old, I nevertheless believe that Piman culture at the time of white contact was a watered-down version of the Hohokam system. In general terms they had an elected head chief, elected village leaders, community councils, patrilocality, a number of social groups which exerted no strong restraints on marriage or other social customs. Religion was mainly person-oriented, and there were few community rituals. Public opinion was a strong force in determining personal relationships, and life and property were secure. Sensitivity toward group welfare, and a feeling of individual responsibility, particularly in agricultural pursuits, were probably more important than was strongly developed political leadership.

While one cannot be certain that the Hohokam operated
along these lines, it does seem likely that they were a benign
primitive democracy rather than a theocracy or a strong politi-
cally oriented society. We may assume that the Hohokam were
more ritually directed and their technology was more developed than was the case among the Pima. Social and economic
factors probably superseded all others in determining how the
Hohokam reacted toward each other. The absence of formality
in the village layout and, most of all, the apparent disregard for
house and trash mound placement with respect to ball court
and platform mound, emphasize the secularity of the Hohokam way of life. Rules of residence and lines of descent were
weak (Haury 1976:352–353).

In the mid-1980s Hohokam origins are still a problem much in
dispute. There are probably more proponents for a Hohokam derivation out of the earlier Archaic people than there are for my proposal that they were an immigrant group from Mexico already fully
equipped with the knowhow and the cultural hardware to establish
themselves in the harshness of the Sonoran Desert. But what I see
coming out of the ground, as at Matty Canyon and in late Archaic sites
nearby, does not dissuade me from my view. The richness of the oldest
Hohokam ceramic tradition, their lithic technology, irrigation ca-
pability from the start, and echoes of Mesoamerican beginnings per-
suade me to hold fast. What the late Archaic people had and did and
what the oldest Hohokam had and did were so contrasting that a continuity is difficult to perceive. But as the inventory of radiocarbon and
archaeomagnetic dates grows, it is increasingly apparent that the
spread in years between Hohokam and Archaic is short and, indeed,
that the chronologies may overlap. The latter phenomenon appears
to be true, given the likelihood of the near correctness of my proposed 300 B.C. beginning date for Hohokam and the first century B.C.
dates for Matty Canyon. My question, therefore, is: If Matty Canyon
is representative of a late Archaic horizon at about the time of Christ,
how, then, can we believe that the Hohokam were derived from them,
even if their beginning date is moved forward three centuries?

Expansion and Decline

In contrast to my development of ideas on Hohokam origins, my
views on their expansion and ultimate decline have remained relatively unchanged. The question of Hohokam colonization is closely

linked to the character of their adaptation and to the nature of the contact with other southwestern peoples. Looking at colonization, one observes that

> Pioneer period remains are mainly confined to the Phoenix, Sacaton, and Tucson areas of the Salt, Gila, and Santa Cruz rivers respectively. Radiations northward up the Agua Fria, New, and Verde rivers, going as far as Flagstaff, and eastward into the Tonto Basin and beyond, up the Gila River to Safford, and southward into the valleys of the San Pedro and Santa Cruz rivers, and even into Papagueria, are identified as having taken place in the Colonial period, an aptly named segment of Hohokam history. It is probably no accident that territorial expansion coincided with the climaxing of Hohokam culture. The nature of the mixing that took place with other people in the fringes of this large part of the arid Southwest does not impress one as having been a matter of conquest, but rather the peaceful expansion into new valleys by extending their irrigation technology. It seems to have been a case of a gentle but stubborn breed of people soft-selling their way of life and in the process achieving some degree of cultural blending. In a few instances, as at Winona and Ridge ruins east of Flagstaff and Walnut Creek near Young, factors other than irrigation practices ruled. Application of water-control knowledge was no longer important in those environments. All evidence points to the fact that the Hohokam were more versatile and adaptable to changing habitats than has seemed apparent until now (Haury 1976:355).

In the mid-1980s a popular alternative to the geographic expansion of Hohokam people was to view Snaketown as a trading center,

> as a home base for organized groups trafficking with neighbors in ideas and commodities. Our failure to find large stocks of raw materials as, for example, marine shells, does not support this idea. Furthermore, looking at the complexion of Hohokam society, at least as we see it from highly sketchy information, this kind of commercial endeavor would not appear to have fitted their pattern. Normal, or unorganized, trade, engaged in by individuals rather than groups, can be visualized as the mechanism whereby the Hohokam reached other people. That influences did extend out is demonstrable, and the consequence could be made the subject of a detailed study. A fascinating aspect of cultural diffusion from the Hohokam to the

Anasazi, for example, is the lag time between possession and acquisition. Why should it have taken perhaps as long as seven hundred years for the knowledge of pottery making to have spread from southern to northern Arizona? Or a lesser, but still a long, time for the transmission of cotton? These delays in acquisition of highly useful cultural attributes by the Anasazi and to a somewhat lesser extent by the Mogollon, emphasize the ineffective, unorganized status of Hohokam commercialism. In actuality, the major impact of the Hohokam seems not to have been felt by neighbors until after A.D. 700 when optimum development had been reached by them. It was then that highly specific elements were borrowed, cribbed, or traded, making the identification of cross-cultural contacts less speculative.

The significant change in the Hohokam regime came after Snaketown as a coherent village was abandoned. Satellite communities did spring up in the east and west margins of the 250-acre village; but the settlement pattern had changed from open rancheria to compact, contiguous-roomed residence units, a shift associated with other introductions, namely, polychrome pottery, inhumation, and doubtless a different social order. This was the so-called Salado intrusion, best exemplified by such places as Casa Grande and Los Muertos (Haury 1945[c]: 204–210). A pronounced change in Hohokam painted ceramics took place as a related phenomenon. In terms of this discussion the change was due to the arrival of a new cultural element, not to internal or direct environmental forces. The withdrawal of the Puebloid people close to A.D. 1450 brought the pattern of the big village, of the centers with high population density, to a close. The people left behind, the residual Hohokam, continued dispersed rancheria living in a manner that lasted into the nineteenth century.

The reasons for decentralization and community break-up in the fifteenth century have been much debated. Our work at Snaketown produced no new insights to the problem. The most frequently heard reasons given for the collapse were water logging and salt concentration in the fields due to over irrigation, thereby making the soil unfit for cultivation. While these conditions may have been factors, I cannot accept them as the sole ones. Communities not dependent on canal irrigation, as those in Papagueria, fell victim to the same fate. Of more importance is the fact that the collapse was taking place over much of the Southwest, affecting settlements in the mountains and on the plateau where different living patterns were followed. Without attempting to identify causes, whatever the forces were, these had to be broad in nature, cutting across cultural and environmental boundaries.

In summary, the Hohokam record illustrates a not uncommon growth and decline pattern: a thousand years of slow ascendancy, peaking from A.D. 700–900; followed by a population rise but with an associated decline in aesthetic values; the infusion of a new cultural system, the Salado, which materially altered settlements; and with their withdrawal, a weakened Hohokam left behind. It was they who survived to modern times by dint of will and an illustrious inheritance to become the Pima. As far as we know now, greater Snaketown can lay claim to having been the longest continuously inhabited open site in the desert, if not in the Southwest: from about 300 B.C. to A.D. 1450, followed by a hiatus and a reoccupation by the Pima Indians in the nineteenth century. Apart from the interest factor, this underlines a kind of stable living that I believe to be directly correlated with the successful merging of technology and environment. Unhappily, we do not yet have adequate data about climatic fluctuations, about variations in plant and animal communities, to talk about how these may have influenced the life of the Hohokam (Haury 1976:355).

In retrospect, I might comment that, even though my observations of the Hohokam have provoked controversy and disagreement, and will continue to do so for years to come, they have served to orient research that eventually will provide a clearer understanding of Hohokam prehistory.

MOGOLLON AND ANASAZI

Many debates grew from the proposal in 1936 that the remains of Mogollon culture found in the mountains of the Southwest were dissimilar to those of the Basketmaker-Pueblo on the Colorado Plateau and to those of the desert-dwelling Hohokam. These debates, which continued into the 1940s and 1950s, were based on the important question of the relative ages of these complexes. Dates ranging from A.D. 200 to A.D. 300 were an important element in the original arguments proposed in the Bluff Site report (Haury and Sayles 1947), but these early dates were ignored or little mentioned in the ensuing literature. Indeed, it seemed that because the Bluff Site dates were as early as (or perhaps earlier [than]) the oldest date published for Basketmaker II, eschewing them was the easy way out of a dilemma. Yet the solid evidence of early age provided by the Bluff Site was eventually one of the keys leading to the acceptance of the Mogollon as a cultural, as well as a taxonomic, unit. . . .

The proximity of the Forestdale Valley to the Anasazi domain made the contrast between the two sets of cultural materials available for study all the more impressive. Martin's work, with that of his colleagues, added territorial breadth and helped confirm the time-depth of the remains attributed to the Mogollon, and also further refined the concept. Wheat's (1955) synthesis and more recently Martin's (1979:61–74) summation have imbued the Mogollon concept with an aura of respectability, and . . . its pedigree has been strengthened further by conferences solely devoted to it. With this amount of attention, the concept is certain to be altered and embellished far beyond the original formulation of the 1930s.

Apart from the sharply contrasting environments between the Colorado Plateau and the mountain zone, the material remains of the former inhabitants also show substantial differences that, taken with the demonstrably great antiquity for the Mogollon complex, add validity to the separation of the groups, at least taxonomically, and probably in reality.

As time passed, the Anasazi bloomed with exceptional cultural vitality, resulting in architectural, ceramic, and other material advances as well as enriched ritual symbolism, far outstripping their southern neighbors in sophistication. Considering what appears to have been the receptor nature of the more colorless Mogollon people, one may infer that they viewed the Anasazi achievements with favor and adopted some of them. This process led to the transformation of traditional pit house living to pueblo living, with its concomitant change in attitudes of residence, that is, a shift from an uncongested life style based on the open deployment of buildings to a cheek-by-jowl existence in multistoried buildings. Along with that came the adoption of new ceramic techniques, especially for the production of "fancy" pottery, while the essential fabric of the utility wares was retained. A person knowledgeable in Anasazi remains, taken blindfolded to such sites as Grasshopper, or the late and large (800-room) Point of Pines Ruin and the Classic sites of the Mimbres, surely would say, on the basis of the architecture, blindfold removed, that those were sites of the Anasazi.

One hears references to the "swamping" and "takeover" of the Mogollon by the Anasazi and the inclusion of ruins and complexes within the Mogollon rubric that do not seem to belong there. I cringe, for example, when the large, late pueblos like Tundastusa, Grasshopper, Kinishba, and Point of Pines Ruin are labeled as Mogollon, or when St. Johns Polychrome is called a Mogollon pottery type.

There appears to be little difficulty with calling the Basketmaker pit-house-to-pueblo transition Anasazi; there are problems, however, with saying the Mogollon pit-house-to-pueblo transition is solely Mogollon. Both continua involve more than just architecture, because other Mogollon attributes survive late in time and the resulting cultural amalgam shares something of both. A useful descriptive compromise label for the communities in the eleventh century and later that contain features of both cultures is Mogollon-Pueblo, first suggested by Joe Ben Wheat in 1955. It is less acceptable to call them Mogollon, glossing over the highly indicative and readily identifiable attributes that spell an Anasazi heritage.

These problems, and more, should lead eventually to a reevaluation of the Mogollon idea. Not to do that means that Mogollon encompasses so much that it becomes meaningless and, at the same time, what we think of as Anasazi has been seriously impaired by nibbling away at it.

Having expressed that view, it seems appropriate for me to restate what I perceive the outstanding Mogollon characteristics to have been. But capturing the essence of a people in words from their meagre remnants, the mode of living, the relation to the earth, the outlook, and much more, is not an easy task. How does one distinguish the Visigoths from the Catalans, the Aztec from the Chibcha? And how different were the Mogollon from the Hohokam and the Anasazi? The archaeologist is denied the criteria such as language, social customs, political and religious systems, and view of self that are used to differentiate living societies. Hence, the determinations are less precise, but I believe them to be real, nonetheless.

The most striking of Mogollon attributes was a preference for a mountain habitat. Their range encompassed most of the mountainous terrain in the Greater Southwest, as much or more than the homelands of the Anasazi and Hohokam combined. This territorial homogeneity is coupled with a long tenancy, beginning at least at the time of Christ and stretching down through the centuries little changed until, as a receptor

people, they absorbed many dominant elements of the Anasazi
and thereby lost much of their identity. Their social values dictated pit house living, the houses dispersed openly in what appear to have been autonomous villages, usually associated with
an impressively large structure presumed to have had ritual
uses. Stable village life was based on an agricultural economy
supplemented richly with other natural plant resources and
the products of the hunt. They buried their dead, varying locally as to manner. The details of their domestic structures and
their crafts, notably pottery, differ markedly from the equivalent products of the Anasazi and Hohokam, providing the archaeologist with the most readily identifiable criteria. The pottery was a brown ware oxidized fabric, in early times much of it
receiving intentional smudging, texturing, and occasionally a
red slip; and only some centuries into pottery-making was it
painted in simple red patterns on polished brown surfaces. Although the Mogollon people may have inspired pottery production among the Anasazi by about A.D. 400, a topic that
needs further exploration, they had little else to give their
neighbors, and as a consequence were willing absorbers of the
advantages offered by others. Compared with the Hohokam
and Anasazi, their material culture was lustreless. During the
eleventh century A.D., they ceased to exist as a discrete Mogollon
people. By then, pueblos were being built, and black-on-white
and polychrome pottery was being made in what was once
Mogollon territory. Although the roots of the original culture
were still there, they were plated with the elements of another
people to the extent that they had given up their birthright.

I do not pretend to know what linguistic, racial, and genetic
factors may have separated Mogollon from Anasazi people, or
even if those distinctions existed; but it is clear that the styles,
most of the material possessions, and doubtless the psychologi-
cal outlook of the people who lived in a place like Grasshopper
Pueblo, were Anasazi and not Mogollon. The problem boils
down to the academic question of whether or not, and when,
the life of the people changed to more resemble one or the
other. To say that thousands of people who inhabited the many
late and large pueblos in the White Mountain region, as well as
the Salado people who lived in myriad pueblo communities
during the thirteenth and fourteenth centuries in central and
southern Arizona, were Mogollon, is to water-down the con-

cept of Mogollon so far that it loses its meaning. If one believes—and there is some support for the idea—that remnants of the thousands of pueblo-dwelling White Mountain and Salado people of the fifteenth century survived in the late prehistoric and early historic villages of the Zuni, then the proponents of the more inclusive Mogollon concept would have to say that Zuni is Mogollon and I doubt if there is any enthusiasm for that.

The observation is in order that if the modern pueblos carry the legacy of the people who built the many notable ruins on the Plateau, cause for little argument, and if the Pima-Papago are the likely candidates as modern representatives of the Hohokam, the Mogollon of Arizona and New Mexico then are left without equally obvious or eligible descendants. The easy answer is that, indeed, there may have been a "swamping" of these Mogollon by the Anasazi and their absorption was so complete that we see no regional survivors. However, to the south, in Mexico, a different picture emerges. The 50,000 or more people who inhabit the backbone of the Sierra Madre Occidental, the Tarahumara, are a conservative, change-resistant, mountain-dwelling people. They are agricultural, and while they keep domestic animals, they eat little meat. Much that they have and do, and notably their ceramics, fits the template devised for the Mogollon. Even their little dependence on meat seems to match the scarcity of bones in most Mogollon sites. I hypothesize that the Tarahumara are in contention as descendants of a broad-based Mogollon cultural group, whose territory at one time far exceeded in extent the relic Sierra Madre area inhabited today. Perhaps the Mogollon-Anasazi controversy will be illuminated when some imaginative and industrious investigators dig in the still-inhabited caves of the Tarahumara, linking their culture stratigraphically and typologically with the archaeological remains in Chihuahua, identified as Mogollon years ago (Sayles 1936:88; Gladwin 1936:94; Lister 1958:110 ff), and from there establishing connections with the Mogollon who once lived in New Mexico and Arizona. It may even be that such investigations could cause us to reassess our notions of Mogollon territoriality, and that what we see as Mogollon north of the International line was in truth no more than a robust arm from a heartland centered in the Sierra Madre Occidental of Mexico.

A large homeland, community living based on the family as suggested by the architecture, an apparent easy adaptability to variations in the environment, and a long unbroken heritage tell us that the Mogollon were in prehistory the kind of "enduring" people Ned Spicer saw the Yaqui to be in history (Haury, unpublished manuscript, 1979*).

The views expressed above still seem valid to me in the mid-1980s. Point of Pines appeals to me as one of the choice places where the transition from a dominant Mogollon complex to one overridden by Anasazi elements can be best illustrated. Regrettably, the findings of fifteen years of Field School endeavors there have been slow in appearing in print. Much of the information is surely at hand, and some day someone with a keen interest in the problem will delve into the records and bring clarity to the issue, a task that I had long envisioned for myself, but which now is no longer possible. The potential of clearing up that issue is the real legacy of Point of Pines; once articulated, it will be a fitting tribute to the more than three hundred students who shared in the task of acquiring the information.

APPROACHES TO PREHISTORY AND ARCHAEOLOGY

Most archaeologists have a deep personal stake in what they are doing. The consuming drive to do the best one knows how in the process of learning about other peoples, times, and places is based on the fantasy that sometime, somewhere one will stumble on a real bonanza—the prize of all places. Ventana Cave was such a place for me. Even before Snaketown, did I hear someone say? Yes!

Given my interest in developing the past human history of an area to the fullest extent possible, the reason for my choice is apparent, for Ventana Cave held within its sheltering walls an amazingly near-continuous record of man's tenancy of Papagueria, a span of roughly 10,000 years. Its condition of vertically stratified remains in five meters of trash is rarely encountered in the Southwest, and it means that the excavator has the privilege of piecing together a succession of stages of human development laid one on top of another and of eliminating the need to bring information from many separate sites together in a less certain way.

---

*This manuscript, *Mogollon Culture in the Forestdale Valley, East-Central Arizona*, by Emil W. Haury, was published by the University of Arizona Press in 1985.

But associated with that good feeling about Ventana Cave is also one of my greatest regrets: Ventana Cave was excavated thirty years too soon. Radiocarbon dating, the systematic extraction of pollen from earthen deposits, and numerous refinements in excavating methods and concepts had not yet been developed. Hence, although we learned much, the yield of information would have been greater if the work had been done later. Yet, that can be said about all excavations, for there never is an ideal time. I take some solace from believing that had the cave not been studied when it was, in 1939–1940, the unusually rich cultural deposits would almost surely have fallen victim to vandals' shovels and all might have been lost.

My personal position on how one approaches the study of prehistory has long been known to the many students in my seminar classes through the years. While supporting the premise that we must continually strive to improve our analytical procedures, to establish a higher level of credibility in what we do, and to be more "scientific," I cannot lose sight of the fact that archaeology is and always will be a humanistic study, that much of its infinite content can never be recovered, and that the fraction available to us must be treated with a mixture of skills of the artist and the scientist in order to extract its essence. Much to the annoyance of students and younger colleagues, I have often said that archaeology is 90 percent art and 10 percent science, and, while I am disinclined to debate the correctness of the percentages, the difference is still there.

I see the principal steps in the archaeological process—namely, investigation, analysis, interpretation, and peer evaluation—not as a closed circle but as an open spiral which, upon repetition, reaches ever forward. Without fresh data and refined techniques, we operate within a closed circle. Until unimpeachable new information comes to light or gross errors in earlier calculations are demonstrated, my stance is firm, though listening. An unsettling truth of archaeology is that we may never possess the answers to prehistory in a way satisfactory to everyone.

The search for clarification of prehistory inevitably comes down to the elemental position that the starting point demands the establishment of three dimensions: first, the place or the space occupied by the phenomenon being dealt with; second, the age or the time of the subject material; and, third, its nature, the cultural content. Without knowing those, not much can be made to fall into place. With them, the door is opened for considerations of problems going beyond the how, where, when, and what; the why follows as a logical sequel.

My views of the Paleoindian, the Archaic, the Hohokam, Mogollon and Anasazi complexes, even the Chibcha of Colombia have been shaped by operating from that eclectic platform, and it is reassuring to think that some of the findings going back as far as the 1930s have stood the test of time. Examples are: development of the ceramic sequence in the Mimbres Mogollon area, recognition and dating of the early stages of Mogollon prehistory in the Forestdale Valley, and the Hohokam story as revealed at Roosevelt 9:6 and Snaketown, though a few doubts surround the interpretation of Snaketown. I know full well that those were only the beginning steps and that, as the story is fleshed out by additional studies, changes will be made. Such must be the nature of progress.

Lest the investigators of the 1930s be accused of being nonprogressive, of being interested in classification only for its own sake, I would like to note in their defense that they saw such classification not as an end, but as a means of organizing information so that other problems might be addressed. The current generation of young and eager archaeologists is sometimes prone to find fault with the archaeologists of earlier years because, they say, the views held of archaeology were too limited and narrow. While it can be said that research goals, research designs, and explorations of theoretical and philosophical positions were not always adequately articulated, nevertheless, a thorough reading of the writings of earlier archaeologists reveals that they were thinking along much the same lines as the investigators of today. The vocabularies and modes of expressing thoughts were different; the aims were not. While the decades after 1950 did not have a monopoly on ways to enlighten the past (a statement with which some might disagree), progress in archaeology would have stalled if new learning had not occurred.

The subject of learning prompts an additional observation. Fears of training too many archaeologists have proved groundless. Yet, with the expanded promise of employment, I sense the emergence of a more serious problem—students electing to move into the job market before they are properly trained, technically and theoretically. I must explain that the situation is not unique to any one institution, but it exists nationwide. The hope, of course, is that time will diminish the problem by bringing about a better articulation between the work to be done and the talents of the worker.

Experiences during my introduction to the discipline of archaeology told me that several conditions needed to be met if one wanted to be proficient as a student of the past. First, broadly based training in the substance of archaeology, normally gained through classroom work in an institution of higher learning, was necessary. Second was fulfillment of the dream of getting into the field, where it all starts; there is no substitute for the thrills of uncovering remnants of life left by others, and nothing can take the place of the intimate knowledge gained by observing how things occur in the ground. The interpretive process begins with that comprehension. Beyond the discovery process, and almost as important, was the knack of getting along in the field, often in remote places, where the necessities of life and smooth relationship with the local population might not come easily. Early in the game it became apparent to me that unless those problems were solved quickly, no work would get done. The ability to meet these conditions, interests that made one feel at home grubbing in the garbage and houses of others, and the skills to articulate one's findings made, in my view, the Complete Archaeologist.

But, alas, times have changed that. Those archaeologists who have worked diligently to expand the reservoir of knowledge from which all of us must operate have been joined by other investigators who do not contribute fresh data, but thrive by reworking the information obtained by others. While they have spared themselves the discomforts of the field and the task of acquiring the information, they are the poorer for not having experienced how evidence of the past is collected, for this experience is an essential ingredient in the interpretive process. My plaint is not that these colleagues are not needed, but that they often gain a prominence denied the suppliers of the data with which they work. Apart from the fact that a second-hand review of data can and has been useful, I would feel better about it if those who fit the category had demonstrated a capacity to collect information at the grass-roots level in the first place.

During more than four decades of teaching, advising students on a variety of subjects came to be an integral part of the process. On looking back, I do not recall ever discussing a topic which has vexed me on more occasions than one, so now seems to be a good moment to offer a word of friendly counsel to those students who may read these pages.

Conflicts in ideas between two active archaeologists are often seen as evidence of deep personal animosities. A strange quirk in human behavior encourages some bystanders to enlarge on a presumed unfriendliness by reporting things which are imagined or fabricated and which needlessly drive a wedge between them. I speak with feeling about this because it was well known that certain ideas of Charles Di Peso's and mine clashed, though our personal relationship was of the finest kind. Yet, in the minds of students we were mortal enemies. A long evening of candid exchanges involving our two families was needed to resolve what came to be a stressful situation created and fueled by the foolish words of others. Professional differences at the substantive level should be seen for what they are and left at that.

Having introduced the subject of controversy, I am prompted to carry it a bit further. A goodly share of writing in my career of nearly sixty years has struck sparks. That is as it should be. The development of the phase sequence at Snaketown and the dating of the Hohokam at that well-known village, as published in 1937, brought me into almost immediate conflict with Gladwin, even though his name appeared as senior author on the initial publication. Gladwin's opposition was followed by a host of others who had other alternative views. My follow-up work in 1976 fared little better. Formalization of the Mogollon concept in 1936 produced its share of outcries. And there have been debates about other topics, some of them extending over many years. My purpose in bringing this up is not to review those differences, but to respond to the question recently put to me: "How does one endure controversy?"

My innate tendency is to side-step controversy if it is not likely to lead anywhere. I learned early in the pursuit of archaeology that the same body of information may result in as many conclusions as there are people viewing it. So from the start, my visceral feeling was to let it be until new data showed me to be wrong. Except for clarifying one's position, disputation without new supportive information is usually a waste of energy and certainly of space on the printed page if the debate is published. Public criticism may take several forms. Honest differences are often resolved by time. Malicious diatribes are best not dignified by responses and mischievous vexations ought to be ignored.

In the BC (Before Contracts) days of archaeology, we were lured to places to dig either because the ruins were impressive in size and setting or because they promised a rich yield of information and material. The days of probing at Pecos, Pueblo Bonito, Casas Grandes, or Snaketown with substantial funding may not be gone, but the opportunities to do so are waning. Other circumstances, such as clearing a path for a freeway (as at Las Colinas and La Ciudad in Phoenix) now dictate where we dig.

Who would have thought in 1933 that Franklin D. Roosevelt's launching of New Deal politics—putting hundreds to work in the South as a way of relieving the sting of the Depression—would be the first step in the process that determines what we do today in archaeology? In the years immediately following World War II, the nation's return to peaceful pursuits, such as building roads and dams, posed a new threat to remains of the past. As we saw those remains disappearing before our eyes, the chance to recover what we could before all was lost was enough to cheer about. Although the public money invested in archaeology now stems from legislation sensitive to the preservation of our archaeological and historical resources, federal support remains the essential ingredient.

Having promoted federal support for archaeology through service for several decades on the Committee for the Recovery of Archaeological Remains (CRAR) and otherwise, I would be the first to say that the archaeologist desperately needed federal awareness and intervention in the problem. Increasing legislation since 1966 has reflected that awareness and has brought us millions of dollars annually under contract arrangements, where before we were fortunate if we had thousands.

My position on contract work lies between the two extremes of those who see no alternative to it and those who would have no part of it. We have learned much that otherwise would have received no attention, and more people than ever before are working in archaeology, but I hold that we are paying dearly for the change in regimen because a precious tradition has been lost. Our institutions devoted to anthropology have succumbed to the lure of dollar riches to build larger, but not necessarily better, programs of investigation. We are in the process of giving up the key ingredient of science: the freedom to follow a course dictated by our findings and goals. A lingering question haunts me: when funding in the magnitude that we know in the

1980s dries up—and I think surely that it will—can our institutions revert to the formerly held schedule?

The words "management," "conservation," and "rescue" have been used with increasing frequency to describe types of archaeology. Such terms reflect clearly the consequences of our dwindling resources and of federal attempts through legislation to further safeguard our national prehistoric treasures. Along with this protectionism has grown a new philosophy about digging in ruins: dig less rather than more and, by the application of "models" and refined analytical tools, get more substance out of these smaller data sets. I have no quarrel with digging less and learning more by refining our methods, and, indeed, it seems certain that the days of hurried, broadside mega-digging—except as forced by threats of total loss— are behind us. But it is bothersome in the extreme when one is so enslaved by an adopted coordinate system that only half of a pit house can be dug when all of it is there to give the archaeologist a complete picture. It is ludicrous in the extreme to agonize over what the undug part of the house was like when a few more shovel strokes would have removed all doubts.

Surveying a region for its archaeological remains has fallen prey to a false protectionism as well. I refer to the notion that nothing—no potsherds or other vestiges of past life—is to be collected in the field; only observations and on-site identification of pottery types are allowed. This procedure precludes any verification later; it depends implicitly on the skills of the survey team to make technical decisions which are often in doubt even in the minds of experts, and, in effect, it condemns irreplaceable archaeological remains to complete loss in many cases. The only evidence we now have of thousands of village sites destroyed by a variety of twentieth-century land uses consists of the survey collections and notes in the archives of anthropological institutions. My plea is to strike a course of judicious digging and collecting to insure the maximum return of information. If we must, we should even go to the extreme of sacrificing some of the resources if something can be learned: in simple terms, it is better to know something about an artifact by destroying a bit of it for detailed analysis rather than to have it repose in a specimen cabinet and not know the elemental truths about it.

As a member of that select but ever-growing club, the Octogenarians, and as witness to and participant in the march of archaeology for six decades, I am tempted to back off and look at what we have been doing from as detached a vantage point as possible. Balancing the pluses against the minuses on a broad scale, the sum comes out positive. The discipline is in good health and I see a new receptiveness to archaeology by the public at large. Yet, there are some concerns, and a few have already been voiced. Even though much of what and where we dig is dictated by twentieth-century circumstances, far more investigations are being carried out than would otherwise be the case. But mass is good only if it is matched by quality. On that issue my judgement finds a greater disparity today than was the case some decades ago. The ogre is the contract environment in which we operate—not as much the constraints of money as of time. In earlier years money was tight but time was flexible. Now, the two are reversed, and the pressure of time in many cases has eroded the quality of results.

On the plus side, the excavation techniques have been improved vastly, even though much that is being done, while appearing to be sophisticated and "scientific," is little more than reinventing the wheel. The costs in human energy and dollars are in no way justified by the returns coming from some of our ventures or by the contributions being made to our basic understanding of human behavior. Laboratory procedures also have advanced, but with the pronounced drawback that the field investigator and the author too often work from computerized printouts prepared by others, rather than having the chance to observe first-hand the material excavated. I have concerns about this situation particularly because, in my experience, laboratory personnel who are less than experts in the material culture involved are placing incorrect data into the information bank. Imprecisions in judgment are often converted to precise values in the mindless atmosphere of the computer.

Positive advances have been made in some of our philosophical premises, in the logic of our deductions and theoretical positions, but needed are more sensitive perceptions of the soundness of inferences drawn from the residues of culture and a better awareness of the built-in limits of how far the archaeologist can go in speaking for other people. Above all, we need more intelligible prose to communicate the meaning of our findings to others. These are some of the challenges that lie before us.

Our successes in illuminating the past will be better served when we see our role as a living part of the society in which we operate, rather than as something apart from it. Even though public interest in archaeology remains high in the mid-1980s, the image of the archaeologist has become tarnished because of his aloofness to societal needs and his unwillingness to see compromise as a way of settling issues. There are, of course, many exceptions, but impressions are often formed by the exceptional and not the usual. The future of archaeology is not in jeopardy, but it is time that we reexamine our role as social scientists and our responsibility to society at large. Heavily dependent on public monies, we cannot afford to do less.

About the Contributors

BRYANT BANNISTER, professor of dendrochronology at the University of Arizona, was director of the Laboratory of Tree-Ring Research at the University of Arizona from 1964 to 1981. During his years as director he supervised a massive updating and review of the entire southwestern tree-ring chronology. He studied under Emil Haury and received his doctoral degree in 1960 from the University of Arizona.

JEFFREY S. DEAN, professor of dendrochronology in the Laboratory of Tree-Ring Research at the University of Arizona, has focused his research on Anasazi prehistory in northern Arizona and on the theory of archaeological dating. He studied southwestern archaeology under Emil Haury and received his doctoral degree from the University of Arizona in 1967.

C. VANCE HAYNES has been professor of anthropology and geosciences at the University of Arizona since 1974. His research has combined his geological perspective with his archaeological training under Emil Haury to investigate the earliest southwestern people and their environment. He received his doctoral degree from the University of Arizona in 1965.

STEVEN A. LEBLANC conducted research in the Mimbres Valley from 1974 to 1979 under the auspices of the Mimbres Foundation, which he established and which he continued to direct in 1985. He received his doctoral degree in 1971 from Washington University in St. Louis, and in 1983 became curator of archaeology at the Southwest Museum, Los Angeles.

WILLIAM J. ROBINSON, professor of dendrochronology, became director of the Laboratory of Tree-Ring Research at the University of Arizona in 1982. His research interests in tree-ring-date interpretations and applications of dendrochronology developed under Emil Haury at the University of Arizona, where he received his doctoral degree in 1967.

E. B. SAYLES was curator of the Arizona State Museum at the University of Arizona before his death in 1977. He pioneered archaeological research into the early cultures of the Southwest.

WILLIAM W. WASLEY was archaeologist of the Arizona State Museum at the University of Arizona at his death in 1970. His extensive interest in southwestern archaeology developed under Emil Haury at the University of Arizona, where he received his doctoral degree in 1959.

Bibliography of the Works of Emil W. Haury

1928   A Navaho healing ceremony. *The Mennonite Weekly Review.* Nov. 21. Newton, Kansas.

1928   The succession of house types in the pueblo area. MA thesis, University of Arizona, Tucson.

1930   A sequence of decorated redware from the Silver Creek Drainage. *Museum Notes* 2(11):4. Flagstaff: Museum of Northern Arizona.

1931   Minute beads from prehistoric pueblos. *American Anthropologist* 33(1): 80–87.

1931   Kivas of the Tusayan Ruin, Grand Canyon, Arizona. *Medallion Papers* 9. Globe, Arizona: Gila Pueblo.

1931   Pinedale Polychrome, and Four-Mile Polychrome. *In* Some southwestern pottery types, Series II, by Winifred and Harold S. Gladwin. *Medallion Papers* 10. Globe, Arizona: Gila Pueblo.

1931   (with L. L. Hargrave) Recently dated pueblo ruins in Arizona. *Smithsonian Miscellaneous Collections* 82(11). Washington, D.C.: Smithsonian Institution.

1932   Roosevelt:9:6, a Hohokam site of the Colonial Period. *Medallion Papers* 11. Globe, Arizona: Gila Pueblo.

1932   The age of lead glaze decorated pottery in the Southwest. *American Anthropologist* 34(3):418–425.

1934   Archaeology and life. *Bethel College Monthly* 39(10):4–8.

1934   Climate and human history. *Tree-Ring Bulletin* 1(2):13–15. Flagstaff: The Tree Ring Society.

1934   The Canyon Creek Ruin and the cliff dwellings of the Sierra Ancha. *Medallion Papers* 14. Globe, Arizona: Gila Pueblo.

1935   Dates from Gila Pueblo. *Tree-Ring Bulletin* 2(1):3–4. Flagstaff, Arizona: The Tree Ring Society.

1935   Tree-rings: The archaeologist's time-piece. *American Antiquity* 1(2): 98–108.

1936   Some southwestern pottery types. Series IV. *Medallion Papers* 19. Globe, Arizona: Gila Pueblo.

1936   The Mogollon Culture of southwestern New Mexico. *Medallion Papers* 20. Globe, Arizona: Gila Pueblo.

1936   A glimpse of the prehistoric Southwest, *Indians at Work* 4(9):15–22. Washington, D.C.: U.S. Department of the Interior, Office of Indian Affairs.

1936   Vandal Cave. *The Kiva* 1(6):1–4.

1936   The Snaketown Canal. *In* Symposium on prehistoric agriculture. *University of New Mexico Bulletin, Anthropological Series* 1(5):48–50. Albuquerque: University of New Mexico.

1936   Review of *The Ruins at Kiatuthlanna, Eastern Arizona,* by Frank H. H. Roberts, Jr. *American Anthropologist* 38(1):116–117.

1936   Review of *Dating Pueblo Bonito and Other Ruins of the Southwest,* by A. E. Douglass. *American Antiquity* 1(3):248–249.

1937   A pre-Spanish rubber ball from Arizona. *American Antiquity* 2(4):282–288.

1937   (with Harold S. Gladwin, E. B. Sayles, and Nora Gladwin) Excavations at Snaketown, material culture. *Medallion Papers* 25. Globe, Arizona: Gila Pueblo. Second edition, 1965, third editon, 1975. Tucson: University of Arizona Press.

1937   (with I. F. Flora) Basket-maker III dates from the vicinity of Durango, Colorado. *Tree-Ring Bulletin* 4(1):7–8. Tucson, Arizona: The Tree Ring Society.

1938   Southwestern dated ruins: II. *Tree-Ring Bulletin* 4(3):3–4. Tucson, Arizona: The Tree Ring Society.

1938   Legged vessels from the Southwest. *American Antiquity* 3(3):264–265.

1938   Review of *Lowry Ruin in Southwestern Colorado,* by Paul S. Martin. *American Antiquity* 3(3):288–290.

1938   (with C. M. Conrad) The comparison of fiber properties of Arizona Cliff Dweller and Hopi Cotton. *American Antiquity* 3(3):224–227.

1939   Progress report on excavations at Forestdale. In *Yearbook of the American Philosophical Society,* pp. 232–233. Philadelphia: American Philosophical Society.

1939   Article IX. The Builders of Our First Apartment Houses. *In* United States Department of the Interior, Memorandum for the Press. Mimeographed, pp. 1–9.

1940   Progress report on excavations at Forestdale. In *Yearbook of the American Philosophical Society,* pp. 186–188. Philadelphia: American Philosophical Society.   .

1940 How ancient timbers gave clues to long sought dates. *The Science Counselor* 6(4):95–96, 115–117.

1940 New tree-ring dates from the Forestdale Valley, east-central Arizona. *Tree-Ring Bulletin* 7(2):14–16. Tucson, Arizona: The Tree Ring Society.

1940 Excavations at Forestdale. *The Kiva* 6(2):5–8.

1940 Excavations in the Forestdale Valley, east-central Arizona. *University of Arizona Bulletin* 11(4), *Social Science Bulletin* 12. Tucson: University of Arizona.

1941 Progress report on excavations at Forestdale. In *Yearbook of the American Philosophical Society*, pp. 222–225. Philadelphia: American Philosophical Society.

1941 Review of *Style Trends of Pueblo Pottery in the Rio Grande and Little Colorado Cultural Areas from the 16th to the 19th Century*, by H. P. Mera. *American Anthropologist* 43(2):285–286.

1941 Review of *Field Manual of Prehistoric Southwestern Pottery Types*, by Florence M. Hawley. *American Anthropologist* 43(2):286–287.

1942 Recent field work by the Arizona State Museum. *The Kiva* 7(5–6):17–24.

1942 The Arizona State Museum: The present and the future. *The Kiva* 7(7–8):31–32.

1942 Some implications of the Bluff Ruin dates. *Tree-Ring Bulletin* 9(2):7–8. Tucson, Arizona: The Tree Ring Society.

1942 Review of *An Archaeological Site Near Gleeson, Arizona*, by William S. Fulton and Carr Tuthill. *American Anthropologist* 44(4):701–702.

1943 A possible Cochise-Mogollon-Hohokam sequence. *In* Proceedings of the American Philosophical Society 86(2):260–263. Philadelphia: American Philosophical Society.

1943 The stratigraphy of Ventana Cave, Arizona. *American Antiquity* 8(3):218–223.

1943 A proposal for the development of a corn exchange. *Clearing House for Southwestern Museums Newsletter* 65:229–230. Denver: Clearing House for Southwestern Museums.

1943 Review of *Distribution and Significance of Ball Courts in the Southwest*, by Chester S. Chard. *American Anthropologist* 45(1):132–133.

1943 Mexico and the Southwestern United States. In *El Norte de Mexico y El Sur de Estados Unidos, Tercera Reunion de Mesa Redondo Sobre Problemas Antropologicos de Mexico Y Centro America, August 25–September 2*, pp. 203–205. Mexico, D. F.: Sociedad Mexicana de Antropolpgia.

1944 Anthropology in the Southwest. *Phi Kappa Phi Journal* 24(3):95–97.

1944 Tree-rings continue to tell their story. *The Kiva* 9(2):10–14.

1944 Arizona State Museum, 1943–44. *The Kiva* 9(4):29–31.

1944 Review of *Dating Prehistoric Ruins by Tree-Rings*, by W. S. Stallings, Jr. *American Antiquity* 10(1):106–107.

1945 Painted Cave, northeastern Arizona. *Amerind Foundation* 3. Dragoon, Arizona: The Amerind Foundation.

1945 The archaeological survey on the San Carlos Indian Reservation, *The Kiva* 11(1):5–9.

1945 Dating early man in the Southwest. *Arizona Quarterly* 1(4):5–13.
1945 The excavation of Los Muertos and neighboring ruins in the Salt River Valley, southern Arizona. *Papers of the Peabody Museum of American Archaeology and Ethnology* 24(1). Cambridge: Peabody Museum, Harvard University.
1945 Arizona's ancient irrigation builders. *Natural History Magazine* 54(7): 300–310, 335.
1945 The problems of contacts between Mexico and the southwestern United States. *Southwestern Journal of Anthropology* 1(1):55–74.
1946 Summer activities at Point of Pines. *The Kiva* 12(1):3–5.
1946 (with E. B. Sayles) Review of *The SU Site: Excavations at a Mogollon Village, Western New Mexico, Second Season, 1941*, by Paul S. Martin. *American Anthropologist* 48(2):251–253.
1947 A large pre-Columbian copper bell from the Southwest. *American Antiquity* 13(1):80–82.
1947 (with E. B. Sayles) An early pit house village of the Mogollon Culture. *University of Arizona Bulletin* 18(4), *Social Science Bulletin* 16. Tucson: University of Arizona.
1948 Foreword. *In* The Jornada branch of the Mogollon Culture, by Donald J. Lehmer. *University of Arizona Bulletin* 19(2), *Social Science Bulletin* 17. Tucson: University of Arizona.
1948 The 1948 Southwestern Archaeological Conference. *El Palacio* 55(11): 357–358.
1949 The 1948 Southwestern Archaeological Conference. *American Antiquity* 14(3):254–256.
1949 The 1948 Southwestern Archaeological Conference (U.S.A.) *Boletín Bibliográfico de Antropología Americana* 11:120–121. Mexico, D. F.
1949 Review of *Archaeology of Alkali Ridge, Southeastern Utah, with a Review of the Prehistory of the Mesa Verde Division of the San Juan and Some Observations on Archaeological Systematics*, by John Otis Brew. *American Antiquity* 15(1):64–66.
1950 *The Stratigraphy and Archaeology of Ventana Cave, Arizona*. Tucson and Albuquerque: University of Arizona Press and University of New Mexico Press (joint publication). Second edition, 1975. Tucson: University of Arizona Press.
1950 A sequence of great kivas in the Forestdale Valley, Arizona. In *For the Dean*, pp. 29–39. Tucson and Santa Fe: Hohokam Museums Association and Southwestern Monuments Association (joint publication).
1950 Archaeology in Arizona. *Bethel College Bulletin* 37(5):5–7.
1950 Foreword. *In* A report on the excavation of a small ruin near Point of Pines, east-central Arizona, by Fred Wendorf. *University of Arizona Bulletin* 21(3), *Social Science Bulletin* 19:7–10. Tucson: University of Arizona.
1950 (with Gordon C. Baldwin and Jesse L. Nusbaum) Prehistory of man. In *A Survey of the Recreational Sources of the Colorado River Basin*, pp. 79–101. Washington, D.C.: U.S. Department of the Interior, National Park Service.
1952 Exploring the corridors of time. *The Kiva* 17(3–4):1–28.

1952 The Naco mammoth. *The Kiva* 18(3–4):1–20.

1952 Review of *Investigaciones arqueológicas en el Departamento del Magdalena 1946–1950*, by Gerardo y Alicia Reichel-Dolmatoff. *American Antiquity* 18(2):182–183.

1953 Some thoughts on Chibcha Culture in the High Plains of Colombia. *American Antiquity* 19(1):76–78.

1953 (with Ernst Antevs and John F. Lance) Artifacts with mammoth remains, Naco, Arizona. *American Antiquity* 19(1):1–24.

1953 (with Julio César Cubillos) Investigaciones arqueológicas en la sabana de Bogotá, Colombia (Cultura Chibcha). *University of Arizona Bulletin* 24(2), *Social Science Bulletin* 22. Tucson: University of Arizona.

1954 Selected bibliography. "Southwest Issue," edited by Emil W. Haury. *American Anthropologist* 56(4):728–731.

1954 Comment on Time depths of American linguistic groupings, by Morris Swadesh. *American Anthropologist* 56(3):372–373.

1954 Selected bibliography. "Southwest Issue," edited by Emil W. Haury. *American Anthropologist* 56(4):728–731.

1955 Archaeological theories and interpretations. *Yearbook of Anthropology* 1:115–132. Baltimore: Wenner-Gren Foundation for Anthropological Research.

1955 A mammoth hunt in Arizona. *Archaeology* 8(1):51–55. Reprinted 1967 in *Conquistadors Without Swords: Archaeologists in the Americas*, edited by Leo Deuel, pp. 505–508. New York: St. Martin's Press, Inc.

1955 Archaeological stratigraphy. *Geochronology, University of Arizona Bulletin* 26(2), *Physical Science Bulletin* 2, pp. 126–134. Tucson: University of Arizona.

1956 Archaeological theories and interpretations. In *Current Anthropology*, edited by William L. Thomas, Jr., pp. 115–132. Chicago: University of Chicago Press.

1956 The Lehner mammoth site. *The Kiva* 21(3–4):23–24.

1956 Speculations on prehistoric settlement patterns in the Southwest. *In* Prehistoric settlement patterns in the New World, edited by G. R. Willey. *Viking Fund Publications in Anthropology* 23:3–10. New York: Wenner-Gren Foundation for Anthropological Research.

1956 (with Robert L. Rands, Albert C. Spaulding, Walter W. Taylor, Raymond H. Thompson, and Robert Wauchope) An Archaeological Approach to the Study of Cultural Stability. *Society for American Archaeology Memoir 11. American Antiquity* 22(2):31–57.

1957 An alluvial site on the San Carlos Indian Reservation, Arizona. *American Antiquity* 23(1):2–27.

1957 Operation: Pick 'n shovel. *Arizona Alumnus* 34(3):10–13.

1957 The problem of obtaining adequate identification. *In* The identification of non-artifactual archaeological materials. *National Academy of Science–National Research Council* 565:17. Washington: National Academy of Science and National Research Council.

1957 The tree-ring laboratory and the geochronological program, University of Arizona. *In* The identification of non-artifactual archaeological materials. *National Academy of Sciences–National Research Council* 565: 30–31. Washington: National Academy of Sciences and National Research Council.

1957 Foreword. In *Southwest Indian Painting*, by Clara Lee Tanner. Tucson: University of Arizona Press, and Arizona Silhouettes.

1958 Two fossil elephant kill sites in the American Southwest. *In* Proceedings of the Thirty-Second International Congress of Americanists. *University of Arizona Program in Geochronology Contribution 4*, pp. 433–440. Copenhagen, Denmark.

1958 Post-Pleistocene human occupation in the Southwest. *In* Climate and man in the Southwest, edited by T. L. Smiley. *University of Arizona Program in Geochronology Contribution 6. University of Arizona Bulletin* 28(4):69–75. Tucson: University of Arizona.

1958 Evidence at Point of Pines for a prehistoric migration from northern Arizona. *In* Migrations in New World culture history, edited by R. H. Thompson. *University of Arizona Bulletin 29:2, Social Science Bulletin* 27:1–8. Tucson: University of Arizona. Reprinted in *The Bobbs-Merrill Reprint Series*, A-304, 1966. Indianapolis. Reprinted in *In Search of Man*, edited by Ernestene Green, pp. 381–388, 1973. Boston: Little, Brown and Company.

1958 Review of *Late Mogollon Communities: Four Sites of the Tularosa Phase, Western New Mexico*, by Paul S. Martin, John B. Rinaldo, and Eloise R. Barter. *American Anthropologist* 60(1):197–198.

1958 Review of *Klamath Prehistory: The Prehistory of the Culture of the Klamath Lake Area, Oregon*, by L. S. Cressman. *American Antiquity* 23(3):318–320.

1958 Review of *Abriss der Vorgeschichte*, by Karl J. Narr, Willy Schulz-Weidner, Christoph von Fürer-Haimendorf, Anthony Christie, Max Loehr, Karl Jettmar, Oswald Menghin. *American Antiquity* 24(2):196–197.

1959 Scientific sleuthing. "Arizona Days and Ways." *Arizona Republic*, December 13:9–10. Phoenix, Arizona.

1959 Review of *Pleistocene Man at San Diego*, by George F. Carter. *American Journal of Archaeology* 63(1):116–117.

1959 Review of *Digging into History*, by Paul S. Martin. *Science* 129(3360): 1419–1420.

1959 Review of *Pecos, New Mexico: Archaeological Notes*, by Alfred Vincent Kidder. *American Antiquity* 25(2):281–282.

1959 (with Carol A. Gifford) A thirteenth century "strongbox." *The Kiva* 24(4):1–11.

1959 (with Edwin B. Sayles and William W. Wasley) The Lehner mammoth site, southeastern Arizona. *American Antiquity* 25(1):2–30. Reprinted in *The Bobbs-Merrill Reprint Series*, A-305, 1966. Indianapolis.

1960 Before history. In *Arizona: Its People and Resources*, edited by J. C. Cross, E. H. Shaw, and Kathleen Scheifele, pp. 17–27. Tucson: University of Arizona Press. 2d ed., 1972. Reprinted in *Indians of Arizona: A Contemporary Perspective*, edited by Thomas Weaver, pp. 7–25. Tucson: University of Arizona Press, 1975.

1960 Association of fossil fauna and artifacts of the Sulphur Spring stage, Cochise Culture. *American Antiquity* 25(4):609–610.

1960 Review of *Approach to Archaeology*, by Stuart Piggott. *Science* 131(3413): 1605.

1961 Archaeology. In *20th Annual Report on the Foundation's Activities, 1941–1961*. New York: Wenner-Gren Foundation for Anthropological Research. Small Grants: Pro (from "Archaeology") reprinted in Foundation News. *Bulletin of the Foundation Library Center* 3(1):7. Baltimore: Foundation Library Center.

1961 The engineer and archaeology. *Division of Engineering and Industrial Research Newsletter* 3:2. Washington: National Academy of Sciences.

1962 The greater American Southwest. In "Courses Toward Urban Life," edited by Robert J. Braidwood and Gordon R. Willey. *Viking Fund Publications in Anthropology* 32:106–131. New York: Wenner-Gren Foundation for Anthropological Research.

1962 HH-39: Recollections of a dramatic moment in Southwestern archaeology. *Tree-Ring Bulletin* 24(3–4):11–14. Tucson, Arizona: The Tree Ring Society.

1962 Review of *Black Sand*, by Harold S. Colton. *Science* 135(3502):425.

1963 Axel L. Wenner-Gren, 1881–1961. *American Antiquity* 29(1):90.

1965 Snaketown: 1964–1965. *The Kiva* 31(1):1–13.

1967 The Hohokam: First masters of the American desert. *National Geographic Magazine* 131(5):670–695.

1968 So you want a research grant? *Western Museums Quarterly* 5(2):15–16.

1968 Report on the annual meeting of the Committee for the Recovery of Archaeological Remains. In *Report of the Executive Board, American Anthropological Association*, p. 17. Washington: American Anthropological Association.

1969 (with Sidney Brinckerhoff, Gordon Heck, David Mackie, and Richard Morse) Historic architecture in Tucson. In *A Report by the Historic Preservation Consultants*, vols. 1 and 2, edited by Emil W. Haury. Tucson: Tucson Urban Renewal.

1970 Report on the annual meeting of the Committee for the Recovery of Archaeological Remains. In *Report of the Executive Board, American Anthropological Association*, pp. 41–42. Washington: American Anthropological Association.

1970 (with V. Bucha, R. E. Taylor, and Rainer Berger) Geomagnetic intensity: Changes during the past 3000 years in the western hemisphere. *Science* 168(3927):111–114.

1972 Report on the annual meeting of the Committee for the Recovery of Archaeological Remains. In *Report of the Executive Board. American Anthropological Association*, pp. 29–30. Washington: American Anthropological Association.

1972 (with B. Fontana and T. Weaver) Edward P. Dozier. *Indian Programs* 2(3):6–8.

1973 Hohokam. *Encyclopædia Britannica* 11:586–587. Chicago.

1974 Report of the representative of the Committee for the Recovery of Archaeological Remains. *1973 Annual Report, American Anthropological Association*. Washington: American Anthropological Association.

1975	The Anasazi of Arizona. In *The Ascent of Man*, edited by John F. Hena-han, pp. 59–62. Boston: Little, Brown and Company.

1975	Metric Slips (Letters Section). *Science* 190(4212):324.

1975	Recipe for Wetherill stew. *A Matter of Taste Cook Book*, p. 63. San Diego: Klee Wyk Society of the Museum of Man.

1975	Cuicuilco in retrospect. *The Kiva* 41(2):195–200.

1975	(with Isabel Fathauer) *Tucson, From Pithouse to Skyscraper*. Tucson: Tucson Historical Committee.

1976	*The Hohokam: Desert Farmers & Craftsmen; Excavations at Snaketown, 1964–1965*. Tucson: University of Arizona Press.

1976	Salado: The view from Point of Pines; and Comments on papers. *In* "The 1976 Salado Conference," edited by David Doyel and Emil W. Haury. *The Kiva* 42(1):81–84, 125–126.

1977	Uncovering the story of man (transcription of taped conversation). In *This Land, These Voices*, by Abe and Mildred Chanin, pp. 55–64. Flagstaff: Northland Press.

1978	Concluding thoughts. *In* The Hodges Ruin, A Hohokam Community in the Tucson Basin, by Isabel T. Kelly, edited by Gayle H. Hartmann. *Anthropological Papers of the University of Arizona* 30:126–128. Tucson: University of Arizona Press.

1978	Discussant. *In* Proceedings of the 1973 Hohokam Conference, edited by Donald E. Weaver, Jr., Susan S. Burton, and Minabell Laughlin. *Contributions to Anthropological Studies* 2. Albuquerque: Center for Anthropological Studies.

1978	Snaketown's Longevity. *Popular Archaeology* 7(1–2):9, 11. Arlington. (Excerpted from *The Hohokam: Desert Farmers & Craftsmen*, 1976)

1979	(with George J. Gumerman) Prehistory: Hohokam. *Handbook of North American Indians*, edited by William C. Sturtevant, Vol. 9, pp. 75–90. Washington: Smithsonian Institution.

1980	Early goals of the Arizona State Museum. *In* The Arizona State Museum Archaeological Site Survey System, compiled by Lawrence E. Vogler. *Arizona State Museum Archaeological Series* 128:155–159. Tucson: Arizona State Museum, University of Arizona.

1980	Foreword. *In* Archaeological Explorations in Caves of the Point of Pines Region, by James C. Gifford. *Anthropological Papers of the University of Arizona* 36:ix–x. Tucson: University of Arizona Press.

1980	On the discovery of Ventana Cave, pp. 123–130; and Elephant bones and amateurs: An Arizona safari, pp. 140–144. In *Camera, Spade and Pen*, by Marc and Marnie Gaede. Tucson: University of Arizona Press.

1980	Foreword. *In* Ceramic Sequence in Colima: Capacha. An Early Phase, by Isabel Kelly. *Anthropological Papers of the University of Arizona* 37:vii. Tucson: University of Arizona Press.

1980	Comments on the Hohokam Symposium. *In* Current Issues in Hohokam Prehistory. Proceedings of a Symposium, edited by David Doyel and Fred Plog. *Arizona State University Anthropological Research Papers* 23:113–120. Tempe: Arizona State University.

1983	Obituary. Madeleine Appleton Kidder, 1891–1981. *American Antiquity* 48(1):83–84.

1983 Foreword; and Concluding remarks. *In* The Cochise Cultural Sequence in Southeastern Arizona, by E. B. Sayles. *Anthropological Papers of the University of Arizona* 42:ix, 158–166. Tucson: University of Arizona Press.

1983 Foreword. In *Those Who Came Before*, by Robert H. and Florence Lister, pp. 8–10. Tucson: Southwest Parks and Monuments Association and the University of Arizona Press.

1983 Foreword. *In* Cultural and Environmental History of the Cienega Valley, Southeastern Arizona, by Frank E. Eddy and Maurice E. Cooley. *Anthropological Papers of the University of Arizona* 43:vii–viii. Tucson: University of Arizona Press.

1984 The Search for Chichilticale, in Coronado's Footsteps. *Arizona Highways* 60(4):14–19.

1985 *Mogollon Culture in the Forestdale Valley, East-Central Arizona.* Tucson: University of Arizona Press.

1985 Reflections: Fifty Years of Southwestern Archaeology. *American Antiquity* 50(2):383–394.

1985 (Obituary, with J. Jefferson Reid) Harold Sterling Gladwin, 1883–1983. *The Kiva* 50(4):271–280. Tucson: Arizona Archaeological and Historical Society.

1985 Wetherill Stew. In *The Chacmool Field Cook Book*, pp. 77–78. Calgary, Alberta: Archaeological Association of the University of Calgary.

1986 *Emil W. Haury's Prehistory of the American Southwest*, edited by J. Jefferson Reid and David E. Doyel. Tucson: University of Arizona Press.

1987 Comments on Symposium Papers. *In* The Hohokam Village: Site Structure and Organization, edited by David E. Doyel, pp. 249–252. *Southwestern and Rocky Mountain Division of the American Association for the Advancement of Science: AAAS Publication* 87-15.

1988 Recent Thoughts on the Mogollon. *The Kiva* 53(2):195–196. Tucson: Arizona Archaeological and Historical Society.

1988 Epilogue. In *Pecos: Gateway to Pueblos and Plains; The Anthology*, edited by John V. Bezy and Joseph P. Sanchez, pp. 132–136. Tucson: Southwest Parks and Monuments Association.

1988 Gila Pueblo Archaeological Foundation: A History and Some Personal Notes. *The Kiva* 54(1). Tucson: Arizona Archaeological and Historical Society.

1989 Point of Pines, Arizona: A History of the University of Arizona Archaeological Field School. *Anthropological Papers of the University of Arizona* 50. Tucson: University of Arizona Press.

1991 Afterword. In *The Hohokam: Ancient People of the Desert*, edited by David Grant Noble, pp. 69–73. Santa Fe: School of American Research Press.

1991 The Search for Chichilticale. In *In Coronado's Footsteps*, by Stewart L. Udall, pp. 25–31. Tucson: Southwest Parks and Monuments Association.

References Cited

Abbott, Charles C., and Frederick W. Putnam
  1879 Implements and weapons made of bone. *U.S. Geographical Survey West of the Hundredth Meridian* 7. Washington, D.C.

Antevs, Ernst
  1949 Geology of the Clovis sites. *In* Ancient man in North America, by H. Marie Wormington. Denver Museum of Natural History, Popular Series 4. 3rd edition. Denver: Denver Museum of Natural History.
  1952 Arroyo-cutting and filling. *Journal of Geology* 60:375–385.
  1953 Artifacts with mammoth remains, Naco, Arizona. II. Age of the Clovis fluted points with the Naco Mammoth. *American Antiquity* 19(1):15–17.
  1955 Geologic-climatic dating in the West. *American Antiquity* 20(4): 317–335.

Anyon, Roger
  1980 The Late Pithouse period. In *An Archaeological Synthesis of South Central and Southwestern New Mexico*, edited by Steven A. LeBlanc and Michael E. Whalen, pp. 141–255. Albuquerque: Office of Contract Archaeology, University of New Mexico.
  1984 Mogollon Settlement Patterns and Communal Architecture. Master's thesis, University of New Mexico, Albuquerque.

Anyon, Roger, Patricia A. Gilman, and Steven A. LeBlanc
  1981 A reevaluation of the Mogollon-Mimbres archaeological sequence. *The Kiva* 46(4):209–225.

Anyon, Roger, and Steven A. LeBlanc
  1980 The architectural evolution of Mogollon-Mimbres communal structures. *The Kiva* 45(3):253–277.
  1984 *The Galaz Ruin: A Prehistoric Mimbres Village in Southwestern New Mexico.* Albuquerque: Maxwell Museum of Anthropology Publication Series, University of New Mexico Press.
Aveleyra Arroyo de Anda, Luis
  1955 El segundo mamut fósil de Santa Isabel Iztapan, México, y artefactos asociados. *Instituto Nacional de Antropología e Historia, Dirección de Prehistoria, Publicaciones* 1. Mexico City: Instituto Nacional de Antropología e Historia.
Aveleyra Arroyo de Anda, Luis, and Manuel Maldonado-Koerdell
  1952 Asociación de artefactos con mamut en el Pleistoceno Superior de la Cuenca de México. *Revista Mexicana de Estudios Antropológicos* 13(1), Mexico City.
Baby, Raymond S.
  1954 Hopewell cremation practices. *Ohio Historical Society, Papers in Archaeology* 1. Columbus: Ohio Historical Society.
Bannister, Bryant
  1969 Dendrochronology. In *Science in Archaeology*, edited by Don Brothwell and Eric Higgs, pp. 191–205 (revised edition). London: Thames and Hudson.
  1977 Tree-ring dating of the archaeological sites in the Chaco Canyon Region, New Mexico. *Southwest Parks and Monuments Association Technical Series* 6(2). Globe, Arizona: Southwest Parks and Monuments Association.
Bannister, Bryant, Jeffrey S. Dean, and William J. Robinson
  1968 *Tree-Ring Dates from Arizona C-D: Eastern Grand Canyon, Tsegi Canyon, Kayenta Area.* Tucson: Laboratory of Tree-Ring Research, University of Arizona.
Bannister, Bryant, John W. Hannah, and William J. Robinson
  1966 *Tree-Ring Dates from Arizona K: Puerco, Wide Ruin, Ganado Area.* Tucson: Laboratory of Tree-Ring Research, University of Arizona.
  1970 *Tree-Ring Dates from New Mexico M-N, S, Z: Southwestern New Mexico Area.* Tucson: Laboratory of Tree-Ring Research, University of Arizona.
Bartlett, John R.
  1854 *Personal Narrative of Explorations and Incidents in Texas, New Mexico, California, Sonora, and Chihuahua, Connected with the United States and Mexican Boundary Commission, During the Years 1850, 1851, 1852, and 1853.* New York: D. Appleton and Co.
Bartlett, Katharine
  1933 Pueblo milling stones of the Flagstaff Region and their relation to others in the Southwest. *Museum of Northern Arizona Bulletin* 3. Flagstaff: Museum of Northern Arizona.
  1934 The material culture of Pueblo II in the San Francisco Mountains,

Arizona. *Museum of Northern Arizona Bulletin* 7. Flagstaff: Museum of Northern Arizona.

Beals, Ralph L.
1932 The comparative ethnology of northern Mexico before 1750. *Ibero-Americana* 2. Berkeley: University of California Press.

Bieber, Ralph P., and A. B. Bender, editors
1938 Cooke's journal of the march of the Mormon Battalion, 1846–1847. In *Southwest Historical Series* 7:63–240. Glendale: Arthur H. Clark Co.

Bolton, Herbert E.
1948 *Kino's Historical Memoir of Primería Alta.* Berkeley: University of California Press.

Bradfield, Wesley
1931 Cameron Creek Village: A site in the Mimbres area in Grant County, New Mexico. *Monographs of the School of American Research* 1. Santa Fe: School of American Research.

Braidwood, Robert J.
1948 Prehistoric men. *Chicago Natural History Museum Popular Series, Anthropology* 37. Chicago: Chicago Natural History Museum.
1958 Near eastern prehistory. *Science* 127(3312):1419–1430.

Breternitz, David A.
1956 The archaeology of Nantack Village, Point of Pines, Arizona. Master's thesis, University of Arizona, Tucson.

Brew, John O.
1946 Archaeology of Alkali Ridge, southeast Utah. *Papers of the Peabody Museum of American Archaeology and Ethnology* 21. Cambridge: Peabody Museum, Harvard University.

Bryan, Bruce
1927 The Mimbres expedition. *The Masterkey* 1(3):21–24.

Bryan, Kirk
1925 Date of channel trenching in the arid Southwest. *Science* 62(1607): 338–344.
1929 Flood-water farming. *Geographical Review* 19:444–456.
1950 Geological interpretation of the deposits. In *The Stratigraphy and Archaeology of Ventana Cave, Arizona*, by Emil W. Haury, pp. 75–126. Tucson and Albuquerque: University of Arizona and University of New Mexico (joint publication).

Bryan, Kirk, and James W. Gidley
1926 Vertebrate fossils and their enclosing deposits from the shore of Pleistocene Lake Cochise, Arizona. *American Journal of Science* 11(5):477–488.

Bullard, William R., Jr.
1962 The Cerro Colorado Site and pit house architecture in the southwestern United States prior to A.D. 900. *Papers of the Peabody Museum of American Archaeology and Ethnology* 44(2). Cambridge: Peabody Museum, Harvard University.

Byers, Douglas S.
1954   Bull Brook—A fluted point site in Ipswich, Masssachusetts. *American Antiquity* 19(4):343–351.
1959   Radiocarbon dates from the Bull Brook Site. *American Antiquity* 24(4):427–429.
Campbell, Elizabeth W. C., and William H. Campbell
1940   A Folsom complex in the Great Basin. *The Masterkey* 14(1):7–11.
Campbell, Elizabeth W. C., William H. Campbell, Ernst Antevs, Charles A. Amsden, Joseph A. Barbieri, and Francis D. Bode
1937   The archaeology of Pleistocene Lake Mohave. *Southwest Museum Papers* 11. Los Angeles: Southwest Museum.
Castetter, Edward F., and Willis H. Bell
1942   *Pima and Papago Indian Agriculture.* Albuquerque: University of New Mexico Press.
Childe, V. Gordon
1950   The urban revolution. *Town Planning Review* 21(1):3–17.
1952   *New Light on the Most Ancient East.* 4th edition. London: Routledge and Kegan Paul.
Clark, Grahame
1946   Farmers and forests in neolithic Europe. *Antiquity* 19:57–71.
Colton, Harold S.
1932   Sunset Crater: The effect of a volcanic eruption on an ancient pueblo people. *Geographical Review* 22(4):582–590.
1936   The rise and fall of the prehistoric population of northern Arizona. *Science* 84(2181):337–343.
1938   Names of the four culture roots in the Southwest. *Science* 87(2268): 551–552.
1939   Prehistoric culture units and their relationships in northern Arizona. *Museum of Northern Arizona Bulletin* 17. Flagstaff: Museum of Northern Arizona.
1956   Pottery types of the Southwest: Wares 5A, 5B, 6A, 6B, 7A, 7B, 7C, San Juan Red Ware, Tsegi Orange Ware, Homolovi Orange Ware, Winslow Orange Ware, Awatovi Yellow Ware, Jeddito Yellow Ware, Sichomovi Red Ware. *Museum of Northern Arizona, Ceramic Series* 3C. Flagstaff: Museum of Northern Arizona.
Cooke, P. St. George
1848   Report of Lieutenant Colonel P. St. George Cooke of his march from Santa Fe, New Mexico, to San Diego, Upper California. *30th Congress, 1st Session, House Executive Document* 41:549–562. Washington, D.C.
Cosgrove, Cornelius B.
1947   Caves of the Upper Gila and Hueco areas in New Mexico and Texas. *Papers of the Peabody Museum of American Archaeology and Ethnology* 24(2). Cambridge: Peabody Museum, Harvard University.
Cosgrove, Harriet S., and Cornelius B. Cosgrove
1932   The Swarts Ruin: A typical Mimbres site in southwestern New Mexico. *Papers of the Peabody Museum of American Archaeology and Ethnology* 15(1). Cambridge: Peabody Museum, Harvard University.

Crook, Wilson W., Jr., and R. K. Harris
  1958 A Pleistocene campsite near Lewisville, Texas. *American Antiquity* 23(3):233–246.
Cruxent, J. M., and Irving Rouse
  1956 A lithic industry of Paleo-Indian type in Venezuela. *American Antiquity* 22(2):172–179.
Cushing, Frank H.
  1890 Preliminary notes on the origin, working hypothesis, and primary researches of the Hemenway Southwestern Archaeological Expedition. *Proceedings of the 7th International Congress of Americanists*, pp. 151–194. Berlin, 1888.
Daifuku, Hiroshi
  1952 A new conceptual scheme for prehistoric cultures in the southwestern United States. *American Anthropologist* 54(2):191–200.
  1961 Jeddito 264: A report on the excavation of a Basketmaker III-Pueblo I site in northeastern Arizona with a review of some current theories in southwestern archaeology. *In* Reports of the Awatovi Expedition 7. *Papers of the Peabody Museum of Archaeology and Ethnology* 33(1). Cambridge: Peabody Museum, Harvard University.
Daugherty, Richard D.
  1956 Early man in the Columbia intermontane province. *University of Utah Anthropological Papers* 24. Salt Lake City: University of Utah.
Dean, Jeffrey S.
  1978 Independent dating in archaeological analysis. In *Advances in Archaeological Method and Theory*, Vol. 1, edited by Michael B. Schiffer, pp. 223–255. New York: Academic Press.
  1981 Chronological analysis of Tsegi Phase sites in northeastern Arizona. *Papers of the Laboratory of Tree-Ring Research* 3. Tucson: University of Arizona Press.
Dice, Lee R.
  1943 *The Biotic Provinces of North America.* Ann Arbor: University of Michigan Press.
Dick, Herbert W.
  1952 Evidences of early man in Bat Cave and on the plains of San Augustin, New Mexico. *In* Indian tribes of aboriginal America, edited by Sal Tax. *Selected Papers of the 29th International Congress of Americanists* 3:158–163. Chicago: University of Chicago Press.
  1954 The Bat Cave complex: A note on its distribution and archaeological significance. *El Palacio* 61(5):138–144.
Dillon, Lawrence S.
  1956 Wisconsin climate and life zones in North America. *Science* 123(3188):167–176.
Di Peso, Charles C.
  1953a Clovis fluted points from southwestern Arizona. *American Antiquity* 19(1):82–85.
  1953b The Sobaipuri Indians of the Upper San Pedro River Valley, southeastern Arizona. *Amerind Foundation* 6. Dragoon, Arizona: The Amerind Foundation.

Di Peso, Charles C. (*continued*)
  1956 The Upper Pima of San Cayetano del Tumacacori: An archaeo-historical reconstruction of the O'otam of the Pimería Alta. *Amerind Foundation* 7. Dragoon, Arizona: The Amerind Foundation.
  1958 The Reeve Ruin of southeastern Arizona: A study of a prehistoric Western Pueblo migration into the middle San Pedro Valley. *Amerind Foundation* 8. Dragoon, Arizona: The Amerind Foundation.
  1974 Casas Grandes: A fallen trading center of the Gran Chichimeca, Volume 3. *Amerind Foundation* 9. Dragoon, Arizona: The Amerind Foundation.

Douglass, Andrew E.
  1929 The secret of the Southwest solved by talkative tree-rings. *National Geographic Magazine* 56(6):736–770.
  1935 Dating Pueblo Bonito and other ruins of the Southwest. *National Geographic Society Contributed Technical Papers, Pueblo Bonito Series* 1. Washington, D.C.: National Geographic Society.

Doyel, David E.
  1979 The prehistoric Hohokam of the Arizona Desert. *American Scientist* 67:544–554.
  In press Current directions in Hohokam research. *The Arizona Archaeologist*.

Doyel, David E., and Emil W. Haury, editors
  1976 The 1976 Salado Conference. *The Kiva* 42(1).

Doyel, David E., and Fred Plog, editors
  1980 Current issues in Hohokam prehistory. *Arizona State University Anthropological Research Papers* 23. Tempe: Arizona State University.

Eggan, Frederick R.
  1950 *Social Organization of the Western Pueblos.* Chicago: University of Chicago Press.

Ellison, Glenn R. "Slim"
  1968 *Cowboys Under the Mogollon Rim.* Tucson: University of Arizona Press.

Evans, Glen L.
  1951 Prehistoric wells in eastern New Mexico. *American Antiquity* 17(1): 1–9.

Ferdon, Edwin N., Jr.
  1955 A trial survey of the Mexican-Southwestern architectural parallels. *Monographs of the School of American Research* 21. Santa Fe: School of American Research.

Fewkes, Jesse W.
  1900 Tusayan migration traditions. *Annual Report of the Bureau of American Ethnology* 19. Washington, D.C.: Smithsonian Institution.
  1911 Antiquities of the Mesa Verde National Park. Cliff Palace. *Bureau of American Ethnology Bulletin* 51. Washington, D.C.: Smithsonian Institution.
  1912 Casa Grande, Arizona. *Twenty-eighth Annual Report of the Bureau of American Ethnology*, 1906–1907:33–179. Washington, D.C.: Bureau of American Ethnology.

1914   Archaeology of the lower Mimbres Valley, New Mexico. *Smithsonian Miscellaneous Collections* 63(10). Washington, D.C.: Smithsonian Institution.

Figgins, Jesse D.
1931   An additional discovery of the association of a "Folsom" artifact and fossil mammoth remains. *Proceedings of the Colorado Museum of Natural History* 10(2). Denver: Colorado Museum of Natural History.
1933   A further contribution to the antiquity of man in America. *Proceedings of the Colorado Museum of National History* 12(2). Denver: Colorado Museum of National History.

Fitting, James E., editor
1973   *The Development of North American Archaeology: Essays in the History of Regional Traditions.* Garden City, New York: Anchor Books.

Fulton, William S.
1934a   Archaeological notes on Texas Canyon, Arizona. *Contributions from the Museum of the American Indian* 12(1). New York: Heye Foundation.
1934b   Archaeological notes on Texas Canyon, Arizona. *Contributions from the Museum of the American Indian* 12(2). New York: Heye Foundation.

Gazin, C. Lewis
1942   The Late Cenozoic vertebrate faunas from the San Pedro Valley, Arizona. *Proceedings of the United States National Museum* 92(3155): 475–518. Washington, D.C.: Smithsonian Institution.

Gidley, James W.
1922   Preliminary reports on fossil vertebrates of the San Pedro Valley, Arizona, with descriptions of new species of rodentia and lagomorphia. *U.S. Geological Survey Professional Paper* 131-E:119–131. Washington, D.C.: U.S. Geological Survey.
1926   Fossil Proboscidea and Edentata of the San Pedro Valley, Arizona. *U.S. Geological Survey, Professional Paper* 140-B:83–94. Washington, D.C.: U.S. Geological Survey.

Gifford, Edward W.
1928   Pottery-making in the Southwest. *University of California Publications in American Archaeology and Ethnology* 23(8):353–373. Berkeley: University of California Press.

Gifford, James C.
1957   Archaeological explorations in caves of the Point of Pines Region, Arizona. Master's thesis, University of Arizona, Tucson.
1980   Archaeological exploration in caves of the Point of Pines Region, Arizona. *Anthropological Papers of the University of Arizona* 36. Tucson: University of Arizona Press.

Gilder, R. F.
1909   Excavation of earth lodge ruins in eastern Nebraska. *American Anthropologist* 2(1):56–79.

Gladwin, Harold S.
1928   Excavations at Casa Grande, Arizona. *Southwest Museum Papers* 2. Los Angeles: Southwest Museum.

Gladwin, Harold S. (*continued*)
 1936 Discussion. *In* An archaeological survey of Chihuahua, Mexico, by Edwin B. Sayles. *Medallion Papers* 22:89–107. Globe, Arizona: Gila Pueblo.
 1942 Excavations at Snaketown III: Revisions. *Medallion Papers* 30. Globe, Arizona: Gila Pueblo.
 1945 The Chaco Branch: Excavations at White Mound and in the Red Mesa Valley. *Medallion Papers* 33. Globe Arizona: Gila Pueblo.
 1946 Tree-ring analysis: Problems of dating II: The Tusayan Ruin. *Medallion Papers* 36. Globe, Arizona: Gila Pueblo.
 1948 Excavations at Snaketown IV: Review and conclusions. *Medallion Papers* 38. Globe, Arizona: Gila Pueblo.
 1957 *A History of the Ancient Southwest.* Portland, Maine: Bond Wheelwright Company.
 1979 Mogollon and Hohokam A.D. 600–1100. *Medallion Papers* 40. Globe, Arizona: Gila Pueblo.
Gladwin, Harold S., Emil W. Haury, Edwin B. Sayles, and Nora Gladwin
 1937 Excavations at Snaketown, material culture. *Medallion Papers* 25. Globe, Arizona: Gila Pueblo.
Gladwin, Winifred, and Harold S. Gladwin
 1928 A method for designation of ruins in the Southwest. *Medallion Papers* 1. Globe, Arizona: Gila Pueblo.
 1929a The Red-on-buff Culture of the Gila Basin. *Medallion Papers* 3. Globe, Arizona: Gila Pueblo.
 1929b The Red-on-buff Culture of the Papagueria. *Medallion Papers* 4. Globe, Arizona: Gila Pueblo.
 1930a The western range of the Red-on-buff Culture. *Medallion Papers* 5. Globe, Arizona: Gila Pueblo.
 1930b An archaeological survey of the Verde Valley, 1930. *Medallion Papers* 6. Globe, Arizona: Gila Pueblo.
 1930c Some southwestern pottery types: Series I. *Medallion Papers* 8. Globe, Arizona: Gila Pueblo.
 1933 Some southwestern pottery types: Series III. *Medallion Papers* 13. Globe, Arizona: Gila Pueblo.
 1934 A method for designation of cultures and their variations. *Medallion Papers* 15. Globe, Arizona: Gila Pueblo.
 1935 The eastern range of the Red-on-Buff Culture. *Medallion Papers* 16. Globe, Arizona: Gila Pueblo.
Guernsey, Samuel J.
 1931 Explorations in northeastern Arizona: Report on the archaeological fieldwork of 1920–1923. *Papers of the Peabody Museum of American Archaeology and Ethnology* 12(1). Cambridge: Peabody Museum, Harvard University.
Hack, John T.
 1942 The changing physical environment of the Hopi Indians. *Papers of*

the *Peabody Museum of American Archaeology and Ethnology* 35(1). Cambridge: Peabody Museum, Harvard University.

Hargrave, Lyndon L.

1930   Prehistoric earth lodges of the San Francisco Mountains. *Museum Notes* 3(5). Flagstaff: Museum of Northern Arizona.

1932   Guide to forty pottery types from the Hopi country and the San Francisco Mountains, Arizona. *Museum of Northern Arizona Bulletin* 1. Flagstaff: Museum of Northern Arizona.

1933   Pueblo II houses of the San Francisco Mountains, Arizona. *Museum of Northern Arizona Bulletin* 4. Flagstaff: Museum of Northern Arizona.

Harrington, Mark R.

1920   Certain Caddo sites in Arkansas. *Contributions from the Museum of the American Indian* 10. New York: Heye Foundation.

Haury, Emil W.

1928   The succession of house types in the Pueblo area. Master's thesis, University of Arizona, Tucson.

1931   Kivas of the Tusayan Ruin, Grand Canyon, Arizona. *Medallion Papers* 9. Globe, Arizona: Gila Pueblo.

1932   Roosevelt 9:6: A Hohokam site of the Colonial period. *Medallion Papers* 11. Globe, Arizona: Gila Pueblo.

1934a   Climate and human history. *Tree-Ring Bulletin* 1(2):13–15. Flagstaff: The Tree Ring Society.

1934b   The Canyon Creek Ruin and cliff dwellings of the Sierra Ancha. *Medallion Papers* 14. Globe, Arizona: Gila Pueblo.

1935   Tree-rings: The archaeologist's time-piece. *American Antiquity* 1(2): 98–108.

1936a   The Mogollon Culture of southwestern New Mexico. *Medallion Papers* 20. Globe, Arizona: Gila Pueblo.

1936b   Vandal Cave. *The Kiva* 1(6):1–4.

1936c   The Snaketown canal. *In* Symposium on prehistoric agriculture. *University of New Mexico Bulletin, Anthropological Series* 1(5):48–50. Albuquerque: University of New Mexico.

1936d   Some southwestern pottery types: Series IV. *Medallion Papers* 19. Globe, Arizona: Gila Pueblo.

1940   Excavations in the Forestdale Valley, east-central Arizona. *University of Arizona Bulletin 11(4), Social Science Bulletin* 12. Tucson: University of Arizona.

1942   Some implications of the Bluff Ruin dates. *Tree-Ring Bulletin* 9(2): 7–8. Tucson: The Tree-Ring Society.

1943   A possible Cochise-Mogollon-Hohokam sequence. *Proceedings of the American Philosophical Society* 86(2):260–263. Philadelphia: American Philosophical Society.

1945a   Painted Cave, northeastern Arizona. *Amerind Foundation* 3. Dragoon, Arizona: The Amerind Foundation.

Haury, Emil W. (*continued*)

1945b The problems of contacts between Mexico and the southwestern United States. *Southwestern Journal of Anthropology* 1(1):55–74.

1945c The excavations of Los Muertos and neighboring ruins in the Salt River Valley, southern Arizona. *Papers of the Peabody Museum of American Archaeology and Ethnology* 24(1). Cambridge: Peabody Museum, Harvard University.

1950a *The Stratigraphy and Archaeology of Ventana Cave, Arizona.* Tucson and Albuquerque: University of Arizona and University of New Mexico (joint publication).

1950b A sequence of great kivas in the Forestdale Valley, Arizona. *For the Dean*, pp. 29–39. Tucson and Santa Fe: Hohokam Museums Association and Southwestern Monuments Association (joint publication).

1956 Speculations on prehistoric settlement patterns in the Southwest. *In* Prehistoric settlement patterns in the New World, edited by Gordon R. Willey. *Viking Fund Publications in Anthropology* 23:3–10. New York: Wenner-Gren Foundation for Anthropological Research.

1957 An alluvial site on the San Carlos Indian Reservation, Arizona. *American Antiquity* 23(1):2–27.

1958a Post-Pleistocene human occupation of the Southwest. *In* Climate and Man in the Southwest, edited by T. L. Smiley. *University of Arizona Program in Geochronology*, Contribution 6, *University of Arizona Bulletin* 28(4):69–75. Tucson: University of Arizona.

1958b Two fossil elephant kill sites in the American Southwest. *In* Proceedings of the Thirty-Second International Congress of Americanists. *University of Arizona Program in Geochronology*, Contribution 4:433–440. Tucson: University of Arizona.

1958c Evidence at Point of Pines for a prehistoric migration from northern Arizona. *In* Migrations in New World culture history, edited by R. H. Thompson. *University of Arizona Social Science Bulletin* 27. Tucson: University of Arizona.

1962a The Greater American Southwest. *In* Courses Toward Urban Life, edited by Robert J. Braidwood and Gordon R. Willey. *Viking Fund Publications in Anthropology* 32:106–131. New York: Wenner-Gren Foundation for Anthropological Research.

1962b HH-39: Recollections of a dramatic moment in Southwestern archaeology. *Tree-Ring Bulletin* 24(3–4):11–14. Tucson: The Tree-Ring Society.

1975 *The Stratigraphy and Archaeology of Ventana Cave, Arizona.* Tucson: University of Arizona Press.

1976 *The Hohokam, Desert Farmers and Craftsmen: Excavations at Snaketown, 1964–65.* Tucson: University of Arizona Press.

1983 Concluding remarks. *In* The Cochise Cultural Sequence in Southeastern Arizona, edited by E. B. Sayles. *Anthropological Papers of the University of Arizona* 42:158–166. Tucson: University of Arizona Press.

1985 *Mogollon Culture in the Forestdale Valley, East-Central Arizona.* Tucson: University of Arizona Press.

Haury, Emil W., and Edwin B. Sayles
1947 An early pit house village of the Mogollon Culture, Forestdale Valley, Arizona. *University of Arizona Social Science Bulletin* 16. Tucson: University of Arizona.

Haury, Emil W., Ernst Antevs, and John F. Lance
1953 Artifacts with mammoth remains, Naco, Arizona. *American Antiquity* 19(1):1–24.

Hawley, Florence M.
1934 The significance of the dated prehistory of Chetro Ketl, Chaco Canyon, New Mexico. *The University of New Mexico Bulletin* 1(1). Albuquerque: University of New Mexico.
1937 Pueblo social organization as a lead to pueblo history. *American Anthropologist* 39(3):504–522.

Haynes, C. Vance
1982 Archaeological investigations at the Lehner Site, Arizona, 1974–1975. *National Geographic Society Research Reports* 14:325–334. Washington, D.C.: National Geographic Society.

Hodge, Frederick W.
1920 Hawikuh bonework. *Contributions from the Museum of the American Indian* 3(3). New York: Heye Foundation.

Hoover, J. W.
1941 Cerros de trincheras of the Arizona Papagueria. *Geographical Review* 31(2):228–239.

Hough, Walter
1907 Antiquities of the Upper Gila and Salt River Valley in Arizona and New Mexico. *Bureau of American Ethnology Bulletin* 35. Washington, D.C.: Smithsonian Institution.
1914 Culture of the ancient pueblos of the Upper Gila River region, New Mexico and Arizona. *U.S. National Museum Bulletin* 87. Washington, D.C.: U.S. National Museum.
1919 Exploration of a pit house village at Luna, New Mexico. *Proceedings of the United States National Museum* 55(2280):409–431. Washington, D.C.: U.S. National Museum.

Howard, Edgar B.
1935 Evidence of early man in North America—based on geological and archaeological work in New Mexico. *The Museum Journal* 24(2–3): 53–171. Philadelphia: The University of Pennsylvania Museum.

Hrdlicka, A.
1927 Catalogue of human crania. *Smithsonian Publication* 2631. Washington, D.C.: Smithsonian Institution.

Huckell, Bruce
In press Review of *The Cochise Cultural Sequence in Southeastern Arizona*, by E. B. Sayles. *The Quarterly Review of Archaeology.*

Humphrey, Robert R.
1958 The desert grassland: A history of vegetational change and an analysis of causes. *Botanical Review* 24(4):193–252.

Hutton, N. H.
  1859   El Paso and Fort Yuma wagon road. U.S. Congress, *35th Congress,
         2nd Session, House Executive Document* 108:77–100. Washington,
         D.C.: U.S. Government Printing Office.
Janmart, Jean
  1952   Elephant hunting as practiced by the Congo Pygmies. *American An-
         thropologist* 54(1):146–147.
Jenks, Albert E.
  1928   The Mimbres Valley expedition. *Bulletin of the Minneapolis Institute
         of Arts* 17(31). Minneapolis: Institute of Arts.
Jennings, Jesse D.
  1957   Danger Cave. *Memoirs of the Society for American Archaeology* 14. Salt
         Lake City: Society for American Archaeology.
Jennings, Jesse D., and Edward Norbeck
  1955   Great Basin prehistory: A review. *American Antiquity* 21(1):1–11.
Jennings, Jesse D., editor
  1956   The American Southwest: A problem in cultural isolation. *In* Semi-
         nars in archaeology: 1955, edited by Robert Wauchope. *Memoirs of
         the Society for American Archaeology* 11:59–127. Salt Lake City: So-
         ciety for American Archaeology.
Jochelson, Waldemar
  1907   Past and present subterranean dwellings of the tribes of north-
         eastern Asia and northwestern America. Fifteenth Session of the
         Congress International des Americanistes. Quebec.
  1928   Archaeological investigation in Kamchatka. *Carnegie Institu-
         tion of Washington Publication* 388. Washington, D.C.: Carnegie
         Institution.
Judd, Neil M.
  1924   Two Chaco Canyon pithouses. *Annual Report of the Smithsonian In-
         stitution for 1922* (2740):399–413. Washington, D.C.: Smithsonian
         Institution.
  1954   The material culture of Pueblo Bonito. *Smithsonian Miscellaneous
         Collections* 124. Washington, D.C.: Smithsonian Institution.
Karns, Harry J.
  1954   *Unknown Arizona and Sonora, 1693–1721.* Tucson: Arizona
         Silhouettes.
Kelly, Isabel
  1980   Ceramic sequence in Colima: Capacha, an early phase. *Anthropologi-
         cal Papers of the University of Arizona* 37. Tucson: University of Ari-
         zona Press.
Kidder, Alfred V.
  1924   *An Introduction to the Study of Southwestern Archaeology.* New Haven:
         Yale University Press.
  1927   Southwestern archaeological conference. *Science* 66(11):489–491.
  1932   The artifacts of Pecos. *Papers of the Phillips Academy Southwestern Ex-
         pedition* 6. New Haven: Phillips Academy.
  1936   *The Pottery of Pecos.* Volume II. New Haven: Yale University Press.
  1937   Foreword. *In* Excavations at Snaketown II: Comparisons and The-

ories, by H. S. Gladwin. *Medallion Papers* 26:vii–x. Globe, Arizona: Gila Pueblo.

1939 Review of *Starkweather Ruin, a Mogollon-Pueblo Site in the Upper Gila Area of New Mexico and Affiliative Aspects of the Mogollon Culture*, by Paul H. Nesbitt. *American Anthropologist* 41(2):314–316.

1962 *An Introduction to the Study of Southwestern Archaeology.* New Haven: Yale University Press (reprint of the 1924 edition).

Kidder, Alfred V., and Samuel J. Guernsey

1919 Archaeological explorations in northeastern Arizona. *Bureau of American Ethnology Bulletin* 65. Washington: Smithsonian Institution.

Kirchhoff, Paul

1954 Gatherers and farmers in the greater Southwest: A problem in classification. *American Anthropologist* 56(4):529–550.

Krieger, Alex D.

1953 New World culture history: Anglo-America. In *Anthropology Today: An Encyclopedic Inventory*, edited by A. L. Kroeber, pp. 238–264. Chicago: University of Chicago Press.

Kroeber, Alfred L.

1917 Zuni kin and clan. *Anthropological Papers of the American Museum of Natural History* 18(2). New York: American Museum of Natural History.

1928 Native culture in the Southwest, *University of California Publications in American Archaeology and Ethnology* 23(9):375–398. Berkeley: University of California Press.

1939 *Cultural and Natural Areas of Native North America.* Berkeley and Los Angeles: University of California Press.

Krogman, Wilton M.

1949 The human skeleton in legal medicine: Medical presentation. In *Symposium on Medicolegal Problems*, edited by S. A. Levinson, Series 2, pp. 1–92. Philadelphia: J.B. Lippincott.

Lance, John F.

1953 Artifacts with mammoth remains, Naco, Arizona, III: Description of the Naco Mammoth. *American Antiquity* 19(1):19–24.

Lawton, H. W., P. J. Wilke, Mary DeDecker, and W. M. Mason

1976 Agriculture among the Paiute of Owens Valley. *The Journal of California Anthropology* 3(1):13–50.

LeBlanc, Steven A.

1975 *Mimbres Archaeological Center: Preliminary Report of the First Season of Excavation, 1974.* Los Angeles: The Institute of Archaeology, University of California.

1980a The Early Pithouse period. In *An Archaeological Synthesis of South Central and Southwestern New Mexico*, edited by Steven A. LeBlanc and Michael E. Whalen, pp. 91–141. Albuquerque: Office of Contract Archaeology, University of New Mexico.

1980b The dating of Casas Grandes. *American Antiquity* 45(4):799–806.

1982 Temporal change in Mogollon ceramics. *In* Southwestern ceramics: A comparative review, edited by Albert H. Schroeder. *The Arizona Archaeologist* 15:107–128.

Libby, Willard F.
1952   *Radiocarbon Dating.* Chicago: University of Chicago Press.
1955   *Radiocarbon Dating* (2nd edition). Chicago: University of Chicago Press.
Lindsay, Alexander J., Jr.
1958   Fossil Pollen and its bearing on the archaeology of the Lehner Mammoth Site. Master's thesis, University of Arizona, Tucson.
Lister, Robert H.
1958   Archaeological excavations in the northern Sierra Madre occidental, Chihuahua and Sonora, Mexico. *University of Colorado Studies, Series in Anthropology* 7. Boulder: University of Colorado.
McGregor, John C.
1930   Tree-ring dating. *Museum of Northern Arizona Museum Notes* 3(4). Flagstaff: Museum of Northern Arizona.
1941   *Southwestern Archaeology.* New York: John Wiley and Sons.
McGuire, Randall H., and Michael B. Schiffer, editors
1982   *Hohokam and Patayan: Prehistory of Southwestern Arizona.* New York: Academic Press.
Mangelsdorf, Paul C., and C. Earle Smith, Jr.
1949   New archaeological evidence on evolution in maize. *Harvard University Botanical Museum Leaflet* 13(8):213–247.
Mangelsdorf, Paul C., and Robert H. Lister
1956   Archaeological evidence on the evolution of maize in northwestern Mexico. *Harvard University Botanical Museum Leaflets* 17:151–178.
Martin, Paul Schultz
1958   Pleistocene ecology and biogeography of North America. *In* Zoogeography, edited by C. L. Hubbs. *American Association for the Advancement of Science, Symposium Volume* 51:375–420. Washington, D.C.: American Association for the Advancement of Science.
Martin, Paul Schultz, and James Schoenwetter
1960   Arizona's oldest cornfield. *Science* 132(3418):33–34.
Martin, Paul Schultz, James Schoenwetter, and B. C. Arms
1961   *Southwestern Palynology and Prehistory: The Last 10,000 Years.* Tucson: Geochronology Laboratories, University of Arizona.
Martin, Paul Sidney
1940   The SU Site: Excavations at a Mogollon village, western New Mexico, 1939. *Field Museum of Natural History Anthropology Series* 32(1). Chicago: Field Museum.
1943   The SU Site: Excavations at a Mogollon village, western New Mexico, second season, 1941. *Field Museum of Natural History Anthropological Series* 32(2). Chicago: Field Museum.
1979   Prehistory: Mogollon. In *Handbook of North American Indians: Southwest*, edited by Alfonso Ortiz, pp. 61–74. Washington: Smithsonian Institution.
Martin, Paul Sidney, and Fred Plog
1973   *The Archaeology of Arizona.* Garden City, New York: Doubleday/ Natural History Press.
Martin, Paul S., and John B. Rinaldo

1947　The SU Site: Excavations at a Mogollon village, western New Mexico, third season, 1946. *Field Museum of Natural History Anthropology Series* 32(3). Chicago: Field Museum.

1950　Sites of the Reserve phase, Pine Lawn Valley, western New Mexico. *Fieldiana: Anthropology* 38(3). Chicago: Field Museum.

Martin, Paul S., John B. Rinaldo, Elaine Bluhm, Hugh C. Cutler, and Roger Grange, Jr.

1952　Mogollon cultural continuity and change. The stratigraphic analysis of Tularosa and Cordova caves. *Fieldiana: Anthropology* 40. Chicago: Field Museum.

Martin, Paul S., John B. Rinaldo, and Ernst Antevs

1949　Cochise and Mogollon sites, Pine Lawn Valley, western New Mexico. *Fieldiana: Anthropology* 38(1). Chicago: Field Museum.

Martínez del Río, Pablo

1952　El mamut de Santa Isabel Iztapan. *Cuadernos Americanos* 64(4): 149–170.

Mason, Otis T.

1896　Influence of environment upon human industries or acts. *Smithsonian Institution Annual Reports, 1895*, pp. 639–665. Washington, D.C.: Smithsonian Institution.

Mason, Ronald J.

1958　Late Pleistocene geochronology and the Paleo-Indian penetration into lower Michigan peninsula. *Anthropological Papers, Museum of Anthropology, University of Michigan* 11. Ann Arbor: Museum of Anthropology, University of Michigan.

Meinzer, O. E., and F. C. Kelton

1913　Geology and water resources of Sulphur Spring Valley, Arizona. *United States Geological Survey, Water-Supply Paper* 320. Washington, D.C.: U.S. Geological Survey.

Mera, Harry P.

1935　Ceramic clues to the prehistory of north central New Mexico. *Technical Series Bulletin* 8. Santa Fe: Laboratory of Anthropology.

Miller, Carl F., Jr.

1934　Report on dates on the Allantown, Arizona, Ruins. *Tree-Ring Bulletin* 1(2):15–16. Flagstaff: The Tree Ring Society.

1935　Additional dates from Allantown. *Tree-Ring Bulletin* 1(4):31. Flagstaff: The Tree Ring Society.

Mindeleff, Cosmos

1900　Localization of Tusayan Clans. *Annual Report of the Bureau of American Ethnology* 19. Washington, D.C.: Smithsonian Institution.

Mindeleff, Victor

1891　A study of pueblo architecture: Tusayan and Cibola. *Annual Report of the Bureau of American Ethnology* 8:3–228. Washington, D.C.: Smithsonian Institution.

Minnis, Paul E.

1981　Economic and organizational responses to food stress by non-stratified societies: An example from prehistoric New Mexico. Doctoral dissertation, University of Michigan, Ann Arbor.

Morris, Earl H.
   1927   The beginnings of pottery making in the San Juan area: Unfired
          prototypes and the wares of the earliest ceramic period. *Anthropo-
          logical Papers of the American Museum of Natural History* 28(2). New
          York: American Museum of Natural History.
   1939   Archaeological studies in the La Plata district, southwestern Colo-
          rado and northwestern New Mexico. *Carnegie Institution of Washing-
          ton Publication* 519. Washington, D.C.: Carnegie Institution.
Morris, Earl H., and Robert F. Burgh
   1941   Anasazi basketry, Basket Maker II through Pueblo III. *Carnegie In-
          stitution of Washington* 533. Washington, D.C.: Carnegie Institution.
   1954   Basket Maker II sites near Durango, Colorado. *Carnegie Institution
          of Washington* 604. Washington, D.C.: Carnegie Institution.
Morss, Noel
   1931   The ancient culture of the Fremont River in Utah: Report on the
          explorations under the Claflin-Emerson fund, 1928–29. *Papers of
          the Peabody Museum of American Archaeology and Ethnology* 12(3).
          Cambridge: Peabody Museum, Harvard University.
Movius, Hallam L., Jr.
   1950   A wooden spear of Third Interglacial Age from Lower Saxony.
          Southwestern Journal of Anthropology 6(2):139–142.
Murdock, George P.
   1934   *Our Primitive Contemporaries.* New York: Macmillan.
Nesbitt, Paul H.
   1931   The ancient Mimbrenos based on the investigations at the Mat-
          tocks Ruin, Mimbres Valley, New Mexico. *Logan Museum Bulletin* 4.
          Beloit: Logan Museum.
Nichol, A. A.
   1952   The natural vegetation of Arizona, revised by W. S. Phillips. *Uni-
          versity of Arizona, Agricultural Experiment Station, Technical Bulletin*
          127. Tucson: University of Arizona.
Palerm, Angel
   1955   The agricultural basis of urban civilization in Mesoamerica. *In* Irri-
          gation civilizations: A comparative study, edited by Julian H. Stew-
          ard, pp. 28–42. *Social Science Monographs* 1. Washington, D.C.: Pan
          American Union.
Parke, J. G.
   1857   Report of explorations for railroad routes. U.S. Congress, *33rd
          Congress, 2nd Session, Senate Executive Document 78*, Vol. 7. Washing-
          ton, D.C.: U.S. Government Printing Office.
Parry, C. C.
   1854   General geological features of the country. *In* Report on the United
          States and Mexican Boundary Survey, edited by W. H. Emory. U.S.
          Congress, *34th Congress, 1st Session, Senate Executive Document 108*
          1(2):1–23. Washington, D.C.: U.S. Government Printing Office.
Parsons, Elsie C.
   1939   *Pueblo Indian Religion.* Chicago: University of Chicago Press.

Pepper, George H.
1920 Pueblo Bonito. *Anthropological Papers of the American Museum of Natural History* 27. New York: American Museum of Natural History.
Plog, Fred
1980 Explaining change in the Hohokam pre-Classic. *In* Current Issues in Hohokam Prehistory, edited by David E. Doyel and Fred Plog. *Arizona State University Anthropological Research Papers* 23:4–22. Tempe: Arizona State University.
Redfield, Robert
1953 *The Primitive World and Its Transformations.* Ithaca: Cornell University Press.
Reed, Erik K.
1942 Implications of the Mogollon concept. *American Antiquity* 8(1): 27–32.
1958 Comment. *In* Migrations in New World culture history, edited by Raymond H. Thompson. *University of Arizona Social Sciences Bulletin* 27:7–8. Tucson: University of Arizona.
Ritchie, William A.
1957 Traces of early man in the Northeast. *New York State Museum and Science Service Bulletin* 358. Albany: University of the State of New York.
Roberts, Frank H. H., Jr.
1929 Shabik'eshchee Village: A late Basket Maker site in the Chaco Canyon, New Mexico. *Bureau of American Ethnology Bulletin* 92. Washington, D.C.: Smithsonian Institution.
1930 Early pueblo ruins in the Piedia district, southwestern Colorado. *Bureau of American Ethnology Bulletin* 96. Washington, D.C.: Smithsonian Institution.
1931 The ruins at Kiatuthlanna, eastern Arizona. *Bureau of American Ethnology Bulletin* 100. Washington, D.C.: Smithsonian Institution.
1935 A survey of Southwestern archaeology. *American Anthropologist* 37(1):1–35.
1939 Archaeological remains in the Whitewater district, eastern Arizona: Part I. House Types. *Bureau of American Ethnology Bulletin* 121. Washington, D.C.: Smithsonian Institution.
Robinson, William J.
1967 Tree-ring materials as a basis for cultural interpretations. Doctoral dissertation, University of Arizona, Tucson.
Russell, Frank
1908 The Pima Indians. *Annual Report of the Bureau of American Ethnology* 26. Washington, D.C.: Smithsonian Institution.
Sauer, Carl O.
1952 *Agricultural Origins and Dispersals.* New York: American Geographical Society.
1954 Comments on *"Gatherers and Farmers in the Greater Southwest: A Problem in Classification,"* by Paul Kirchoff. *American Anthropologist* 56(4): 553–556.

Sayles, Edwin B.
 1935 An archaeological survey of Texas. *Medallion Papers* 17. Globe, Arizona: Gila Pueblo.
 1936 An archaeological survey of Chihuahua, Mexico. *Medallion Papers* 22. Globe, Arizona: Gila Pueblo.
 1945 The San Simon Branch: Excavations at Cave Creek and in the San Simon Valley. *Medallion Papers* 34. Globe, Arizona: Gila Pueblo.
 1983 The Cochise cultural sequence in southeastern Arizona. *Anthropological Papers of the University of Arizona* 42. Tucson: University of Arizona Press.
Sayles, Edwin B., and Ernst Antevs
 1941 The Cochise Culture. *Medallion Papers* 29. Globe, Arizona: Gila Pueblo.
Schmidt, Erick F.
 1928 Time-relations of prehistoric pottery types in southern Arizona. *Anthropological Papers of the American Museum of Natural History* 30(5):247–302. New York: American Museum of Natural History.
Schroeder, Albert H.
 1957 The Hakataya cultural tradition. *American Antiquity* 23(2):176–178.
 1960 The Hohokam, Sinagua, and Hakataya. *Society for American Archaeology, Archives of Archaeology* 5. Madison: Society for American Archaeology.
 1965 Unregulated diffusion from Mexico into the Southwest prior to A.D. 700. *American Antiquity* 30(3):297–309.
 1966 Pattern diffusion from Mexico into the Southwest after A.D. 600. *American Antiquity* 31(5):683–704.
Sellards, Elias H.
 1938 Artifacts associated with fossil elephant. *Bulletin of the Geological Society of America* 49:999–1010.
 1952 *Early Man in America: A Study in Prehistory.* Austin: Texas Memorial Museum.
Shelford, Victor E., editor
 1926 *Naturalist's Guide to the Americas.* Baltimore: Ecological Society of America.
Soday, F. J.
 1954 The Quad Site: A Paleo-Indian village in northern Alabama. *Tennessee Archaeologist* 10(1):1–20.
Stallings, William S.
 1933 A tree-ring chronology for the Rio Grande drainage in northern New Mexico. *Proceedings of the National Academy of Sciences* 19(9): 803–806. Washington, D.C.: National Academy of Sciences.
Steward, Julian H.
 1933 Archaeological problems of the northern periphery of the Southwest. *Museum of Northern Arizona Bulletin* 5. Flagstaff: Museum of Northern Arizona.
 1937 Ecological aspects of Southwestern society. *Anthropos* 32:87–104.

1938 Basin-plateau aboriginal sociopolitical groups. *Bureau of American Ethnology Bulletin* 120. Washington, D.C.: Smithsonian Institution.

Strong, William D.
1927 An analysis of Southwestern society. *American Anthropologist* 29(1): 1–61.
1933 The Plains culture area in the light of archaeology. *American Anthropologist* 35(2):271–287.
1935 An introduction to Nebraska archaeology. *Smithsonian Miscellaneous Collections* 93(10). Washington, D.C.: Smithsonian Institution.

Thornthwaite, C. W.
1948 An approach toward a rational classification of climate. *Geographical Review* 38:55–94.

Thwaites, Reuben G., editor
1905 Pattie's personal narrative. In *Early Western Travels, 1748–1846*, Vol. 18. Cleveland: Arthur H. Clark Co.

Trischka, Carl
1933 Hohokam: A chapter in the history of Red-on-buff Culture of Arizona. *The Scientific Monthly* 37:417–433.

Turney, Omar A.
1929 *Prehistoric Irrigation in Arizona*. Phoenix: Arizona State Historian.

Wagoner, Jay J.
1952 History of the cattle industry in southern Arizona, 1540–1940. *University of Arizona Social Science Bulletin* 20. Tucson: University of Arizona.

Wasley, William W.
1957 *The Archaeological Survey of the Arizona State Museum*. Tucson: Arizona State Museum, University of Arizona.
1962 A ceremonial cave on Bonita Creek, Arizona. *American Antiquity* 27(3):380–394.

Waters, Michael R.
1983 *The Late Quaternary geology and archaeology of Whitewater Draw, Southeastern Arizona*. Doctoral dissertation, University of Arizona, Tucson.

Wauchope, Robert, editor
1956 Seminars in Archaeology: 1955. *Memoirs of the Society for American Archaeology* 11. Salt Lake City: Society for American Archaeology.

Webb, George Ernest
1983 *Tree-Rings and Telescopes: The Scientific Career of A. E. Douglass*. Tucson: University of Arizona Press.

Wedel, Waldo R.
1935 Contributions to the archaeology of the upper Republican Valley, Nebraska. *Nebraska History Magazine* 15(3):133–209.

Wheat, Joe Ben
1952 Prehistoric water sources of the Point of Pines area. *American Antiquity* 17(3):185–196.
1954 Crooked Ridge Village. *University of Arizona Social Science Bulletin* 24. Tucson: University of Arizona.

Wheat, Joe Ben (*continued*)
  1955 Mogollon Culture prior to A.D. 1000. *Memoirs of the Society for American Archaeology* 10. Salt Lake City: Society for American Archaeology.
Whitaker, Thomas W., Hugh C. Cutler, and Richard S. MacNeish
  1957 Cucurbit materials from three caves near Ocampo, Tamaulipas. *American Antiquity* 22(4):352–358.
Wilcox, David R., and Charles Sternberg
  1983 Hohokam ballcourts and their interpretation. *Arizona State Museum Archaeological Series* 160. Tucson: Arizona State Museum, University of Arizona.
Wilcox, David R., and Lynette Shenk
  1977 The architecture of the big house and its interpretation. *Arizona State Museum Archaeological Series* 115. Tucson: Arizona State Museum, University of Arizona.
Willey, Gordon R.
  1953 Prehistoric settlement patterns in the Viru Valley, Peru. *Bureau of American Ethnology Bulletin* 155. Washington, D.C.: Smithsonian Institution.
Willey, Gordon R., and Philip Phillips
  1955 Method and theory in American archaeology: II. Historical-developmental interpretation. *American Anthropologist* 57(4):723–819.
  1958 *Method and Theory in American Archaeology.* Chicago: University of Chicago Press.
Wilson, Thomas
  1899 Arrowpoints, spearheads, and knives of prehistoric times. *Report of the U.S. National Museum for 1897*, pp. 811–988. Washington, D.C.: U.S. National Museum.
Wise, Edward N., and Dick Shutler, Jr.
  1958 University of Arizona radiocarbon dates. *Science* 127(3289):72–73.
Wissler, Clark
  1922 *The American Indian: An Introduction to the Anthropology of the New World.* 2nd edition. New York: Oxford University Press.
Wittfogel, Karl A., and Esther S. Goldfrank
  1943 Some aspects of pueblo mythology and society. *Journal of American Folklore* 56:17–30.
Witthoft, John
  1952 A Paleo-Indian site in eastern Pennsylvania: An early hunting culture. *Proceedings of the American Philosophical Society* 96(4):464–495. Philadelphia: American Philosophical Society.
Woodbury, Richard B.
  1961 Prehistoric agriculture at Point of Pines, Arizona. *Memoirs of the Society for American Archaeology* 17. Salt Lake City: Society for American Archaeology.
  1973 *Alfred V. Kidder.* New York: Columbia University Press.
  1983 Looking back at the Pecos Conference. *The Kiva* 48(4):251–266.

Woodward, Arthur
    1930   Buried treasure. *Los Angeles County Employee*, June.
    1931   The Grewe Site, Gila Valley, Arizona. *Los Angeles Museum of History, Science, and Art, Occasional Papers* 1. Los Angeles: Los Angeles Museum of History, Science, and Art.
Wormington, H. Marie
    1949   Ancient Man in North America. *Denver Museum of Natural History, Popular Series* 4. 3rd edition. Denver: Denver Museum of Natural History.
    1957   Ancient Man in North America. *Denver Museum of Natural History, Popular Series* 4. 4th edition. Denver: Denver Museum of Natural History.
Wyllys, Rufus K.
    1931   Padre Luis Velarde's "Relación of Pimería Alta, 1716." *New Mexico Historical Review* 6(2):111–157.

Acknowledgments

We are, indeed, grateful to the many staff members and students of the Department of Anthropology and the Arizona State Museum of the University of Arizona and the staff of the University of Arizona Press who contributed their expertise, time, and considerable energy to the preparation of this anthology. Their contributions testify to Emil Haury's impact upon southwestern archaeology and its practitioners and friends. The idea for this anthology was suggested to the senior editor by Raymond H. Thompson, who provided support and encouragement throughout its development. We are especially indebted to Barbara Klie Montgomery for editing assistance, a role that kept her moving from word processor to drafting table, from the library to the copy machine, and always back to the manuscript for one more check of the figures and references. Her efforts and, ultimately, the completion of this anthology were made possible through a grant from the Agnese Lindley Foundation. Assistance with the many illustrations was essential; Julie Lowell, among numerous other helpful activities, located the original negatives; Ellen Horn assisted the file search and facilitated the production of photographs, which were printed by Helga Teiwes and Michael Barton; and additional photographic assistance was provided by Kathy Hubenschmidt and Elizabeth Gibson. George Michael Jacobs and Daphne Scott, as always, provided help in ways too numerous to list. Elizabeth Pate and Teresa Reichhardt helped in the early stages of compiling the bibliography. Roger Anyon provided comments incorporated as footnotes to Chapter 13. Carol Gifford shared her valuable editing experience and inspiration, Doris Ann Sample contributed her expertise with the processed word, and Stephanie Whittlesey and Sharon Debowski provided support and encouragement. To all we extend sincere thanks.

J. JEFFERSON REID
DAVID E. DOYEL

Index